Nova Scotia's Massachusetts

Nova Scotia's Massachusetts

A Study of Massachusetts-Nova Scotia Relations

1630 to 1784

GEORGE A. RAWLYK

McGill-Queen's University Press
Montreal and London 1973

Legal Deposit fourth quarter 1973

This work has been published with the help of
a grant from the Social Sciences Research Council of Canada
using funds provided by the Canada Council.

Design by Carl Zahn
Printed in Canada by The Bryant Press Limited

For

MURRAY TOLMIE   MASON WADE   PETER WAITE
who had faith when others doubted

Contents

Maps

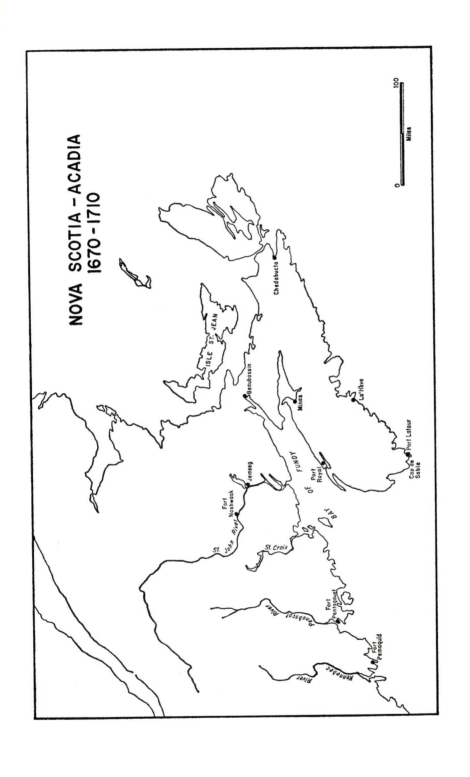

NOVA SCOTIA – ACADIA
1670 – 1710

ISLE ST. JEAN

Chedabucto

Beaubassin

Minas

La'Hève

Cap de Port Latour
Sable

Port Royal

OF

BAY

FUNDY

Jemseg

Fort
Nashwaak

St. John River

St. Croix

Penobscot River

Fort
Pentigouet

Fort
Pemaquid

Kennebec
River

0   100
Miles

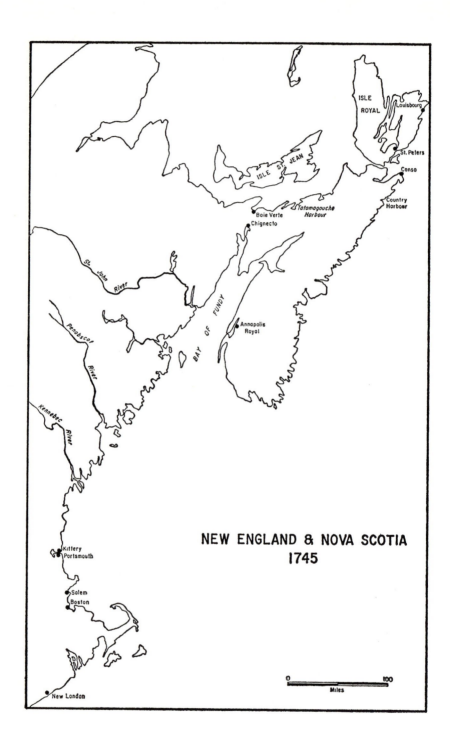

ISLE ROYAL

Louisbourg

St. Peters

Canso

Country Harbour

ISLE ST. JEAN

Totamagouche Harbour

Boie Verte

Chignecto

St. John River

BAY OF FUNDY

Annapolis Royal

Penobscot River

Kennebec River

Kittery
Portsmouth

Solem
Boston

New London

NEW ENGLAND & NOVA SCOTIA
1745

0   100
Miles

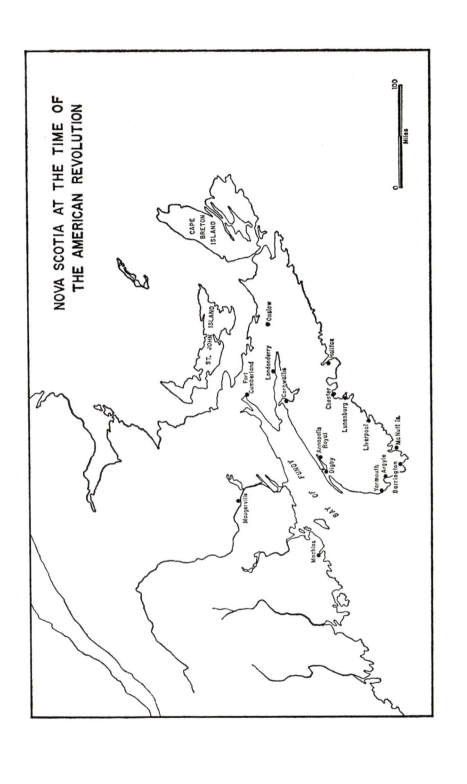

NOVA SCOTIA AT THE TIME OF
THE AMERICAN REVOLUTION

CAPE BRETON ISLAND

ST. JOHN ISLAND

●Onslow

Fort Cumberland

Londonderry

Cornwallis

Halifax

Chester

Lunenburg

Annapolis Royal

Digby

Liverpool

McNutt Is.

Yarmouth

Argyle

Barrington

Mougerville

FUNDY

OF

BAY

Machias

Miles

0   100

Preface

This book is not intended as an exhaustive examination of every aspect of Massachusetts' relationship with Nova Scotia–Acadia for the entire 1630 to 1784 period. Rather, it is primarily concerned with describing and attempting to account for, first, the continuing economic hammerlock Massachusetts had during most of the period from 1630 to 1784 over the neighbouring colony and, second, the various military thrusts sent from New England to the region to the northeast. Around these military expeditions are to be found clustered the various individuals and interested groups concerned with what may be referred to as Nova Scotia–Acadia (all of present-day New Brunswick and Nova Scotia).

What is particularly significant about the 1630–1784 Massachusetts–Nova Scotia relationship is that it was emphatically not one of equals. Nova Scotia's population was always merely a small fraction of that of Massachusetts. In 1670, for example, after four decades of existence, Massachusetts had over 30,000 settlers, while Nova Scotia had fewer than 500. Forty years later, in 1710, Massachusetts had approximately 62,000 inhabitants and Nova Scotia, 1,700. In 1750, five years before most French-speaking Acadians of Nova Scotia were expelled, there were almost 190,000 Massachusetts residents, while the Nova Scotia population consisted of an estimated 10,000 Acadians and approximately 2,000 newly arrived British immigrants in the vicinity of Halifax. There were, in addition, about 4,000 French inhabitants on the French-controlled island colony of Cape Breton. By 1770, Massachusetts had a population of 235,000, in sharp contrast to Nova Scotia's fewer than 15,000 citizens.[1] Taking into account these population statistics, one is hardly surprised that there was a widespread ignorance and indifference in Massachusetts concerning Nova Scotia and Nova Scotia affairs. Apart from a relatively small number of fishermen, traders, and governmental officials, few Massachusetts residents, except briefly during periods of war, wished to involve themselves or their government in affairs involving the neighbouring colony.

Massachusetts' interest in and concern with the Nova Scotia region probably peaked in 1690 with the Phips expedition, and again in 1745 with the amazing capture of Louisbourg, the so-called French Gibraltar of North America. What these and other Massachusetts military thrusts against the French seemed to show was that military expansion into Nova Scotia would happen only if there was some initial encouragement from Great Britain or from British officials and supporters in Massachusetts, who possessed a somewhat grandiose vision of an Anglo-American empire. In addition, it was essential to have the support of the fishing interests of Essex County, of the Boston merchants, and often that of the northeastern frontier interests. When these interests and pressure groups fused during periods of war, they cleverly utilized propagandists initially to create public enthusiasm and then to channel that enthusiasm into active participation and support. This enthusiasm and support, however, was never translated into any permanent form of Massachusetts imperialism vis-à-vis Nova Scotia. Instead, the military expeditions were short-lived outbursts of temporary concern. After King George's War and the Seven Years' War, a few outcroppings of a new and bitter hostility towards Nova Scotia were to be observed within the prevailing bedrock of Massachusetts indifference. Thus, by the outbreak of the American Revolution, most Massachusetts residents probably viewed the neighbouring colony through a conceptual filter clogged by scorn, ignorance, or apathy. It was clear that during the years following King George's War, Nova Scotia was no longer seen as "New England's Outpost," as had been the case in the seventeenth century. Instead, it was viewed by some influential Massachusetts inhabitants as a backward Anglophile colony incapable and unworthy of political redemption.

This book, obviously, owes a great deal to J. B. Brebner's two outstanding volumes, *New England's Outpost* and *The Neutral Yankees of Nova Scotia*.[2] I have, however, tried to do more than to fill some of the gaps which may be found in Brebner's work. It is evident that less than 20 percent of both *New England's Outpost* and *The Neutral Yankees of Nova Scotia* deals implicitly or explicitly with what may be called Massachusetts–Nova Scotia relations. The bulk of Brebner's work is concerned with the political and cultural history of Nova Scotia–Acadia written from the vantage point of Annapolis Royal or Halifax. In *New England's Outpost*, Brebner set out to explain, as he cogently put it, how and why "New England . . . stimulated and carried out the expulsion of the Acadians in 1755."[3] But even in trying to find answers to this fascinating historical problem, he seemed content to concentrate his attention on the Nova Scotia scene, especially on the Acadians, during the years from 1710 to 1756. In a similar manner, his *Neutral Yankees of Nova Scotia* is primarily a book about the "Yankees" in Nova Scotia and why they did not join the American Revolution. For Brebner, the Yankees, despite their New England heritage, were forced by external and domestic circumstances, to walk the knife-edge of neutrality as had their immediate predecessors, the French-speaking Acadians. Locked into his neutrality paradigm, Brebner viewed all events in pre-1755 New England–Nova Scotia relations as leading inevitably to the expulsion. He then threw the net of neutrality forward from his location in time in 1755 to catch all the Nova Scotia residents during the revolutionary war.

Brebner's brilliant and suggestive neutrality thesis certainly provides a meaningful overview for an otherwise extremely confused relationship. Only recently it has been referred to as the "classic and satisfactory" interpretation.[4] Yet in spite of my own original predilection towards the Brebner approach to the study of prerevolutionary Nova Scotia, my research has led me in a somewhat different direction. Instead of seeing what Brebner called the "expanding energies" of New England leading "inevitably and naturally" to the expulsion, I perceived a Massachusetts interest in the area as suddenly declining after the Louisbourg episode of 1745. And, so far as I could determine, the so-called expanding energies of New England had nothing to do with the expulsion. Instead of being giant steps leading towards *le grand dérangement*, the military expeditions of 1654, 1690, 1704, 1707, 1710, 1745, 1746, and 1755 really reflected the ebb and flow of a rather limited Massachusetts interest in Nova Scotia. They certainly did not represent a growing Massachusetts or New England imperialism. Finally, the original response of the Nova Scotia Yankees to the Revolution seemed to me more one of confusion than of neutrality. This acute disorientation was symptomatic of a collective identity crisis, which was resolved for many when they became part of the Great Awakening of Nova Scotia led by the young, charismatic evangelist Henry Alline. This religious revival, one of the most significant social movements in the long history of Nova Scotia, was the means by which a significant number of Nova Scotians extricated themselves from the domination of New England. By creating a religious ideology that was specifically geared to conditions in the northern colony, the Great Awakening enabled some residents to regard themselves as a people with a unique history, a distinct identity, and a special destiny.[5]

Savage Harbour
P.E.I.
August, 1971

Acknowledgements

I am very much indebted to various librarians and archivists in New England and Canada who have made my research both possible and enjoyable. Mr. and Mrs. Leo Flaherty of the Massachusetts Archives, Boston, were especially helpful to me as were Dr. Bruce Fergusson and Miss Phyllis Blakeley of the Public Archives of Nova Scotia, Halifax, and Mr. Tom Adams of the John Carter Brown Library in Providence, Rhode Island. In addition, I owe a great deal to the staffs of the Public Archives of Canada, the Massachusetts Historical Society, the Maine Historical Society, and the American Antiquarian Society.

Many kind friends have helped me to write this book. Mrs. Susan Warram of Boston provided me with research assistance as well as her special brand of hospitality. Professor Robin Winks of Yale University, Professor Richard Bushman of Boston University, Professor Alice Stewart of the University of Maine, Professor Gordon Stewart of Michigan State University, Professor Gerald Craig of the University of Toronto, and Professor R. A. MacLean of St. Francis Xavier University read part or all of an early draft of this study. They all provided me with invaluable advice and what was even more important to me — encouragement. My colleague Professor Jim Nuechterlein has worked hard on the final revision of the manuscript and has helped me to clarify numerous themes.

I also owe a great deal — more than they will ever realize — to the graduate students who have taken my History 823 Seminar at Queen's University. They have tested many of my poorly conceived hypotheses dealing with Massachusetts–Nova Scotia relations and, in the process, have provided me with insights, constructive criticism, and a huge supply of valuable historical information. They have forced me to clarify my thinking, and have also, at times of profound discouragement, given me renewed confidence and enthusiasm.

The chairman of the University of Maine Studies, Professor Edward Schriver, has permitted me to use material originally published in my book *Yankees at Louisbourg*. For this I am very grateful.

Without the generous financial assistance provided by the Canada Council and the John Carter Brown Library, it would not have been possible for me to have done the basic research for this volume. And for the three scholars who made it all possible when others had lost faith, I set aside a separate page.

1

John Winthrop and Nova Scotia, 1630–1649

At two o'clock in the afternoon on Sunday, June 6, 1630 (O.S.), a few excited men on the decks of the *Arbella* were the first to see land and North America. The 350-ton vessel was the flagship of the Massachusetts Bay Company's main colonizing expedition to the New World. A persistent fog had slowly lifted in the early afternoon, and the blurred contours of the tip of southeastern Nova Scotia could barely be seen some eighteen miles away.[1] Those on board the *Arbella* had endured two months packed in a foul-smelling ship tossed about by the merciless Atlantic. Now the end of their confinement was in sight. The landmass of peninsular Nova Scotia, which thrusts itself like a giant disfigured foot into the North Atlantic, welcomed the Puritan immigrants to their "Citty upon a Hill."[2]

For John Winthrop, the leader of the expedition and the first governor of the Massachusetts Bay Colony, Nova Scotia – Acadia was not alien territory. Winthrop knew in June, 1630, that the area was no longer in French hands but was being colonized by the Scot, Sir William Alexander. This realization, together with the fact that Nova Scotia was the "good land" first perceived by the Puritans,[3] encouraged Winthrop to see a special relationship between his colony and neighbouring Nova Scotia. This attitude, which other settlers must have shared with the extraordinarily gifted Winthrop, was significantly strengthened on Monday, June 7, when the rich natural resource of the region was discovered — "the knob-headed, richly fat, and succulent codfish."[4] Winthrop noted in his journal: "The wind S. About four in the morning we sounded and had ground at thirty fathom, and was somewhat calm; so we put our ship a-stays, and took, in less than two hours, with a few hooks, sixty-seven codfish, most of them very great fish, some a yard and a half long, and a yard in compass. This came very seasonably; for our salt fish was now spent."[5] It is not surprising therefore that Nova Scotia was soon regarded as the natural vantage point of Massachusetts' northeastern frontier. The neighbouring area could be early fitted into the Puritan special sense of mission. God's "eies," Winthrop was sure, were focused on Massachusetts, and as the century unfolded, at least a few Massachusetts' "eies" would be glued on Nova Scotia.

In January, 1633, Winthrop was compelled to reconsider his attitude to Nova Scotia. On January 17 he observed that he had been informed "from the east, that the French had bought the Scottish plantation near Cape Sable, and that the fort and all the ammunition were delivered to them, and that the cardinal [Richelieu], having the managing thereof, had sent some companies already, and preparation was made to send many more the next year and divers priests and Jesuits among them."[6] Winthrop's intelligence was accurate.

According to the Treaty of Saint-Germain-en-Laye signed March 23, 1632, Nova Scotia was returned to the French and Alexander's Scottish settlement was abandoned. Cardinal Richelieu, in his capacity as general superintendent of navigation and commerce, appointed his cousin, Isaac de Razilly, lieutenant-general for Acadia. Razilly's right-hand man was his cousin, Charles de Menou d'Aulnay, de Charnisay. Richelieu assumed that Charles de La Tour, who had been named "Lieutenant-General of the country of Acadia, Fort Louys, Fort de La Tour" in 1631, would come under Razilly's jurisdiction. But La Tour, who had received as well a baronetcy from Sir William Alexander in May, 1630, had other ideas.[7] La Tour, who was involved in the Nova Scotia fur trade, especially in the St. John River valley area, refused to be subservient to any one man or to any one nation. He had his own pockets to fill and his own ego to satisfy.

In late August, Razilly, d'Aulnay, six Capuchins, and some 300 settlers had landed at La Hève harbour near present-day Bridgewater. A blockhouse had been constructed in preparation for the long winter siege. The fleur-de-lis once again flew over peninsular Nova

Scotia. On hearing of the French expedition, Governor Winthrop immediately "called the assistants to Boston, and the ministers and captains, and some other chief men, to advise what was fit to be done for our safety." Winthrop believed that the French were "like to prove ill neighbours (being Papists)."[8] The Puritan leaders were unusually agitated and frightened and their intense fear fed on exaggeration and rumour. The "Citty upon a Hill" had been originally built as "a bulwarke against the kingdom of Antichrist which the Jesuits labour to rear up in all places of the world."[9] Now the forces of Antichrist threatened the very existence of Massachusetts Bay. Winthrop and his colleagues felt helpless. All they could do was to agree to build a plantation and fort at Nantasket at the mouth of Boston harbour, "partly to be some block in an enemy's way . . . and especially to prevent an enemy from taking this passage." In addition, the Boston fort was to be completed and the land about Ipswich settled "(being the best place in the land for village and cattle), lest any enemy, finding it void, should possess and take it from us."[10] The plan adopted was largely inadequate to deal with any major French assault. The Boston deliberations of January 17, 1633, revealed how militarily vulnerable the colony actually was and how easily the reservoir of anti–Roman Catholic fear could be tapped in moments of crisis.

Of course, the Puritans brought with them to the New World a finely developed suspicion, fear, and sometimes hatred of Roman Catholicism. In 1630 nowhere in Europe did Protestantism appear safe, and this was particularly the case in France where Richelieu had been able the previous year to impose a victorious peace on the Huguenots. The importance of the impact of this suspicion and fear of the power of Catholicism on the New England mind is most difficult to evaluate. What seems clear, however, is that as the Massachusetts population grew and as the threat of French military and economic expansion from Nova Scotia appeared to disappear, anti-Catholicism became much less intense. Prejudice remained, but it was never strong enough to preclude commercial or diplomatic relations. It was not until the 1680s that anti–Roman Catholicism would emerge as a powerful factor in Massachusetts' relations with Nova Scotia. In that decade many people of Massachusetts believed that their traditional way of life, and their hard-won liberties, were being threatened from within by the arrogant Roman Catholic James II and his colonial henchmen and from without by Louis XIV, who was eager to use his North American colonists and Indian allies to annihilate the New Englanders. Under these special circumstances, when their existence appeared threatened, the passions of the people of Massachusetts could be stirred by an emotional appeal to their latent anti–Roman Catholic and anti-French feeling.

By 1633, then, the French had regained their hold, however tenuous, over Nova Scotia, whose western boundary was considered to be in the general area of the Penobscot and St. John rivers. Between this colony and Massachusetts Bay, there stretched a long coastline open to the exploitations of both. Almost immediately, English and French fur traders pushed into this area. The English were led by a few men from the Plymouth Colony, Pilgrim neighbours of Massachusetts, and the French by the energetic La Tour. Using his base at the mouth of the St. John River, La Tour was eager to confine the commercial activities of the English to the region west of the Penobscot. In December, 1633, La Tour destroyed the "trading wigwam" belonging to an Isaac Allerton at Machias, north of the Penobscot, and killed two of his men.[11] But since Allerton had in some way alienated Governor Bradford and other Plymouth merchants, little notice was apparently taken of the incident. Winthrop probably felt that Allerton received what he deserved and that the episode was simply what one could expect from two unprincipled and greedy entrepreneurs.

In 1635 further French commercial expansionism in the Penobscot-Kennebec area forced Winthrop to reconsider his policy vis-à-vis the neighbouring colony and raised in Massachusetts new fears of possible French aggrandizement. In January, 1635, Winthrop had been informed that La Tour "had authority from the king of France, who challenged all from Cape Sable to Cape Cod, wishing them to take notice, and to certify the rest of the English, that, if they traded to the east of Pemaquid [Kennebec River], he would make prize of them. Being desired to show his commission, he answered, that his sword was commission sufficient."[12] Within less than two years, apparently, La Tour had pushed the western boundary of Nova Scotia from the Penobscot to the Kennebec. It would only take him another year or so to jump to the Charles. In August, possibly in an attempt to undermine La Tour's growing power in the western part of Nova Scotia, Governor Razilly sent d'Aulnay, his deputy, by ship to attack a Plymouth fur trading post at the mouth of the Penobscot. In spite of the fact that he had received orders to assist in the attack, La Tour refused to participate. But d'Aulnay had no difficulty in capturing the fort. While there he reiterated La Tour's contention that the English had no right to expand beyond the Kennebec.

The Plymouth Colony had ignored La Tour's attack on Allerton in December, 1633, but the French offensive of 1635 was far too serious to disregard. Pride and an undetermined fur hinterland were at stake. The leaders of the Plymouth Colony therefore sent a small naval force to recapture the Penobscot fort, but the expedition was an embarrassing failure. Stung by the unexpected defeat, Governor Bradford wrote to the Massachusetts General Court, requesting immediate military assistance. The Bay colony was not insensitive to the dangers of French encroachments, but the settlers in Massachusetts Bay, unlike their Plymouth neighbours, had no economic investments to protect in the northeastern frontier area. In spite of this, they saw the need to push back the Gallic invaders.

On October 9, 1635, Winthrop, together with ten other Massachusetts officials, penned their signatures to the following letter to Plymouth:

Worthy Srs:
Upon the reading of your letters, and consideration of the waightiness of the cause therein mentioned, the courte hath joyntly expressed their willingness to assist you with men and munition, for the accomplishing of your desires upon the French.

Massachusetts was apparently quite willing to provide men and supplies for a joint expedition, but only on the clear understanding that Plymouth would eventually pay all expenses involved. Nothing more was done by either side. Plymouth did not have sufficient funds, and by October 16 any Massachusetts enthusiasm for the venture had disappeared. There were two reasons which may help to explain the sudden change in the policy of the Massachusetts General Court. First, its members came to realize "we had then no money in the treasury, neither could we get provision of victuals, on the sudden, for one hundred men, which were to be employed. So we deferred." Second, and perhaps most important, a group of Massachusetts merchants decided that the time was propitious for them to displace the Plymouth fur trading interests in the "Esterne plantations."[13] These

Massachusetts interests did not wish to see the Plymouth fur trading post re-established under any circumstances. Instead, they intended to work closely with the French, thereby funnelling Nova Scotia furs through Boston to the European markets. In the process, of course, badly needed hard currency would be pumped into the Massachusetts economy.

The timing of the Massachusetts move into the Penobscot-Kennebec area could not have been any more fortuitous, for in November, 1635, Razilly suddenly died, leaving d'Aulnay as his successor. The next fifteen years witnessed a bitter struggle between d'Aulnay and La Tour for control of Nova Scotia. D'Aulnay was supreme in the Port Royal— La Hève section of the peninsula, while La Tour was master of the St. John River area. Only the death of d'Aulnay in 1650 and the marriage of his widow to the triumphant La Tour finally brought the vicious civil war to an end. While La Tour and d'Aulnay were at each other's throats, Massachusetts fur trading and fishing interests were free to push gradually into what La Tour and d'Aulnay, at least, considered to be French territory.[14]

Any successful colony must, among other things, find an adequate economic base. During the first ten years of its existence, Massachusetts Bay prospered by supplying the material needs of the tremendous influx of new settlers. But 1640 spelled the end of the "Great Migration to New England,"[15] and the beginning of a severe economic crisis. This crisis accelerated changes that were already taking place in the Massachusetts economy. Two of the most significant of these changes involved the enlargement of the merchant fleet and the rapidly expanding fishery. Massachusetts traders developed further their coastal trade into the Nova Scotia area where furs were looked for and southward to the West Indies and Virginia. This southward trade was of far greater economic importance than was that with Nova Scotia—Acadia. At the same time fishing entrepreneurs were following the cod northeastward to Brown's Bank, Roseway Bank, and La Have Bank, a relatively short distance from the speck of land sighted by Winthrop in June, 1630. Offshore fishing in Massachusetts no longer provided sufficient cod, and by 1640 and 1641 the fishermen had learned that with the coming of spring the cod moved north and that southeastern Nova Scotia provided hundreds of commodious harbours where the cod from the new unfished banks could be dried and salted.[16] By moving into Nova Scotia waters, the Massachusetts fishermen were not only able to extend their fishing season into the early autumn, but they were also forced to spend some of their time on Nova Scotia land – d'Aulnay's territory. Thus by the early 1640s a few Massachusetts fur traders were taking the initiative from the French and moving into the bitterly contested frontier region to the northeast, while some Massachusetts fishermen were taking temporary possession of a few harbours in southeastern Nova Scotia. While d'Aulnay and La Tour were battling for supremacy in Nova Scotia, each man was being threatened by a different economic thrust from Massachusetts.

La Tour reacted quickly to the crisis that confronted him. Fully aware of the growing strength of Massachusetts and shrewdly assessing economic, military, and religious realities, he sent a "Monsieur Rochett," a Huguenot, to Boston in November, 1641, to negotiate a commercial treaty and to obtain military assistance against d'Aulnay. In order to neutralize any religious hostility, Rochett emphasized the fact that La Tour was sympathetic to the Protestant cause, while d'Aulnay was surrounded and manipulated by a host of Roman Catholic priests. Rochett also argued that since d'Aulnay was determined to prevent the New Englanders from participating in the fur trade in the Penobscot area, close commercial relations with La Tour would enable them to continue their activities in the northeastern frontier region. Besides, La Tour was willing to promise them access to the rich fur area of the St. John River valley.

The Massachusetts officials eagerly accepted the proposal providing for "liberty of free commerce." They refused, however, to ally themselves militarily with La Tour against his rival. Freedom of trade they were pleased to grant – trade was what they wanted – but they would go no further. They knew they were in a strong bargaining position and so did La Tour. Nevertheless, this did not prevent him from trying again in October, 1642, to persuade Massachusetts to provide him with support. In that month Governor John Winthrop made this comment in his *Journal*:

> *6 Here came in a French shallop with some 14 men, whereof one was La Tour his lieutenant. They brought letters from La Tour to the governor, full of compliments, and desire of assistance from us against Monsieur D'Aulnay. They staid here about a week, and were kindly entertained, and though they were papists, yet they came to our church meetings; and the*

La Tour's "lieutenant" left Boston with a Protestant New Testament
but with no promise of military assistance. He was, however, followed
to the St. John River by a Massachusetts trading vessel. The vessel
was "welcomed . . . very kindly" by La Tour, but on the voyage
home it was captured by d'Aulnay near Pemaquid. D'Aulnay "wrote
also to our governor," Winthrop noted, "and sent him a printed
copy of the arrest against La Tour, and threatened us, that if any
of our vessels came to La Tour, he would make prize of them."[18]
Winthrop did not appear overly concerned in the autumn of 1642 with
this threat, since he believed that the northern trade was a private
matter and that it therefore did not involve Massachusetts in the
d'Aulnay–La Tour feud. The Massachusetts merchants could take
care of themselves — at least when they were in French territorial
waters.

La Tour, an unusually persistent individual, was not satisfied with
the two negative responses from Massachusetts to his demand for
military aid. Consequently he resolved to visit Massachusetts himself to
persuade the authorities there to assist him. La Tour's 140-ton ship,
the *Saint-Clément*, sailed into Boston harbour on a sunny June afternoon in 1643. On board the *Saint-Clément* were 140 men, many of
whom were tough, experienced Huguenot soldiers. During La Tour's
absence in France, d'Aulnay had blockaded his fort on the St. John
River, and this blockade had forced La Tour to sail to Boston for help.
The *Saint-Clément* "came in with a fair wind, without any notice
taken of them." No armed ship had previously threatened the safety of
Boston, and on June 12, 1643, Winthrop and others seemed to feel
that they were at the mercy of La Tour and his armed force:

> *Divers boats . . . had given notice hereof to Boston and
> Charlestown, [La Tour's] ship also arriving before Boston, the
> towns betook them to their arms, and three shallops with
> armed men came forth to meet the governor and to guard him
> home. But here the Lord gave us occasion to take notice of
> our weakness, etc., for if La Tour had been ill minded
> towards us, he had such an opportunity as we hope neither he*

nor any other shall ever have the like again; for coming by
our castle and saluting it, there was none to answer him, for
the last court had given order to have the castle-Island
deserted, a great part of the work being fallen down etc.

The following day Winthrop hastily summoned an emergency meeting of all available magistrates and deputies to discuss La Tour's request. It was agreed that he would be free to hire as many ships and men in the harbour area as he needed to lift the blockade.[19]

Why did Winthrop and the Massachusetts authorities suddenly reverse the stand taken in 1641 and 1642? There were probably three major reasons for the sudden change in policy.[20] First, La Tour's unexpected arrival gave him the element of surprise and struck fear into the hearts of the Puritans. They considered themselves to be at his mercy, especially when they saw his confident troops exercising on the commons and going through complex military manoeuvres. Concessions were necessary under these circumstances or else, as one contemporary asserted, a "store of blood would be spilled in Boston."[21]

Second, it seems that Winthrop and some of his colleagues were persuaded during this period of acute anxiety that an alliance with La Tour would result in considerable trade with Nova Scotia. This increase in trade would be particularly significant if d'Aulnay were driven from the French colony. Three Massachusetts merchants, Thomas Hawkins, Edward Gibbons, and John Winthrop, Jr., enthusiastically put forward this argument. Hawkins was a London shipwright who had made Boston his shipbuilding and commercial centre. Gibbons was a pre-1630 settler of Massachusetts Bay who had become a Church member and by 1643 was one of the leading merchants in the community. John Winthrop, Jr., was the talented son of the governor. These three men, it should be emphasized, were interested in developing the fur trade in the area north and east of the Penobscot. They were naturally eager to support La Tour against d'Aulnay, who was perceived as a very real threat to their ambitious plan.[22]

Third, in protecting his son's potential commercial interests, Winthrop was also being true to his conviction that a useful and expedient political action had to be "both in tune with the fundamentals of the government, and deduced from the law of God." In aiding La Tour, Winthrop not only had the commercial strengthening and the protection of Massachusetts in mind, but he also was quite explicit in stressing a proper spiritual intention — the Christian rule of charity. Thus Winthrop's "rule of state" was carefully blended into his "rule of charity." This blending process was further encouraged by the fact that Winthrop could not condone isolationism.[23] The future of his colony, he felt, especially during the chaotic Civil War years of the 1640s, depended upon a much closer economic relationship with the outside world — even an "idolatrous Roman Catholic world."[24]

The decision to support La Tour, however, was immediately and violently attacked by some Massachusetts residents. There were those who were vociferously opposed to any alliance with Roman Catholics. There were others, especially in the area north of Boston, who were afraid that the new policy would probably encourage d'Aulnay to attack their isolated settlements. It was fear of the consequences that prompted their protest in the same way that the hope for economic gain encouraged some Bostonians to support La Tour. Richard Saltonstall and other merchants from Ipswich gave the impression that they opposed the pro–La Tour policy because they felt that isolationism was the only viable option open to their colony. As far as they were concerned, there was little to choose between the two Frenchmen, and if offensive action was necessary, Massachusetts should act independently and not be "margent notes upon a French text, which to us is as yet but Apocrypha."[25] Saltonstall's group may have been primarily concerned with the principle of the matter, but its opposition must also have stemmed from the fact that it had its own economic interests to protect. Some in the group wished to develop the western fur trade and did not want to see their competitors who were moving northeastward receive subsidization of any kind from the General Court. Furthermore, there were some Ipswich-area fishermen particularly active in the Cape Sable area of Nova Scotia who were not eager to alienate d'Aulnay.[26] These men were stubbornly tied to the status quo.

In spite of the opposition, La Tour was able to hire four vessels from Thomas Hawkins and Edward Gibbons. These ships carried in all fifty crewmen and thirty-eight cannon, and La Tour promised to pay £940 sterling for them. If he was unable to find sufficient funds, Gibbons and Hawkins were to be granted La Tour's St. John fort as well as much of his claim to Nova Scotia. La Tour also hired an additional fifteen sailors and sixty-eight soldiers, each of whom was to receive forty shillings per month. It was agreed that all the booty taken from d'Aulnay would be shared among those participating in the expedition.[27] On July 14, 1643, La Tour's four-ship flotilla, carrying over 270 men, set sail from Boston for the St. John River.

As far as Hawkins, Gibbons, and John Winthrop, Jr., were concerned, the expedition was both a commercial venture and an expansionist thrust. Their view was probably shared by a majority of the Massachusetts authorities. What the three men were apparently interested in was to establish in Nova Scotia a "sphere of influence open not merely to the commercial exploitation, but also to the political penetration of what was already, next to Virginia, the most populous English plantation on the North American continent."[28]

The La Tour–Massachusetts expedition easily forced d'Aulnay's blockading fleet to retreat to Port Royal, the tiny capital of the French colony. On August 6 the expedition, with Hawkins now commander-in-chief, dropped anchor off Port Royal. D'Aulnay refused to negotiate with the invaders, and as a result, thirty Huguenots and thirty Massachusetts volunteers were sent ashore "to do some mischief to D'Aulnay." A frontal attack involving all the invaders was out of the question, since the Massachusetts men were unwilling to participate. After the sixty-man force had ravaged the outskirts of Port Royal, burning and looting at will, the men returned to their ships and almost immediately sailed to the St. John. The military expedition had been both a success and a failure. D'Aulnay's blockade of La Tour's St. John River fort had been lifted, but d'Aulnay was still in control of Port Royal. All those involved in the expedition, however, were relatively happy. The three Boston entrepreneurs had La Tour financially dependent upon them, and they also had access to what they considered to be a vast virgin fur domain. The Massachusetts volunteers in the expedition had their wages and a share of the considerable booty of "400 moose skins and 400 beaver skins," and supplies captured from one of d'Aulnay's vessels. And of course La Tour and his men were now able to develop further the resources of their region of Nova Scotia. Winthrop and the Massachusetts General Court had other ideas about the expedition, regarding it both as "offensive and grievous." When he had agreed to Massachusetts' participation, Winthrop had assumed that the lifting of the d'Aulnay blockade was the only aim of the expedition. Neither his "rule of charity" nor his "rule of state" could condone offensive raids on d'Aulnay's stronghold.[29]

As would be expected, d'Aulnay was furious with Massachusetts' intervention into the affairs of his colony and he issued commissions of reprisal. His violent reaction was shared by a growing number of prominent people in Massachusetts. Thus in the summer of 1644 when La Tour again requested assistance, it was decided that although trade with him should be continued, no further military aid should be provided. A letter to this effect was sent to d'Aulnay, together with an explanation of the Massachusetts government's criticism of what was considered to be the unjustified and unauthorized attack on Port Royal.[30]

In response to the Massachusetts correspondence, d'Aulnay sent a negotiating team headed by a Mr. Marie to Boston in the autumn of 1644. After protracted discussions, the following treaty of peace was signed on October 8:

The governor and the rest of the magistrates do promise to Mr. Marie, that they and all the English within the jurisdiction of the Massachusetts aforesaid shall observe and keep firm peace with Mr. D'Aulnay, etc., and all the French under his command in Acadie: and likewise the said Mr. Marie doth promise for Mr. D'Aulnay, that he and all his people shall also keep firm peace with the governor and magistrates aforesaid, and with all the inhabitants of the jurisdiction of the Massachusetts aforesaid; and that it shall be lawfull for all men, both French and English, to trade each with other: so that if any occasion of offence shall happen, neither party shall attempt any thing against the other in any hostile manner before the wrong be first complained of, and due satisfaction not given. Provided always, the governor and magistrates aforesaid be not bound to restrain their merchants to trade with their ships with any persons, either French or other.[31]

The signing of the treaty meant, among other things, that Massachusetts Bay was free to trade with either d'Aulnay or La Tour, and as Winthrop observed, "We were freed from the fear our people were in, that Mr. D'Aulnay would take revenge of our small vessels or our plantations, for the harm he sustained by our means the last year."[32] There was also a verbal understanding to the effect that if d'Aulnay seized any supplies being sent to La Tour from Massachusetts, d'Aulnay was to provide compensation for them. D'Aulnay made these concessions because he had been ordered by the French government to adopt a conciliatory attitude to Massachusetts, and because he did not want his enemy to receive any further military assistance from the south. The treaty was, in a sense, a gamble, but d'Aulnay felt he had no other choice.

A few Boston merchants were opposed to the treaty with d'Aulnay. While it was being negotiated, they were attempting to work out a satisfactory commercial arrangement with Lady La Tour, who had arrived in Boston on September 17, eight days after her husband had left Massachusetts Bay. Legal problems made even more difficult Lady La Tour's desperate search for supplies. Finally she was successful in hiring three London vessels laden with supplies in Boston harbour for the relief of her husband's fort.[33] The captains were promised payment with beaver and elk skins and coal once they arrived at their destination. This financial arrangement, together with the lack of any enthusiastic governmental support, probably discouraged any Massachusetts merchants from coming to Lady La Tour's aid.

Soon after Lady La Tour arrived at the fort, d'Aulnay began his siege. In spite of her inspiring leadership in her husband's absence, the fort was captured in April, 1645. La Tour was now a homeless and poverty-stricken adventurer, and following the death of his brave wife in June, a widower. The shattering news reached La Tour in Boston during the summer of 1645. The mood of gloom spread to the business community when it was realized that Edward Gibbons, La Tour's creditor, had lost "more than 2500 pounds . . . ([and] by this loss was now quite undone)."[34]

To show his appreciation to Massachusetts, La Tour, in January of 1646, stole over £400 worth of commodities belonging to some Boston merchants and sailed to Quebec. During the episode, it was rumoured, he shot one New Englander in the face with a pistol and forced four others to fend for themselves near Cape Sable. La Tour's defection forced the disillusioned John Winthrop to observe: "Whereby it appeared (as the scripture saith) that there is no confidence in an unfaithful or carnal man. Though tied with many strong bonds of courtesy, etc. he [La Tour] turned pirate, etc."[35] La Tour's decision to abandon Massachusetts for New France was certainly understandable under the circumstances. He realized that the General Court would not assist him in driving d'Aulnay from the colony, and even if by some sudden change in policy it resolved to do so, his Boston creditors would be the only ones to benefit from the military venture. There was always a chance, however, that from Quebec La Tour would be able to use his considerable persuasive skills to convince the French authorities to re-establish his position in Nova Scotia.

With the capture of La Tour's fort, d'Aulnay confidently resolved to press the Massachusetts authorities for some major changes in the treaty of 1644. Negotiations stretched into 1646, and in the process d'Aulnay began to realize that he would win no major concessions from the English and that he had far more to gain by encouraging peaceful trade with his neighbours than by creating further tension between the two colonies. After laying claim to damages "to the value of 8000 pounds," his agents were content to accept from Governor Winthrop instead "a very fair new sedan (worth forty or fifty pounds where it was made, but of no use to us)."[36] Peace was finally established — a "sedan" peace — and John Winthrop played a key role in bringing it about. He was determined to settle once and for all the problem of Massachusetts' relations with Nova Scotia. His task was enormously simplified because of d'Aulnay's victory and La Tour's defection.

The treaty of 1644 as revised in 1646, on the surface anyway, gave the Massachusetts merchants freedom to trade in Nova Scotia. But it was understood, apparently, that this liberty would not extend to the Indian trade. In the spring of 1647, for example, d'Aulnay confiscated a Boston vessel trading with Micmac Indians in the Cape Sable area. The merchants involved pressured the General Court and Governor Winthrop to strike back, "but the court thought it not safe nor expedient for us to begin a war with the French; nor could we charge any manifest wrong upon D'Aulnay, seeing we had told him, that if ours did trade within his liberties, they should do it at their own peril. . . . And besides there appeared an over-ruling providence in it, otherwise he could not have seized a ship so well fitted, nor could wise men have lost her so foolishly."[37] The ironic twist in the Court's resolution merely underlined the fact that the Massachusetts authorities, in their relations with Nova Scotia, were determined to continue to work within the framework of the 1644–46 arrangements. Any Yankee merchant unwilling to do so would have to face the possible disastrous consequences involved.

Until the death of Winthrop in 1649 and of d'Aulnay in the following year, there were no problems of any consequence between

the two neighbouring colonies. Stability had replaced chaos and
both sides seemed pleased with the amicable arrangement. While in
the New World, most of John Winthrop's energies had been expended
in attempting to build a Puritan "Citty upon a Hill." His spiritual
city could not, however, be separated from the secular one. Neither he
nor his colony could avoid the implications of political responsibility
and the problems involving Massachusetts' relations with the French in
Nova Scotia. Certainly Winthrop could never escape from the shadow
Nova Scotia affairs cast on his North American career. Nor did he
try to avoid this shadow, however small it actually was in terms of the
Massachusetts experience. By the middle of the seventeenth century,
commercial and diplomatic realities, as well as the forces of geography,
had drawn the two colonies together — in spite of the existing fundamental racial and religious differences.[38]

2

Robert Sedgwick, Thomas Temple, and Nova Scotia, 1650-1670

By 1649–50 Massachusetts and Nova Scotia had reached what seemed to be a satisfactory arrangement concerning mutual problems. This amicable relationship was not one involving equals, and this may help to explain why both sides had accepted the 1644–46 treaty. There were fewer than 400 Acadians, the vast majority of whom resided near Port Royal, compared with a population of approximately 15,000 in Massachusetts. For the Acadians good relations with Massachusetts meant the continued existence of their colony; with only a few score fighting men to count on, the Acadians were at the mercy of their English-speaking neighbours. Most Massachusetts inhabitants, for their part, had no desire to involve themselves in military expansion. Those few individuals concerned with developing commercial ties with Nova Scotia had achieved by 1648 much of what they had desired.

Underlying the arrangement between Nova Scotia and Massachusetts were three major considerations. Until the turn of the century, each of these continued to be of considerable importance in determining the relations between the two colonies. First, the Penobscot River was apparently accepted, unofficially at least, as the boundary between English and French settlements. The existence of such a boundary did not in any way in the 1650s or 1660s restrict either Nova Scotia's or Massachusetts' colonization. There were still vast tracts of virgin land contiguous to existing settlements and hundreds of miles from the Penobscot. This boundary line represented to the New Englanders the ultimate limit of French southwestern penetration into North America. French officials in Nova Scotia viewed it in a similar light as far as English northeastern settlement was concerned. Thus, if the boundary was not respected by either side, especially if the larger Massachusetts considered its territorial interests to be threatened, a crisis was bound to ensue. And if this territorial conflict was accompanied by tension regarding economic matters and Indian relations, warfare usually broke out.

The second major consideration was the freedom for Massachusetts traders and fishermen to tap the natural resources of the Nova Scotia area. Fur entrepreneurs continued to have access to the general area, but their trade was usually funnelled through French middlemen. In addition, especially when supply ships from France did not arrive, a not infrequent occurrence, the Acadians were dependent on New England foodstuffs. This dependency at times of crisis significantly strengthened the economic ties between the two regions. As La Tour had learned in the 1640s, Massachusetts could usually be counted on when disaster threatened — particularly if a large profit margin was involved.

Massachusetts fishermen, as well, had little to fear from the Acadians. In fact the fishermen had virtually driven the Acadians from the offshore fishing grounds in the Bay of Fundy and off Cape Sable. Those Frenchmen interested in developing the Nova Scotia fishery were compelled to establish stations in the northeast corner of peninsular Nova Scotia, on Cape Breton Island, and on the north shore of present-day New Brunswick. It was somewhat ironic that the rich fishing areas close to the large French settlement at Port Royal were controlled by New Englanders who had forced the French settlers to become sedentary subsistence farmers. Having developed a deep-rooted pragmatism and a sense of survival, the Acadians were not eager to lose their ships and fishing equipment to the much more numerous and aggressive Massachusetts fishermen. One could easily and safely farm the rich lands of the Fundy shore. As long as the Massachusetts fishermen had the monopoly of the Nova Scotia fishery they were happy and not at all concerned about the existence of a French colony to the northeast. Any sign of French competition could be expected to result in a deep concern about the evils of French imperialism.

The third consideration underlying the amicable relationship reached by the middle of the century was the absence of any tension between the New Englanders and the Indian allies of the French. The frontier areas of Maine and Massachusetts had not suffered from French-Indian raids in the 1640s, and the Nova Scotia French did not appear eager to encourage the Abenakis or Malecites to pursue such a policy. Once Indian attacks came or seemed to be imminent, the French settlements closest to Massachusetts were blamed, and the frontiersmen and others demanded suitable retribution.

With the sudden death of d'Aulnay in a tragic boating accident off Port Royal in May, 1650, chaos threatened once again to engulf Nova Scotia affairs, thereby undermining the amicable relationship achieved between the colony and Massachusetts. Almost single-handedly, d'Aulnay had brought some semblance of stability to the area as well as a prospect for a bright future.[1] But while consolidating his position in the colony, he had been compelled to borrow heavily from Emmanuel Le Borgne, an entrepreneur from La Rochelle. Consequently, when news of d'Aulnay's death reached France, Le Borgne obtained formal recognition from d'Aulnay's sick father, who had succeeded his son to "the government of the said country," that 260,000 *livres* were owed him by d'Aulnay's heirs. Le Borgne was eager to obtain this sum as quickly as possible, and in this hope he organized a trading expedition to the Bay of Fundy in the spring of 1651. His agent was the Sieur de Saint-Mas, who was also appointed d'Aulnay's father's "Lieutenant-General."[2]

While Le Borgne's expedition was being outfitted, the indefatigable Charles de La Tour, having immediately sailed from Quebec on hearing of his rival's death, was in Paris obtaining the Nova Scotia fur monopoly as well as the position of "Governor and Lieutenant-General."[3] In giving La Tour this commission, King Louis XIV was clearly violating the commission he had issued to d'Aulnay years earlier. But during the Fronde almost anything could happen, and any person with money and influential Court contacts could persuade the Council to authorize the most ridiculous decisions.

Shortly after Le Borgne's expedition sailed for Nova Scotia, d'Aulnay's father died. To replace him, the king appointed the Sieur de La Fosse intendant of Acadia until d'Aulnay's eldest son came of age. La Fosse's commission stressed that the d'Aulnays still possessed the fur monopoly, despite the fact that three months earlier Louis XIV had given this right to La Tour.[4] To make even more hopeless an already incoherent and confused situation, the king in February, 1652, declared that since La Tour had usurped the rights of the d'Aulnays, César de Bourbon, Duc de Vendôme, the illegitimate son of Henry IV, was to share the fur monopoly and the government of Nova Scotia with d'Aulnay's widow.[5] Chaos had returned with a vengeance to Nova Scotia.

D'Aulnay's widow, Jeanne Motin, was fully aware of her precarious situation in the spring of 1651 and saw no suitable alternative to cooperating with Saint-Mas. Almost the first thing Saint-Mas and Jeanne Motin did was to send one of Le Borgne's sons from Port Royal to Boston in order to ensure that good relations would continue between the French and the English, so that Massachusetts would not be tempted to fill what could have been regarded as an economic and political vacuum.

Young Alexandre Le Borgne brought three letters to Boston, all of which made the same point. It was important "to renew . . . a good and perfect alliance, friendship and confederation, with protestation, that it shall not be violated in any of those things, which should be kept between good friends allianced and neighbours."[6] Governor John Endecott's replies were brief and to the point. He and his colony wanted good relations with the French settlers. He wrote to Madame d'Aulnay: "We received yours . . . in which you intimated your ready inclination to hold a continued, firm, neighbourly correspondency with us, as usually is between good friends, which hath been always grateful to us to entertain with all men, as much as in us lieth, nor do we know or intend any thing but all neighbourly, loving and friendly compliance with you, unless ought shall proceed from yourselves towards us contrary thereto."[7]

Endecott's sympathetic, yet realistic, response brought much relief to the Le Borgne–d'Aulnay group. But the arrival of La Tour in September, 1651, royal commission in hand, forced Madame d'Aulnay to surrender Fort St. John, at the mouth of the St. John River, to her husband's bitter and long-time foe.[8] The clock had been turned back one decade, but this time La Tour had to cope not only with d'Aulnay's widow but also with the powerful and aggressive Le Borgne.

When Le Borgne heard of the Vendôme-d'Aulnay agreement of February, 1652, he sent another expedition to Port Royal to make sure that his financial interests would be protected. Madame d'Aulnay was forced to give up Port Royal and the seigneurial manor there and also to acknowledge that a debt of 205,000 *livres* was still owed to Le Borgne. She was left with only two small farms, and her future looked extremely bleak. Abandoned to her fate by Vendôme, pillaged by Le Borgne's force, Madame d'Aulnay turned to La Tour for assistance. La Tour had an easy solution to the woman's perplexing problem — marriage. They became man and wife in July, 1653, five months after the complicated "Articles of Marriage" had been signed to ensure, among other things, "the peace and tranquility of the country, and concord and union between the two families."[9]

The aim of the new couple to bring peace and tranquility to Nova Scotia had not taken into account Le Borgne, who arrived at Port Royal on August 20, 1653, and captured the settlement as his force had done the preceding year. La Tour was away and his wife was unable to stop Le Borgne from seizing furs from the storehouse. Next the La Rochelle merchant sent a ship to Cape Breton Island to destroy the fishing settlement being built at St. Peters by a Nicolas Denys. Continuing his efforts to remove forcibly all possible competition, Le Borgne attacked the tiny settlement at Pentagouet at the mouth of the Penobscot and La Hève. He then returned with considerable booty to France. It had been an unusually successful business venture, and it was hoped that Le Borgne's ruthless policy of devastation had frightened all the French settlers, even La Tour, into a subservient position.[10]

Events in Nova Scotia in 1653 did not go unnoticed in Massachusetts. Probably because of pressure from Cromwell, who was anticipating an imminent declaration of war with France, and also because of the entreaties of some of its neighbouring colonies, the Massachusetts General Court decided in May, 1653,

> *for prevention of any such trade as maybe of dajngerous consequence to ourselves, as the strengthening of persons in hostillitje to our nation or ourselves, that from the publication hereof, all persons in our jurisdiccon are prohibitted from carrying provissions, as corne, beefe, pease, bread, or porke, etc., into any of the plantacons of Dutch or French inhabitting in any of the parts of Amerrica; and in case any shall so doe, they shall pay treble the value so traded, uppon legall conviction.*[11]

Such a regulation prohibiting trade with the Dutch, with whom Britain was at war, was quite understandable. But its application to the French, then at peace with Cromwell, seemed inexplicable, especially as far as Massachusetts was concerned. It may have been that the General Court did not want any of the Massachusetts entrepreneurs to be involved in the Le Borgne–La Tour–d'Aulnay controversy. Or it may have been that the General Court wished to exert some control over the Nova Scotia trade and hoped to do so by granting exceptions to the regulation. Two weeks after the new trade restrictions were issued, for example, the General Court resolved to "graunt liberty to Capt. Jno Leverett, Mr. James Oliver and Ensigne Scottou to send forth a vessell of seventeene tonnes, with flower, pease, and such provicons as they have occasion now to send forth, to Mounsr La Tour."[12] A number of weeks later the Court gave Major Gibbons, the prominent Boston merchant to whom La Tour owed over £4,000,[13] "libertje . . . to goe with any vessell or vessells to the sajd French with provissions for trade, and not otherwise, whereby he may endeavor the getting in the sajd debt, not withstanding the sajd prohibition of trade wth the sajd French, which is still contjnewed."[14]

Captain John Leverett and Major Gibbons were close friends and business associates. In 1653 Leverett was an elected deputy for Boston in the General Court, while the influential Gibbons was the commander of the colonial militia. Both men had been unusually active in the Nova Scotia trade, and it is not surprising that the General Court was willing to make special exceptions for them as far as the May regulations were concerned. In making these exceptions, the General Court was in all likelihood opening the Acadian trade to those interests that had virtually dominated it in the pre-1653 period. Perhaps this was precisely what the new regulations had intended to accomplish: the protection of the Gibbons-Leverett monopoly.

In France, in late 1653, when Vendôme heard of La Tour's marriage, the duc immediately allied himself with Le Borgne, who early the next year sent to Port Royal the 300-ton *Châteaufort* laden with merchandise, provisions, and munitions.[15] Le Borgne intended to drive the La Tours permanently from the St. John River valley where they had moved the previous year. By July 13 Le Borgne's force was on the verge of attacking La Tour's fort when the commanding officer decided to delay the attempt indefinitely.[16] The following day, in an ironic twist of fate, an Anglo–New England expedition led by

Robert Sedgwick began the siege of the French fort.[17]

Robert Sedgwick had arrived in Massachusetts in 1636 and had soon become a successful merchant and entrepreneur and an active Church member. In 1653 he was chosen major-general, the officer in charge of the colonial militia,[18] but he surrendered this office to Gibbons during the following year. While visiting England in 1653–54, Sedgwick was appointed by Cromwell the commanding officer of a military expedition against the Dutch colony on the Hudson River. The second-in-command was Captain John Leverett, Sedgwick's son-in-law. Before Sedgwick and Leverett could organize in Boston the assault upon the Dutch, they received word from Cromwell that peace had been declared.[19]

Sedgwick had already discovered that there was little enthusiasm in Massachusetts for the expedition against the Dutch. One of his officers observed that "ye Colonye of ye Masachusets did not act with yt life yt was Expected supposing they had not a just call for suche a worke."[20] But Sedgwick was not content merely to wait eight weeks for a load of masts to be prepared for the return voyage to England. He had at his disposal three ships, the *Augustine*, the *Hope*, and the *Church*, and a small ketch "fitted for the former designe," and he could not comprehend why the Almighty would "see it meett not to imploy us" in some manner.[21] He knew from his instructions from Cromwell that he was empowered to seize "ye shipps of any of ye subjects of ye ffrench King."[22] This of course meant that Sedgwick was able to sail into Nova Scotia waters in search of French ships, even though France was at peace with England. Sedgwick assumed that he was also permitted to attack the French settlements in the area.

Sedgwick badly needed some excitement and perhaps some booty for his Roundhead troops and the 100 Massachusetts volunteers recruited for the Dutch expedition, but there were other reasons why he and Leverett favoured a Nova Scotia expedition. First, as Leverett explained to Cromwell, it was imperative

> in owneing of ye English Interest and enleargling your
> Highness Dominions in these Westerne American parts or
> rather ye Interest of ye Lord Jesus in removeing so many of
> ye locusts as were crept in amongst ye blind Indians to
> deceive them as else where they have ye Nations, and thereby
> vindicated his owne glorious name against ye blasphemyes

of yt deludeing Crew who had given it out among ye Indians;
that ye English were so and so valiant and victorious agt ye
Dutch at Sea, but yt one French man could beat ten English-
men a shoare.[23]

Leverett's men visiting Nova Scotia the previous summer probably brought back this news concerning French anti-English propaganda among the Indians. Like a growing number of Massachusetts residents, especially those residing in the northeastern frontier areas, Leverett was becoming increasingly concerned about a possible French-Indian military alliance. "The great affright of the people" was something he felt compelled to take into consideration.[24] The second reason in favour of the Nova Scotia raid was basically an economic one: to reassert Massachusetts' influence in "tradinge and fishinge."[25] Le Borgne's economic impact had to be neutralized. Leverett certainly had economic interests to protect in Nova Scotia, and it was preferable for him and his friends to have Nova Scotia in English hands rather than in the possession of Le Borgne or even the not-to-be-trusted La Tour.

It would be wrong to assume that the Sedgwick expedition was merely a matter of Cromwellian influence impinging upon North American affairs.[26] The Protector's influence was there, but it should not be forgotten that the leaders of the expedition were Massachusetts men and that many of the troops involved were from the colony. The expedition may be seen as an economic and military thrust from Massachusetts, even though the General Court showed little enthusiasm for it. After Sedgwick's force had returned to Massachusetts, the General Court ordered the commanding officer to inform it, "by what authority or Commission, of which we are yet altogether ignorant, they have surprised the ffrench and possess'd their forts."[27] The independent-minded members of the Court were probably objecting most to the fact that Sedgwick had decided to attack Nova Scotia without first consulting them.

After a three-day siege, La Tour's fort was captured and a "Considerable quantitie of moose skins" confiscated by Sedgwick's 170 troops. La Tour's force was transported to France after being permitted to "march out of ye fort with Collers flying and with Drums." On July 31, 1654, Sedgwick's fleet sailed to Port Royal where Le Borgne's vessel, the *Châteaufort*, was captured "Laden with Brande

french wines, vinegar and salt with som Lining." Port Royal surrendered after the French defenders had been badly mauled by the
experienced "ould England souldiers," who put on a spirited display
for the less venturesome New England volunteers.[28] The captured
French inhabitants were permitted either to remain in Nova Scotia,
where they were promised freedom of worship, or to return to
France.[29]

After leaving a small garrison at Port Royal, as he had also done at
the mouth of the St. John, Sedgwick sailed to Pentagouet on the
Penobscot River — "a place of good trade with ye Indens."[30] Pentagouet was captured on September 2. Sedgwick's expedition had driven
the French military and fur interests from the Bay of Fundy area
and had firmly established English control over it. Only one of his
men had been killed and six wounded. The only significant French
settlement remaining in Nova Scotia was that belonging to Nicolas
Denys on Cape Breton Island,[31] a safe distance from Massachusetts and
of no immediate threat or challenge to the English colony. Sedgwick's
expedition was not only a brilliant military success. It has been estimated that "he plundered the forts of their goods to the value of about
£10,000."[32] The pious Sedgwick was understandably abundantly
blessed with what he called "the vareious and strainge turnes in God's
workings and dealeings."[33]

Until Nova Scotia's final disposition by Cromwell, Leverett was
appointed the military commander of the captured forts, whereas
Sedgwick, after returning to London with La Tour, was ordered to
the Caribbean where he died in 1656. Leverett employed several Massachusetts merchants, notably Captain John Allen of Charlestown, who
had considerable experience in the Acadian trade, in an attempt to
rule the conquered territory. Leverett's potential competitors were
prohibited by the Massachusetts General Court from trading with the
Nova Scotia Indians, since it was hoped that the money spent on
Leverett's garrison would come from the profits of the fur trade.[34] For
the hundreds of French settlers who remained, nothing had changed
very much in Nova Scotia. The only major difference was that the
fur monopoly was now in the hands of an absentee New Englander
whose tiny English-speaking force occupied the three former French
forts. Some of the bucolic Acadians were probably oblivious to the
change; others were indifferent or perhaps secretly delighted. At last
some semblance of stability had returned, and the actual source of

this stability was conceived to be of little consequence.

During the autumn of 1655, the Massachusetts General Court publicly revealed some concern about the future of Nova Scotia. Fearing that Cromwell might return the area to the French, the Court instructed John Leverett to protect Massachusetts' interests "before the Lord Protector and his honnorable council in England."[35] Leverett was to attempt to persuade Cromwell to grant Nova Scotia to Massachusetts, provided that Massachusetts "be free from charges and other ingagements."[36] The General Court was emphatic in its desire to be free of the large La Tour debt to Gibbons, as well as the considerable sum Leverett was demanding to cover the expenses involved in garrisoning the captured colony. Not surprisingly, Cromwell turned down the Massachusetts petition. Instead, probably in early 1656, he began to bargain with La Tour, who had discovered in his almost bottomless pocket the 1630 grant for Nova Scotia, which he had received from Sir William Alexander. Almost overnight, once again, La Tour had transformed himself into an ardent English subject. Some six years earlier he had been in Quebec assisting the Jesuits in the missionary activities and battling against the Iroquois. In 1656 he had become one of Cromwell's supporters.[37]

In arguing that only he deserved to govern the area, La Tour used his extraordinary self-confidence and his knowledge that neither Cromwell nor Massachusetts was eager to colonize Nova Scotia. His chief problem in the negotiations was finances — the money he owed Major Gibbons and the sum demanded by Leverett. La Tour needed a partner with both money and influence. He found such a man in Thomas Temple.

Temple, who always maintained that Charles I had called him "honest Tom," was the nephew of the influential William Fiennes, Viscount Saye and Sele, a member of Cromwell's Council of State.[38] Fiennes, who had a great deal of influence on the Protector's North American policy, played a key role in bringing his forty-two-year-old nephew in contact with La Tour and with William Crowne, a merchant who promised to supply the necessary financing.[39] Thus La Tour provided the opportunity for the new partners to gain control of Nova Scotia: Temple the crucial governmental contact, and Crowne the money.

After agreeing to pay over £5,000 to Gibbons's widow and to Leverett, the three partners were granted the fur monopoly in Nova

Scotia from present-day Lunenburg to the "St. George River" west of the Penobscot. All that the English government was to receive in return was "20 beaver skins and 20 moose skins payable annually."[40] Temple and Crowne wanted La Tour to play a secondary role and they did not wish to be outmanoeuvred by the wily Frenchman. He was therefore persuaded in September, 1656, to surrender his rights to Temple and Crowne on condition that they promise to pay his debts and a yearly 5 percent of the proceeds of the fur trade. Thus Temple, not La Tour, was named governor.

In many respects La Tour had been used as a convenient tool by Cromwell, Temple, and Crowne, and then cast aside once he had served his purpose. He had been beaten at his own game by the Puritans. Cromwell's claim to the Bay of Fundy—Cape Sable area of Nova Scotia apparently demanded a more durable basis than that of the conquest of 1654. This must have been one of the major reasons why so much emphasis was placed on the fact that La Tour's title could be traced directly to the grant made by James I to Sir William Alexander in 1621. Cromwell had at last found the legal justification for Sedgwick's successful expedition.

La Tour returned to the Cape Sable area where he eventually died in 1663. Pragmatic, ruthless, and ambitious, he had lived a life of almost constant controversy. He had a profound impact on Massachusetts—Nova Scotia relations throughout his sojourn in the region. Practical considerations always outweighed his sense of loyalty to any one country. He seemed as much at home in Quebec as in Boston, in London as in Port Royal.

In 1657 Temple arrived in Boston from where he resolved to rule his colony and to exploit its resources. He was accompanied by a large retinue of servants and "was honourably received ashore by the Governor and Company soldiers." When one of Leverett's friends informed Temple that his "noble spirit will not suit with Acadie, or at least the profit of Acadie will not maintain his post," the absentee Nova Scotia governor replied that "he will by degrees clear himself of the unnecessary charge, which he is at by many servants, that he brought over, who will be as drones to eat up all the honey, that others labour for, and that he will have but two at most, to wait upon himself."[41] Temple was learning quickly. He was short of money and needed considerable working capital. The only source of income from his colony was the fur trade, and to carry on this trade a large initial investment was necessary. Goods were needed to exchange for pelts and skins, and experienced men had to be hired to conduct the trade and to man the posts. In addition, of course, the genial governor, possessing many of the traits of the born aristocrat, felt under an obligation to live a life worthy of an English gentleman.

Temple found his financial saviour in Captain Thomas Breedon, a prominent Boston and London merchant. Breedon represented the new group of Massachusetts entrepreneurs who had displaced, by the late 1650s, the first generation of mercantile leaders.[42] In exchange for his financial assistance, Breedon was named by Temple his deputy and lieutenant in Nova Scotia. Two other Boston merchants involved themselves with Breedon, Hezekiah Usher and Thomas Lake (who had been previously associated with Leverett in the Nova Scotia trade).[43] Thus the Boston merchants had once again reasserted their economic control over the Nova Scotia fur trade. Of his treatment by his merchant associates Temple frequently and bitterly complained. He alleged that they not only exacted a 100 percent profit on the goods they sold him but that they also placed their own value on the Nova Scotia furs which they consigned directly to themselves.[44]

Temple's arrangement with Crowne apparently gave Crowne in 1657 control of the territory west of present-day Machias. Three years later Crowne leased his territory to Temple for an annual rent of £110.[45] Crowne's role throughout was peripheral and secondary. After his arrival at Boston, Temple had little time to savour the delights of the Puritan capital. He was forced in 1658 to organize an expedition to drive the stubborn Le Borgne from Nova Scotia. In 1657 Emmanuel Le Borgne had been appointed governor of Acadia by Louis XIV. The following year his son took possession of La Hève and confiscated the pelts that Temple's men had stored there. Eager to assert his sovereignty and compelled to protect his economic interests, Temple showed unusual vigour and foresight in despatching his expedition. The Massachusetts assault on La Hève was thus vividly described by a French inhabitant of the region:

> But the English knowing that Le Borgne was at La Haive [sic] went there to take him. Seeing them coming, Le Borgne retired into the woods with some of his men, of whom much of the greater part remained with Guilbault [Le Borgne's associate] in the fort with the intention of defending it. In fact they resisted an attack by the English of whom several were

killed on the spot, among others their commander. This
compelled them to retire for some time. But Guilbault, who
had no other interest in this affair than to save his goods,
agreed then with the English to deliver the fort into their
hands on condition that everything which belonged to him
. . . should be restored . . . and this was carried out. But the
English having entered the fort, and not having found Le
Borgne there, were not willing that he should be included in
the capitulation. This compelled him, having gone into the
woods without provisions, to come in a little later and give
himself up as a prisoner. They carried him off to Boston,
where [they] kept him under guard for a long time.[46]

While a prisoner in Boston, the young Le Borgne de Belle-Isle
persuaded Temple to do everything in his power to obtain permission
for the Le Borgnes to pursue the cod fishery in the La Hève area. But
apparently nothing came of Temple's request to his uncle Lord
Fiennes. The interest of the Le Borgnes continued in Nova Scotia, and
in 1667 Belle-Isle received a royal commission from the French
monarch as governor and lieutenant-general of Acadia. Belle-Isle
possessed this useless commission for three years until Nova Scotia was
finally returned to the French in 1670.[47]

After the restoration of Charles II in 1660, a host of vociferous
claimants for Nova Scotia appeared, hoping to dispossess those to
whom the area had been granted by Cromwell. To protect his interests,
Temple felt compelled to appoint Breedon to represent him in London.
Breedon soon discovered that a Thomas Elliot, a groom of the bed-
chamber who was supported by the Lord Chancellor Clarendon,
appeared likely to displace Temple. Fearing, perhaps, that he would
lose his own considerable investment in Nova Scotia if Temple lost his
grant, Breedon agreed to recognize Elliot as proprietor and to pay
him £600 yearly if Elliot appointed him governor. The bargain was
struck and for a time Temple was dispossessed. He therefore hurried to
England where he was able to recover his colony on payment of the
£600 yearly to Elliot.[48] As a further indication of royal favour,
Temple was created a baronet of Nova Scotia in 1662. "Honest Tom"
had become Sir Thomas Temple, but at a considerable price.

Temple's relationship at this juncture with Breedon has been
described in this way:

*Doubtless Temple would now have been glad to free himself
from his dependence on one who had betrayed him, but he
was too much in debt to Breedon to be able to do so immediately. Breedon served him both as banker, providing the
necessary capital for carrying on the Acadian trade, and as
business manager, for the Acadian furs were consigned to
Breedon's Boston agents, and it may be inferred from his
English connections that he attended to the disposing of them
in England. Temple, in fact, treated Acadia somewhat as many
an English landlord treated his estate, leaving the management
to others, getting a precarious living from it, and remaining
perpetually in debt.*[49]

Temple complained that the net income from Nova Scotia never
exceeded £900 yearly, of which he had to pay Elliot £600. The
Boston merchants in addition charged him £180 to transfer this money
in British currency to Elliot. Thus Temple, according to his conserva-
tive estimate, had only £120 a year to live on. In fact the Nova Scotia
trade must have brought him much more money, for Temple was
able to accumulate a great deal of valuable property in Boston and
along the Kennebec River. He owned a vessel that was likely engaged
in the Nova Scotia trade. By 1668, furthermore, Temple had finally
succeeded in freeing himself from his financial obligations to Breedon.[50]
This was no mean accomplishment for somebody earning only £120
per year.

The Massachusetts General Court always treated Temple well.
After 1660 it had enough problems of its own with Charles II and had
no desire to appropriate Temple's colony. Besides, because Temple
resided in Boston and was closely associated with many of the capital's
merchants, Nova Scotia was virtually the northeastern extension of
Massachusetts. This close association of Temple with the General
Court was shown on two separate occasions in 1658, and again in 1663
and 1666. In May, 1658, the General Court lent Temple "three hundred
weight of minion shott" for the expedition against Le Borgne. Five
months later the Court declared:

*Whereas the honnorable Colonell Thomas Temple is, by
Commission from his highnes the Lord Protector, constitued
governor of Acady and Nova Scotia . . . and is thereby
impowred to seize and confiscatt the vessells and goods of all*

persons trading peltry or furs with Indians without his licence,
as also to burne, kill and destroy all such as shall resist
him . . . this Court, judging it meete to prevent all forcible
contests or unnecessary losse that maybe occasioned by any
exhorbitant or inconsiderat persons, as also all occasions of
offence betweene this colony and the governor aforesajd,
being also desirous that loving and good correspondency may
be cherrished & majnteyned, doth order, that henceforth it
shall not be lawfull for any person of this jurisdiction to trade
for furrs or peltry with the Indjans within the ljmitts
aforesajd, without licence from the sajd governor; and it shall
be lawfull for the sajd governor, or his attourney, authorized
thereunto under his hand, to arrest, sue & implead any person
or persons that shall be found offending herein in any Court
within the ljmitts of this colony in any action of the case or
trespass, and shall have aequall injustice therein.[51]

Thus the General Court not only showed its concern for good relations
with Nova Scotia but it also asserted that breaking Temple's monopoly
was in a sense an offence against the law of Massachusetts. Temple's
regulations would be enforced in Massachusetts by Massachusetts
courts. Nova Scotia was therefore conceived to be in 1658, at least, the
economic and legal appendage of Massachusetts.

In May, 1663, and again in 1666, the General Court reiterated its
October, 1658, declaration "prohibbiting trade with ye Indians in Nova
Scotia, on ye nation of Sr. Tho. Temple, knight and baronet, gov.
thereof." Moreover, in September, 1666, the Court endeavoured to
implement its Nova Scotia regulations:

On the motion of Sr. Thomas Temple, informing this Court
that severall inhabitants of this jurisdiction have, contrary to
the order of this Court prohibiting all their inhabitants to
make any incroachments on the confines of the sajd Sr.
Thomas Temple, taken upon them to goe into his territorjes,
& there breake open the house of the sajd . . . Temple, and
have despoyled him of his goods, & being come hither some of
them, this Court judgeth it meete to desire Major Generall
Jno. Leverett & Captain Thomas Clarke, who have in
themselves power to exert their authority, to send for such
persons by warrant, to appeare before them as Sr. Thomas

Temple shall informe them to have had any hand in
despoyling him of his goods, & the sajd persons thoroughly
to examine, & if thereupon they finde cause, the sajd persons
to committ to prison.[52]

Nothing more was said about the case in the General Court *Records*.
Perhaps Temple was reimbursed before the threatened trial or perhaps
his evidence left something to be desired. Nevertheless, the incident
was an outward and visible sign of the General Court's concern for
Temple's sovereignty and the dependence of Temple on the Massachusetts authorities.

It was the Anglo-French war of 1666–67 that finally brought
Temple's Nova Scotia venture to an end and ultimately led to his
return to England. It seems likely that by 1666 Temple had come a
long way in extricating himself from his financial difficulties. In
improving his financial position, he had also constructed an almost
ideal relationship, in Massachusetts' eyes at least, between the colony
and Nova Scotia. All trade and profits came to Boston and all administrative and defence costs were shouldered by Temple himself.[53] But
the Anglo-French war and the peace treaty ending it shattered this
idyllic arrangement.

The war of 1666–67 was the first Anglo-French war that involved
Massachusetts. The war must have revealed to at least a few perceptive
residents the multiplicity of serious problems that faced them because
of the presence of the French in New France and in Nova Scotia. In
1666 and 1667 neither was yet a threat to Massachusetts, but French
privateers from the West Indies and New France certainly were. In
their letters from Charles II in which they first learned of the declaration of war with France, Temple and the governors of the various
New England colonies were encouraged to consider plans "for the
reducing Canada."[54] Temple met with John Winthrop, Jr., governor
of Connecticut, and with the governor and Council of Massachusetts.
It was unanimously agreed on September 11, 1666, that "it is not
feasable, as well in respect of the difficulty (if not impossibility) of a
land march over the rocky mounteines & houling desarts about fower
hundred miles, as the strength of the French there according to
report."[55] Temple had his own serious defence problems to worry
about in Nova Scotia, and Massachusetts was not interested in any
imperialist adventure as long as the French were no serious and

immediate threat to the colony's frontiers. With Nova Scotia in English hands, there was little danger from the North American French. Another reason for Massachusetts' lack of response was the fact that the General Court was locked in a bitter dispute with the commissioners of Charles II, who were investigating the colonies, and consequently the Court was in no mood to make any sacrifice in terms of men or money for the king.

If the declaration of the war had shocked Temple and disturbed Massachusetts, news of the peace treaty, the Treaty of Breda, had a traumatic impact. In order to recover the English half of the island of St. Christopher, Charles II had agreed to return Temple's territory to the French. Economically speaking, the exchange undoubtedly favoured the English, but it was a disaster for Temple. Furthermore the return of Nova Scotia to the French had significant economic and strategic consequences for Massachusetts. The Nova Scotia fur trade was now to be a monopoly of the Le Borgnes,[56] and the position of the Massachusetts fishery interests in southern Nova Scotia was threatened.

When it became clear that Temple's strident protests had fallen upon deaf ears, the General Court in May, 1669, bitterly complained to Lord Arlington. This strongly worded protest accurately and forcefully portrayed the dangers to be anticipated from a French-controlled Nova Scotia:

> Should the French have that country it would not only obstruct the trade of peltry, but of fishing, which is most considerable; for when they had possession of it, even in peace, the least occasion was taken by them to make prize of vessels fishing on those coasts, and should there happen a war, how bold their attempts may be to annoy those plantations needs no great forereach to apprehend. It would be doubtless not only a reviving of the French King's withering interest in North America, but a very large augmentation of advantage to their settlement at Kebeck, and become as an half girdle to the English settlements by land, added to their sea advantage for the obstruction of navigation; so that the parting with Nova Scotia or Acadia for St. Christopher's holds slender proportion.[57]

In spite of Massachusetts' vociferous complaint and Temple's desperate manoeuvring, Temple, in 1670, finally surrendered "Pentagoet, St.

John's and Port Royal ... containing the whole country under my command,"[58] to the French governor, Andigné de Grandfontaine. The Nova Scotia fur monopoly was placed temporarily in the hands of the persistent Le Borgnes, who "denied [the Boston merchants] trade with the savages."[59] In addition, it was agreed in Massachusetts, at least, that the boundary between Nova Scotia and New England was to follow the Penobscot River — the pre-1654 line.

Under Temple's absentee rule, Nova Scotia had become an economic and political appendage of Massachusetts. In 1670 Yankee fur traders and fishermen had a virtual monopoly over these resources from the Kennebec to the St. John River and from the St. John to Port Royal and Cape Sable; and at the moment when the French were regaining their former colony, Massachusetts fishermen were beginning to push up the Atlantic coast to Canso and beyond.

The critical problem confronting the returning French — and the issue that would greatly affect Massachusetts–Nova Scotia relations for the rest of the century — was whether Massachusetts' tight economic stranglehold could be broken. In other words, would Nova Scotia be able to declare its economic as well as its political independence from the Puritan colony? It was obvious in 1670 that the Boston-area merchants and the fishermen from Salem and Marblehead were unwilling to abandon, without a fierce struggle, what they perceived to be their God-given area of exploration. Faced with this kind of intransigence and with the fact that the Acadians were hopelessly outnumbered by the Massachusetts inhabitants, French colonial authorities found themselves facing a most perplexing dilemma.

3

Years of Peace and Years of Growing Tension, 1670-1686

In the general context of Massachusetts–Nova Scotia relations for the period 1670 to 1686, the two most influential individuals were Boston's enterprising merchant John Nelson, who was Temple's nephew, and Jean-Vincent d'Abbadie de Saint-Castin, the French soldier and Abenaki chief who lived at Pentagouet. Soon after 1670 these two men, both in their twenties and both vitally interested in the Nova Scotia fur trade, developed extremely close personal and commercial relations. They probably controlled most of the Nova Scotia fur trade, and they were also responsible for providing most of the Acadians with European supplies of one kind and another.[1] In terms of commercial expansion and financial success, Castin and Nelson were completely dependent upon one another. And for much of the period, this dependence strengthened existing ties between Massachusetts and Nova Scotia.

Nelson's involvement in Nova Scotia began in 1674 when on the death of his unmarried uncle in London, he was bequeathed the bulk of Temple's estate, including the disputed claim to Nova Scotia. Nelson, because of his financial contacts in Boston and London, provided the capital and business acumen for the partnership's commercial ventures. Castin, on the other hand, because of his unusually close relations with the Indians of the entire Nova Scotia–Maine region, was able to tap this fur reservoir for himself and for Nelson. In addition,

Castin opened many doors for Nelson among the Acadian settlers as well as in New France. Nelson's large warehouse at Port Royal and his vessels that regularly visited the Nova Scotia settlements were convincing proof that the Temple claim to Nova Scotia was not a dead issue.

A contemporary, who likely knew him well, described Nelson as being an "Episcopalian in principle, and of a gay free temper."[2] Nelson was, it is clear, an opportunistic merchant adventurer. By taking full advantage of his uncle's business contacts and by marrying the daughter of William Tailer, Sr., whose wife was the sister of William Stoughton, land speculator, politician, and judge, Nelson became part of the new Boston commercial and political élite. In the 1670s, as Professor Bernard Bailyn has observed, this élite, "emerging from the constrictions of a medieval social order, was an effective agent of change in the nascent society of colonial New England." Merchants like John Nelson and William Tailer in the 1670s and '80s experienced first-hand the divisive forces of "the widening of commercial contacts and the tightening of the British mercantilist system."[3] For Nelson, however, the latter only infrequently damaged his large yet illegal trade with the French.[4]

Nelson's associate Castin had come to New France in 1665 as an ensign in the Carignan-Salières regiment. When his friend Grandfontaine, a captain in the same regiment, was appointed governor of Nova Scotia, Castin accompanied him to Pentagouet. Here Castin exerted a considerable influence over the Abenaki Indians, especially those who lived along the Penobscot. He "roamed the woods and hunted with them, learned their language, had intercourse with their women . . . and was made a chief."[5] Residing as he did at the southern extremity of the French colony, his relations were more intimate with the English than they were with the French. Nevertheless, he felt no more attachment to the English Crown than he did to Louis XIV. Castin was a Nova Scotian *coureur de bois* whose primary allegiance, as had been La Tour's, was to himself and to the fur frontier.

Andigné de Grandfontaine spent less than three years in Nova Scotia. His commission as governor of the French colony was an embarrassment to him and in most respects a useless piece of paper. He grew completely dependent upon the goodwill of the Massachusetts merchants and tradesmen. To provide communications between Pentagouet, his capital, and Port Royal, Grandfontaine had been compelled to purchase a ketch from Temple.[6] To help with various building projects, the governor had to bring in carpenters from Massachusetts. When short of supplies and food, he sent to Massachusetts for assistance.[7] Because of his dependence on the neighbouring English colony, and because he had been instructed to develop good relations with Massachusetts,[8] Grandfontaine permitted the Massachusetts fishermen to continue with their Nova Scotian dry fishery, that is, in processing their fish on shore. To save some face, the governor announced soon after arriving in Nova Scotia in 1670 that he would require each New England fishing vessel fishing in Nova Scotia waters to pay him a fee of "*vingt cinq éscus.*"[9] But there were no means available for the French to force the fishermen to pay this sum. It is highly unlikely that the tough-fisted Salem and Marblehead fishermen sailed to the Penobscot for the special purpose of making the payment. A few may have paid Temple for their fishing rights,[10] but none would pay a largely helpless French governor.

Fully aware of Grandfontaine's tenuous position and eager to take advantage of it, the Massachusetts General Court in 1671 decided to push its boundaries towards the northeast. The Treaty of Breda had been unusually vague about this line of demarcation. Captain Thomas Clark, who was involved in the Kennebec fur trade, was put in charge of the survey. He persuaded the General Court to expand into the contested area between the Kennebec and Penobscot. Consequently, by 1674 the new county of Cornwall had been established in the Pemaquid region.[11] For Massachusetts, therefore, the southwestern boundary of Nova Scotia was the Penobscot. For Grandfontaine and for Jacques de Chambly, who replaced him in the autumn of 1673, the southwestern boundary was the Kennebec.[12] These two claims, however, conflicted with the grant originally made by Charles II to the Duke of York in 1664 and renewed in 1674. According to this grant, the Duke of York possessed all territory between the Kennebec and the St. Croix.[13]

To add further confusion to a once more chaotic situation, Nova Scotia in 1674 was captured by a Dutch sea-captain, Jurriaen Aernoutsz. With the United Netherlands at war with France and her new ally England, Aernoutsz, early in 1674, was commissioned by the Dutch governor of Curaçao in the West Indies to attack English and French settlements in northeastern North America.[14] Sailing north in the frigate *Flying Horse*, the captain discovered at New York in early

July that England and Holland had already made peace by the Treaty of Westminster. Here also Aernoutsz met the Boston merchant John Rhodes who talked him into attacking the French in Nova Scotia, as Sedgwick had done twenty years earlier under surprisingly similar circumstances. Rhodes, an experienced pilot familiar with the Nova Scotia coast, and some of his friends joined the Dutch expedition.[15] On July 31 Governor Chambly with some thirty men quickly surrendered Pentagouet. Moving in a northeasterly direction, Aernoutsz pillaged various tiny French settlements until he reached the mouth of the St. John River. From this point his men went up the river and captured the small French port of Jemseg near present-day Fredericton.[16]

In all, the Dutch force had spent about a month in Nova Scotia. In that period Aernoutsz had confiscated considerable booty and had captured every member of the French garrison, including the governor, Chambly. In addition, Aernoutsz had been very conscientious, whenever he landed, about burying glass bottles containing copies of his commission and declarations that the territory now belonged to the Prince of Orange. The Dutch officer even renamed the region New Holland. He then sailed to Boston where he sold his plunder, which included the cannon from Fort Pentagouet, and landed his prisoners and John Rhodes, whom he appointed commander of the Dutch colony of New Holland.[17] Rhodes hoped to rule Nova Scotia from Boston as Temple had done.

Governor Frontenac of New France blamed the Massachusetts authorities for organizing the expedition against Nova Scotia,[18] but this charge was without foundation. Rhodes had no connection with the Boston authorities and the plan to attack the French was hatched in New York. A handful of New Englanders was involved because of chance and greedy opportunism, not because of any kind of Massachusetts imperialism. With Nova Scotia firmly under the economic domination of Massachusetts, there was obviously no need for such a thrust.

Rhodes took his Dutch commission as commander seriously. He regarded it as an opportunity for him to fill his pockets by gaining control of the Nova Scotia fur trade, which he considered to be his monopoly. In late autumn Rhodes was in Nova Scotia making life miserable for a number of Massachusetts merchants. In December, 1674, William Waldron, for example, reported that "coming homewards ... Rhodes, and others fired two guns at him [Waldron] and commanded him to anchor; they came on board and forcibly took peltry to the value of about £60, carried himself and goods to their vessel and made him set his hand to a writing drawn by John Rhodes that they had taken nothing but peltry and had taken it in New Holland."[19] Two months later, John Freak, another Massachusetts merchant, complained that "a small vessel of his, under command of George Manning, on the voyage home from the eastward, was, in the river of St. John, by John Rhodes and some Dutchmen, his complices, in December last, piratically seized and the master wounded."[20] At the same time, that is in early 1675, "several others of the Massachusetts jurisdiction also complained, and asked that measures might be taken for security."[21] According to these men, Rhodes was trying to drive Massachusetts merchants from a market that was rightfully theirs, thereby threatening to break the Massachusetts stranglehold on the Nova Scotia fur trade. Would the fishery be next? The Massachusetts Council, subject to considerable merchant pressure, resolved to deal with the situation without delay. Governor John Leverett commissioned Captain Samuel Mosely to capture Rhodes, and by April 12, 1675, Rhodes and his associates were imprisoned in Boston jail.[22] The captives were tried for piracy, and three, including Rhodes, were sentenced to death. But the sentence was never carried out; the men instead were banished from the colony, though as far as Rhodes was concerned, not for long. In 1678 he apparently tried to work out some kind of business arrangement with Castin concerning the Nova Scotia fur trade.[23] This attempt failed since Rhodes was captured by agents of the Duke of York in the Pemaquid region and taken prisoner to New York.[24] Released in October, 1678, he moved to Delaware and in all likelihood never returned to Massachusetts or to Nova Scotia.

It was ironic that the Treaty of Nimwegen of 1678, ending hostilities between France and Holland, did not even mention Nova Scotia. Only Rhodes had taken the Aernoutsz commission seriously. In 1678, under the leadership of Sieur de La Vallière, the new governor, the French re-established their control over Nova Scotia.[25] The Aernoutsz raid revealed that the French hold on Nova Scotia in the 1670s was extremely tenuous. Massachusetts' vigorous response to the Rhodes threat further showed how involved and influential those Massachusetts merchants trading in Nova Scotia actually were. It seems likely that if King Philip's War had not broken out in 1675, these merchants would have pressed the Massachusetts government to fill the power vacuum in Nova Scotia and thus ensure the required stability the French were obviously unable to provide.

By late 1674 two significant northeastern expansionist thrusts were at work in Massachusetts. One, manipulated by a few aggressive land speculators, was directed to the southwestern corner of Nova Scotia. The other, led by some of the Massachusetts merchants, was pointed at all of Nova Scotia. Even without the aid of propagandists and the fishing interests, these two thrusts, for a moment at least, appeared to be providing Massachusetts' northeastern expansion with considerable momentum. "Massachusetts," one contemporary observer complained, "having the preheminence in trade, strength and riches, take the liberty to clayme as farre as their convenience and interest directs, never wanting a pretext of right to any place that is commodious for them, declaring they doe not know the boundaries of their common-wealth."[26]

Massachusetts' territorial expansionism was, without question, dealt a severe blow by King Philip's War, an indigenous uprising of the New England Indians against what they considered to be the shattering impact of European civilization. For some two years almost all of Massachusetts and much of New England was a violent and bloody battleground. Hundreds of Massachusetts residents lost their lives; many families were scattered; homes were destroyed and women and children butchered.[27] The Acadians played absolutely no role in encouraging or in supplying the Indians when fighting began in earnest in Maine in the summer of 1676. Nonetheless, the French were blamed by many Massachusetts residents for the Indian raids. Edward Randolph, special agent of the Lords of Trade in New England, suggested in 1676 that "the government of the Massachusetts hath a perfect hatred for the French, because of their too near neighbourhood, and losse of their trade, and looke upon them with an evill eye, believing they have had a hand in the late warre with the Indians."[28] The Reverend Increase Mather maintained, "It is too evident that a French Coal hath kindled this unhappy fire."[29] Mather and Randolph and others were wrong. Anglo-Saxon callous arrogance had precipitated hostilities, and if anyone could be blamed for supplying the Indians with firearms, it was the New England traders themselves.[30]

By December, 1676, most of the Maine settlements east of the Piscataqua River had been abandoned. The northeastern thrust of expansion had been stopped and even reversed. Governor Edmund Andros of New York saw in the frontier difficulties an opportunity to assert the Duke of York's sovereignty over the disputed area between the Kennebec and the St. Croix. The French, the Dutch, and now Massachusetts had been driven out. As far as Andros was concerned, such an opportunity could not be missed. He informed his British superiors in November, 1677:

> Upon returne of said sloope in January, 1677 being more particularly informed all said Easterne parts were wholly deserted by ye Indyans, and then neglected by Boston, who had usurped itt, butt now lost itt, and told the Inhabitants 'twas the Dukes and nott their businesse, and dayly heareing of ye number of captives, sloope and vessells taken by the Indyans, doing mischeife as farr as Piscattaway; The Governor resolved, and in June 1677 sent a force and strong fram'd Redoutt in four good sloops to take possession and settle in his Royll Highnesse right at Pemaquid, and defend or secure the ffishery giving notice thereof to the Massachusetts and our other neighbours.[31]

The Andros fort at Pemaquid was defended by seven cannon, fifty regular troops, and a four-gun sloop "to attend ye Coast and ffishery."[32]

The New York governor's unilateral decision to provide a buffer between Massachusetts and the French was not favourably received in Boston. This was particularly the case when it was discovered that the New Yorkers claimed the right to control and to license all fishermen and fur traders operating in the Duke of York's huge royal province. The Massachusetts General Court bitterly complained in October, 1677, about Andros's attempt "to inhibitt the people of this jurisdiction from their anntient priviledge and liberty as Englishmen."[33] A new element had been introduced to complicate still further Massachusetts–Nova Scotia relations, for the New Yorkers lacked the pragmatic approach towards the French of the New Englanders, whom they had replaced in this sensitive frontier area. Over the years the Boston authorities and the Massachusetts entrepreneurs had carefully worked out a satisfactory relationship with the Acadians and later with Castin. The Acadians were actually quite different from the inhabitants of New France, but this was not the point of view of the New York authorities who were convinced that all Frenchmen were precisely alike. This inability to distinguish between the two groups of French inhabitants and to view events in the two different areas of North America in quite different perspectives meant that the Pemaquid New Yorkers possessed a distorted picture of Acadian–New England relations. Massachusetts could not control the New Yorkers whose actions and policies could, nevertheless, have a devastating impact on the colony and on its relations with the Acadians and their Indian allies. In a sense then Massachusetts was no longer the effective master of its own special relationship with Nova Scotia.

With Rhodes out of the way, and in spite of the outbreak of King Philip's War, some Boston merchants had returned to the Bay of Fundy region looking for furs.[34] Others, at the moment when their friends in Massachusetts were "like soules distracted running hither and thither for shelter, and no where at ease,"[35] were loading their vessels with coal from the surface seams of northeastern Cape Breton island.[36] Still others were starting to dig some of the readily available gypsum to be found in southeastern Cape Breton.[37]

In the 1670s and 1680s the fur trade, next to the fishery, continued to be the most valuable asset in the Massachusetts–Nova Scotia commercial relationship. Soon after King Philip's War had ended in 1677, and Andros had constructed Fort Pemaquid, John Nelson seems to have succeeded in achieving a dominant position over his fur trade competitors. He did this by his own energetic activity, by taking full advantage of his uncle's Acadian and Indian contacts, and by developing his close relationship with Castin. In January, 1677, the Massachusetts Council issued a proclamation prohibiting all trade with Nova Scotia and the Maine area in the hope of preventing the Indians in the region from receiving guns and ammunition. This embargo marked a response by Massachusetts residents reacting violently to the "Trade, and worldly interest, by whom the Indians have been scandalized."[38] For a brief time Nelson's trade ventures were adversely affected by the embargo.[39] But as tension with the Indians lessened after 1677 and since enforcement of the Council regulation proved so difficult, the embargo, much to Nelson's relief, was lifted.

King Philip's War had not played havoc, either, with what may be considered to be the mainspring of Massachusetts commerce — the cod fishery. In 1676 Randolph reported that despite the war, Massachusetts fishermen had caught 12,000 quintals of cod worth some

£50,000.⁴⁰ Some of this fish, perhaps most of it, had been caught or dried in the Cape Sable region of Nova Scotia. In the summer of 1677 the Nova Scotia fishery was dealt a delayed but minor blow from the Indians. During these months a few "fishing catches about Cape Sable" were captured by the Micmacs.⁴¹ But this was an isolated incident and there apparently was no further difficulty. Certainly the Nova Scotia French were in no way implicated in the incident. Because they were completely dependent upon Massachusetts for supplies and because most of the Acadians distrusted and were fearful of the Micmacs, a Micmac-Acadian alliance was out of the question.

From 1678 to 1682 Massachusetts strengthened even further its economic hold over Nova Scotia. Possibly 100 fishing ketches from Salem and Marblehead freely fished in the "fertile waters of the Acadian Banks, sometimes making two or three voyages in a single summer during which they might garner 1,000 quintals of cod."⁴² Each of these sturdy lateen-rigged vessels of twenty-five to forty tons was manned by a crew of four or five hands. This could mean that at any one time close to 500 New Englanders were involved in the fishery concentrated in the Cape Sable area. For decades most of them had been free of any Nova Scotia or Massachusetts regulations and consequently they coveted their freedom and independence. For them, the Cape Sable area, where they dried their fish and where they sought shelter in bad weather, was Massachusetts territory *de facto non de jure.*

Even though they may have been dependent upon Nelson and Castin, Massachusetts traders and merchants continued in the late seventies and early eighties to dominate the economic life of the French colony. In 1681 Jacques Duchesneau, the intendant of New France, described the dependence of Nova Scotia on Massachusetts this way:

*L'Acadie qui est à nous et qui joint ces pais [Massachusetts]
est presque dans une pareille situation et a les mesmes
advantages. La naviggation y est libre en tout tems, excepté
pendant deux mois seulement en de certains endroits.
Cependant, on n'y faict rien et quoyqu'il n'y ayt environ
que cinq cens François de tous sexes et de tous aages il ne
subsistent que par les Anglois et leur portent avoir leurs
besoings quelques pelleteries qu'ils se contenent de commercer
avec les Sauvages.⁴³*

Governor Frontenac, like Duchesneau, was extremely worried about what he felt was a Massachusetts attempt to push its commercial frontier overland to the south shore of the Gulf of St. Lawrence. He instructed the Sieur de La Vallière, the commandant and governor of Nova Scotia in 1681, to ask the Boston officials for a reason for "ces sortes d'entreprises et la justice qu'ils en veulent faire, puisque leur limittes . . . marquez à la rivière St. George, lesquelles ils outrepassent de plus de cent cinquante lieues venant au Cap Breton."[44] It is noteworthy that Frontenac asserted the French claim to the St. George River, between the Kennebec and the Penobscot, as the southwestern boundary of Nova Scotia. Sometime early in 1682, Frontenac's protest and La Vallière's note reached Massachusetts. In all likelihood it was carried from La Vallière's residence on the Chignecto Isthmus to Boston by John Nelson, Massachusetts' unofficial governor of the French colony.

When Frontenac's protest arrived, the Massachusetts government was deeply involved in a struggle with Edward Randolph, the arrogant representative of Charles II. Randolph's arrival in Massachusetts in June, 1676, had "signalized the home government's new policy of thorough-going imperial centralization."[45] In bitter reaction to Randolph's pressure, the Massachusetts government responded with unusual alacrity to Frontenac's letter. In June, 1682, John Nelson was appointed to sail to Quebec with, it has been argued,[46] the basis for some kind of unofficial trade agreement with the French. In all likelihood, Nelson was making the journey anyway, which helps to explain the General Court's swift response. Then on Nelson's return, or just before, the Massachusetts General Court, on October 11, 1682, resolved:

> This Court, being informed by the Right Honnorible the
> Earle of Frontineac, governor of Canada, and Monsieur De la
> Valier, governor of Accadie, that severall of the inhabitants of
> this colony have committed irregularitjes in their trading,
> making of fish, and fetching of coales within the territories
> belonging to the French, contrary to the treaty and rattifica-
> tion of the articles of peace concluded at Breda. . . . for the
> prevention of the like practice for the future, and the
> preservation of a good correspondence betweene our
> neighbours of Canada and Accadie, above mentioned, and

*ourselves, it is hereby declared, that this Court doth not allow
and approve of any such irregularitjes, and that all persons
so offending are liable to the poenaltjes and forfeitures
provided against them by the lawes of those governments,
where such offenses shall be committed.*⁴⁷

Much has been made of this resolution of the Massachusetts General
Court. It has been contended that Massachusetts was

*stirred by the coincidence of the appearance of Randolph
with a commission as collector of customs, which meant a
vigorous attempt to enforce the Navigation Acts, and the
protest of Frontenac against irregularities in Acadia. It
would never do to have two quarrels on their hands at once.
The obvious thing to do, since there seemed little hope of
an accommodation with England, was at least to come to some
agreement with the French to protect the all important
fisheries against the possibility of interference.*⁴⁸

Such an interpretation, however, distorts somewhat Massachusetts'
actual response to Frontenac's protest. It should be kept in mind that
the resolve of October 11, 1682, was simply a restatement of the
policy John Winthrop and the General Court had decided upon
decades earlier.⁴⁹ Laws had to be obeyed — especially when New
Englanders were caught committing "such irregularitjes." Everyone
knew that the Acadians were, as Governor Bradstreet described them
in 1680, "few and weak."⁵⁰ Nova Scotia was a French colony, and
Massachusetts citizens operating in the French territory had to be
subject to French law in their relations with the inhabitants. This
was not a sudden change in policy; it was the old Winthrop policy
emphasized.

In his negotiations with Massachusetts, Frontenac had endeavoured
to re-establish Grandfontaine's licensing system for Massachusetts
vessels fishing in Nova Scotia waters.⁵¹ These licences were to
be purchased from the omnipresent John Nelson, who became La
Vallière's Massachusetts agent. In all likelihood, Nelson also had
available other licences for those people interested in mining Cape
Breton coal and gypsum. Licences may have been sold in Boston, late
in 1682, but there was nobody there who could or would compel
anyone to purchase them. Nevertheless, the shrewd Massachusetts

observer must have realized in 1682 that the period of French neglect concerning Nova Scotia had come to an end. Massachusetts' suzerainty was at last being challenged, a step at a time, from Quebec and Versailles.

Frontenac's successor, La Barre, continued the licensing policy in 1683 and encouraged La Vallière "to maintain a good correspondence with the English and permit them their former liberties to fish and fetch coals on their coast."[52] Nelson also received another commission to grant licences. La Barre contended that his policy would continue to ensure that the Acadians would be supplied with provisions and merchandise from Massachusetts. "Without their help," he accurately observed in October, 1683, "this country [Nova Scotia] would be abandoned."[53] But La Barre was ignorant of a basic change in Nova Scotia policy then taking place at distant Versailles.

In an *arrêt* issued in February, 1682, by King Louis XIV, Sieur de Bergier, a Huguenot merchant from La Rochelle, and his Paris associates were granted extensive fishing and trading privileges on the Nova Scotia coast. To carry out their endeavour, they organized the Compagnie des Pêches sédentaires de l'Acadie.[54] Bergier, "the driving force in this enterprise,"[55] came over to Nova Scotia later in the year and established his company's base of operations at Chedabucto on the Strait of Canso near present-day Guysborough. Bergier went back to France late in 1682 but returned to Nova Scotia in the following year. He decided to visit all the settlements of Nova Scotia and was apparently successful in encouraging six inhabitants from Port Royal to engage in the offshore fishery.[56] Bergier was eager to drive the New Englanders from what he considered to be his own company's territory. His aggressive policy in southern Nova Scotia, however, met with determined Massachusetts opposition. The six Port Royal fishing vessels were captured in 1683 by William Carter of Salem, who had received a licence from La Vallière the previous year to fish in Nova Scotia waters. Bergier was understandably furious and demanded from Louis XIV a twelve-gun frigate to drive away the Massachusetts interlopers. With a considerable investment to protect and being violently opposed to the La Barre–La Vallière pro-Massachusetts policy,[57] Bergier refused to accept any pragmatic compromise. His strong protest fell upon receptive ears at Versailles; and in March, 1684, the Conseil d'État issued "un arrêt par lequel Sa Majesté declara que les vaisseaux estrangers, qui seroient trouvez faisant le commerce de pelleteries ou la pesche le long de la dite coste [of Nova Scotia] seroient pris et amenez dans les ports de son Royaume pour y estre confisquez."[58] In addition, La Vallière was dismissed from his post and forbidden to issue any licences to the New Englanders.[59] The controversial François-Marie Perrot, former governor of Montreal — a "rogue" according to one modern authority[60] — replaced La Vallière. Until such time as Perrot arrived in the colony, Bergier was to be acting governor.

On the basis of his new royal *arrêt*, Bergier in July, 1684, took the initiative against the New England fishermen. Using his company's bark *St. Louis*, but not supported by the frigate he had requested the previous year, Bergier seized seven fishing ketches and a sloop off Cape Sable and carried the captains to La Rochelle. There the admiralty officials confiscated all but two of the vessels; the captains of these two ships "were found to have permits" from La Vallière.[61] Two aspects of the seizure are noteworthy. First, Bergier maintained that he did not capture the vessels until after he had made public in Massachusetts his "prohibition to foreign vessels to enter within its [Nova Scotia] jurisdiction on pain of confiscation."[62] Second, all the vessels seized came from New Hampshire and only two had licences. It seems remarkable that of the approximately 100 ketches operating in Nova Scotia waters, most of which were from Massachusetts, the eight captured vessels came from New Hampshire. Was this occurrence an accident or were some of the Salem and Marblehead fishermen using Bergier to drive away competitors? It may not be surprising, therefore, that the Bergier capture of the New Hampshire vessels resulted in no official outcry in Massachusetts. Besides, the Massachusetts authorities were concerned with a far more disconcerting development. The Massachusetts Charter was suspended in 1684, and after a prolonged delay, royal government was established early in 1686.

In the absence of governmental restraints and because of the administrative chaos in 1684, 1685, and 1686, the seafaring population of Massachusetts, "like the Elizabethan sea-dogs, proceeded to take the law into their own hands, with the result that the [French] fishing company was a total failure."[63] In 1685, for example, Massachusetts freebooters captured off Cape Breton four vessels belonging to the Compagnie des Pêches.[64] This freebooting offensive destroyed Bergier's aggressive designs and re-established Massachusetts control over

Nova Scotia's fishery and commerce. By 1686 Governor Perrot had come to realize how foolish it had been to resist the inevitable. He asserted that the Massachusetts fishermen should be permitted to dry their fish on the French shores without being required to make any payment whatsoever.[65] In addition, he permitted the Massachusetts merchants to continue to trade in Nova Scotia because without their supplies the Acadians were destitute. Another reason for Perrot's sympathetic policy towards New Englanders may have been that he wanted to tap the rich Nova Scotia–Massachusetts commercial relationship. There is some evidence to suggest that he was eager to displace Nelson and Castin and become the funnel for all Massachusetts–Nova Scotia trade.

Perrot may have been involved indirectly in the summer of 1686 in the confiscation by the New York authorities at Pemaquid of a large shipment of wine and other supplies owned by Castin and Nelson. The vessel was seized in the Penobscot near Castin's residence. Randolph described the incident this way: "Capt. Palmer and Mr. West of New Yorke, who being at the Port of Pemmequid and haveing advice of a ship of Piscattaqua which landed wine at Penobscutt belonging, as they say, to Nova Scotia, they by force went ashoar and took of the wine. . . . The governor of New Yorke, I am told has given them directions to claim all the land as farr eastward as the river St. Croix."[66] Castin was furious since his economic base at Pentagouet was being threatened by New York. His loud outcry received no sympathetic hearing from the new governor of New York, Governor Dongan, who coolly replied to Perrot's formal complaint: "I have received yours of the 29th of August [1686], and am not aware that anything has been done to the French on their territories. But, if you remain on the soil of the King of England's province, you cannot expect peace, nor can I give you any satisfaction."[67]

New York's claim to his territory alienated Castin who reacted by considering returning with hundreds of his Indian allies to the French sphere of influence.[68] It was probably his association with Nelson that stopped him, at least for the time being. But the storm signals were there for the sensitive person to see. There was growing tension on the northeast boundary of Massachusetts and every indication that the French authorities were planning another counterattack against Massachusetts' economic monopoly over Nova Scotia.

It was ironic that at almost the same time that the growing tension on the boundary between Nova Scotia and Pemaquid was threatening to precipitate hostilities, the Treaty of Neutrality was being concluded between France and England. The treaty, it has been argued,

> left the Maine-Acadian boundary question unchanged. With respect to the controversial fisheries, it sought to preserve peace by recognizing an exclusive right on the part of the French to exploit the shores, creeks, harbors, and islands of Acadia, while conceding to the subjects of both Crowns liberty to fish anywhere beyond the marginal waters of the other sovereign's province. The Treaty provided no formula or machinery for handling future disputes over the Acadian fisheries. Indeed, the sole assurance it offered in regard to such likely eventualities was to be found in the broad guarantee that, if the English and French sovereigns should go to war against one another in Europe, the hostilities were not to extend to their respective colonies in North America.[69]

The treaty may have satisfied Charles II and even Louis XIV, but it certainly was viewed with a jaundiced eye by the Massachusetts authorities. What the treaty specifically prohibited was the drying of fish on Nova Scotia soil by Massachusetts fishermen, a drastic measure which, if enforced, would significantly affect the entire Massachusetts economy. The implicit reference to the fact that a declaration of war in Europe between the two powers would not automatically involve Nova Scotia and Massachusetts in hostilities soothed the anxiety of few sensitive souls in either colony. They realized that North America could not be indefinitely isolated from European wars. Besides, the available evidence in 1686 seemed to suggest that North American hostilities would probably precede a declaration of war in Europe.

4

John Nelson, William Phips, and the Capture of Nova Scotia, 1687-1690

The Treaty of Neutrality of November, 1686, marked the beginning of a three-pronged French counteroffensive in the Nova Scotia region.[1] It was the French colonial authorities who mounted this counteroffensive; the Acadians themselves saw no reason to upset the status quo.[2] The Versailles officials and their agents in North America wished to neutralize what they perceived to be dangerous Massachusetts territorial and economic encroachments into French territory. The first aim of the French counteroffensive was to reassert French sovereignty southwestward at least to the Kennebec River.

By 1687 the delicate question of territorial sovereignty in the New World had apparently captured the special interest of the French minister of marine, the official in charge of the colonies. To strengthen their claim to the disputed and strategically located area between the St. Croix (which the governor of the new Dominion of New England, Edmund Andros, now regarded as the Massachusetts eastern boundary) and the Kennebec, the French resolved to cultivate the friendship of Castin and his Indian allies. This was done in two ways. First, Castin was placed under considerable pressure to support the French position. The French estimated that he could bring with him at least 400 "savages . . . who were the natural enemies of the English."[3] He therefore received supplies and ammunition from Port Royal in order to facilitate his espousal of the French cause and to induce the Indians to follow his example. In addition, he was persuaded to sever his commercial ties with New England and to develop new ones with New France, the assumption being that his trading with the French would draw his area into the economic and military orbit of New France and of France. This basic commercial reorientation had begun, by the summer of 1688, to undermine to a considerable extent Castin's business relationship with John Nelson and Massachusetts.[4] Another means used to strengthen the French strategic position in the Kennebec – St. Croix region was the sending of missionary priests; three men, the brothers Bigot and Father Thury, were despatched from Quebec to proselytize the backsliding Castin and his Indian allies for the Roman Catholic and French cause.

The second prong of the new French policy was directed at the Acadian inhabitants of Nova Scotia. It was decided to try to break their economic dependence on New England – a dependence, it was felt, that seriously undermined their attachment and loyalty to the French Crown. In February, 1688, for example, the French minister of marine ordered "to have sent to the inhabitants of Port Royal goods worth 12,000 livres."[5] Not only were the Acadians to be encouraged to trade with what was hoped would be an increasing number of French merchants, but they were also instructed to have nothing to do with the Massachusetts traders. With some assurance that the French authorities could provide them with badly needed supplies and protection, it was apparently anticipated that the Acadians would respond with enthusiasm in any future Anglo-French war. This was a naive expectation and ran counter to a hardened pragmatic tradition that had taken decades to evolve. Unquestioned loyalty to a European monarch was an irrelevant concept in the unpredictable isolation of Nova Scotia.

A limited military thrust was the third feature of the new aggressive French policy. Approximately 100 new reinforcements were sent in 1688 and 1689 to the tiny French forts at Chedabucto and Port Royal. To the latter settlement were also shipped eighteen large cannon and "supplies and munitions of the King." The French wished to transform what the fort's engineer described in 1690 as an "old fort, which was not even large enough to be a simple Acadian dwelling . . . crumbling everywhere" into a defensive stronghold.[6] Moreover, a well-armed frigate was to patrol the Nova Scotia coast to drive away the Massachusetts fishermen and traders. All foreigners found in Nova Scotian territorial waters or on Nova Scotian territory were to be arrested and their property confiscated.

In 1687 the Sieur de Meneval was appointed governor and commander of Acadia with instructions to execute the new policy. To assist Meneval, the French king sent from Rochefort a light frigate, the 150-ton *La Friponne*, "carry[ing] sixteen Gunns, about Sixty men,"[7] under the command of the Sieur de Beauregard. But months before the July arrival of *La Friponne* in Nova Scotian waters, rumours about the new French policy were circulating in the Massachusetts fishing ports. News about the implications of the Treaty of Neutrality blended into the exaggerated stories about a large French fleet to be sent to drive the New Englanders from French territory. Edward Randolph observed on March 14, 1687, "Our trade dayly decayes and the prohibition to fish on the french coast of Nova Scotia . . . will quite destroy our fishery."[8] Two weeks later Governor Andros reported from Boston, "Our fishing parties are afraid of being disturbed in their fishery off the coast [of Nova Scotia] where they find plenty of fish."[9] The French threat was indeed there but *La Friponne* alone could hardly have destroyed the Massachusetts fishery.

In July, 1687, as Beauregard was cruising off Cape Sable, the centre of the Massachusetts fishery, he came across and captured "two fishing Ketches belonging to Salem." While being escorted to Port Royal, one of the captured ketches, owned by Stephen Sewall, the brother of the famous diarist Samuel Sewall, separated "from the Frigat in a Fogg" and returned to Salem. Before its unexpected arrival, Samuel Sewall wrote on August 1 to John Nelson "to see, if Brother might have his Ketch again."[10] The shrewd Sewall knew what Massachusetts resident had his finger near the level of power at Port Royal.

The *La Friponne* incident was also reported to Governor Andros, who immediately placed the Salem protest in the hands of his Council meeting at Boston on August 4. Little time was wasted in debate since Andros and the Council members agreed that the Salem ketch should be restored and suitable compensation provided for its owner. Captain Francis Nicholson, a British army officer, and not a Massachusetts resident, carried the letter of protest to Port Royal. Nicholson was more than a letter carrier; he was also expected to make observations concerning the military strength of the French colony. He was obviously not impressed:

*In the afternoon I went to Towne [Port Royal]. . . . It
stands upon a Small neck of Land about a mile round, there
is the ruine of an old Earthern Fortification (formerly
distroyed by the English) there is about 40 Soldiers whereof
tenn were old ones, the rest came in the man of Warr. . . . I
do not think there were 80 familyes belonging to ye place. . . .
They had there before only three old Guns, but now
brought 15 very fine and large ones, where they will make
their Fortification I could not learne.*[11]

Because of Meneval's absence, Nicholson was unable to confront
the French governor and to obtain from him the concessions Andros
and the Council were demanding. Nicholson could only observe: "I
hope they will not disturbe Our Fishery this year, Though this
late Accident of the two Ketches affrighted most of Our Fishermen
(but at present they are pretty well Satisfyed). If this next year the
French should hinder Our Ketches to fish on the Bankes of Cape
Sables and other their Coasts it will be halfe ruine Our Fishery."
Nicholson's mission had not, however, been a total failure. He brought
with him to Boston valuable intelligence concerning Nova Scotia.
Furthermore, his bellicose representations may have put "the Acadian
functionaries on the defensive." At least the former governor, Perrot,
who had been replaced because of his corruption and his illicit trade
relations with Massachusetts, felt it necessary immediately to clarify his
position. Perrot wrote to Andros, "mak[ing] an Excuse about the
Ketches, and Saith that the man of Warr hath only orders to forbid our
Fishermen to make their fish on Shoar, and that he hath taken care
to forewarn those that had his leave (for which they paid him five
pounds per Ketch)."[12] Perrot was probably responsible then for the
news about the Nova Scotia fishery that had been circulated in the
Massachusetts fishing ports in March. He was merely providing information for his commercial associates, those who provided him with
£5 per ketch for the right to fish and to dry their catch on shore.

But with their friend Perrot no longer a governor and with the
knowledge that *La Friponne* would return the following year, some of
the Massachusetts fishermen must have been understandably concerned
about their economic future in 1688. What may have neutralized
somewhat this sense of concern was the realization that only one of
the scores of Massachusetts fishing vessels had been captured in 1687.

Their worst fears had not been realized, and they therefore saw no good reason to beach their ships. Fishing was a gamble and in 1688 it would be a little more of a gamble.

Governor Andros in 1687 continued the policy of Dongan with respect to Castin and the Penobscot territory. In June, for example, he sent a small ship with "eighty men to take possession of Pentagouet and to lay claim to the entire coast up to the St. Croix, 40 leagues away."[13] Castin was instructed to take no further orders from the French. Not content with this formal ratification of his authority, Andros himself in the spring of 1688 visited the territory east of the Kennebec. An active participant in the expedition described it in this manner:

With the Rose frigate, [the governor] made towards Penobscott; his Excellency had ... appointed Capt. George to speake to Monsieur St. Casteen, and to acquaint him with his comeing, the captain roade with his frigott before Casteen's doore, sent his lieut ashoare, Casteen spoake to him and told him, but upon notice of the Governor's comeing, Casteen and all the Company retired, left the place ... and left his house shutt; the Governor landed, with other gentlemen with him, and went into the house and found a small altar in the common roome, which altar and some pictures and ordinary ornaments, they did not meddle with anything belonging thereto, but tooke away all his armes, powder, shott, iron kettles and some trucking cloath and his chaires, all which were putt aboard the Rose and laid up ... in the forte at Pemmequid ... notice being irregularly given to the Indian Sachem, neighbour to Casteen, that he should have all his goods restored if he would demand them at Pemmaquid and come under obedience to the King.[14]

Even Edward Randolph, one of Andros's closest associates, realized the stupidity of Andros's anti-Castin and expansionist policy. Randolph maintained that Castin "does not well like to live under the French government, desires to live indifferent."[15] But Andros was driving Castin and his Indian allies into the welcoming arms of the French. At this moment of bitter resentment against Andros, Castin was being seduced by the enticing blandishments of the French priests and by more material inducements from Quebec and Port Royal.

What finally drove the reluctant Castin into the French camp was the news that his trading vessel, sailing from Quebec to the Penobscot, had been captured by a New England pirate ship near Canso.[16] As far as Castin was concerned, his archenemy Andros was the villain behind both the pillage of his home at Pentagouet and the capture of his ship. Castin vowed to wreck vengeance on neighbouring Massachusetts in spite of his close commercial ties with the colony. His Indian friends were receptive to his vehement anti-Massachusetts tirades and to those from the three French missionary priests assiduously at work in their midst. It was not surprising, therefore, that in the following year it was reported: "One of our [Massachusetts] privateers on the coast off Pemaquid was told by Indians ashore that an Englishman was left in these parts. The ship was under French colours, and the man spoke French to the Indians, but one of them chancing to speak English was at once attacked."[17]

For Castin's Indian allies in 1689 a Frenchman was automatically a friend, while an English-speaking resident was a detested enemy. Of course Castin did not create the huge reservoir of anti-Massachusetts feeling among the eastern Indians. As the Reverend Cotton Mather perceptively noted, there were five major sources for this undercurrent of hatred which, with Castin's defection to the French, triggered the "long and bloody War":

1) Because the English refused to pay that Yearly Tribute of Corn, agreed upon in the Articles of Peace [of 1678], formerly concluded with them by the English Commissioners.
2) Because they were Invaded in their Fishery at Saco-River, by certain Gentlemen, who stopp'd the Fish from coming up the River with their Nets and Sains. This they were greatly affronted at, saying, They thought (though the English had got away their Lands as they had, yet) the Fishery of the Rivers had been a Priviledge reserved Entire unto themselves.
3) Because they were abused by the English. . . .
4) But the Fourth and Main Provocation was, the Granting or Patenting of their lands to some English; at which they were greatly enraged, threatening the Surveyor to knock him on the Head if he came to lay out any Lands there.
5) To these may be added the Common Abuses in Trading,

*viz. Drunkenness, Cheating, etc. which such as Trade much
with them are seldom innocent of.*[18]

Andros and Randolph also blamed the Massachusetts and Maine
frontiersmen for the outbreak of hostilities. Andros's enemies, on the
other hand, led by Cotton Mather, singled out the governor and his
New York cronies for special blame. These arrogant officials, they
argued, had not fully appreciated the explosive nature of the situation
and had, in fact, precipitated the conflict by alienating Castin who
was the only man capable of keeping the Indians in line. In searching
for the immediate cause of the frontier war, Mather pointed his finger
at Andros. Mather asked:

*[Who] will Enquire whether no body seized a parce of
Wines that were Landed at a French Plantation to the
Eastward? Whether an Order were not obtained from the
King of England, at the Instance of the French Embassador,
to Restore those wines? Whether upon the Vexation of this
Order, we none of us ran a New Line for the Bounds of the
Province? Whether we did not contrive our New Line so as
to take in the Country of Monsieur St. Casteen? Whether
Monsieur St. Casteen, flying from our Encroachments, we
did not seize upon his Arms and Goods, and bring them away to
Pemmaquid? And Who were the We which did these
things? And whether the Indians, who were extremely under
the Influence of St. Casteen, that had Married a Sagamore's
Daughter among them, did not from this very Moment begin
to be obstreperous? And whether all the Sober English in
the Country did not from this very Moment foretel a War?*[19]

The remainder of 1688 witnessed the playing out only of the
preliminaries to the conflict, but in the early months of 1689, the
bloody horror of full-scale Indian war suddenly engulfed the northeastern frontier. It was as if the clock had been turned back some
thirteen years to the devastating time of King Philip's War. It is clear
that in 1689 the vast majority of French settlers in New France and
Nova Scotia, together with most New Englanders, did not want
any kind of war, especially an Indian war, in North America. Yet the
imperial representatives of the two European nations seemed keen to
bring about hostilities. Old World values, in a sense, were in conflict

with New World realities. As A. H. Buffinton has argued: "[In 1688 and 1689] very few of the colonials wanted war. . . . The French of Acadia certainly did not care to fight; they had lived too long on terms of friendly intercourse with Boston. . . . The New England fishermen and traders did not want war, for it would destroy their trade and cripple their fishery."[20]

Even the Abenakis did not really want war. They were forced into it by the English at the same time that they were being gently pushed in this direction by the French. During the winter of 1688/89, determined to protect Maine from Indian attacks, Andros "at the head of one hundred and twenty men" marched into the area "through dismal and almost impossible swamps." Not one Indian was killed during the expedition, but by "recovering divers goods and ammunition taken from the English," Andros had reduced the Indians "to bows and arrows."[21] The difficulties that he and his troops confronted were increased when they realized the actual extent of the illegal trade with the Indians being carried on by some Boston merchants. Andros was fighting so-called friends as well as enemies. John Nelson, for example, was accused of supplying Castin with fourteen barrels of powder and 2,000 cwt. of lead, which Castin in turn had supplied to his Indian allies in their raids against the English.[22] In addition, the well-informed Edward Randolph declared: "The Indians could have been reduced to beg for terms, had not the Foster and Waterhouse, merchants in Boston . . . sent a ship in the Governor's absence with forty tons of ammunition and other goods to trade with these Indians and the French between Port Royal and Penobscot."[23]

After strengthening forts and garrisons at Pemaquid, Casco Bay, Saco, and along the Kennebec and the Damariscotta rivers, Andros left Maine earlier than expected on March 16, 1689. He had heard of William of Orange's invasion of England and realized that trouble was brewing in Boston. A few weeks after his return to the capital, the "Glorious Revolution" came to Massachusetts, and Andros and his followers were thrown into jail on April 18. One of the leaders of the revolution was John Nelson. The Dominion of New England had come to an end, and the old form of government was unilaterally revived.[24] Eighty-seven-year-old Simon Bradstreet, a former governor, was chosen to replace Andros.

The political turmoil at Boston produced chaos on the northeastern frontier. Andros's officers were arrested and sent to Boston but there were no suitable replacements. In early August, 1689, Pemaquid, "the Keay to all the Easterne ports," was captured by some 200 Indians well-equipped with French supplies.[25] Most of the other Maine forts collapsed like a crooked line of dominos, and by the end of autumn only four English settlements remained east of the Piscataqua – Kittery, York, Wells, and Casco Bay. The Indians boasted that "if they had 200 French regulars with them . . . they could sweep to Boston."[26]

After much procrastination, the Massachusetts General Court, under Bradstreet's feeble leadership, ordered militia units into Maine in the late summer of 1689 to check what seemed to be the Indian invasion. In the period of acute disorientation and anxiety, Indian numbers were wildly exaggerated, as was the actual Indian threat to the colony. It was argued that the French were behind the Indian attacks. Governor Bradstreet was convinced that they were "doubtless incited by the French" and "by them supplied with ammunition."[27] There was, of course, more than an element of truth in this observation, but it was also true that Yankee traders continued in 1688 and 1689 to supply the French and Indians, thus facilitating their aggressive designs.[28]

The shrill howls of protest from the frontier inhabitants might have gone largely unnoticed in the colony's capital in the late autumn months of 1689 had it not been for a loud accompanying outcry about Gallic hostility from the influential Salem fishermen.[29] In early September, 1689, two French frigates from Port Royal had captured six Salem fishing ketches and a large brigantine near Cape Sable.[30] The seizure of at least 10 percent of the Salem fishing fleet was a serious blow to the entire Massachusetts fishery.[31] On hearing of the capture of their vessels, the leading Salem citizens urged the General Court to "secure the release of the said men captured and to demand satisfaction." The name of Bartholomew Gedney, a member of the Council who also had real estate interests in Maine, headed the list of petitioners, which also included Stephen Sewall, who had had one of his ketches temporarily captured by the French two years earlier. The Salem residents went on to declare:

We are well assured the french at the Eastward have taken
six of Our Ketches and made Captives about thirty of our men
to the great damage of the persons interested therein, and

also others Concerned in the Imploy of fishing who will be
discouraged for the future in these undertakings unless some
remedy be found to secure them in their Imployments, Or
to obtaine satisfaction for the present damages.

And whereas we are Informed our said Ketches are Carried
into Port Royall by two French friggots of Considerable
strength whereby we are discouraged from setting out our
Vessels the next spring and the being of two such shipps on
the Coasts may be of dangerous Consequence to the whole
Countrey.[32]

Pressure was thus mounting on the Massachusetts authorities to act
with vigour to turn back the French-Indian offensive, and this
pressure was coming from politically influential inhabitants, not from
bucolic frontiersmen. The protests of the fishing entrepreneurs and
various land speculators were not to be cavalierly disregarded. But
what could be done in late 1689 to deal effectively with the perplexing
problems facing the colony? The General Court seemed torn between
the desire to do something about the French and the fear that any
action would make matters even worse. Delay seemed the only
acceptable policy. Refugees from the eastern frontier continued to
flock into the Boston area, but there was little economic activity there
to absorb their energies; everywhere there appeared to be growing
confusion and perplexity. Massachusetts was at war, but war had not
been officially declared by Great Britain. Until news of the declaration
reached Boston, the government refused to attack, on its own initiative,
the French in Nova Scotia who had become almost overnight the
imagined source of all of Massachusetts' woes.

While the Massachusetts officials awaited the formal declaration of
war, which finally arrived in early December, 1689,[33] Governor
Meneval of Nova Scotia was himself bitterly criticizing the French
naval and Indian offensive against Massachusetts. He saw no justification for the capture of the Salem vessels and predicted that a massive
Massachusetts assault would soon be directed against his almost
defenceless colony.[34] Moreover, Meneval must have had serious
reservations about the French policy of encouraging the Indians in
their bloody raids on the isolated Maine settlements. Against whom
would the Yankees retaliate? They would, of course, first strike against
the nearest and most accessible French colony, and that was Nova

Scotia. In his criticism, the Nova Scotia governor was, without question, articulating the point of view of the Acadian inhabitants, who felt that their interests were being sacrificed for some incomprehensible French imperial design.

Only two days after the official declaration of war reached Boston on December 4, 1689, the Massachusetts General Court was petitioned "to inquire into ye present state & condition of our said neighbours ye ffrench; & consider what may be proper & necessary for us to doe respecting them, so as to prevent their being capable to make farther depredations on us, & their assisting & supplying our Indian enemies."[35] Governor Bradstreet and the General Court did not need the prodding of the petitioners. Bradstreet had already decided, largely because of the Salem pressure, "to take revenge upon the ffrench at Nova Scotia for seizing 6 or 7 of their fishing Ketches."[36] The petition merely accelerated the decision-making process. On December 16, 1689, the Court voted that "Voluntiers be Raised by beate of Drum for the Reduceing of Acadia or Els where to the Obedience of there Majties of Great Britain, And that such Commander or Commanders shall be Commissioned by the present Govermt."[37]

This decision marked the point in December, 1689, when a number of forces demanding retaliatory action against the French had converged in Massachusetts. The importance of the influence exerted in the General Court by the fishing interests and by those interested in land speculation in northeastern Massachusetts and Maine should not be underestimated. In tandem the two interest groups possessed formidable political power and they equated their own prosperity with that of their colony. These men took full advantage of the mood of despair and the widely held view that it was incumbent upon Massachusetts to demonstrate its loyalty to the English Crown.[38] This demonstration "of excessive loyalty,"[39] they hoped, would persuade William to restore the old Massachusetts Charter. What better vehicle for the expression of the new Massachusetts loyalty than an attack on the neighbouring possessions of the French king who was harbouring and supporting the royal pretensions of William's rival? Thus, in a sense, the proposed expedition was seen by some to be the means by which Massachusetts might regain its old independence.

The man who played a key role in facilitating the converging of these various pressures and then directing them at the General Court was the ubiquitous John Nelson. Nelson, keen to reassert his uncle's claim to Nova Scotia, realized that his task would be much easier with Nova Scotia in English hands. Furthermore, aware of increased French trading competition in what he considered to be his commercial empire, Nelson wished to destroy his foreign competitors once and for all. His imperial vision was of a Nova Scotia politically and economically subservient to John Nelson.

On January 4, 1690, Nelson took the initiative with respect to Nova Scotia in a closely argued set of "Proposals" to the General Court. He maintained that a well-planned offensive thrust against the French colony was the best possible defence for Massachusetts. Since the public treasury was empty, he and some business associates offered magnanimously "for ye Publique Benefit to carry on this enter prize at theire owne charge, and in such methods as by a Comitty from you Joyned with our selves, may be thought most Convenient, to which Purpose we Apply our selves unto you for Approbation and Countenance, in permitting Volunteers to be levied and Commissions to be granted, to all Necessary and respectable Officers, and such rules and Instructions as may be agreed on . . . for the . . . good of this Expedition."[40] Nelson's offer was enthusiastically received by the General Court, which on January 4 voted to encourage "Such Gentlemen & Merchnts of this Collony as shall undertake to reduce Penobscot St. John Port Royall Gut of Canco etc." They were to be offered the free use of two government-owned "Sloops of Warr," what plunder they could find, and the monopoly of the Nova Scotia trade until such time as the English government would order otherwise.[41] In other words, the General Court had accepted the principle of partially subsidizing a private imperialist venture which promised, among other things, to neutralize the French-Indian threat to the northeast.

The committee requested by Nelson to finalize arrangements met and on January 16 presented its report to the General Court. The members of this committee are of some consequence in showing what groups were most concerned with the conquest of Nova Scotia. Of the seven men, three, Bartholomew Gedney, Benjamin Browne, and Charles Redford, were from Salem and represented the fishing interests of Essex County. The other four, Nathaniel Oliver, John Foster, John Alden, and John Nelson, were prominent Boston merchants. The latter three were widely known for their close commercial ties with Nova Scotia.

The committee strongly endorsed the Nelson proposals of January

4, as well as the resolution of the General Court of the same day. The members, however, wished to obtain some insurance for "such private undertakers . . . or company . . . that this Country [Massachusetts] will make some publick Act whereby to assure unto the Gentlemen that shall undertake, a full & real reimbursement of what the plunder etc. shall fall short of the principall Summe, in case the ffrench Country be wrested out of their hands by any accident before the first disbursement can be or is discharged." This clause was, without question, a concession to Nelson and his merchant associates Alden and Foster and was probably drafted by them. To balance matters, and to keep the coalition of interests locked together, the Salem fishing interests, in exchange for their offer of transportation vessels for the "expedition," were to be promised that "one or both of the Sloops . . . be well fitted and prepared for the defence of our fishery along the Coast of Cape Sables."[42]

It was not until February 6 that the General Court considered the committee's recommendations. There was no explanation for this long delay, but it was probably brought about by a growing opposition in the Court to the aspirations of the Nelson group. On February 6 the Court adamantly refused to change the policy it had adopted a month earlier and rejected the new proposals that had been inserted by the committee. The Court declared:

It is Agreed and Ordered that permission be given for the raysing of volunteers for that Expedition and that Commissions from this Governmt be granted to all necessary Officers for that Service.

That one of the Sloops now in the Country's Service be lent them gratis for two or three months and the other Sloop for lesser time as shalbe limited.

That the sole benefit and profits of the sd ffrench Country when reduced be appropriated unto the Undertakers or Company waiting his Maties Commands and Settlement for the future disposal that is to say, the Indian Trade and what plunder may be reasonably made both of Stores of warr & otherwise (saveing the performance of all such Articles as may be concluded with the Inhabitants upon Surrender) this Governmt to have the first tender and refusal of the great Artillery if drawn off the place.[43]

No mention was made of either the possible governmental financial subsidy or the protection of the Cape Sable fishery. Without these two commitments from the General Court, Nelson's side of the bargain was not to be honoured, and his plan became a dead issue.

Why did the members of the General Court in early February, 1690, vote against their committee's recommendation? What had apparently happened was that in the first week of February the county members had shouldered out of their earlier position of dominance the representatives of the commercial élite. Inspired by the Reverend Cotton Mather, these men were suspicious of Nelson — an Anglican who was also opposed to the re-establishment of the Old Charter form of government. When the General Court realized that Nelson in fact wished to be "generalissimo" of the planned expedition, his critics, observed one contemporary, exclaimed that "he was a merchant and not to be trusted."[44] How could a non-Puritan, recently charged with trading illicitly with the eastern Indians, be given the command?

When the General Court looked about for a suitable replacement willing to work within the framework recently laid down, it could find no one. Consequently, by the end of the first week of February, Nelson's scheme lost whatever momentum it had once possessed. It now seemed certain that there would be no Nova Scotia expedition. Then the unexpected occurred and Nelson discovered that there was still some life in his proposals. On February 24 Boston learned of the bloody French-Indian assault on Schenectady. The sensitive Samuel Sewall noted in his diary: "Schenectady, a village 20 miles above Albany, destroy'd by the French. 60 Men, Women and Children murder'd. Women with Child ripp'd up, Children had their Brains dash'd out. . . . Just about dinner time Mr. Nelson comes in and gets me to subscribe £100 to the Proposals against the French. I thought 'twas time to doe something, now were thus destroy'd by Land too."[45]

It is impossible to ascertain how many other Bostonians Nelson approached for funds for his proposals. The fierce Schenectady raid had suddenly revived Massachusetts' waning interest in the Nova Scotia enterprise, and Nelson wished to channel this enthusiasm for his own benefit. Would the frontier settlements of Massachusetts be the next target for the vicious enemy? This question must have been asked by thousands of residents of the colony, and one which Nelson and his supporters doubtlessly emphasized. In March they received their answer when the unsuspecting residents of Salmon Falls, New Hamp-

shire, were attacked by another French force despatched by Governor
Frontenac of New France. At "ye dreadfull destruction of Salmon
ffalls" thirty persons were killed and another fifty-four taken prisoner.[46] It was rather ironic that Frontenac maintained that this assault
was a calculated move "to make a diversion which may prevent the
invasion of Port Royal, which is defenceless."[47] The Salmon Falls
episode did not deflect New England's military thrust away from
"defenceless" Nova Scotia; indeed, together with the Schenectady raid,
it was largely responsible for the renewed interest in Massachusetts
for an invasion of the neighbouring French colony.

On March 18, the day before the news from Salmon Falls reached
Boston, Bartholomew Gedney, the Salem entrepreneur who had for
years been involved in the Nova Scotia fishery, was chosen by the
General Court "to be Commander in cheife of the forces designed for
an Expedition against the French."[48] Gedney, though far more acceptable to the nonmerchant members of the Court than Nelson, refused
to serve as commander and was replaced on March 21 by a Captain
Townsend, who was commander-in-chief for about twenty-four hours.
On Saturday, March 22, he "relinquished with Thanks" the commission
to Sir William Phips.[49] On being informed of the Court's decision,
the disillusioned Nelson "refused with scorn to serve under him."[50]
Nelson felt cheated of what was rightfully his. Had he not virtually
singlehandedly coaxed into existence the enthusiasm in the colony for
the Nova Scotia venture? Then just at the moment when he expected
to receive the mantle of leadership from the Court, it was suddenly
thrown upon the shoulder of Phips — the protégé of his archenemy
Cotton Mather.

William Phips was certainly a strange and a remarkable man. Born
near the mouth of the Kennebec River in 1651, the former shepherd
and ship's carpenter won widespread fame, fortune, and a knighthood
by his remarkable feat of recovering in 1687 treasure valued officially at
over £207,600 from the wreck of a Spanish galleon in the West
Indies.[51] When he returned to Massachusetts in 1688, he became a
popular hero. He was, as Samuel Sewall described him, the New
World's "Jason fetching the Golden Fleece."[52] Having converted
Phips to the Christian faith early in 1690, Cotton Mather thrust him
forward as the saviour of Massachusetts. Phips and his "golden touch"
alone, it was argued, could attract volunteers for the expedition. An
aura of success seemed to hang over the man, and his amazing career

was convincing proof that the Almighty had singled him out to accomplish great things for Massachusetts. Phips himself had more mundane reasons for leading the expedition. He was interested in the anticipated booty at Port Royal, and he also wished to obtain as his reward a lucrative imperial appointment – perhaps even a governorship.

In spite of Phips, the blandishments of the General Court, and the propaganda barrage provided by Cotton Mather and others, recruiting was difficult. One critic observed: "Drums beat for recruits; some few enlist and then change their minds and desert; and no one dares to question them. . . . About eighty in a body deserted with huzzas on being told that they must find their own arms."[53] In order to encourage volunteers to enlist, the Court promised to pay them the same wages the impressed frontier soldiers were receiving. In addition, they were to obtain "the just Half of all Plunder taken from ye Enemy . . . shared among the Officers & Souldiers, (Stores of Warr only excepted)." Widows of volunteers who might be killed in the assault were to be given their husbands' share of the booty.[54]

Cotton Mather viewed the expedition as a religious crusade and used his considerable rhetorical skills to persuade Massachusetts residents to enlist. He declared, "He is no New Englander (not worthy of the Name) who at such a Time as this, will not Venture his All, for this Afflicted people of God." For Mather the war in North America was a battle between Satan and Christ, and Massachusetts was battling for the Lord. If the French could be beaten, according to Mather, "then, *A Golden Age*, will arrive to this place." In 1690 Massachusetts was the centre of a cosmic drama and its procrastination concerning the French threat had deep spiritual significance: "The Question which we have now before us, in short is This, *Whether we will venture All, with an Hope to Preserve All, or Whether we will keep All, with an Assurance to Loose All. . . . Who is on the Lord's side?* Even so, *Who is for Jesus, against Satan, and Who is for the true Christian, Protestant Religion against Popery and Paganism?*" Mather drove home this point time and time again in his sermons, and the implication was always clear. Those who followed Phips were not only obeying Christ's command but they were also helping to accelerate the entire redemptive process. Mather concluded by attempting to channel his emotional appeal into the recruiting campaign: "Let us not lose our Time, that we may not Lose our All. . . . Everything loudly calls upon us, make haste. . . . Common prudence now calls for Expedition

& all things concur in that Advice unto us, *Be up and be doing*. Shall we be drawing *Circles* in the Earth, when the City is just falling into the Hands of its Enemies."[55]

It is impossible to ascertain how effective Mather's propaganda actually was. It may have persuaded some of the more pious to volunteer, but the limited available evidence suggests that the expectation of considerable booty was probably far more important. Whatever their motives, when the expedition finally left Boston in April, there were 736 men on board the seven vessels, which were defended by a total of seventy-two cannon.[56]

Professor J. B. Brebner accurately described the Phips expedition as "an affair of pure pillage."[57] The fleet sailed from Boston on April 28 and carefully moved up the coast of Maine to *"Mount-Desart,* which was the place appointed to Rendezvous."[58] Some plunder was seized in the region beyond the Penobscot, but little contact was made with either the Indians or the French. On May 9 the Massachusetts fleet anchored off Port Royal. The following day a boat was sent ashore "with a Demand to the Governor to surrender the Fort." Phips's ultimatum was obviously designed to frighten the French into submission. If they refused his honourable terms, he resolved, "by the help of God, on whom alone I trust for Assistance, to attacque, kill, burn & destroy, and then you may when too late, wish for that favour which you now refuse." Meneval quickly capitulated, agreeing to give up "all the great Artillery, small Arms and stores of War, and whatever else belongs to the French King." The invaders were not, however, to touch the private property of the Acadian inhabitants.

The actions of the Massachusetts troops on Nova Scotia territory after the official surrender reveals a great deal about their real reason for joining the expedition. They completely disregarded the capitulation terms and seized from every conceivable source all available plunder. Phips innocently observed in his journal: "Monday 12. This Morning, we went a-shoar to search for hidden goods. . . . We cut down the Cross, rifled the Church, Pulled down the High-Altar, breaking their Images; and brought our Plunder, Arms and Ammunition into Mr. Nelson's Storehouse. Tuesday 13. And so kept gathering Plunder both by land and water, and also under ground in their Gardens, all the next day." When the New Englanders finally exhausted themselves in their search for plunder, their officers managed to direct them to rather more mundane military matters. The fortifications were levelled, the cannon removed, and the prizes in port suitably rigged. Then the oath of allegiance was administered to the settlers in the naive hope that a few meaningless words would transform the Acadians into ardent supporters of "their most Excellent Majesties William & Mary."

Phips ordered two of his officers, Captain John Alden, Nelson's business associate, and Captain Cyprian Southack, to attack the remaining French settlements in Nova Scotia and "to Summon the French in all these places as you go along, to take the Oath of Allegiance to the Crown of England." Alden was to concentrate his efforts in the Bay of Fundy, while Southack was to sail as far as Chedabucto. Southack left a fascinating account of his expedition which was designed to drive away French competitors from the Nova Scotia fishery. At Chedabucto:

> We sallyed up at the Fort at Once and they killed me three men, and wounded me six, so we fought them Six houres, and they beat us off from the Fort, and about Pistol shot from the Fort, we gott into a Great house, where I found 4 barrells of Gun Powder, and I made fire balls and Arrows, and we sallyed up againe to the Trenches, and there got in my self with 4 men more, so that their Great Guns could not hurt us, and we threw severall balls into the Fort, at last it got into the House of Guard and set Fire, and in One houres time the Fort was all on Fire. And then the Govr struck the Flag, and he with his Souldiers and the Priests came out, and then the Fort in One half houres time blew up with the Powder that was in it . . . so I was 5 days demolishing of it. . . . I have seized severall Ships of the French which I will give a full account of by the first Oppertunity.[59]

It was not the volunteers alone who benefitted from the plundering of Nova Scotia. The gouty Meneval presented Phips with his not inconsiderable personal possessions — for safekeeping of course — desiring that Phips's wild troops not get their hands on his "Two dressing gowns of linen, trimmed with lace, A grey vest, entirely new. Three new wigs — Three pair of new shoes . . . Four pair of silk garters . . . Twelve cravats of lace . . . Four nightcaps, with lace edgings . . . Twelve pair of new socks." Phips evidently agreed to the request, but when Meneval in Boston demanded the return of his property, Phips refused. He retained Meneval's household goods, his silverware, "Six silver spoons. Six silver forks. Two large silver tumblers," his fancy clothing, his liquor, as well as "Four hundred and four pistoles, the balance of five hundred and four pistoles."[60]

Despite the losses suffered by the French, it is debatable whether the expedition was a sucessful financial venture for Massachusetts. A Boston merchant, James Lloyd, maintained that the enterprise had cost "£3,000 more than the value of the plunder."[61] If it was a business failure, the expedition was a disaster for New England "imperialism." The arrangements made by Phips to ensure that Nova Scotia remain an English possession were simple. First, he compelled as many Acadians as possible to swear allegiance to the British Crown. Second, he hoisted the Union Jack over Port Royal, and third, he implemented a simple system of indirect rule. A president, who was a French sergeant in the Troupe de la Marine, and six Acadian councillors were chosen "for the Conservation of the Peace among the said Inhabitants." These men were to establish a new society in Nova Scotia; they were to ensure

> that you take care to prevent all prophaneness, Sabbath breaking, Cursing, Swearing, Drunkenness, or Theeving, and all other Wickedness, and punish those that you shall find guilty.
>
> That you do not impose upon any person in point of Conscience, to constrain him to the way of Worship . . . we hope you will all ere long learn better than hitherto you have been Taught.
>
> That all Contest between Man and Man about his Land may be laid aside, and every man maintained in the quiet Enjoyment of what men possess of. . . .
>
> That you Send an account to the Governor of Massachusetts, from time to time, how Matters are with you, in order to your Receiving further instructions, and you may rest well-assured that if you be faithful to our Government, they will seek your peace & prosperity as their own.[62]

Immediately after the brief swearing-in ceremony, Phips and his men set sail for Boston on May 21, after only a short sojourn in Nova Scotia.

No Massachusetts troops were left to defend Port Royal. Surrounded by people they had recently plundered and with the Indians lurking nearby and French warships expected at any moment, no New Englander in his right mind wanted to garrison Port Royal. Theirs had been a plundering adventure, not an exercise in Massachusetts imperialism. The expedition, in fact, was of questionable strategic importance. With the St. Lawrence area still in French hands, Massachusetts remained threatened. To underline this point, while Massachusetts troops were active in Nova Scotia in May, a Frontenac-inspired raid was devastating Fort Loyal, now Portland, Maine. Phips had tried to cut off a weak French branch; the St. Lawrence trunk, however, remained.

5

John Nelson
and
Benjamin Church,
1690-1697

Phips's military success against Nova Scotia was followed by his and Massachusetts' abysmal failure to capture Quebec in the autumn of 1690. While Phips was experiencing first-hand the Almighty's "Spit in our Face" and "the awfull Frowne of God,"[1] the French were regaining possession of Nova Scotia and John Nelson and his associates were planning the economic and political take-over of the French colony. Apparently, in spite of the Phips expedition, things had changed very little in Nova Scotia.

Only a few days after Phips's departure from Port Royal on May 21, Joseph Robineau de Villebon, Meneval's lieutenant, returned to Nova Scotia from France. With his magnificent army consisting of what he referred to as "5 . . . of my soldiers," he reasserted French control over the colony. But seeing the hopelessness of defending Port Royal, he decided to establish the major French military outpost at Jemseg, some fifty miles inland on the St. John River.[2] At this location Villebon felt that he could not only deal more effectively with potential Massachusetts invaders, but he could also participate fully in the fur trade of the region.[3] In addition, and possibly the most important reason for moving to Jemseg, Villebon was here much closer to his anti-Massachusetts Indian allies.

During the war years, but especially after 1691 when he was finally appointed governor of Acadia, Villebon tried to implement an aggressive policy against Massachusetts. In so doing, he was merely obeying instructions received from both Frontenac and the minister of marine. The Indian allies, the Abenakis, the Malecites, and the Micmacs, provided the personnel for the land offensive, and the French supplied them with some military leadership, guns, ammunition, and other inducements such as "5 chapeaux bordez d'or faux, 10 chemises . . . 10 paires de bas . . . 5 couvertures de Rouen."[4] In addition, a few French privateers were encouraged to prey upon Massachusetts shipping, which they did with amazing success. One of these, for example, Pierre Maisonnat Baptiste, captured in a brief period of time approximately twenty vessels going to or coming from Massachusetts. It was hoped that the constant pressure put on Massachusetts by the Indians and privateers would prevent the New Englanders from mounting any further expeditions against New France. The landmass that was Nova Scotia with its handful of Acadians could, as far as Frontenac and his French superiors were concerned, be callously sacrificed for the greater good of the French North American empire.

It is noteworthy that Villebon was genuinely concerned about the plight of the Acadians, whom he perceived to be hopelessly caught "between the hammer and the anvil." He did everything in his power not to undermine the Phips arrangement as it applied to peninsular Nova Scotia where the vast majority of Acadians lived. For example, in late June, 1692, Villebon freely admitted that the French sergeant appointed in 1690 by Phips to be in command at Port Royal continued in this capacity "only with my approval." The French governor then went on to describe cogently the dilemma he faced: "Without these compromises it would be impossible to exist in this country, where I am without troops, and these unfortunate people, living so far from help, are exposed to every attack. The English also provided a flag to be hoisted for ships and other English vessels which might come in. I have not deemed it advisable to remove it, for it is of no consequence."[5]

Villebon later maintained that the Acadians were "to obtain all the assistance possible from the English until they received other orders."[6] Because supplies from France were being used to retain Indian support, Villebon felt it necessary actually to encourage the Acadians to trade with Massachusetts. Thus during most of the war, Yankee merchants supplied the growing Acadian population with badly needed merchandise, while the French authorities, much relieved because of the unexpected Massachusetts benevolence, were able to channel most of their goods to the Indians who were encouraged to attack Massachusetts. Furthermore, some of the Massachusetts goods obtained by the Acadians eventually made their way to the Indians — especially the guns and ammunition. Some Massachusetts merchants, then, were playing a key role in helping to destroy their own colony.

After his return from Quebec, Phips found himself embroiled in a violent controversy with Meneval and Nelson about the ownership of Meneval's considerable Port Royal possessions. Phips was supported by the Massachusetts rank and file, while Meneval and Nelson were backed by most of the Council members and the Boston merchants, who resented Phips's sudden and dramatic rise to a position of influence and power. When Phips left for England during the winter of 1690/91, the issue had not been adequately resolved.[7] Phips did not return to the colony until May, 1692, when he came as the royal governor appointed to administer the new Charter, which among other things gave to Massachusetts "the lands and hereditaments lying and being in the country or territory commonly called Accada or Nova Scotia."[8]

While Phips was otherwise engaged at Quebec and England, Nelson and John Alden had begun to try to renew their commercial relations with Nova Scotia. In early November, 1690, the Massachusetts General Court permitted Alden "to visset Port Royall to inquire into the State of the people there being subjected to the obedience of the Crown of England, and to carry some provisions for their supply. Liberty is granted him to proceed accordingly at his own charg, Not to carry with him any ammunition more then for the Necessary use of the vessell."[9] It would seem that Alden and the Acadians were not considered entirely trustworthy by the members of the General Court — and for good reason. Far too frequently, in 1688 and 1690, Massachusetts guns and ammunition had ended up in the possession of the Indians raiding the frontiers of the colony.

Again in March, 1691, Alden was sent by the General Court to Port Royal to discover how loyal the Acadians actually were. Alden had other reasons for the trip as well. Marke Harrison, a prisoner of the northeastern Indians in 1690/91, commented caustically concerning Alden's voyage:

Last winter and spring [1690/91] both French and Indians were forced to eat their dogs, since having no powder or shot they could not kill a fowl, though they swarmed in numbers before their doors. In March, however, Mr. Alden arrived in

*the St. John's river ... and brought them supplies of food and
ammunition, without which they would have perished. He has
been with them often since the war began. ... Mr. Alden ...
said he came to trade, not to redeem captives.*[10]

Alden's trips indicated that the General Court was not completely
indifferent to the situation in Nova Scotia. By early June, 1691, this
passive concern had grown into a conviction that some direct permanent Massachusetts control over Nova Scotia was essential, provided it
cost the Court nothing. In mid-1691 the Massachusetts authorities were
being pressured from at least three directions to do something about
establishing some kind of military, economic, and political presence in
the neighbouring colony. Some of the Acadian inhabitants, who had
sworn allegiance to the English Crown in 1690, wanted suitable protection from the Indian allies of the French as well as a sure supply of
much-needed goods.[11] If the Acadians were in fact English subjects,
they wished to partake of all the advantages of their new nationality.
Pressure was also being exerted on the Court by the beleaguered
frontier inhabitants, who continued naively to hope that with Nova
Scotia firmly under Massachusetts control, the Indian raids would soon
stop. The third source of pressure was John Nelson and his merchant
friends. These men, fully aware of the economic potential of Nova
Scotia and realizing that some Massachusetts competitors such as
Andrew Faneuil were beginning to establish commercial relations with
Nova Scotia, were intent on obtaining a monopoly of the trade.[12]
What better way to accomplish this end than to have the Nelson
group take over the actual government of the colony? Taking advantage of the absence of his bitter enemy Phips, Nelson used his influence,
especially in the Council, to persuade its members that what was good
for him was also best for the military and political well-being of
Massachusetts.

During the first week of June, 1691, therefore, John Nelson and
six other merchants offered to build a fort at Port Royal and to
garrison it at their own expense, provided that the General Court
gave them a five-year monopoly over the entire Nova Scotia trade.[13] It
was assumed, of course, that Nova Scotia was in fact Massachusetts
territory. In an attempt to meet the criticism directed against the
imposition of this tight monopoly, Nelson encouraged other Massachusetts merchants to become associated with his company. Twenty-

two persons eventually subscribed " £46 each" and among the later subscribers was John Alden.[14] After some negotiations, the Council agreed to the Nelson proposal, and Colonel Edward Tyng, the chief military officer in Maine under Andros, was appointed commander of Port Royal and governor of Nova Scotia.[15] Nelson, the originator of the scheme and the man who had earlier seemed so intent upon obtaining the governorship, had apparently come to realize, along with the Council, that his being appointed governor would alienate a large segment of the population and serve possibly to focus its vitriolic reaction on the Council decision to involve Massachusetts officially in Nova Scotia affairs. Nelson was therefore satisfied with his role as the éminence grise behind his friend and associate Tyng. This was a small price to pay for the monopoly of the Nova Scotia trade.

Nelson further proposed that an offer be made by the Massachusetts authorities to his old friend Castin that if he would submit to the English and persuade his Indian allies to do so, he would then "have security for his person and property and the privilege of continuing his trade with the Indians."[16] Nelson expected that his company would supply Castin with merchandise for the Indian trade as Nelson had done before the outbreak of hostilities.

The attempt to accomplish by private enterprise what the Massachusetts government was not willing to do with its own resources was not successful. Castin showed no interest in Nelson's proposal; he must have been unimpressed with Tyng's army of "twenty centinels" who were alone "to garrison" Nova Scotia. After arriving at Port Royal "where they dealt for £1,200 but did nothing for the King," Nelson, Tyng, Alden, Alden's son, and the company's mercenaries sailed for the St. John River. While trading at the mouth of this river, the men from Massachusetts were captured in early October by a French vessel, the *Soleil d'Afrique*, commanded by a Captain Bonaventure. The ship was carrying Governor Villebon and a cargo of munitions, supplies, and presents for the Indians. Nelson, Tyng, and Alden's son were kept as hostages, and the remainder of the Massachusetts inhabitants were sent back with the elder Alden, who was instructed to secure the return of the French soldiers from the Port Royal garrison still incarcerated in Boston.[17] Nelson and Tyng were taken to Quebec. Tyng died in custody but Nelson, despatched to France in 1693, eventually returned to Massachusetts after the end of King William's War. Even confinement in the Bastille in the 1690s did not destroy Nelson's continuing obsession with Nova Scotia.[18]

It was a strange conjunction of events in October, 1691, when at the very time the Lords of Trade and Plantations added Nova Scotia to Massachusetts, Villebon, the new French governor of Nova Scotia, captured Colonel Tyng, the Massachusetts-appointed governor of the same colony, as well as John Nelson, the one man who seriously threatened the French commercial position in Nova Scotia. Almost immediately after seizing these prizes, Villebon was in contact with Father Thury on the Penobscot, encouraging the priest to lead his Indians against the New Englanders.[19] There followed as a direct consequence, on Candlemas Day, 1692, what has been called "the greatest tragedy of Colonial Days in New England,"[20] the massacre at York. Thury with approximately 200 Indians "Killd & Carried Captive 140 — 48 of which are killed." The Reverend George Burroughs, a contemporary eyewitness, graphically described the devastation: "The Pillours of Smoke, ye rageing of ye mercyless flames, ye insultations of ye heathen enemy, shooting, hacking, (not haveing regard to ye earnest supplication of men, women, or Children, with sharpe cryes & bitter teares in most humble manner,) & dragging away others, (& none to help), is most affecting ye heart."[21] To show his delight with the raid, Villebon welcomed with enthusiasm some of Thury's Indians in April, 1692, and "harangued them and gave them presents, and this was followed by a magnificent feast."[22]

When Phips returned as governor in May, 1692, he was particularly disturbed at Villebon's aggressive policy. Almost immediately, therefore, Phips sent troops to the northeastern frontier under the command of the experienced Indian fighter, Benjamin Church. Phips accompanied this force as far as Pemaquid, where he began to construct a fort. Church continued to the Kennebec but came into contact with few Indians. The most encouraging aspect of the expedition as far as Church was concerned was the discovery of "considerable quantities of plunder, viz., beaver, moose skins etc."[23] Phips's show of strength definitely impressed and frightened many of the Indians. As a result of his policy, by the summer of 1693 most of the principal Indian leaders, who were formerly French allies, signed a peace treaty with Massachusetts.[24]

In addition to his successful military counteroffensive into Maine, Phips despatched two ships to Port Royal to proclaim formally that the region now belonged to Massachusetts and that the Acadian inhabitants could expect to have their problems sympathetically dealt with in Boston. When the forty-six-gun frigate and the eight-gun brigantine arrived at Port Royal, the English, according to Villebon,

> tried to induce the settlers to take up arms against all Frenchmen who might come from Europe. They refused to do this, or to interfere with my privateers; and very resolutely told the captain that it could only cost them their lives if he chose to use violence, for on this they were resolved. They were, however, willing to promise that they would not interpose and would welcome the English unless they came with the intention of doing damage; if they wished to establish a garrison, as they had long since promised to do, they might take any action they chose about the French vessels, but they themselves would remain neutral. The English tried to make them sign a guarantee for their people against the Indians in case a garrison should be sent there. But the settlers replied, as I had told them to do, that far from being able to answer for them, they would be the first victims if the Indians came to regard them as friends of the English.[25]

The pragmatic Acadians felt that they had no other choice but to proclaim their own special brand of neutrality. On the one hand, they were adamant in refusing to fight against their fellow countrymen; on the other, they seemed to indicate that they would welcome a New England garrison. But once the troops arrived, they were not to expect military assistance in any dispute with the Indians. The Acadians were, therefore, content to remain as passive Massachusetts subjects, but only if the Indians did not "regard them as friends of the English." It was a matter of survival, and in late seventeenth-century Nova Scotia, only those capable of walking the knife-edge of neutrality between the Yankees and their French and Indian enemies could hope to survive — or so it seemed.

Phips's show of force in Nova Scotia and particularly in Maine in 1692 was not the only reason for the temporary return of peace to the northeast frontier region in the following year. In March, 1693, the Massachusetts General Court, in an attempt to neutralize the activities of French privateers who were seen to be encouraging Indian depredations, sent out three guard vessels, the *William & Mary*, the *Mary*, and the *Hopewell*, to protect Massachusetts shipping "towards the Eastward." Cyprian Southack, the captain of the *William & Mary*, who had participated in Phips's 1690 Nova Scotia expedition, received these instructions:

> *Whereas this Coast has lately been annoyed by a Vessell man'd with French men and others comeing from Port Royal on St. Johns River, who have committed divers Spoyles, and Surprised several vessells with their goods belonging to their Maties Liege people of this place [you are] . . . to pursue and attack the said Enemy, and for the recovery of said Vessells and goods and the doing of such further service against their Maties Enemies ffrench or Indians as you may be capable of and shall have opportunity for.*[26]

The Court was particularly concerned about the activities of Captain Baptiste, who in the spring of 1692 had captured, within sight of Boston, a forty-five-ton brigantine from Pennsylvania, laden with 2,500 bushels of wheat and eight small barrels of flour, and a ketch from Jamaica.[27] During 1693 the three New England vessels successfully protected Massachusetts shipping from Nova Scotia–based privateers and in this way helped to consolidate the peace treaty of August of that year.

When Frontenac heard from Villebon about the peace negotiated by the Massachusetts authorities with the Indians at Pemaquid, he was outraged. He ordered Villebon in May, 1694, "to make every effort to stop the negotiations between the Indians and English," and arrogantly added that if the English were resolved to strike a momentous blow against the French in North America, "let them come to Quebec." Quick to respond to his superior, Villebon exerted all available pressure upon the Indians to break the treaty they had negotiated with the Massachusetts authorities. Not all of the chiefs responded to the intense French pressure, but a sufficient number did to carry out an attack on July 18, 1694, on Oyster River in New Hampshire. Villebon estimated that about 100 New Hampshire inhabitants were killed and 60 taken prisoner.[28] The eighteenth-century historian Jeremy Belknap described the slaughter: "They entered . . . without resistance . . . killed fourteen persons, one of them being a woman with child, they ripped open. . . . Drew surrendered his garrison on the promise of security, but was murdered when he fell into their hands; one of his children, a boy nine years old, was made to run through a lane of Indians as a mark for them to throw their hatchets at, till they had dispatched him."[29]

Villebon in 1694 also unleashed his aggressive privateer, Captain Baptiste. In early July Baptiste returned to the St. John River, "having captured five prizes." In spite of the three Massachusetts guard vessels, Baptiste had been able to seize a ship "on its way from Barbados to Boston, loaded with rum and molasses" and another "loaded with cloth from Lancaster in England."[30] The French privateer was primarily interested in capturing English vessels carrying valuable foodstuffs and merchandise, supplies which could be used to buttress the French position in the Nova Scotia region. He had little enthusiasm for seizing the Massachusetts fishing ketches with their smelly and virtually useless cargoes. Nevertheless, his activities frightened most fishermen into the protective safety of their home harbours.

In 1695 an epidemic swept through the ranks of the Indian allies of the French and appeared to drain away much of their fighting energy. The politician-scholar Thomas Hutchinson observed, "The year 1695 passed away, with less molestation from the enemy, then any year since 1688."[31] Not only were the Indians subdued but Captain Baptiste's corvette *La Bonne* was captured in May, 1695, "in Musquash Harbour by an English frigate of 36 guns and another armed vessel." In August Villebon lamented in his journal that "since the loss of the corvette, there have been many English fishermen along the coast."[32] For the Nova Scotia governor, the situation had changed so drastically by the summer of 1695 that he felt it necessary to make a remarkable proposal to Frontenac and the minister of marine, Count Pontchartrain. After informing his superiors that he had received a letter from the Salem and Marblehead fishermen requesting permission to fish in Nova Scotia waters on payment of "ten pistoles for each vessel," Villebon reported that he had sent word to Essex County that "while waiting an authorization, they might send delegates to discuss the matter with me, and if they were willing to set aside a fund of 2000 piastres, I should be able to gratify them." In justification for his action, he argued that if a large number of New England fishermen were employed in Nova Scotia waters catching cod, readily available men would be lacking for anti-French expeditions. Villebon went on to explain that the French were "not sure of capturing all those who go without permission to the coast of Acadia, and who, at a given point, become legal prizes, for a French privateer seldoms overhauls a fishing smack because it provides only a cargo of green fish for which he has no use." It was far better, therefore, in the face of practical considerations, for the French to obtain a licensing fee from the Massachusetts fishermen who were going to swarm into the region anyway. He concluded with the strongest arguments in simple economic prose: "During summer it would deprive the coast near Boston of its best men, and enable the Indians to attack their settlements more boldly. It would guarantee the safety of the French settlements in Acadia, because they would not dare to attempt anything for fear of reprisals on the fishermen and the loss of these privileges." Villebon's scheme was not accepted immediately by the Salem and Marblehead interests, "because Baptiste was captured about that time and they believed that they had nothing more to fear."[33] But his proposal does suggest that he was clearly on the defensive in the summer of 1695 and that he was desperately trying to find peace and stability for his colony.

The capture of *La Bonne* and Villebon's admission of weakness resulted, in the early summer of 1695, in the return of large numbers of Massachusetts fishermen to the Cape Sable region as well as in the resolution of the Court to encourage extensive trade with Nova Scotia.[34] But in early September a French privateer, François Gayon, ignorant of Villebon's eagerness to work out a special arrangement with Massachusetts, captured nine Yankee fishing smacks off Cape Sable. Five of these were "to be ransomed for 1500 *livres*; in one he had sent the English home, and the others he had brought home."[35] Gayon had, however, carefully avoided confronting two Massachusetts frigates cruising in Nova Scotia waters — the forty-gun *Sorlings* and the twenty-four-gun *Newport*. Gayon's unanticipated privateering activities completely and quickly undermined Villebon's conciliatory policy and triggered a demand in Essex County that Massachusetts destroy, once and for all, the French threat in Nova Scotia.

With Phips having died in London early in 1695, William Stoughton, the lieutenant-governor, was now in charge of Massachusetts. Reflecting the revived anti-French mood of the seaboard, Stoughton was determined to carry out the wishes of the Essex County fishing interests. In November, 1695, he declared that "the French [privateers] having the advantage of so many harbours and Islands Eastwards to shelter themselves and lie undiscovered, makes it more difficult to surprize them. I am of opinion We cannot be free from annoyance by them unless the Garrison at St. Johns be divested and removed which I hope to see attempted by God's blessing in the Spring."[36]

Who was to lead, "by God's blessing," Stoughton's proposed expedition? The acting governor's eyes and those of most members of the General Court focused on Benjamin Church, a member of the Court and an unusually popular and famous Indian fighter. Fifty-six years old, somewhat corpulent, Church exerted a great deal of influence in southeastern Massachusetts, especially among the Christianized Indians of the area. On being selected, he proceeded to "raise volunteers; and made it his whole business, riding both east and west in our province [Massachusetts] and Connecticut, at great charge and expense."[37] Church offered his volunteers the promise of booty and the opportunity to obtain bounties for Indian scalps. The reward for the scalp of an Indian adult male was to be £100 but only "Fifty Pounds pr head for any Indian Woman or Child Male or Female, under the Age of 14."[38] In about a month's time, Church raised what he considered to be a sufficient number and marched them down to Boston. About half of Church's 300 volunteers were Indians.[39]

While waiting for the "whale boats, and other necessaries," at Boston, Church heard early in August, 1696, of the capture of Pemaquid by a combined French naval and Indian land assault. The French expedition had been organized by Frontenac, and Villebon had played only a minor role in it.[40] With the easy capture of the fort near the mouth of the Kennebec, there seemed to be no military or strategic rationale for the proposed Church expedition. The two French warships involved in the Pemaquid assault had been sent from France via Quebec. Even if the French had been previously driven from the St. John River valley, the two French vessels could still have attacked Pemaquid. Moreover, the Indians had been stirred into action by Frontenac in Quebec. Stoughton should have listened to Cotton Mather's declaration:

> It was Canada that was the chief Source of New-England's Miseries. There was the main Strength of the French; there the Indians were mostly supplied with Ammunition; thence Issued Parties of Men, who uniting with the Salvages, barbarously murdered many Innocent New-Englanders, without any Provocation on the New-English part ... and as Cato could make no Speech in the Senate without that

Conclusion, Delenda est Carthago; *so it was the general Conclusion of all that Argued sensibly about the safety of that Country,* Canada must be Reduced.[41]

Under the circumstances, it is difficult to be certain what Stoughton hoped to accomplish by sending Church's force to Nova Scotia. There was no mention in Church's very vague official instructions of a specific attack on Jemseg or Fort Nashwaak, about thirty miles west of Jemseg.[42] Perhaps it was hoped that a Massachusetts show of force in the Maine–Nova Scotia region would help to counter some of the advantages the French had gained from their unexpected capture of Pemaquid. Perhaps Stoughton felt powerless to hold back Church's motley collection of volunteers intent upon seizing booty and scalps.

After picking up a few recruits at Piscataqua, Church's flotilla moved northeastward looking for Indian scalps. None was found so Church ordered his men to row towards the Acadian settlement of Chignecto near present-day Sackville, New Brunswick. When the invaders reached the undefended settlement, the Acadians "carried all or part of their goods with them." Church's men searched for Indians and booty and found little of either. For amusement the volunteers "chopped and hacked with hatchets" the "cattle, sheep, hogs, and dogs" belonging to the defenceless and bewildered French inhabitants.[43]

Church gathered the Acadian inhabitants together and explained to them why the expedition had been organized and also gave them a stern warning:

The Major told them [that] he did not design the savages should hurt them; but it was to let them see a little what the poor English felt, saying [that] it was not their scalps [that] he wanted, but the savages; for he should get nothing by them. . . . But the Major bid them tell their fathers, (the friars and Governours), that if they still persisted, and let their wretched savages kill and destroy the poor English at that rate, he would come with some hundreds of savages, and let them loose amongst them, who would kill, scalp, and carry away every French person in those parts; for they were the root from whence all the branches came, that hurt us.[44]

When Church had completed his work at Chignecto on September 20, he "concluded to go to St. Johns river." At the mouth of the river his men discovered "twelve great guns which were hid in the beach, below high water mark. (The carriages, shot, and wheelbarrows, some flour and pork, all hid in the woods)." This material was intended for the new French fort planned at the mouth of the St. John River. Church had considered launching an attack on Villebon's fort up the St. John River, but he felt that the water level in the river was too low to permit him to approach the fort. Besides he was not, to use his own words, "willing to make a Canada expedition" of his enterprise.[45] In other words, he was not intending to court military disaster by striking inland against the French capital.

While returning to Boston, Church was amazed to meet three Massachusetts vessels carrying 100 men under the command of Colonel John Hathorne of Salem, a member of the Massachusetts Council. Hathorne had been appointed the new commander-in-chief of the expedition and had orders to attack Fort Nashwaak and to capture "the ordnance, artillery, and other warlike stores, and provisions, lately supplied to them from France."[46] Church was, as he put it, "not a little mortified" at what he considered to be the inexperienced Hathorne's effrontery in shouldering aside the famous Indian fighter. Church argued that his troops had had enough of Nova Scotia, and "having their faces towards home, were loath to turn back"— but turn back they did, at least as far as the mouth of the St. John River.[47] Hathorne's October assault on Nashwaak was a failure; he should have remained in Salem where his military skill might have been of some value. After a desultory thirty-six hour siege, his force meekly withdrew to the mouth of the river where it joined the rest of the volunteers and hurried back to Boston.[48] Much to the unhappiness of Church, it had in fact been "a Canada expedition."

The Hathorne-Church fiasco disgusted many members of the Massachusetts General Court and the general populace. It seemed to be convincing proof that Massachusetts lacked even the necessary military resources to deal effectively with the tiny French force in Nova Scotia. The fiasco appeared to drain away whatever might have remained of Massachusetts' expansionist independence. By the early autumn of 1696, therefore, in this period of acute collective self-doubt, the colony desperately turned to King William for assistance. The "most humble and distressed Subjects," according to the General Court, demanded:

Royal Aid, humbly praying That yor Majesty would be graciously pleased to order ... That Port Royal and St. Johns

in Accadia or Nova Scotia may be Setled by Erecting of a
regular Fortification furnished with all necessary warlike
Provisions and Stores and a Suitable number of Souldiers
posted in Garrison at each of the said places at the charge of
yor Matys Exchequer; which is apprehended will be a greater
bridle upon the Enemy by reason of their Scituation, than
Pemaquid could be.[49]

Nova Scotia was no longer conceived to be Massachusetts' special responsibility; rather, the "greater bridle upon the enemy" was to be forced upon the region by the troops of King William. A colonial mentality had returned to Massachusetts and was accompanied by a pervasive mood of isolation. Nova Scotia was to be avoided at all costs. In December, therefore, the General Court prohibited absolutely all trade and contact with Nova Scotia, "Forasmuch as it is very Evident, That both the French and the Indian Enemy are releive'd and Succourd by the Supplys transmitted, from hence."[50]

Virtually powerless in 1697, Massachusetts was expecting either massive English military assistance or a large-scale French assault on Boston. Most residents seemed content to wait passively for one of the two inevitable happenings to occur. But neither did. Instead, on December 9, Boston heard the glorious news that peace had finally come. A jubilant Samuel Sewall wrote in his diary: "Mr. Jno Willard brings the Order for proclaiming the Peace here, which was done between 3 and 4 p.m. Eight or 10 Drums, Two Trumpets: Prisoners released."[51]

If there was a winner in the war in the Massachusetts–Nova Scotia region, it was the French-Indian side. Fewer than 1,000 Indians and Frenchmen had played havoc with the Maine frontier and with Massachusetts commerce and the fishery. Massachusetts had entered the war full of self-confidence, intent upon impressing the mother country. By 1697 the Massachusetts economy was on the verge of collapse, and there was the stench of defeat in the air: hundreds had died during the war, many frontier settlements had been destroyed, and the General Court had, in desperation, turned to England for salvation. Massachusetts' economic suzerainty over Nova Scotia at the end of the seventeenth century was not enough to lock the French territory into a political and military subjugation.

6

Joseph Dudley, 1698-1707

By restoring the status quo ante, the Treaty of Ryswick of 1697 ignored the essential sources of Anglo-French territorial conflict in northeastern North America. Seven years of often bitter warfare in the Massachusetts–Nova Scotia region had been disregarded by the European-oriented French and English authorities. The peace was not considered as a time to build good relations between the two nations in either the Old or New World. Rather, it provided an opportunity to prepare for what both sides hoped would be a decisive war that would decide once and for all which country would be supreme in Europe. Obviously, within this tight strategic framework, North America was still conceived to be of peripheral and limited importance.

The first full year of peace, 1698, provided convincing proof of the continuing unshakable economic hold of Massachusetts over Nova Scotia. Scores of Salem and Marblehead fishermen, no longer paralyzed into inactivity by the threat of French privateers, sailed once again to the Cape Sable area. A few Massachusetts merchants, looking for the furs which had accumulated during the war years in various Indian settlements, also pushed northeastward but veered into the Bay of Fundy. Other traders provided supplies for a number of Acadian inhabitants, some of whom, at least, had in their possession hard currency obtained from the French military during the war years. Within less than a year, therefore, Massachusetts merchants and fishermen had re-established the status quo ante in their commercial relations with Nova Scotia. The forces of economic continuity had engulfed Nova Scotia.

Under heavy pressure from the French minister of marine, Governor Villebon attempted in the late summer of 1698 to turn back the Massachusetts economic offensive, even though he must have been aware of the utter hopelessness of his situation. In a sharply worded letter to Lieutenant-Governor Stoughton, he warned that the French would seize and confiscate all property belonging to those Massachusetts inhabitants trading or fishing in Nova Scotia territory. Villebon further declared that he had received "special instructions" to maintain the Kennebec as the eastern boundary of his colony. As a consequence, he expected that Stoughton "will forbear in future to treat the Indians settled there as your subjects, in order to avoid regrettable consequences."[1] Villebon had but a meagre force of some seventy soldiers to implement his tough anti-Massachusetts policy. What he threatened, he could not in fact carry out. And what he officially asserted he would do, he privately questioned, since he realized how dependent his tiny colony was on Massachusetts.[2] Some Massachusetts officials, however, unable to distinguish between his half-hearted bluster and the reality of the situation, felt compelled to respond to the "pretensions of the French."[3]

On November 19, 1698, the Massachusetts General Court drafted a detailed representation to King William regarding "ye Insults of the French in their ungrounded and unreasonable pretensions." The General Court seemed particularly worried about the threat to the Cape Sable fishery and the unilateral declaration that all territory east of the Kennebec was French. It maintained that if both of the French "groundless pretexts and Claims" were accepted, the Massachusetts economy would be seriously undermined and the colony's north-eastern frontier settlements would be constantly harassed by the Indian allies of the French. In an unsubtle attempt to strike a responsive chord in governmental circles in England, it was contended that French pretensions in the Massachusetts region were, in essence, a threat to the mother country's interests: "Your Matys Revenue will be greatly endamaged thereby; Considerable quantitys of Bullion will be hindred from coming into your Matys Kingdoms, Trade and Navigation much ruined, a multitude of Familys cut off from the means of their subsistance, and a nursery for the training up of seamen to serve in your Matys Royal Navy will be dissolved."[4]

Having become sensitive during King William's War of their limited military power and of their increased dependence upon the mother country, the members of the General Court were not embarrassed in persisting in their application of pressure on the imperial authorities at another period of crisis. These men realized that the initiative for "the bold Insolences of the French" came from Versailles, not from Villebon's tiny post on the St. John River. Only European diplomacy at the highest level, they argued, could effectively protect Massachusetts' interests. The king therefore was urged to assert his sovereignty over the disputed Kennebec territory and to defend "your Matys good Subjects in the peaceable enjoyment and exercise of their ancient and indubitable priviledge of Fishing in the seas off the Coast of Accadie or Nova Scotia."[5] A pro-Massachusetts stability had to be imposed on the area from the two European capitals.

John Nelson, who had returned to Massachusetts sometime in the late summer of 1698 from imprisonment in France, played a key role in the drafting of the representation, feeling that "nothing but a vigorous assertion of our rights will save us."[6] He lost little time in reasserting his own "rights" in the Nova Scotia trade; in early November he visited his old friend Villebon,[7] though it is impossible to determine what precise impact his visit had on the French governor.

It is clear, however, that a great deal of Massachusetts' concern about the French counteroffensive had apparently disappeared by 1699, and that this change in mood owed much to the return of Nelson and his visit to Villebon. Confronted by a serious shortage of supplies and concerned about the vociferous Massachusetts reaction to his letter, Villebon resolved to make one major public concession to the Massachusetts government. In private he was even willing to question the French claim to the Kennebec and to close his eyes to the activities of Massachusetts traders.[8] In all likelihood, Villebon was determined to encourage Massachusetts commerce not only because of the shortage of supplies in his colony but also since he was personally involved with Nelson in the trade. Villebon's major public concession, it should be emphasized, dealt with the fishery. The French govenor saw no reason for interfering with the Massachusetts fishermen as long as they did not dry their fish on Nova Scotia territory. He pointed out that he had discovered that the fishermen had "offered to pay the . . . toll . . . 50

francs for the privilege of getting wood and water." He even qualified his earlier opposition to the drying of fish on shore by asserting that if the Massachusetts fishermen "were granted permission to establish curing stations they would pay a larger amount, without any rights to trade either with the Indians or with His Majesty's subjects." Villebon calculated that if his licensing system was established, "four to five thousand livres each year" would be raised, money which could be spent on fortifying the colony. He felt that the New Englanders "should not be excluded completely from the country," for if they were, "they might secretly instigate some freebooter . . . to harry our young settlements, without appearing to have had anything to do with the matter." While the money from the Massachusetts fishermen was being used to fortify Nova Scotia against possible Massachusetts attacks, the Massachusetts fishermen were to be encouraged to train Acadians in cod fishing techniques so that the Acadians could eventually drive the New Englanders from Nova Scotia waters.[9]

Villebon's scheme was a somewhat naive attempt to come to grips with what he considered to be economic and political reality as well as his own desire to make quick profits. He wished to alienate neither the powerful Massachusetts fishing interests nor the Versailles authorities. But Villebon died in late June, 1700, before the French minister of marine's rejection of the scheme arrived in Nova Scotia.[10] Count Pontchartrain was willing to concede only that as long as the Massachusetts fishermen were out of sight of shore were they to be permitted to fish the banks off Nova Scotia.[11] Pontchartrain's concession was no concession as this had been French policy since 1686. The minister of marine's refusal to permit the Massachusetts fishermen to salt and dry their catch ashore, for a price, may have been of little real consequence anyway, since some New Englanders had already changed their practice and were drying their cod on safe Massachusetts soil.

The new governor of Massachusetts, Lord Bellomont, who had arrived in Boston in May, 1699, a year after he had received his royal commission,[12] was not immediately made aware of Villebon's informal concessions, and in an attempt to establish his authority, he bellicosely echoed the General Court's earlier concern about the French policy regarding the Kennebec boundary and the fishery. Bellomont seemed particularly worried about "the designs and measures of the French in fortifying the eastern frontier of New England." In late February,

1700, he reported that French priests were encouraging the frontier Indians to organize "a general insurrection and rebellion." He predicted that "if the Five Nations should at any time, in conjunction with the Eastern Indians, and those that live within these Plantations, revolt from the English to the French, they would in a short time drive us quite out of this Continent."[13]

Realizing how important it was to neutralize the efforts of the Jesuit missionaries working among the northeastern frontier Indians, especially after the death of the pliable Villebon, Bellomont and the Massachusetts Council proposed two possible solutions. The governor pleaded with his British superiors to provide him with sufficient funds to build a large fort on the St. Croix River. Such a fort, he was certain, would overawe the Indians in the region, drive the French back into the interior of Nova Scotia, and, in addition, encourage large-scale English settlement in that "noble tract of country of 190 miles in length." The Council, on the other hand, proposed that "three able, learned, orthodox Ministers . . . have their residence among the Eastern Indians,"[14] and use the Puritan gospel to make Massachusetts allies of the aborigines. But suitable frontier missionaries were not to be found and Bellomont received no support for his offensive policy. Before he was able to do anything of consequence about what he regarded as the growing Indian menace and the imminent threat of renewed warfare, Bellomont died in March, 1701.

Until the arrival in Boston on June 11, 1702, of Joseph Dudley, Bellomont's successor as governor of Massachusetts, the colony's affairs were in the hands of Lieutenant-Governor Stoughton and the Council, and after Stoughton's death in July, 1701, in those of the Council members alone.[15] During this fifteen-month period of instability, many people in the colony daily expected to hear of "a rupture betwixt the Crown of England and France." Rumours about a declaration of war circulated freely. Stoughton accurately reflected the mood of the colony when he reported on April 10, 1701: "The rumours of a new War likely to commence do's smartly alarm us and fill us with no little consternation at the pre-apprehensions of the distresses, wherein this Province will unavoidably be merged. . . . For we may expect no other but that the Indians will be instigated by the French to make fresh inroads on our frontiers and our Plantations. The wounds we formerly received by them being still recent, the People will be extreemly discouraged to be again embroyl'd and harassed by those bloody savages."[16]

When the Council members learned in early August that the new governor of Nova Scotia, Governor Brouillan, had arrived at Port Royal with what was estimated as a force of 600 soldiers, they expected a major French-Indian offensive against Massachusetts.[17] When anticipating an outbreak of hostilities with the French or Indians, Massachusetts residents were prone to exaggerate wildly the potential military strength of their enemies. This tendency reflected their own acute sense of anxiety at the beginning of a period of collective disorientation. In late August, 1701, in response to the news from Nova Scotia, the fortifications of Castle Island at Boston were immediately "with all manner of application" prepared for action and a spy ship was sent to Port Royal "to make discovery of the posture and proceedings of the French there."[18] What was effectively hidden from the men on the spy vessel was the fact that Brouillan's entire military force at Port Royal numbered fewer than 200 men.[19] Only approximately 100 reinforcements had accompanied the new governor to Nova Scotia.

Massachusetts residents may have exaggerated Brouillan's military strength, but the French governor was far more realistic and accurate in assessing his situation. He had few soldiers and had just begun to construct his major fortress at Port Royal. Moreover, he had discovered that many of the Acadian inhabitants, whom he described as being "demy-republicans," were disconcertingly sympathetic to the New Englanders.[20] Since he expected Massachusetts to learn first of any declaration of war from Europe, he understandably feared that any Massachusetts invading force, taking full advantage of the element of surprise, could easily capture the largely defenceless Port Royal. Sensing the weakness of his position, he made a surprising proposal to the Massachusetts government on July 28. Brouillan asked Massachusetts to consider a special treaty of neutrality with Nova Scotia which would be binding on both colonies should war break out in Europe. If after signing such a document, the two colonies were ordered to fight by the mother countries, the French in Nova Scotia were to "make to you as we expect you will to us, a public declaration, before we enterprize anything which may break our Treaty of Union and good correspondence." So that the Massachusetts officials would not conclude what was in fact the case, that his proposal was an indication of French weakness, Brouillan simultaneously warned

Massachusetts fishermen "from coming to fish in sight of the lands of this Province."[21]

When Brouillan's letter reached Boston, the Council had become the sole executive arm of government. It returned a cautious, but not unfavourable, reply to the effect that since a new governor was expected at any moment, the Council members were reluctant to make any binding decision concerning the neutrality agreement. Nevertheless, it did promise "whilst on your side all acts of hostility shall be forborn, we shall not be forward to the Aggressors, or to enterprize anything to interrupt our mutual quiet and repose." The Council concluded its reply by sharply criticizing Brouillan's fishery policy, which, it said, was contrary to "the accustomed indubitable right and priviledge of the English to fish . . . on that coast for time out of mind."[22]

Brouillan considered that Massachusetts' response was at least tacit consent to his suggestion. In May of the following year, 1702, he showed that he was willing to compromise on his tough fishery stand in order not to alienate Massachusetts. In the southeast corner of Nova Scotia at Port Latour, three Salem ketches had been captured and one of the fishermen killed by a band of Micmacs. The Salem fishermen had been "forced by bad weather to put in for shelter" and then had been attacked by the Indians. When the Council was informed of the incident, it immediately sent a messenger to Brouillan, demanding that the vessels be restored and that "justice be done."[23] Despite the fact that the Salem fishermen had disregarded his orders and those of his immediate predecessor, the French governor quickly agreed to release the vessels. He also reasserted his desire to live at peace and in harmony with his Massachusetts neighbours.[24]

While the Council was in the midst of its negotiations with Brouillan, Governor Joseph Dudley arrived in Boston on June 11, 1702. A robust man of fifty-five years, Dudley was returning to his native Massachusetts. He was the son of Thomas Dudley, the second governor of the colony. A Harvard graduate and successful colonial politician, Dudley had earned the enmity of most Massachusetts residents because of his unqualified support of the detested Andros administration. During his long political exile in England, from 1693 to 1702, the shrewd, energetic, and ambitious Dudley had served first as deputy-governor of the Isle of Wight and then as a Member of Parliament for Newton. He wished to follow in his father's footsteps, and largely because of his persistence and the influence of his close friend William Blathwayt, clerk of the Privy Council and one of the Lords of Trade, he was finally appointed to the governorship.[25] He was an excellent administrator, but a man who, in the words of one of his successors, "had as many virtues as can consist with so great a thirst for honour and power."[26]

Dudley had missed a decade of Massachusetts development; he had not experienced first-hand the full effects of the frightening impact of the Indian raids on the frontier or the depredations of the French privateers during the latter years of King William's War. He could not therefore appreciate the considerable appeal Brouillan's neutrality scheme must have had for many Massachusetts inhabitants. As Thomas Hutchinson perceptively observed concerning Massachusetts in 1702, "It is certain that the Massachusetts government would have been content (provided the Eastern Indians had continued at peace with the English) that they should not be obliged to go to war against the French."[27] But from the outset, Dudley, who tended to look at Massachusetts' problems through English eyes, had little enthusiasm for any kind of neutrality. In order to please his English superiors and to add lustre to his own reputation, he wished to strike hard and successfully at the French. On hearing on June 19, 1702, of the declaration of war between France and England, Dudley immediately announced his intention of encouraging the "merchants to equip some of their ships on H.M. Service, for the annoying of H.M. enemies."[28] And within less than a month at least four Massachusetts vessels were cruising against the French.[29] By September 17 these privateers had captured at least fourteen French vessels, nine in the Port Royal–Cape Sable region, three at the mouth of the St. Lawrence, and two off the east coast of Newfoundland.[30] The seizure of the French fishing ships in early August near Cape Sable had effectively destroyed the Acadian fishery.[31] By the end of the year four more French ships had been captured. Dudley proudly confided to the Earl of Nottingham: "The three last were one with arms, clothes and provisions sent from Quebeck to the Kennebeck Indians, according to articles lately made between the Indians and the Governor of Canada, upon which the Indians were universally to rise upon the English; the other two were brigantines sent from Quebeck with suitable provision to Placentia, there to take in 50 men each, to cruise upon our coasts for provisions, which are much wanted in all the French settlements, especially at Port Royal, the next settlement to the English pale."[32]

Dudley's military strategy had begun to crystallize by the closing months of 1702. His prime concern was to keep the northeastern Indians neutral, not only by preventing their receiving supplies and encouragement from the French in Nova Scotia and Quebec but also by negotiating directly with them.[33] Furthermore, by sending reinforcements to the northeastern settlements and by stressing the importance of the rebuilding of Fort Pemaquid, Dudley hoped to keep the wavering Indians in line.[34] The peace and stability of the northeast frontier for the remainder of 1702 was convincing proof to Dudley and others that his military strategy had been successful, at least in the short run. To ensure that the stability would be permanent, the governor proposed that Port Royal be attacked by "a small fleet of but three or four men-of-war . . . with assistance of some H.M. people here [Massachusetts] for the land part."[35] He wanted the major initiative for the expedition to come from England, perhaps because he felt that only under these circumstances would the mother country effectively garrison the French colony. If the English navy captured Port Royal and continued to hold it for the duration of the war, Massachusetts would be shielded from French privateers and the Indians, and there was a much better chance that the English would want to keep possession of the area after the end of hostilities. For Dudley, another Phips-like expedition would be a waste of manpower and energy. Besides, if a popular local hero successfully led such an assault, then Dudley's position as governor might be threatened. Dudley could not easily forget the sudden rise to power of William Phips.

Always concerned with pleasing and impressing the members of the Council of Trade, Dudley announced to them in November that since the Indians and French were no longer a major threat to his colony, he planned to send "two companies of volunteers as H.M. has commanded for the service in the West Indies."[36] This decision revealed how delighted and satisfied Dudley actually was in November, 1702, with the success of his French-Indian policy. His own rhetoric and actions had lulled him into a profound sense of security and self-satisfaction.

Dudley's privateering offensive should, it would seem, have convinced Brouillan that his neutrality scheme was a dead letter. Yet the

French governor apparently considered the agreement to be still in force as late as September, 1702, for in that month he asked Dudley to return the Acadian vessels and men mistakenly captured by the Massachusetts "private ships of warr."[37] He blamed the rapacious privateersmen, not the Massachusetts government, for the attacks. For his and his colony's well-being he wanted to remind the Massachusetts authorities that a short time earlier they had promised not "to be the Aggressors; or to enterprize anything to interrupt our mutual quiet and repose."[38] But Brouillan was bravely whistling in the Nova Scotia dark, and by the early part of October he had reluctantly come to the conclusion that Massachusetts was determined to shatter his dream of "mutual quiet and repose."

To deal with the serious threat of Massachusetts aggression, Brouillan asked for massive military assistance from France and, if this was not possible, for some well-equipped privateers. He also began to apply pressure on the northeastern Indians to take the offensive against the English.[39] Aware of his own weakness and vulnerability, and fighting against fantastic odds, the desperate Brouillan further urged Governor Vaudreuil of New France "to send some Canadians to Kinnebequi, to try and induce these Indians to break with these Bostonians."[40] In effect Dudley had forced Brouillan to urge the implementation of that policy which the French had used so well during King William's War.

From Brouillan's counteroffensive, Massachusetts in 1703 felt first the effects of some of the French privateers. The Massachusetts House of Representatives, spurred to action by shipowners and fishermen, was quick to respond and on March 25 urged Dudley to organize an expedition against Port Royal. The Representatives presented Dudley with their motion:

Whereas we are daily infested by the enemy liveing at Port Royal and likely to be deprived of our provisions that we have our great dependance upon for our subsistance by their vessels that are continually taking their opportunitys to surprize the same; and are thereby forced to be at great cost and charge to provide ships and forces for our security therefrom, we are of opinion that an essay should be made for the takeing of Port Royal and the places adjacent, and that encouragement be given to such volunteers as may present to engage in that service by allowing them all the plunder

thereof, saving the rights of H. M., and that the Province
shall supply them with victuals for carrying on the said
expedition.

Dudley and the Council, however, refused to accept the House
proposal unless two amendments were added. First, if 1,000 volunteers
were not found, the deficit would have to be made up of impressed
soldiers "drawn out of the several Regiments for the Province."
Second, there were to be at least three warships in the expedition and
a sufficient number of supply vessels manned by "300 sailors taken up
for the service."[41] In a fit of pique, the House rejected the amendments
and withdrew its original proposal. It is impossible to be certain why
Dudley and the Council did not accept the plan of the House of
Representatives for a volunteer army unsupported by warships. It
may have been that the egocentric governor resented a move by the
Representatives into what he regarded as his own special area of
responsibility. Or unwilling to be associated in any way with a military
fiasco, he may have thought that a sufficient number of volunteers
could not be raised to capture Port Royal. But Dudley must have
realized that the time was ripe for a swift assault on Port Royal. The
fort was in disrepair. Of the 200 or so soldiers, over 50 "appeared to
be weak and infirm,"[42] and reports seemed to suggest that many
Acadians, to quote Brouillan, "if the English appear . . . would join
them."[43]

The collapse of the Port Royal scheme had little apparent effect on
Dudley who by June of 1703 was content to concentrate his efforts
on placating the frontier Indians. Even with Port Royal in French
hands, he felt confident that his tongue could control the Indians. On
June 30 he met at Falmouth with representatives of the Penobscots,
Norridgewocks, Androscoggins, Sacos, and Penacooks. The proceedings ended with the Indians declaring that "as high as the sun was
above the earth, so far distant was their design of making the least
breach of the peace."[44] Six weeks later the Indian sun suddenly fell
from the skies as an estimated 500 warriors, led by a small group of
Frenchmen sent by Governor Vaudreuil at Brouillan's request, ravaged
the frontier area from the Connecticut River to Casco Bay.[45] Some 130
New Englanders were killed or taken prisoner and "terror and confusion" swept all of Massachusetts.[46] What prevented the attacking
Indians from making further inroads into the colony was Dudley's

strong counterattack, facilitated somewhat by the General Court's decision to give £40 for every Indian scalp possessed by a Massachusetts resident.[47]

Incensed at the failure of the governor's frontier policy and convinced that the Nova Scotia French were responsible for the August raids, the Representatives in early September, 1703, once again urged the governor to strike with a volunteer force at what they considered to be the root cause of the colony's difficulties — Port Royal.[48] Dudley once again disregarded their proposal. It was not until after the news of the Deerfield massacre had reached Boston some six months later on March 5, 1704,[49] that Dudley became a little more sympathetic to the Port Royal policy of the House. His sympathy suddenly evolved into enthusiastic support when he was informed on March 9 that "100 French and 200 Indians from Quebeck" were marching "to joyne the Eastern Indians to make in all 1,000" for a spring offensive against northern Massachusetts. Dudley saw in a Nova Scotia expedition an opportunity to channel the violent anti-French sentiment, as well as criticism of himself which had been brought suddenly to the surface by the Deerfield episode. Furthermore, he believed that such an expedition, properly timed and intelligently aimed, would compel the invading Franco-Indian force to defend the Kennebec–Nova Scotia area rather than to attack Massachusetts.[50]

On March 20, 1704, the General Court, this time with the encouragement of Dudley, enunciated its new Nova Scotia policy. A force of 600 volunteers was to be raised, "the Officers and Soldiers to fit out themselves at their own Charge without Pay to range the Coast and Woods of these Provinces, and to Insult the Eastern Coast of Nova Scotia, and Port Royal." The only financial inducement was the promise of a fair share of all plunder taken and £100 for every Indian scalp "above ye age of ten years."[51] No explicit mention, it should be noted, was made of three warships to accompany the expedition or of the possible use of the draft. The March 20 proposal, therefore, seemed to represent a victory of the House of Representatives over the Council and Dudley.

Who could and might want to raise 600 volunteers from an area not immediately threatened by Indian raids? Dudley's answer was the quixotic Major Benjamin Church, the sixty-five-year-old military hero from southeastern Massachusetts. An adroit persuasive salesman, Church used every means at his disposal, especially liquor and cash, to raise some 500 English and Indian volunteers from Plymouth, Barnstable, and Bristol counties.[52] Church's inability to fill his quota of 600 suggests that at the grass-roots level, tremendous popular enthusiasm for the venture was not to be found in Massachusetts.

Despite Church's eagerness to attack Port Royal, Dudley, who was in control of military policy in the colony, excluded it from Church's objectives, using the feeble excuse that he was awaiting further instructions on what to do about Port Royal from the English authorities.[53] No one will ever know precisely what Dudley's motives were for excluding Port Royal. In September, 1702, and again in December of the same year, Dudley had vigorously advocated an expedition against Port Royal provided that three or four warships were made available. In early May, 1704, Dudley had his three warships and at least 500 volunteers; he had, furthermore, resolved to use the fourteen-gun *Province Galley* and two English frigates, one of forty-eight guns and the other of thirty-two, in the expedition. Dudley's enemies would later argue that the governor wanted to spare Port Royal because he was involved in illegal trade with the French fort.[54] There may have been some incriminating evidence there, the discovery of which could have destroyed his career. The Reverend Cotton Mather, for example, was suspicious of Dudley and rebuked the governor: "When Church [wanted to go] . . . to Port royal . . . you absolutely forbad him, you peremptorily forbad him. The cause you assigned was, because the matter had been laid before the queen, and the queen had sent over no orders for it. . . . But the story grows now too black a story for me to meddle with — The expedition baffled — The fort never so much as demanded. . . . A nest of hornets provoked to fly out upon us — A shame cast upon us that will never be forgotten — I dare not, I cannot meddle with these mysteries."[55]

When the troops in fourteen small transports accompanied by the three warships sailed from Boston on May 15, Church had in his possession detailed instructions from Dudley. These instructions went far beyond the Court's March proposal. After searching for Indian scalps and booty in the Passamaquoddy area, Church was to raid the Acadian settlements at Minas and Chignecto and "use all possible methods for the burning and destroying of the enemies houses, and breaking the dams of their corn grounds in the said several places, and make what other spoils you can upon them, and bring away prisoners."[56] The prisoners were important for exchange purposes because of the large number of Massachusetts captives in New France. After four to six weeks in Nova Scotia, Church was to return to the Kennebec River, where his troops were to prevent the Indian allies of the French from mounting any new offensive against Massachusetts.

Church followed his instructions carefully and his men ravaged Chignecto and Minas, burning the houses of the inhabitants, destroying their complicated system of dykes, slaughtering their livestock, and getting wildly drunk on the French brandy and claret.[57] One New England contemporary maintained that the Indian allies of the French were "driven into such confusion, that they left their Wigwams and retired into private Cells."[58] While Church's force was at Minas and Chignecto, the *Province Galley* and the two English warships were cruising off Port Royal. They had been sent there by Dudley ostensibly "to wait the coming of some store ships."[59] But Dudley may have sent the ships to Port Royal for yet another reason: to capture the French fort without firing a shot and without Church's assistance. On June 24 the two English captains and Cyprian Southack, the commander of the colonial vessel, demanded that Brouillan surrender his fort within forty-eight hours. If he refused to do so, 1,500 New Englanders, led by "200 Sauvages," would make a frontal assault on the fort and give no quarter.[60] In spite of the almost nonexistence of adequate fortifications and with fewer than 150 able-bodied soldiers at his command, Brouillan called the bluff of the three captains. Nothing happened after forty-eight hours and nothing occurred on July 4, nine days after the beginning of the naval siege when Church and his men arrived in the vicinity of Port Royal. It was decided at a council of war not to attack the French fort "for this reason, that we judge ourselves inferiour to the strength of the enemy; and, therefore, the danger and risk we run, is greater than the advantage we can, or are likely to obtain." No reason was given for Church's decision to disregard his instructions and to consider the feasibility of an assault on Port Royal. He may have gotten wind of Dudley's intelligence to the three captains, or he may have read greater freedom of action into the clause of his original instructions: "Notwithstanding the particularity of the aforegoing [orders] . . . I lay you under no restraint."[61]

Church next made his way via Chignecto to the Penobscot, and after scouring the countryside for scalps, he sailed for Casco Bay and then back to Boston.[62] The expedition had, at least within the context of Dudley's instructions and strategy, been remarkably successful.

There were considerable booty and a large number of French prisoners, though few scalps; the Acadian settlements had been successfully ravaged and only six Massachusetts volunteers had been killed during the raids.[63] The frontier Indians had been put on the defensive, and as late as February 1, 1706, Dudley could boast: "The . . . Indians . . . are fled to Canada, and for want of their usual support are in a starving discontented condition among the French . . . the people are easy and the masting in the deepest woods has been so well guarded that there is no complaint."[64]

All was not rosy, however, in Massachusetts in the immediate post-expedition period. There was a bitter dispute over the distribution of the plunder, with Dudley's enemies asserting that he and his cronies "Cut off the Army of Half that the *Public Faith* had Engaged them."[65] The volunteers were furious, and with good reason, and so was their commanding officer who, "for all his great expenses, fatigues and hostilities . . . received of his excellency *fifteen pounds*."[66] It would not be as easy to obtain volunteers for such an expedition the next time. There were those who bitterly criticized Dudley for showing so little initiative in attempting to capture Port Royal. This failure meant, among other things, that French privateers could still play havoc with Massachusetts commerce and the fishery. Furthermore, the Indian allies of the French would continue to be encouraged in their anti-English policy because of the military presence, however weak, of the French in Nova Scotia.

The year 1705 was a time of relative peace and stability for Massachusetts, both on the northeastern and western frontiers and on the Atlantic, and this situation seriously weakened the position of Dudley's critics. He took advantage of the period of calm to exchange prisoners with Governor Vaudreuil of Quebec. During these negotiations Vaudreuil asked the Massachusetts governor to consider signing a treaty of neutrality which would, together with ensuring peace, facilitate close commercial relations between the two colonies.[67] Dudley and the General Court refused to carry on negotiations, and this decision was one major reason why French-Indian raids against the colony's frontiers and French privateering attacks on Massachusetts commerce were renewed in earnest in the spring and summer of 1706. The beginning of the new French-Indian offensive coincided with the discovery in Massachusetts that six Boston merchants, Samuel Vetch, John Borland, Roger Lawson, William Rouse, John Phillips, Jr., and

Ebenezer Coffin, were involved in large-scale illicit trade with the French and Indians of Nova Scotia. To make matters even more serious, Dudley was charged with being involved with the six merchants.[68] A bitter fear of conspiracy swept much of the colony.

In the General Court, representatives from the now-beleaguered frontier areas were particularly incensed on hearing the evidence about the illegal trade, and in Boston, as John Winthrop, Jr., observed, there was "a horrid combustion in town about it." Arms and ammunition had not been included in the invoice of goods shipped by Rouse to Port Royal, but the invoice in the governor's handwriting referred to "Eighty Thousand of Shingle Nails. Twenty Thousand Shingle Boards, One Dozen . . . Table Knives . . . Butter . . . Mackerel . . . Searge . . . Wine . . . Some Rice."[69] Two acts of Parliament of 1705 had forbidden "trade and commerce with France" and "all traitorous correspondence with H.M. enemies."[70] New England merchants might have been accustomed to disregard parliamentary commercial regulations, but as far as the General Court was concerned, there was no excuse for putting "knives into the hands of those barbarous infidels to cut the throats of our wives and children."[71] Many members of the Court had had enough of what seemed to them to be unprincipled Boston entrepreneurs. Bypassing the regular courts, the General Court fined the merchants sums ranging from £50 to £1,100.[72] Dudley permitted this unusual procedure to take place knowing that it would likely be repealed in England, as it was, in 1707. Even though nothing more was done about the case in Massachusetts, a bitter suspicion about the incident lingered.

The 1706 controversy over illicit trade had two important consequences relating to Massachusetts–Nova Scotia relations. First, it was responsible for Samuel Vetch's journey to England to seek a reversal of his sentence, and while in England, Vetch was able to play a key role in persuading the English authorities to become militarily involved in North America. Second, the controversy influenced Dudley to make a serious effort to capture Port Royal without English aid. He felt compelled to do so in order to convince a growing number of enemies and critics that he was as anti-French as any man in Massachusetts and that he had nothing to hide at Port Royal.

The evidence is conclusive that the idea for a 1707 expedition against Port Royal originated with Dudley and was merely his 1702 plan revived unchanged. In February, 1707, he wrote to Governor

Fitz-John Winthrop of Connecticut concerning his intention to attack the French fort and settlement with "a thousand men, with two or three ships of strength." Dudley asserted that "there seems a great inclination to it in the trading part in these provinces."[73] When the General Court met early in March, Dudley put forward his proposal, and after considerable bickering between the House and Council regarding recruiting policy and the division of booty, an expedition was agreed to on March 21.[74] It was decided that "if the abovesd numbers of Souldiers and seamen, do not offer themselves voluntarily what are wanting be equally Impressed, out of Such Towns, as are not ffrontiers, by land, so that the number of Souldiers impressed do not Exceed Three Hundred."[75] Dudley and the Council had finally dragged the reluctant representatives to a policy position they had earlier vigorously opposed, especially the part dealing with the possible use of nonvolunteers.

The general mood of Massachusetts about the expedition in March and April, 1707, is not easy to gauge. Some people, no doubt, shared Governor Winthrop's reservations expressed in a letter to Dudley:

Some may insinuate that tho' wee should succede in the designe, yet if upon the conclusion of a peace (wch one would think not far off) it should be restored to them, the honr of our success will soone be forgotten, and wee should much resent that we have lavisht our blood and treasure. And tis not unlikely but others will consider that at this tyme, when wee are every day alarmed and expect considerable partyes of the enemy from Canada to infest our frontires, it be hazardous to draw out of the country soe many choice men . . . proper to carry on the designe.[76]

According to the contemporary diarist John Marshall, in late March "people weer genrally dissatisfyed . . . about a descent on poor Port royal."[77] Cotton Mather, speaking of the Port Royal affair, called it "the uncertain Expedition; Pray'd God not to carry his people hence." For Mather, the expedition was not a Puritan crusade directed by the Almighty but rather an attempt by the governor to atone for his and his lackeys' commercial sins. On the other hand, two Boston Congregational ministers, Reverend Mr. Noyes and Reverend Mr. Bridges, preached sermons "Encouraging the Expedition." Noyes contended that those who would participate in the assault on Port Royal were like the Old Testament heroes Gideon, Barak, Samson, David, and Samuel, who "quenched raging fire, escaped the edge of the sword, won strength out of weakness, became mighty in war, [and] put foreign armies to flight." Bridges, using the 149th Psalm as the inspiration for his address, declared that God had put "two-edged swords in their hands, to wreck vengeance on the nations."[78]

Few in Boston, apparently, were inspired to action by the rhetoric of preachers like Bridges and Noyes. Most of the men who took part in the expedition came from Essex County and from the area to the immediate southeast of Boston.[79] Some of these men were not volunteers but were impressed from their militia regiments because of the general lack of enthusiasm for the venture.[80] As would be expected, most came from those areas where fishing was the major occupation and where the previous Nova Scotia expeditions had attracted most of their volunteers. The commander-in-chief was John March, a close friend of the governor, who, according to Francis Parkman, "was personally brave, but totally unfit for his present position."[81] March's colourless personality attracted few volunteers, and the bitterness engendered by the controversy over the distribution of Church's booty in late 1704 also discouraged others from volunteering.

When the expedition was finally assembled in Boston early in May, it was composed of 1,111 New England soldiers and 250 sailors. The fleet consisted of twenty-four vessels, including the twenty-four-gun *Province Galley* commanded by Cyprian Southack, a veteran of two previous Nova Scotia assaults, and the fifty-gun man-of-war, the *Deptford*, under Captain Charles Stukely. To ensure that the spiritual needs of the men would be properly dealt with, no fewer than five chaplains accompanied the troops.[82] That some 1,300 men could be raised in Massachusetts for the expedition, despite the opposition to it, indicated how effective Dudley and the General Court's recruiting program actually was. The necessary widespread use of impressment, however, had dangerously undermined the morale of the troops.

When they had agreed to support the expedition, the members of the General Court had insisted that Dudley use his influence to persuade the neighbouring New England colonies to participate. New Hampshire, where Dudley was also governor, provided sixty men and the usually recalcitrant Rhode Island, eighty,[83] but Connecticut politely rejected Dudley's request.[84] Each New England colony's contribution to the expedition may have reflected the concern of its inhabitants regarding the French threat at Port Royal. The expedition was clearly a Massachusetts expedition; the feeble New Hampshire and Rhode Island response only underlined this fact.

With the help of "an easy southwest wind," the fleet sailed from Boston on May 13 and arrived off Port Royal on May 26.[85] Viewing the large flotilla of ships, the 400 or 500 French within Port Royal, including some recently arrived reinforcements, were, according to one of them, "*fort intimidés.*"[86] But most of the troops and the inhabitants had great confidence in their new governor, Auger de Subercase, who was both a brilliant military strategist and a shrewd administrator. The Massachusetts troops were landed late on May 26 in two groups; 320 men disembarked above the fort and 750 men, under the command of March, below the fort. Despite the well-planned guerilla-like tactics of the French, the invaders were soon within cannon shot of the walls of the fort and began to entrench themselves in a semicircle before it, preparing platforms for the siege artillery still loaded on the ships. However, Colonel John Redknap of the Royal Engineers, commander of the ordnance, and Captain Stukely of the *Deptford* maintained that "it was morally impossible to send the artillery . . . which must pass within command of the fort." Therefore at a council of war on May 31, it was decided, against the wishes of only three New England officers, that the opinion of the regular English officers should be accepted, the siege lifted, and the fleet despatched "to Menis, and Seconnecto, and try what they could do there." Most council members believed that Port Royal was too strongly fortified and the invading troops incapable of conducting a proper siege.

After the council of war was adjourned, March met with one of the chaplains, Harvard-trained John Barnard. Barnard recorded the fascinating confrontation for posterity.

General March . . . took me aside, and said to me "Don't you smell a rat?" I, who knew not what he intended, answered, "No, sir." "Why," said he, "Col. Appleton is for staying to break ground, only to have his wages increased. . . ." He then said to me, somewhat roughly, "I have heard you should say the artillery might be brought" . . . and I said to him, "Sir, I think it may." "Well, then" said he, "if it should be attempted, you shall be one that shall bring it up. . . ." I then said, "Sir,

you are perfectly well acquainted with the design you came
hither upon; you know how much the welfare of your
country, and your own honor lays at stake. I am afraid some
of you connected with, are not so much concerned for either
of them as I could wish. I beseech you, sir, to consider, if you
return with the forces (somewhat of whose vigor and bravery
you have seen) without doing anything farther, whether all
the fault will not be thrown upon you, as the head of all?"[87]

Barnard had struck some responsive chord in March, who, after giving
the chaplain a vigorous bear hug, immediately called another council
of war. At this council on June 3 it was "concluded to stay, get up the
artillery, and attack the fort." But the decision was reversed again
almost immediately, and the next day the troops re-embarked and the
fleet sailed from Port Royal.

The Port Royal fiasco revealed, among other things, sharp differences of opinion between the English regular officers, "Redknap and
the martinets of the *Deptford,*" as they were called, and some of the
Massachusetts militia officers. The regulars regarded the New Englanders as incompetent amateurs, while the Yankees considered the
regulars as arrogant scheming cowards. Of perhaps greater consequence was the fact that the fiasco had undermined further the already
low morale of the rank-and-file troops. These men were incensed at the
unexpected and crude machinations of their officers. One volunteer,
for example, observed: "Never did man in ye world do more bravely
nor boldier & would possitively have gone into ye fort had or officers
had ye skill and conduct to have headed & led you on But yr spirrit
was Wanting. I must boldly say or men will fight if they be well
carried on, for I am sure or officers had more difficulty to bring ym
off yn to carry ym in."[88] Others concluded that the fort was not
bombarded because Dudley wished to capture it intact. Once this was
done, it was rumoured, he intended to garrison it by impressing men
from the ranks for an indefinite period of time. No Massachusetts
soldier in his right mind wished to be incarcerated at Port Royal as an
imperial agent of his governor.

Instead of returning to Boston to face an enraged populace, which
was already celebrating the taking of Port Royal, the fleet sailed to
Casco Bay. A special four-man delegation was sent to the Massachusetts
capital to obtain further instructions from Dudley. When the delega-

tion arrived at Boston in June, it received a tumultuous reception from an aroused and angry populace:

> *They landed at Scarlet's wharfe, where they were met by severall women, who saluted ym after his manner: "Welcome, souldiers!" & presented ym a great wooden sword & said with all "Fie, for shame! pull off those iron spitts wch hang by yor sides; for wooden ones is all ye fashion now." At wch one of ye officers said, "Peace, sille woman, etc." wch irritated ye female tribe so much ye more, yt they cal'd out to one another as they past along the streets, "Is yor piss-pot charg'd neighbor? Is yor piss-pot charg'd neighbor? So-ho, souse ye cowards. Salute Port-Royal. Holloo, neighbor, holloo"; with a drove of children & servts with wooden swords in their hands, following ym with ye repeated salutations "Port-Royal! Port-Royal!" . . . by ye afternoon there was some hundreds of boys gathered together into a company, & ye people about had furnisht allmost all of ym wth wooden swords or old stocks of guns, a drum & a red piece of cloth fastned upon a stick for an ensign, and in this equipage they marcht through ye towne, hollowing "Port-Royall! Port-Royall!"*[89]

John Winthrop, grandson of John Winthrop, Jr., who was an eye-witness to the popular outburst, observed, "Never did poor men receive so many affronts from an insulting rabble. . . . They had better have been whipt than ever have come to towne to be so greeted."[90] Boston had experienced an unprecedented outburst of public indigna-tion. This explosion of frustration, anxiety, anger, and fear revealed something about the nature of the collective mentality of many of the inhabitants under stress, and their obsession with gaining some kind of military victory. In the psychological sense, therefore, what had happened at Port Royal had a great impact on Massachusetts.

Aware of the "generall discontent & dissatisfaction thro ye whole Province," Dudley decided to send reinforcements to Casco Bay and ordered the fleet back to Port Royal. But his impressed reinforcements did not want to go and many clandestinely returned to their homes. Only the threat that "some of ym yt dissented may be hang'd" finally persuaded two companies of fifty men to join March,[91] which as one participant reported, "did not near make up the number of our deserters, since we lay at Casco."[92]

When the fleet finally sailed for Port Royal on July 24, a major change had been made in its leadership. Since a single commanding officer had failed to capture the French capital, Dudley decided, under some public pressure, that a committee of three might. He therefore selected from the General Court Colonel Elisha Hutchinson, Colonel Pen Townshend, and John Leverett to supervise the expedition, and March was placed under their control. Within a short time, March, a broken and disillusioned man, was replaced by Colonel Francis Wainwright of Ipswich.[93] With the inexperienced triumvirate in command, and with the rank and file understandably suspicious of the motives and military capabilities of their company and regimental officers, it is not surprising that there was a "mutionous disposition of the men" which "foreboded no good by going."[94]

The second Massachusetts assault on Port Royal was no more successful than the first. There was no regular siege, no cannon was landed, and Subercase kept the invaders off balance with his well-conceived offensive thrusts. On Sunday, August 24, the invading fleet weighed anchor and made for Boston. There they were met by the angry mob; the troops were "despised and insulted" and called "wooden swords."[95] It was an experience that few would soon forget. They had returned home bitter and disillusioned men, and the general populace shared their shame and discontent. For some the episode had showed "much . . . divine anger." For others it had "drained the inhabitants of this province of 22,000 pounds and more of their money," had cost seventeen lives,[96] and had achieved nothing. A few wanted to court-martial the leading officers, but this search for scapegoats failed, since Dudley refused to act, realizing that the trail might eventually lead to him.[97] He had no other choice but to wait out the difficult situation.

Dudley's Port Royal expedition had been a disastrous failure and for obvious reasons. Unbelievably incompetent Massachusetts and English military leadership and the skill of Subercase, among other factors, had led to the aborted sieges. It was incredible that a ramshackle fort with crumbling walls, defended by only a few hundred men, most of whom were inexperienced soldiers, could not have been captured by an invading force of almost 1,500 men. Dudley had learned from his various Nova Scotia ventures that it was hopeless to undertake any serious military expedition against the French with only colonial troops under incompetent New England officers. Moreover, there was insufficient popular enthusiasm in Massachusetts for Anglo-American imperialistic designs. Impressment of colonial troops merely seemed to exacerbate existing tensions. Thus in a "Memorial referring to the French Settlements in America," written not long after the return of the Port Royal force, Dudley asked the Board of Trade for 2,000 English regulars supported by five or six frigates to drive the French from North America.[98]

7

Samuel Vetch
and
Francis Nicholson,
1708-1717

While Dudley was licking his wounds over his disastrous Port Royal fiasco of 1707 and fighting for his political life in the face of intense criticism, Samuel Vetch was in London defending himself in person against the charges laid against him during the previous year by the General Court. Vetch was also trying to persuade the British government, as Dudley had resolved to do, to organize unilaterally an expedition to drive the French from North America. Vetch, the son of a Scottish minister, had served in the English army on the continent during King William's War, 1689–97. At the end of hostilities, he had joined the ill-fated Scottish Darien expedition to establish a colony near present-day Panama. In 1699 he had come to New York where he married the daughter of an important merchant, Robert Livingstone. Before very long Vetch was actively engaged in illicit trade with the French in New France and by 1705 had moved to Boston where he continued his illegal commercial pursuits and where he became a close associate of Joseph Dudley. In late 1707 Vetch, not yet forty years old, was a bold, enterprising, adaptable adventurer who had the unusual ability to absorb the ideas of those about him and to view commercial problems in their larger imperial context.[1]

Sometime before, in late 1705, Vetch had suggested to John Chamberlayne, the influential secretary of the Society for the Propagation of the Gospel in Foreign Parts, that Scots be used to conquer and settle New France and Nova Scotia. Vetch compared Nova Scotia's impact on New England "as Dunkirk to England, from whence they fit out privateers and infest our coast." The capture of Nova Scotia, he argued, would bring peace to New England, provide naval stores and commodious harbours for the British navy and coal for the English North American colonies, and also secure a rich fishery and vast areas of productive agricultural land.[2] In proposing a Darien-like enterprise for the New France–Nova Scotia region, Vetch endeavoured to use the kind of strategic and economic arguments he thought the English authorities wished to hear. But they had other more important things on their minds.

On July 27, 1708, the persistent Vetch, still looking for the main chance, presented a much-revised version of his 1705 plan to the Board of Trade. The timing of his presentation could not have been more propitious, for a few weeks earlier Marlborough had won his third victory at Oudenaarde and British troops had successfully invaded French soil. The Whig ministry, with final victory in Europe apparently in sight, felt that it was now free to concentrate more attention on North American affairs. Those Whig politicians interested in channelling Scottish nationalism into their government, those eager to strengthen the navy, to expand North American commerce, and to encourage colonization, and also those who wanted an easy but impressive military victory, saw in Vetch's "Canada Survey'd" the means by which they could accomplish their various objectives.[3]

In approaching the Board of Trade, Vetch was clearly acting on his own initiative. His plan, however, reflected the thinking of the merchant community in Boston as well as that of the Massachusetts governor. Once before the Board, Vetch's scheme, which he hoped would eventually bring him a colonial governorship, took precedence over all other proposals. By a strange coincidence, Dudley's "Memorial referring to the French Settlements in America" reached the Board about one week before Vetch put forward his proposal.[4] Furthermore, on July 6, three weeks earlier, George Vaughan, New Hampshire's agent in London, had strongly urged the same Board that "ye two nests of French, (vizt.) Canada and Port Royall setled on ye backs of ye English on ye mainland of America be rooted out, wch. is ye only ready and certain way to procure peace."[5] Vetch's "Canada Survey'd" superseded the two earlier proposals not only because it was far more detailed and persuasively argued but also because Vetch apparently left no palm untouched in his search for support from the individuals responsible for colonial policy matters. The energetic Scot was a one-man lobby, and his desire for colonial office and for new commercial frontiers to conquer, as well as his vision of a Greater Britain in North America, drove him to feverish activity.

Most of Vetch's long and skilfully conceived arguments dealt with the need to capture New France. He, nevertheless, placed some emphasis on the acquisition of Nova Scotia. For him, Nova Scotia in French hands was a serious threat to Massachusetts because of "the ravaging of the frontiers" and the destruction by French privateers of shipping and "the chief branch of the New England trade, their fishery." Vetch perceived Nova Scotia in British hands as a colony with some economic potential. To "effectuate" his "great enterprise," Vetch proposed that in late spring of 1709 two battalions of British regulars and six men-of-war, "joyned from New England with 1000 of their best men," attack Port Royal and then Quebec. In addition, 1,500 troops from "Nework, Jersey, and Connecticout" and some Indians were to march up the Lake Champlain – Richelieu River route, seize Montreal, and sweep to Quebec. This two-pronged offensive was, of course, a plan of action that had been advocated for decades by various officials in New York and Massachusetts. But Vetch, by his brilliant use of propaganda techniques, transformed the old plan into what seemed to be a daring and imaginative new proposal. In an obvious attempt to take advantage of some of the possible political ramifications of the union of England and Scotland, Vetch reasserted in the concluding section of his plan his 1705 contention that the Scots should colonize the captured French territory. Such a develop- ment, as far as Vetch was concerned, would "make Canada a Noble Colony, exactly calculate for the constitution and genius of the most Northern of the North Brittains."[6]

The Board of Trade, in examining the scheme, consulted, among others, Colonel Francis Nicholson, the former governor of Maryland and Virginia who had visited Port Royal in 1687. In spite of his limited military experience, the fifty-three-year-old unemployed governor was favourably impressed with the plan and volunteered his services in the proposed expedition.[7] In November, 1708, the Board asked Vetch to elaborate further on the strategic plans. With respect to the New England contribution to the Port Royal – Quebec expedition, Vetch proposed that "1000 of their best disciplined men" be raised in Massachusetts, New Hampshire, and Rhode Island, "with three months' provisions, transports and pilots . . . those all to be ready about the end of April to embark."[8] It is noteworthy that the Port Royal assault received so little attention and that almost all of the "explanatory supplement" dealt with the two-pronged attack on New France. This was, without question, Vetch's main concern. For him, the capture of Nova Scotia was merely a necessary step in the direction of taking essential control of the French St. Lawrence empire. Vetch was quite familiar with both French colonies, and for him Nova Scotia, though it possessed strategic importance, was, when compared with New France, of limited economic significance. In this view, Vetch was reflecting the view of many of his friends in New York.

At approximately the same time that Vetch was enunciating what may be considered the New York view of, and solution for, the French problem in North America, the Massachusetts General Court was declaring that its major and immediate military concern was the French presence in Nova Scotia. The disaster of 1707 had substantially intensified the colony's concern with the neighbouring French. The Court's address to Queen Anne revealed, among other things, Massachusetts' colonial mentality — a lack of self-confidence and a concomitant growing dependence on the mother country. In 1690 Massachusetts was determined, through the Phips expeditions, to demonstrate to the English monarch how brave, loyal, and self-sufficient the colony in reality was. In 1708 Massachusetts petitioned Queen Anne to show "Royal consideration" and save her helpless subjects from the depredations of the French privateers and the frontier raids. Port Royal was described as "a Dunkirk to us with respect to navigation, it lying to apt and commodious for the intercepting of all shipping coming to or going from hence to the eastward, and is a fit receptacle for privateers, who can soon issue out thence, and are near hand to send in their prizes, as also to annoy our Fishing, whereof we have had frequent experience." The General Court urged the queen "by your Royal Armes to reduce that Countrey and take it by force out of the French hands."[9] Massachusetts had tried hard and sacrificed much in order to deal with the Nova Scotia French, but all the colony had to show for its endeavours was ignominious military failure in Nova Scotia and a profound sense of disenchantment and disgust at home.

The exigencies of English politics and Vetch's propagandizing, together with Massachusetts' increasingly suppliant petitions, had by early 1709 radically transformed the English government's attitude towards North American military questions. It is not surprising that at the end of February, 1709, Vetch had in his possession the instructions for his proposed expedition, a commission as colonel "with the post of adjutant general to the British field officer who would be in chief command, and the promise of the governorship of Canada after it was taken."[10] Vetch's two-year sojourn in England had been extraordinarily successful. When he sailed from England on March 11, 1709, with his right-hand man, the mercurial Francis Nicholson, Vetch looked forward to the implementation of his "Glorious Enterprise" in the "New World."

On April 28 the H.M.S. *Dragon* carrying Vetch and Nicholson anchored in Boston harbour. The news about the expedition delighted Dudley and the Council members, who were quick to respond to the royal instructions to raise in Massachusetts 900 troops "to be at Boston by the middle of May with 3 months provisions and ships to transport them with able pilots."[11] On May 9 Dudley, Vetch, and Nicholson signed a proclamation calling for volunteers. The inclusion of the latter two signatures underlined the fact that the initiative for the expedition came from London. The General Court had been carefully excluded from the planning and the implementing of the scheme. The volunteers were to be "undr the command of their own proper Officers during the sd Expedition," and each man was to receive on enlistment "a good new firelock, Cartouch-box, Flints and Ammunition . . . to be his own forever thereafter." Colonial officers were promised "a preference both with Regard to the Syte and Trade of the sd Country [New France and Nova Scotia], before all other of her Matys Subjects Whatsoever."[12]

Dudley and the Council may have been enthusiastic about the expedition, but their enthusiasm did not accurately reflect the mood of the colony. Many Massachusetts citizens could not readily forget the events of 1707, or even of 1704. In most areas, since men did not enthusiastically rush forward to volunteer, "a general Impress for souldiers for her majestie's service ran through this province." It was rumoured that "every tenth man was taken to serve in this expedition."[13] It may have been, as was the case in New Hampshire, that the Massachusetts residents "were so much exhausted, and . . . had been so ill paid before" that they refused to volunteer.[14]

After Vetch and Nicholson had left Massachusetts on May 12 to drum up support in Rhode Island, Connecticut, and New York, Dudley continued to seek recruits and to obtain supplies and vessels for the expedition. Most of the 900 men were in the Boston area by May 20.[15] They received forty shillings a month wages, eightpence a day living expenses, and were "Quartered on private families, at the Direction of the Select men, not exceeding Two to a Family (without ye Consent of the Masters or Mistresses of Such Families)." When the fleet did not appear in May, the House of Representatives, in order to appease the recruits, "Ordered That a Coat Not exceeding twenty Shillings in value be given to each of them, to be paid out of the public Treasury."[16]

When Vetch returned to Boston early in July, he was happily surprised to discover that the troops "both do the manuall exercise and fire in platoons and battalion equal to most regiments in the service."[17] There were two Massachusetts regiments, one under the command of Sir Charles Hobby and the other under the future lieutenant-governor of the colony, William Tailer. Hobby, an Anglican merchant from Boston, was "a gay man, a free liver" who was active in the local militia and Artillery Company.[18] Tailer was connected by marriage to the old Massachusetts Stoughton family.[19] What these two men had in common was military inexperience, commercial interests in Boston, and a close relationship with Dudley. Lieutenant Paul Mascarene, who would one day be the commander of the British forces at Port Royal, had accompanied Vetch and Nicholson to Boston and was put in charge of the artillery train. His was a critically important and extremely difficult assignment: to train a select group of colonials in the use of siege cannon and mortars.[20]

Vetch may have been pleased with the military skill of many of the recruits, but he was very much disturbed with certain other things. He was particularly worried that "the too late arrivall of the Fleet would be the last disappoyntment to all H.M. Colonies who have so heartily and at so vast an expense complyed with Her Royall orders."[21] He did not know how long the troops could be kept in Boston if they were not soon supported by English regulars and warships. He was also aware of the bitter opposition in the General Court to the quartering of colonial troops in the Boston area.[22] Moreover, he could not escape the growing criticism in Massachusetts to the recruiting tactics used by Hobby and Tailer. There were those who complained "of ye Evil practice of persons in raising of Forces for ye prest

Expedition by dismission of those imprison for Sums of Money," and about the "Extream Disorder" brought about because of the enticing into the regiments of a large number of "minors." There were others, especially among the wealthy in Boston, who attacked "the unlimited Liberty taken by our servants . . . to list themselves in the Services."[23] From some of the petitions sent to the General Court, it might appear that the two Massachusetts regiments were largely made up of minors, ex-prisoners, servants, draftees, and only a few volunteers.

To prevent the further deterioration of morale among the troops, Vetch felt compelled to maintain that the fleet would certainly arrive sometime in July, only two months late. But there was no fleet in July or in August or even in September. Finally, on October 11, 1709, intelligence arrived from England "importing that for divers weighty considerations H.M. had thought fit to lay aside at this time the designed Expedition to Canada, etc." but that if it was felt expedient, Port Royal was to be attacked "without delay."[24] The decision had been made in late May, but a ship to carry the message to Boston was not made available by the Admiralty until August and the *Enterprize* had spent a lazy two months on a routine patrol in the North Atlantic before finally dropping anchor at Boston.[25]

Dudley, Vetch, and Nicholson, who on the urging of the New York authorities had become the commander-in-chief of the "Glorious Enterprise," decided to organize an emergency meeting on October 14 at Rehoboth in southern Massachusetts to consider the feasibility of a Port Royal assault. Eager to salvage something from what Samuel Sewall referred to as "the vast expense and Disgrace of the Disappointed Expedition against Canada,"[26] representatives from Rhode Island, Connecticut, New Hampshire, and Massachusetts decided that Port Royal be attacked "forthwith" provided that the assistance of the six British warships in New England waters might be obtained.[27] Any hope of capturing Port Royal disappeared when only one of the six British captains, the one stationed in Boston, would agree to assist the New Englanders. The other five asserted that they had orders to sail elsewhere. And sail elsewhere they did.[28]

In late autumn, 1709, the troops remaining in the two regiments were disbanded, and the Massachusetts General Court discovered to its horror that almost £31,000 had been wasted on the aborted expedition.[29] For five months the Massachusetts government had paid thousands of pounds in wages and subsistence for 973 officers and soldiers for an enterprise, in a sense, imposed upon the colony by London. While Massachusetts waited for the British fleet and squandered its money, hoping to be soon reimbursed by London, at least thirteen of its vessels were being captured by French privateers from Port Royal.[30] Governor Subercase of Nova Scotia, writing about the privateers, proudly declared, "They have desolated Boston."[31] Fearing further depredations and concerned about the "impoverished and enfeebled" state of the colony, Vetch, Dudley, and other leading Massachusetts citizens urged Nicholson, who was planning to return to England, to "renew the intended Grand Expedition the next year, or at least to order then an expedition be formed against Port Royal as before projected."[32]

Three groups in Massachusetts by late October, 1709, were applying considerable pressure on the Board of Trade to ensure that British warships and regulars would be made available early in 1710 for a Port Royal expedition. They had had enough of the grandiose rhetoric of Vetch's "Glorious Enterprise." They simply wanted the French driven from Nova Scotia. Only when this was accomplished would they seriously begin to consider a further offensive thrust into the St. Lawrence region. The first Massachusetts group preoccupied with Port Royal was the colonial administrators led by Dudley and Vetch. These men regarded Port Royal as "another Dunkirk" and argued "that unless this place be reduced, this country must be abandoned as to it's trade." They requested "four frigatts with a detachment, if it were but of 500 marines, or other regular troops, together with a bomb ketch, and two large morters . . . to be at Boston by the latter end of March."[33] The difficulties confronted by Nicholson's land force south of Lake Champlain in the summer and fall of 1709, and the inability of the British navy to keep to any prearranged schedule, had persuaded Vetch in particular that he would have to be satisfied, at the beginning at least, with merely carrying out the peripheral Nova Scotia venture. The second group consisted of the "principal inhabitants and merchants" in Boston, sixty-seven in number, who in late October "humbly prostrate[d] themselves at the feett of your most excellent Majesty." They claimed that the French privateers had captured many of their vessels and threatened to destroy the economic foundation of the colony.[34] The Boston merchants were enthusiastically supported by the Salem fishing interests, the third Massachusetts group, who wished "to have the free liberty of fishing on those coasts, harbours, etc.," and who also demanded access to the "sea-coale" and "mast trees" of Nova Scotia.[35]

By late October, 1709, in spite of the criticism over the costs involved in paying for an expedition which had not materialized and in spite of the obvious absence of popular enthusiasm for the venture, a powerful new coalition had emerged in Massachusetts pressing for a major Port Royal assault in early 1710. The politically influential Boston merchants and Salem fishermen, together with Dudley, Vetch, and their friends, had come together to forge a new alliance. Economic motives and self-interest undoubtedly dominated the thinking of the first two groups. For his part, Dudley realized that unless something was done about Nova Scotia, his position as governor could become extremely tenuous, while Vetch wanted any colonial governorship, even that of Nova Scotia.[36] Then with the former French colony acting as a giant stepping-stone, he and the Anglo-Americans could sweep into New France.

The alarmist petitions from Massachusetts and Nicholson's convincing arguments persuaded the British to plan yet another major offensive in North America, but this time only against Port Royal. On March 18, 1710, Nicholson received the royal commission as "Commander-in-Chief of our fforces to be employ'ed in the reduction of Port Royal and other places in Nova Scotia." He was ordered to Boston with 500 marines "with a Considerable Quantity of warlike Stores of all sorts and a Bomb Ketch." These troops were to be joined by recruits from the New England colonies according to the quotas set the previous summer. Final military decisions were to be determined by a council of war consisting of Nicholson, Vetch, "the eldest Coll," the governors of the four colonies, the "eldest Capt. of the Marines and the senior sea captains." Once Port Royal was captured, Vetch was to be named governor, and he was expected to defend the new British colony "from the designs of the enemy."[37] It was intended that five British warships would participate in the expedition. The *Falmouth* and *Dragon* were to accompany Nicholson to Boston where they were to be met by the two station ships assigned to New York, the *Feversham* and *Lowestaft*, as well as the *Chester* of Boston.[38]

Nicholson's instructions clearly indicated that the Board of Trade was directly responsible for the Port Royal expedition. The mother country seemed determined to protect the interests of her struggling New England colonies and to provide them with badly needed military leadership. What had been for decades Massachusetts' almost natural northeastern thrust into Nova Scotia had been appropriated by default, in 1709 and 1710, by Great Britain. Various developments since 1690 in the wartime relations between the two colonies, in addition to changing policies in Westminster, had drawn the British government into the military affairs of the region.

In the middle of May, Nicholson set sail for Boston. On his embarkation he discovered that there were only 397 marines "Nigh halfe of these . . . new raised men." It was an inauspicious beginning for the expedition. After battling strong head winds, Nicholson finally arrived at Boston on July 15.[39] Here he received an enthusiastic welcome from the Massachusetts General Court, whose members were overwhelmed by this manifestation of "Royall favour."[40] They were particularly effusive in their praise of the queen "for the obtaining sea and land forces from Great Britain for the reducing of Port Royal . . . thereby to rescue us from the insults of our ill neighbours the French on that side, [this] demands our most humble recognition, with the highest gratitude to the best of Queens, whose innate diffusive goodness inspires Her royal breast with Most gracious dispositions to hear and grant the humble supplications of the meanest of her subjects, and to have regard to such as are far distant from the royal throne." The General Court went on to declare that Nova Scotia must "be restored to your Majesty's Empire. . . . And that it may always hereafter be continued a British colony." Massachusetts did not want to absorb the French territory. Rather, the Court was explicit in its recommendation that the British government should defend and develop Nova Scotia.[41] If this happened, Massachusetts could only benefit from the arrangement; it would have none of the burdens of responsibility and all the advantages of propinquity.

The Massachusetts General Court, in spite of the enthusiasm of some of its members, found it difficult to implement Nicholson's commands. "The vast expence and disappointment of last year," Nicholson reported in September, "made it a busseness of some time to get their troops, transports and provisions ready, the last being very scarce and dear."[42] To encourage volunteers, the General Court decreed that all volunteers should receive in advance a coat worth thirty shillings, a month's wages of forty shillings, and a firelock and ammunition. In addition, the recruits were to be exempt from all impresses for the following three years. But if a sufficient number did not volunteer from the various militia companies, officers were "to Proceed in their Draught in the most equall indifferent manner that may be."[43] The draft and impressment were widely used since rank-and-file interest in the expedition was apparently not very great.[44] For example, John Marshall of Weymouth observed in his diary: "Aug 7 a Genral muster of our regiment at Weymouth in order to expedition. I was drawn off and impressed. 8 – 9 weer idle days seeking to hire a man. . . . 11 – 12 about getting a man, at last I got Clement Cook for 12 pound but he was not accepted. So we got Natll Owen."[45] Those who could afford it hired healthy replacements, but poor draftees had to swallow their better judgment and reluctantly join the volunteers. Societal pressure, which encouraged obedience to governmental regulations, helped to overcome the absence of popular enthusiasm for the venture.

Those who volunteered and those drafted were relieved to discover from their officers that "they would meet with no great difficulty" in their attack on Port Royal. The French fort, they were told, was inadequately fortified and defended and, besides, it was expected that the British regulars and those colonials trained in siege warfare by Mascarene would do all the hard fighting.[46] When Nicholson's fleet set sail from Boston on September 18, the fleet consisted of thirty-six vessels carrying some 900 troops from Boston, 180 from Rhode Island, 300 from Connecticut, and 100 from New Hampshire. In addition to the five British warships and the Massachusetts *Province Galley*, there were thirty colonial transport vessels. As had been the case the previous year, the two Massachusetts regiments were commanded by Hobby and Tailer.

The fleet made its way slowly up the coast to Passamaquoddy where the ships anchored on September 21. Three days later they passed through the narrow "Gutt" at the entrance to Annapolis Basin and soon the troops sighted Port Royal.[47] One Massachusetts transport vessel, the *Caesar*, sank in the treacherous waters at the "Gutt" and some twenty-five men were drowned.[48] The following day, September 25, Nicholson began to land his troops. Since he had certain reservations about the military prowess and fighting spirit of the colonials and also since he wished to have British troops lay their, not New England's, claim to French territory, the marines were landed first. They went ashore on the south side of the river, the side on which the French fort stood. Then a company of Mascarene's grenadiers, colonial troops in the pay of the English government who had been trained and disciplined by a British regular officer for over a year, landed on the north side. Once these troops had decided on camp sites and suitable landing areas, orders were given for the colonials to land. Tailer's Massachusetts regiment disembarked from its whaleboats on the north side where it was "saluted by Monsieur Subercase from the Fort, with three guns and a shell, without doing us any damage." Hobby's regiment was then sent to reinforce the marines on the fort-side of the river. By four in the afternoon all the troops were on Nova Scotia territory. To celebrate the occasion, the "Bomb Ship . . . Saluted the Fort with seven Shells."[49]

What must have amazed Nicholson was the fact that Subercase had provided no opposition to the invaders. A strong sortie properly timed might have driven the marines, at least, from their exposed bridgehead. But the French commander could not trust the loyalty of either the Acadian inhabitants in the fort or his regular troops and "was persuaded that any men he might send out of the fort would not come in again."[50] With fewer than 300 men under his command, a smaller number than in 1707, and with most of these on the verge of mutiny, he decided to defend the fort solely by using his cannon and mortars. All he could hope for was that such a defensive holding operation, together with the anticipated Anglo-American incompetence in siege warfare, would eventually save his fort.

Without any French sorties to contend with, the invaders began to prepare for the siege. On the twenty-sixth Nicholson ordered "a party of Grenadiers as an advanced Guard to march on within 400 paces of the Fort, which they did, Capt. Powell being ordered with 60 marines to joy'n them where they Intrench'd." By the twenty-ninth the cannon and mortars were landed and final preparations were made "to cut Fascines" for the siege batteries. Two days later Nicholson observed in his official journal: "The Lord's day October the 1st. The Great Guns were placed by the Engineers Forbes and Redknap, on their Batteries, the Mortars in another place, and the 24 Cochorn Morters in a third place not far from the outward Barrier of the Fort, within a hundred yards of it, all of which fired against the Fort, whereof six of the Guns and 12 Mortars entered the Fort, the French at the same time firing their great Guns and Mortars at us." Not wanting to destroy the French fortifications and sensing that surrender was imminent, Nicholson sent a summons to Subercase "To deliver up the Fort." On the following day, October 2, the capitulation terms were agreed upon by the two commanding officers. The French garrison was to be permitted, according to military custom, to "march out with their Arms and Baggage, Drums beating, and Colours flying" and were then to be transported in British ships to France. The Acadians within "three English miles" of the fort were to be allowed to "remain upon their Estates, with their Corn, Cattle and Furniture, During two years."[51] Nothing was said about the other Acadian inhabitants of the colony, but it was assumed that they would remain under their new masters.

On October 6 the formal take-over of the fort occurred with the marines and grenadiers leading the way into the renamed Fort Anne. On the little bridge at the entrance to the fort the keys of the fort were "immediately delivered to Col. Vetch, as Governor of the Fort, by virtue of her Majesty's Instructions."[52] Then the "army marched into the fort, hoisted the Union Flag, and drank the Queen's Health, firing all the Guns round the Fort, as likewise did the Men of War and the other vessels in the River."[53]

To emphasize the non–New England nature of the capture of Port Royal, Nicholson arranged that the first Protestant sermon preached in Nova Scotia was given by the Church of England chaplain to the marines, the Reverend Thomas Hesketh. Hesketh's sermon was dedicated to Nicholson and Colonel Robert Reading of the marines, the two men he considered responsible for one of the key "defalcations from the *Gallick Empire*." These men, according to Hesketh, had been used by "Providence" to seize "a Place of such vast importance to the *British Empire*." The Massachusetts contribution was not even mentioned by the Anglican priest.[54] Hesketh was quite justified in stressing the important role played by the British. The men-of-war, the marines, and the British-trained-and-paid grenadiers had landed first and had constructed the siege batteries. They deserved the praise. The New Englanders had merely provided numerical support for the cutting edge of the British offensive.

When Nicholson's fleet sailed for Boston on October 15, Vetch remained behind with a force of 200 marines and 250 New England volunteers. He had in his possession a proclamation of the council of war that all commerce to and from Nova Scotia was to be channelled through Port Royal, renamed Annapolis Royal. Vetch, Hobby, and their Boston associates were to have the monopoly over the Annapolis Royal trade. Their involvement in the expedition had been suitably rewarded; they were, in late October, 1710, at least theoretically in economic and political control over Britain's and not Massachusetts' Nova Scotia.[55]

As would be expected, the people of Massachusetts were at first delighted on hearing of the capture of Port Royal. Dudley issued a proclamation for a general thanksgiving, "It having pleased Almighty God, Graciously to favour us with signal Instances of the smiles of His Merciful Providence."[56] But the delight of some Massachusetts residents must have been transformed into bitterness when they heard the returned British naval captains arrogantly declaring, "The Fleet was a Chief Mean of Taking Port Royal." "Reason of State," moaned the sensitive Samuel Sewall, "require the overlooking many grievous Things."[57] The British regulars could have been more sensitive to Massachusetts feelings; nevertheless, their assessment of what had happened at Port Royal was substantially correct. What the New Englanders had failed to do in 1707, the British were able to accomplish with little apparent effort three years later.

Port Royal in British hands did not put a stop to the frontier raids on Massachusetts, but it did cut down on their number and ferocity. Massachusetts fishermen quickly returned in force to Nova Scotia waters, and the merchants, carefully avoiding Annapolis Royal, carried on extensive trade with the Acadians and Indians.[58] The clock had been turned back a decade and the only difference was that Anglo-American, not French, troops were defending the dilapidated fort at Port Royal.

Vetch did not last long as governor of the colony. After participating in the ill-fated Walker expedition of 1711 to Quebec and after receiving information about the Treaty of Utrecht which granted "all Nova Scotia . . . with its ancient boundaries" to the British but left Cape Breton Island in French hands, Vetch was removed from office in 1713. He was replaced by his former close associate, the darling of the Tories then in political power, Francis Nicholson, who had led the movement to oust him. While in London, Vetch successfully defended himself against Nicholson's "fury, malice, and madness," and with the defeat of the Tories by the Whigs in January, 1715, he regained the governorship.[59] However, he did not return to North America and in 1717 was superseded by Governor Richard Philipps, who was selected to implement the Board of Trade's new Nova Scotia policy.[60]

The protracted Vetch-Nicholson controversy over who was to

govern Nova Scotia provided an ironic end to a decade of British involvement in the area. The two men had significantly affected the relationship of Massachusetts with Nova Scotia during these critical years by providing a peculiar new twist to the old relationship. Massachusetts' response to British imperialism regarding Nova Scotia in 1709 and 1710 showed the extent to which the New England colony had, by the end of the first decade of the eighteenth century, grown dependent on the mother country's military leadership. A distinction was clearly drawn between military-political responsibilities and economic benefits. And after 1710, as had been the case since soon after the founding of Massachusetts, some of the colony's merchants and fishermen were determined to exploit Nova Scotia's natural resources.

8

Massachusetts, Canso, Annapolis Royal, and Louisbourg, 1718-1744

After the signing of the Treaty of Utrecht, only a relatively few Massachusetts fishermen and traders seemed especially concerned with matters relating to Nova Scotia – Cape Breton, and these men were merely asserting the traditional Massachusetts commercial hegemony over the region. During the more than three decades of peace between Britain and France ushered in by the treaty, the people of Massachusetts seemed content to see the frontiers of settlement pushed northeastward to the Penobscot River, up the Connecticut Valley, and westward to the Berkshires and beyond.[1] There was virtually no interest, at any level, in the Massachusetts settlement of peninsular Nova Scotia. For some, largely because of the animosities engendered by the sending of various expeditions from Boston against the French, Nova Scotia was conceived to be an alien land carefully to be avoided at all costs. But there were other, more substantial reasons for the prevailing mood of apathy concerning the new British colony. There was still fairly good land available in the Massachusetts area; moreover, there was little enthusiasm for living permanently contiguous to the Micmacs and the Roman Catholic French-speaking Acadians. The absence of representative government and the apparent political importance of the military at Annapolis Royal further discouraged Massachusetts residents from emigrating to Nova Scotia.

By 1715, at the latest, a small number of Massachusetts fishermen had already begun to fish at Canso, located at the northeastern extremity of peninsular Nova Scotia. In that year it was reported that "ye Great and Many damages" had been "sustained by N.E. fishermen from Indians and others." "Ye Fishermen in Giveing of the them to[o] Much Liquor" were considered by some to be responsible for "ye unhappy Action."[2] Despite this incident, however, Massachusetts–Cape Breton relations were remarkably amicable during the years immediately following the signing of the Treaty of Utrecht. In August, 1718, for example, the former governor of New Hampshire, George Vaughan, who was visiting the Canso region, discovered "all things peaceable and quiet, the French and English fishing with all friendship and love."[3] But by early September, Vaughan's peace and quiet had suddenly disappeared.

Sometime during the summer of 1718, Governor Samuel Shute, who had succeeded Dudley, received a memorial from five Massachusetts fishermen at Canso. These men bitterly complained that the French had "seized the best places to make their fish and threaten the English with a removal pretending what they act is by the advice and direction of the Governor of Cape Britton."[4] It is noteworthy that the Massachusetts fishermen at Canso approached the governor of Massachusetts, not the British authorities at Annapolis Royal, to redress their grievances. These fishermen viewed Canso as an economic appendage of their home colony, and Governor Shute agreed with their assessment of the situation. Moreover, Shute was determined to assert Massachusetts' commercial control over this disputed border area within miles of huge supplies of cod.[5] On receiving the memorial, the governor immediately ordered Thomas Smart, commander of H.M.S. *Squirrel*, a British frigate then stationed at Boston, to sail to Canso. The British captain was accompanied by Cyprian Southack, possessing "the vote of the [Massachusetts] Council." Southack, who had participated in various New England military ventures against the French in Nova Scotia, was regarded as Massachusetts' authority on all matters concerning the new British colony and Cape Breton. Shute explicitly ordered Smart "to do nothing of moment without his [Southack's] assistance."[6]

Shute not surprisingly instructed Smart to adopt an aggressive policy against the French intruders. If they refused to withdraw from Canso, he was "to seize upon what fish and other effects you find within the English limits and bring it of[f] with you and to demolish whatsoever buildings the French have sett up there and compel the French people to quit the said place, except such as are friendly to the English."[7] When Smart and Southack arrived at Canso on September 6, they found "a French ship, a brigantine and sloop, and about 30 French shallops a fishing." After visiting Louisbourg, where Governor St. Ovide de Brouillant refused to accept Anglo-American sovereignty over the disputed territory, Smart angrily returned to Canso. Here he "made seizures of the french ship, brigantine and sloop and some fish of the french on the shoor belonging to the ship and the other French inhabitants and some other goods."[8] Then Smart and Southack, having completely destroyed all vestiges of French settlement ashore, set sail on September 25 for Boston with plunder valued by the French at 200,000 *livres*.[9]

The Smart-Southack expedition seemed to have been extraordinarily successful. Not only was there some 200,000 *livres* worth of plunder taken to Boston but Governor St. Ovide, apparently frightened by the Massachusetts show of strength, decided officially to accept Massachusetts' right to possess Canso.[10] The Council of Trade was delighted with the Massachusetts involvement in the expedition. It reported:

Capt. Smart's proceedings in this affair were by order of the Govr and Council of the Mass. Bay, who we presume believed it was their duty to assert, in this manner H.M. right to ye lands or islands where the seizure was made, and altho a gentler method might possibly have been more advisable at so critical a juncture, yet we cant help thinking that Col. Shute and H.M. Council of the Mass. Bay have expressed on this occasion a very laudable zeal for H.M. service.[11]

The Smart episode may have indeed intimidated the governor of Louisbourg, but it failed to stop large numbers of French fishermen from coming back to the Canso region. In October, 1720, Captain Benjamin Young, after a short sojourn at Canso, reported:

But what excells them all is Canso, which is invaluable for its Fishery. Tis here such great quantitys of Codd herring and Macrell swarm amongst the Islands that when I was there in his Majesty's ship Rose there was then Ninety six sail of English and 200 French makeing their voyages, the English

vessels from 50 to 70 Tonns the French small shallops and
when fish is scarce at other places here they are always plenty
for on letting the line down they draw up Two and two as fast
as they can pull it. . . . When a ship of warr is not there or
anything to hinder the French fishing among us then our
fishing Vessells cannot take 4 fish when they will take tenn.
They fish with fresh and we with Salt Bait we come 180
leagues they but 7: they in small Boats we in Large Sloops.[12]

While the French continued to fish off Canso, some New Englanders used Isle Madame across the Gut of Canso, which was unquestionably French territory, as the base for their fishery. It appears that in 1720 most of the French and Massachusetts fishermen had hammered out an arrangement whereby "the fishing was held in common" on both sides of the boundary line between Cape Breton and Nova Scotia, the Gut of Canso.[13]

Even though their French allies had worked out with the New Englanders what appeared to be an amicable and satisfactory relationship, the Micmacs bitterly resented the encroachments of the Massachusetts fishermen on what the Indians considered to be Micmac territory. The Micmacs felt betrayed by the French. On August 8, 1720, therefore, without any encouragement from the Louisbourg French, the Nova Scotia Indians attacked the Massachusetts fishermen. One participant described the incident:

About one or two in the morning the Indians sprang on the
English fishermen, scarcely giving some of them time to put
on their breeches, and making many prisoners. . . . Everything
was pillaged – fish, goods, clothes, bedding and even pockets,
the loss being said to amount to about £ 18,000. . . . During
this affair 2 Englishmen were shot dead in escaping to the
boats and one was drowned.[14]

In spite of what they regarded as the Indian outrage, no fewer than eighty-eight Massachusetts fishing schooners, with a total number of 602 men aboard, made their way to Canso in the following year, 1721.[15] They may have been encouraged by the decision made by Governor Philipps of Nova Scotia in late 1720 and early 1721 to station three companies of his troops at Canso and to construct a small fort there.[16] Philipps, who was visiting his colony for the first time when the

Micmacs raided Canso in 1720, realized that the frontier fishing outpost was by far the most important commercial centre in Nova Scotia, and he was determined to protect the New Englanders from depredations of any kind.

Canso's new defensive strength and Philipps's military skill were both tested in 1722 when the Micmacs, together with the Indians of Maine, began a major offensive against Massachusetts. During the summer of 1722 it was reported that the Indians had captured "18 tradeing vessells in the Bay of Fundy" and a further eighteen fishing schooners between Cape Sable and Canso.[17] The Massachusetts General Court reacted quickly to the Indian offensive by sending hundreds of troops into northern and eastern Maine and by despatching sixty men to the "Coast of Cape Sable to recover the Fishing Vessels."[18] Before the Massachusetts force could do anything about the eighteen captured fishing schooners, however, Governor Philipps at Canso took the initiative against the Micmacs. "By this time," he explained, "we were in the middle of the fishery and the harbour full of ships wayteing their loading, when fresh advices came that the Indians were cruiseing upon the Banks with the sloopes they had taken assisted by the prisoners whom they compell'd to serve as marriers, and gave out that they were to attack this place with all their strength, which alarm'd the people to that degree, bringing to mind theire sufferings two yeares agoe." To meet what he was certain would be an imminent attack, Philipps persuaded the Massachusetts fishermen to agree to the "fitting and manning out two sloopes to protect the Fishery, and haveing reinforced each of them with a detachment of the Garrison and an Officer, it had that good effect that in three weekes time I retooke all the vessells and prisoners, except foure which the N. England people poorly ransom'd."[19] The quick implementation of Philipps's scheme by the Massachusetts fishermen must have been encouraged by the letter he had received from Governor Shute "with a Declaration of Warr by that Government agt the Indians"; the letter also contained a request urging the enthusiastic support of the Massachusetts fishermen in the war effort.[20] Massachusetts had, without prior consultation, declared war on the Micmacs, who lived in another British colony. Thus, Nova Scotia was dragged by the neighbouring colony of Massachusetts into what came to be known as Dummer's or Lovewell's War.

The often bloody frontier conflict continued until August, 1726, when a formal peace treaty was agreed upon. At the negotiations at Falmouth, Maine, Nova Scotia was represented by Major Paul Mascarene, who had played a key role in the capture of Port Royal in 1710. Mascarene, a Council member, participated fully in the ratification of the treaty.[21] One of the clauses stipulated: "We, the said . . . delegates from the said tribes of Penobscott, Naridgwalk, St. John's, Cape Sable, and other tribes inhabiting within his majesty's said territories of Nova Scotia or Accadie, and New England Do, in the name and behalf of the said tribes we represent, acknowledge his said majestie king George's Jurisdiction and Dominion over the territories of said province of Nova Scotia."[22] The treaty of 1726 finally brought peace to Nova Scotia and it re-emphasized and underlined Massachusetts' profound influence on Nova Scotia affairs. The treaty moreover ushered in the Golden Age of the Massachusetts Canso fishery.

In 1729 there were an estimated 223 Massachusetts schooners at Canso with 1,118 men, who caught 51,749 quintals of cod. In 1732 there were 80 schooners, 450 men, and 25,176 quintals of cod caught; in 1733, 121 schooners, 740 men, and 46,000 quintals; in 1735, 58 Massachusetts fishing schooners; in 1736, 46; and in 1737, 65. In addition to the fishing schooners coming to Canso, there were 19 Massachusetts whaling vessels in 1735, 10 in 1736, and 10 again in 1737. The scarcity of whales off Canso, however, resulted in 1737 in the whalers' decision to move their operations northward to "Davis straits."[23]

It is clear from the official records that the Massachusetts Canso fishery reached its peak in 1729. In any given year the New Englanders spent only the months from March to October in and around Canso and returned to Massachusetts for the winter season.[24] No man would have chosen to spend twelve consecutive months on the isolated, fog-shrouded settlement. By 1737 Canso was a mere shadow of its former importance; it certainly was no longer "New England's cod capital."[25] The declaration of war between Spain and Britain in 1739 dealt a fatal blow to Canso. In that year Captain Peter Warren of the Royal Navy noted, "The English Fishery at Canceaux is much decayed in proportion to the improvement and increase of the French Fishery within these Ten years past."[26] Warren placed the blame on the French fishermen. He would have been more accurate if he had stressed the fact that the Massachusetts Canso fishermen, after 1739 at least, were afraid of a massive French attack from Louisbourg, once the long-anticipated war between France and Britain was finally declared. Furthermore, Warren could have emphasized the adverse effect on Canso of a glutted European and West Indian market in the late 1730s, as well as the effective economic counteroffensive mounted by the Marblehead and Gloucester fishermen against the Essex County fishing interests who were especially active at Canso.[27]

By the early months of 1744, even the British government, often decades late in perceiving actual changes occurring in the North American colonies, had finally come to take it for granted that "there is no Fishery now at Canceu."[28] There was only a handful of fishermen together with four incomplete companies of Governor Philipps's regiment left at Canso in 1744. Of the eighty-seven soldiers, "one third was sick or lame" and the others were poorly armed and badly trained. These men, their sizeable families, and a small number of fishermen-settlers were housed in rude shelters on the various islands in the harbour and along the nearby rocky mainland. Canso's only defence work was now a totally inadequate blockhouse built of timber donated by grateful fishermen. How the mighty had fallen! Massachusetts' former "cod capital" was, in the early 1740s, nothing more than a dilapidated British military outpost. Anticipating an imminent declaration of war between France and Britain, Massachusetts had pragmatically thrust the main military burden for the defence of Nova Scotia to the mother country. In this respect military realities perfectly coincided with commercial considerations and a prevailing lack of interest in Nova Scotia affairs.

From 1718 until the early months of 1744, the policies adopted by the Massachusetts General Court, as well as the matters publicly discussed in debate, clearly reflected the widespread indifference in the colony towards Nova Scotia, especially that part of the colony excluding Canso. For example, the only mention of the Annapolis Royal region during these years in the *Journals* of the House of Representatives was on November 11, 1724. On that day the members of the House refused to act on a request from Lieutenant-Governor John Doucett of Nova Scotia for "a Supply from this Govt. of Thirty men" to help in the defence of Annapolis Royal.[29] Obviously, they felt that the redcoats and not the Yankees had the special responsibility to defend Nova Scotia's capital.

The lack of official concern showed by the Massachusetts General Court in Nova Scotia did not mean, of course, that everybody in

Massachusetts steered clear of the new colony. Nor did it mean that the Nova Scotia authorities willingly accepted their official status in relation to Massachusetts. In 1720, Governor Philipps made certain interesting observations concerning the nature of the commercial relationship between Nova Scotia, excluding Canso, and Massachusetts. These observations, which may have exaggerated the importance of the fur trade and the profits involved, nevertheless cogently described the way in which some Massachusetts merchants had been able to re-establish their traditional commercial control over the region. From Annapolis Royal Philipps reported in August, 1720:

> *As to the trade of this country . . . It is intirely hitherto in favour of Boston . . . the furr trade is carryed on by four or five sloops who make three voyages in the yeare, bringing . . . mostly West Indie commodityes, and provissions of New England with some European goods, all which they put off here sometimes at 4 or 500 pr. cent. and carry away by computation 9 or £10,000 worth of furrs yearly, without paying the least duty or import towards the support of this government. . . . There is likewise in the upper part of the Bay a very good coal mine, which the people of Boston fetch at their pleasure not only without paying any acknowledgement to the Lords of the Mannor (His Majesty) but without the good manners to ask his leave.*[30]

A little more than a decade later the Nova Scotia Council declared that "as to the trade in this part of the Province, but very little the same being carried on by only four or five coasting Vessells from Boston hither, which supply the ffrench Inhabitants with European and West India goods who make two or three trips annually and carry from hence some time grain a few fish but chiefly furrs."[31] Things had not changed that much since 1720 or, for that matter, since the 1640s.

In 1732 the Nova Scotia Council resolved to do something to encourage large-scale Massachusetts involvement in its colony, hoping that in the process governmental concern and interest in the region would grow. A major attempt was made to encourage Massachusetts emigration, and some Boston merchants received permission to develop "the Coaliary Near to Chickenectua, as it was promis'd them in writing [in 1731] by Govr. Philipps."[32] Paul Mascarene was chosen in

September, 1732, to mastermind the drive to obtain immigrants in Massachusetts. The immigrants were to be settled in large townships "twelve miles square." The land was not free, but there was to be "perpetual quit rent of one penny per acre after the first three years, subject also to a further levy of not more than 1d. per acre annually over and above said quit rent. Non-payment of quit rent for three years makes the patents void." In addition, the land had to be improved, "one-tenth of acreage at least within three years from grant of patent."[33]

Mascarene failed to recruit even one Massachusetts settler. What evidently discouraged immigration was the "penny an acre quit rent and the possible tax of another penny," the absence of a House of Representatives, and finally a widely held view that the Acadians already possessed all the good land. At any rate these were the explicit reasons given by Mascarene for his failure. He could have also mentioned that he had had an uphill battle trying to neutralize the bad image of the colony held by many Massachusetts inhabitants, including the colony's governor, Jonathan Belcher. As far as Belcher was concerned, there was no good reason for Massachusetts residents, who already possessed "an easy, civil government," to emigrate to Nova Scotia. According to Belcher, "By what I heard the government of the paultry Province of Nova Scotia has been but one constant source of tyranny. . . . God deliver me & mine from the government of soldiers."[34]

The Nova Scotia Council's coal policy was a little more successful in Massachusetts but did not substantially alter the prevailing negative stereotype of the northern colony. "Major Henry Cope and Company of Boston, New England," was granted the sole right to develop the mine near present-day Amherst, Nova Scotia.[35] Here Cope and associates constructed an impressive complex. One Massachusetts traveller noted: "The Coal which they dig about 7 miles below ye Place, they bring hither in 2 Lighters and throw up into Cribs which they have cut down ye Sodd or Marsh so as to make a Wharff and so low that a Vessel can go in a little before highwater. . . . One Man will dig many Chaldron of this Coal in a day. . . . They a Sergeant . . . & 6 Soldiers more from Annapolis; they employ besides about 10 or 12 Frenchmen, besides the men who go in the Lighters."[36] Possibly five or six Massachusetts ships each year loaded coal from Cope's mine. These ships, together with the "four or five coasting Vesssells from

Boston," represented the extent of Massachusetts' involvement in Nova Scotia outside of Canso. But what is revealing is that even this relatively insignificant commercial contact was sufficient to make Nova Scotia's officials believe that their capital was merely a territorial outpost of Massachusetts. Even the most minor legal question, for example, could not be settled at Annapolis "till such time" as advice was received "of some persons there [Boston] learned in the Knowledge of the Law," concerning "what coud be legally done."[37]

The Massachusetts General Court may have cared very little about Nova Scotia during the pre-1744 period. A significant number of merchants, however, became very involved in illicit commerce with the French in Cape Breton. Even before the French began to construct Louisbourg in 1720, Massachusetts entrepreneurs had begun trading with the inhabitants of Cape Breton. It is difficult to measure accurately the extent of this growing illicit trade. French trade statistics always underestimated the volume of Massachusetts commerce and the Massachusetts authorities had no records concerning the trade. But from carefully analyzing existing data, one can see that the trade was quite extensive.[38] Only once before the outbreak of hostilities with the French in 1744 did the Massachusetts House of Representatives indicate its policy with respect to the illicit trade with Cape Breton. In early December, 1720, Governor Shute had proposed that an act be passed "to Prevent the carrying on an Illegal Trade to Cape Breton, alias Lewis-bourg."[39] The House of Representatives, however, refused to pass such legislation, since most of its members felt that Massachusetts had no legal right to enforce trade regulations with the neighbouring French colony.[40] Besides, it saw no good reason to undermine a commercial relationship which promised to pump badly needed life into the Massachusetts economy.

Reports made by two British Canso officials, one in 1726 and the other in 1743, clearly indicated the large volume of New England trade with Louisbourg. In 1726 Captain John Bradstreet stated:

> When I have been cruizing on the Banks and sent express into Louisbourg, I have seldom failed of meeting the vessells of the people of New England, some laden with cattle, some with boards, shingles etc., and others with beef, pork and other provisions, bound for Cape Britton tho' cleared out for Canso, and particularly last August I saw ten New England

sloops and schooners, and one ship in the harbour of
Louisbourg, all to be sold to the French both vessells and
cargoes; which occasioned some plenty of provisions there,
that the price of one sheep at Canso was equivalent to that of
two at Cape Britton.[41]

In 1743 Hibbert Newton observed:

After your departure the sloops, schooners and other vessels
some now at this place [Canso] and others going daily from
some part or other of His Majesty's Plantations, besides 18
sail we know to be at Lewisburg at this time, will without any
Restraint Load and carry from thence to several Ports in his
Majesty's Plantations, Brandy, Wine, Iron, Sail cloth, Rum,
Molasses and several other French commoditys with which
there is some 80 to 90 Sail generally load with in a year, these
vessels generaly carry lumber, Bricks and live stock there,
they commonly clear out for Newfoundland tho never design
to go farther than Lewisburg, often they sell their vessels as
well as cargoes there, and are paid for all they sell in the
above mention'd goods. . . . At a moderate computation they
yearly carry from Lewisburg 6,000 Hhds of Rum and
Milasses, besides the Brandy, etc.[42]

Louisbourg from the 1720s to the early 1740s had become an
important trading entrepôt in the northwestern Atlantic; the available
evidence suggests that the French, because of the inadequacies of
imports from France, New France, and from the Acadians, were
becoming increasingly dependent on supplies from New England. It
has been estimated that in 1733, of the 158 vessels arriving officially at
Louisbourg, 46 were from New England and Nova Scotia, 70 from
France, 17 from New France, and 25 from the French West Indies.
Ten years later, in 1743, of the 175 vessels, 78 were from New England
and Nova Scotia, only 58 from France, 7 from New France, and 32
from the French West Indies. Every year in the ten-year period from
1730 to 1740, the number of New England ships, most of which came
from Massachusetts, was second only to those coming from France.
By 1743 the number of New England vessels trading with Louisbourg
was not only greater than that from France, but also greater than the
combined number from New France and the French West Indies.[43]

Within an economic context even considering the fact that the Yankee ships were much smaller than most of the French vessels, it may be argued that by 1744 Louisbourg was on the verge of becoming yet another of "New England's Commercial Outposts." But before Massachusetts could further extend its commercial influence over Louisbourg and transform it into a new Port Royal, war broke out between France and Great Britain early in 1744.

On May 23, 1744 (N.S.), a merchantman from Glasgow arrived at Boston with intelligence that war had finally been declared.[44] Governor William Shirley of Massachusetts had long anticipated the outbreak of hostilities and had worked hard, after his appointment in 1741 as governor, to strengthen the colony's defences. British-born, Shirley had immigrated to Massachusetts in 1731, and the influence of his patron, the Duke of Newcastle, eventually got him the governorship. In early 1744 Shirley was not yet fifty years old; he was a calculating politician and an administrator with many of the traits of Joseph Dudley. Shirley's shrewd grasp of complex Massachusetts politics and his almost intuitive strategic sense and "Imperial Vision" were invaluable assets in 1744.[45]

As early as 1743 Shirley was anticipating attacks by Indian allies of the French on the exposed western, northern, and northwestern frontiers of Massachusetts, as well as French naval assaults upon the eastern seaboard of his colony. In October, 1743, he had therefore ordered the militia commanders residing in the frontier areas "to advertise the exposed towns and settlements hereof, and to take proper care that the inhabitants secure themselves and families against any sudden assault from the Indians, and that they do not expose themselves by being too far from home in this time of danger, and that the companies in your regiment that are not much exposed, be in readiness to relieve any of the neighbouring places in case there should be any occasion for it."[46] In addition, Shirley had adopted a conciliatory policy towards the traditionally pro-French tribes, the Penobscots, Pigwackets, Norridgewocks, St. Francis, and Malecites. By providing them with presents and by carefully regulating their trade with the New England merchants, he had hoped to court their favour and support, or at least their neutrality, in case of a rupture with France. But since Shirley could not count upon the success of this pacification policy, he had also encouraged the construction of small forts, especially in Maine where the French-Indian threat seemed most serious.[47]

Shirley not only wished to protect Massachusetts from French aggression, but he also wanted to see the French driven from North America and supplanted by the British. By implementing his defensive-offensive policy he hoped to add substantially to his political power. His plan for achieving this political end began with his ambitious and imaginative defence policy, which he expected would produce a significant reservoir of patronage for him to dispense as the colony's commander-in-chief. The careful distribution of military appointments, supply contracts, and other favours would lead, he hoped, to the desired control over the General Court.[48]

On June 11, the day after the first meeting of the General Court in Boston for the year 1744, Shirley clearly enunciated his war policy to the members of the House of Representatives and the Council. After discussing the frontier defence question and the threat posed to his colony by French privateers, Shirley maintained that the successful defence of Massachusetts was linked with keeping Nova Scotia in British hands. He therefore proposed that Massachusetts troops be sent immediately to Annapolis Royal. He pointed out that "ever since it's first settlement by the French," Nova Scotia had been "a Point of the greatest Importance to the Welfare and Safety of this Province." Striking deep into the historical heritage of his colony, Shirley observed that during former periods of warfare, huge sums of money had been spent by the General Court for numerous "Expeditions . . . for reducing that Place, and recovering it out of the Hands of the French." In order to prevent history from repeating itself and in order to protect Massachusetts, the governor stressed that it was the General Court's duty "to preserve it [Nova Scotia] for his Majesty." In conclusion, having learned something from Joseph Dudley's bitter experience, Shirley urged the Court "to pass a Law, prohibiting upon great Penalties all Trade with our Enemies, and more especially the supplying them with Arms, Ammunition or Provision of any Kind whatsoever."[49] He did not wish to see his French-Indian enemies, using British arms and ammunition supplied by avaricious Yankee merchants, terrorize the Massachusetts inhabitants.

The General Court responded quickly and with considerable enthusiasm to Shirley's call for men to be sent to the exposed frontier regions of the colony. By the end of June some 3,000 troops had been ordered to serve their colony in this defence capacity.[50] The sending of these troops, together with Shirley's conciliatory Indian policy, kept the Penobscots, Pigwackets, Norridgewocks, and St. Francis Indians, all traditional allies of the French, at peace throughout 1744. To deal with the French privateering threat, the House of Representatives agreed late in July to add a tiny ship, armed with eight four-pound carriage guns and eight swivel guns and manned by some fifty seamen, to the colony's unimpressive two-vessel fleet. Faced by a serious shortage of funds, the General Court had decided to rely largely upon New England privateers to keep the sea-lanes to the colony clear and to protect the eastern seaboard from French naval assaults. The vital role played by the Massachusetts privateers during the early months of the war with France should not be underestimated, and it showed the extent to which Yankee private enterprise could be channelled to achieve the public good.[51]

The French at Louisbourg had first heard about the declaration of war on May 3, some three weeks before the news had reached Boston.[52] As would be expected, French privateers had been quick to take full advantage of the element of surprise. From May 31 to June 12, at least ten Massachusetts fishing vessels, ranging in size from twenty-eight to fifty tons, had been captured near Canso and Cape Sable by two enterprising French privateers armed only with muskets. The ease with which the fishing schooners had been captured persuaded the Louisbourg privateers to move their operations further south, where they could tap the busy shipping lanes to and from Boston.[53] During the first week of July, a French privateer captured three Massachusetts vessels within twelve leagues of Cape Cod. During the same week a Louisbourg privateer was captured approximately fifteen leagues from Cape Cod by Captain Tyng, commanding officer of the *Prince of Orange*, one of the colony's three-vessel fleet.[54]

In early July there were only three French privateers in New England waters, but they had almost paralyzed the maritime trade and the fishery of Massachusetts. The Boston merchants and the Essex County fishing interests, however, refused to be intimidated for long. Privateers were hurriedly fitted out and it has been estimated that by August five Boston ships were under sail against the French. These Massachusetts privateers were supported by no fewer than eight from Rhode Island and one from New Hampshire.[55] By early August French privateers were no longer an immediate threat to Massachusetts. Instead, the New Englanders had boldly forced their way into the French waters about Cape Breton and by September were playing havoc with French shipping to and from Louisbourg. Apparently dissatisfied with the lack of suitable French shipping, at least one privateering captain landed his crew on Cape Breton and "plundered some villages, and had the good fortune to surprise some Traders, from whom he took Gunpowder and other Goods to a Great Value."[56] Some other enterprising Massachusetts privateers even began to prey upon French shipping in the Gulf of St. Lawrence.[57]

In 1744 the privateering war between Louisbourg and Boston was in one sense won by the French. Some thirty-six prizes were declared in Louisbourg, of which twenty-six were, in all likelihood, Massachusetts ships. The number of Cape Breton prizes taken by Massachusetts privateers was only a small fraction of the French number. In controlling the seas, however, New England numbers were eventually more than a match for Gallic audacity; by the autumn of 1744 French privateers had been virtually driven from North Atlantic waters into their Louisbourg nest.[58]

Though William Shirley was delighted with the success of the privateering counteroffensive and with the effectiveness of his Indian pacification policy, he nevertheless remained of the opinion that in the long run the successful defence of Annapolis Royal was the most effective way to prevent the French from encroaching upon Massachusetts territory and from undermining its commerce. He felt that a British Annapolis Royal possessed considerable symbolic and strategic importance which critically impinged upon Massachusetts affairs. Annapolis Royal represented British military power in Nova Scotia, whose vast expanse in Shirley's eyes stretched from the Penobscot to Canso. If Annapolis fell to an invading French force, Shirley was certain that the tenuous ties binding the thousands of Acadian inhabitants to the British Crown would be permanently severed. Furthermore, he feared that the fall of Annapolis Royal would immediately destroy the delicately balanced neutrality of the Indian tribes along the Massachusetts northern and northeastern frontiers and throw them into the welcoming arms of the French. Annapolis had become a symbol of British military might to these Indians, and as such, a significant reason for their succumbing to Shirley's blandishments. If the fort was captured, their respect for British military power would probably immediately disappear, and they would do everything in their power to ingratiate themselves with the French. What better expressions of their loyalty to the French could they offer than a string of Massachusetts scalps and a number of devastated frontier settlements? By this kind of analysis, it is not surprising that for Shirley Nova Scotia was indeed Massachusetts' outpost.

Sometime between June 15 and June 22 news of the fall of Canso had reached Boston. On May 24, 350 men from Louisbourg had easily captured the poorly defended British outpost.[59] Shirley and many Massachusetts residents realized that Annapolis Royal would be the next target for French aggression.[60] On June 23, therefore, the House of Representatives, spurred by the Canso news, finally decided to act upon Shirley's request for the despatch of reinforcements to Nova Scotia. The House asserted that since the successful defence of Annapolis Royal was "an Affair of great Importance to the Crown, and in particular to the respective Governments of New England," it was imperative to send "some immediate relief." It was resolved:

> *That his Excellency the Captain General be desired to give orders for raising two independent Companies of Voluntiers, consisting of sixty Men each, exclusive of Officers, to be sent to Annapolis Royal, as soon as may be, at the Charge of the Province: And for Encouragement to good and effective Men to inlist in this Service, that there be and hereby is granted to be paid out of the Province Treasury to each Man that shall inlist twenty Pounds old Tenor ... and that they be freed from all ordinary Impresses within this Province for the space of three Years after their Return.*

The House further emphasized that after the troops arrived at Annapolis Royal, they were to receive neither wages nor supplies from the Massachusetts government. The governor was urged "to use his good offices with the Commander of that Fortress in obtaining Pay and Subsistence for the said Companies from the Crown until they return home."[61]

At first, few men volunteered to serve at Annapolis in spite of the seemingly attractive bounty of £20, in spite of Shirley's promise that the British government would provide the reinforcements with "both Pay and Subsistence" once they were in Nova Scotia, and in spite of the commitment that the men would not be impressed in Massachusetts for a period of three years after their return. It was obvious that the general populace was not as concerned with the French threat as were Shirley and a growing number of members of the General Court. At the popular level, there was to be found a continuing apathy towards Nova Scotia. Realizing the strength of their bargaining position, those Massachusetts inhabitants interested in volunteering demanded even more bounty money before they would enlist. But during the remainder of June, the House of Representatives stubbornly refused to increase the bounty money, and the recruiting campaign for the Annapolis force was an embarrassing failure. Then on the last day of the month, Shirley informed the House that he had just received a disconcerting letter from Paul Mascarene.[62] The new military and civil chief of Annapolis Royal had stressed "the Danger they are in, of being speedily attacked by the Enemy, and the present Weakness of the Garrison there, and requesting that we would send speedy Succours to them of at least two Hundred Soldiers well arm'd and victualled for some Months." Shirley appealed to the members to deal immediately with Mascarene's request so "that no Disaster may happen." On the following day the House acted, but not precisely in the way Shirley wished it to proceed. It was ordered that "each able body'd effective Soldier on his Inlistment for Annapolis Royal receive five pounds old Tenor, for their Encouragement, and that the Sum of twenty Pounds of old Tenor be paid them on their being muster'd in the Town of Boston, or such other place as his Excellency shall appoint, under their proper Officers compleat in their Arms at their own Charge." The House had refused to increase the number of reinforcements from some 120 men to 200, and it had also refused to provide the two companies with supplies for an indefinite period of "some months."[63] Most members of the House still felt that their main concern was the defence of the immediate boundaries of their colony; they had serious misgivings about defending inadequately armed outposts of British imperialism, in spite of Shirley's seemingly persuasive arguments. There still seemed to be, in early July, a prevailing mood of indifference towards the French threat among the rank and file of Massachusetts, at least as reflected in their representatives in the General Court.

As would be expected, Shirley was dissatisfied with the response of the House of Representatives, and he continued to apply steady pressure on its members to raise at least another company of reinforcements and to provision the troops during their entire Nova Scotia sojourn. The House finally agreed on July 4 to grant "a Bounty of twenty-five Pounds . . . for an Encouragement to one Hundred and eighty Soldiers to inlist . . . for the Defence of Annapolis Royal." The House, however, continued to refuse to supply the troops with provisions.[64] As far as its members were concerned, they had made their last concession to the governor concerning his cherished project.

The extra £5 of bounty money aided the recruitment drive but not sufficiently to fill all available openings. On July 12 some seventy men sailed for Annapolis Royal, and their arrival four days later was perfectly timed to raise the sagging morale of Mascarene's force of 100 troops, 20 or 30 of whom Mascarene considered to be "utterly invalides."[65] The day of the disembarkation of the Massachusetts troops witnessed the retreat of some 300 Micmacs who had been besieging the fort since July 11.[66] All the Annapolis Royal British inhabitants shared Mascarene's thoughts when he wrote to Shirley on July 18, "I can hardly find expressions to thank you for the seasonable succour you have sent us."[67] On July 31 a further fifty-three reinforcements, a score of whom were probably Pigwacket Indians, sailed for Annapolis.[68]

The sending of the Pigwackets marked a definite change in Shirley's thinking regarding the Annapolis Royal reinforcement problem. By the closing days of July it was clear to Shirley, as it must have been to most Massachusetts officials, that the available supply of Massachusetts men who were willing to serve in Nova Scotia had quickly dried up. A new source had to be found and Shirley discovered the source among the friendly Pigwackets. On July 29 Shirley informed the General Court that he was determined "to consider in what Manner these Indians may be best disposed of to save Charge to the Province, and to make them in some Measure useful to us."[69] What better way was there to make the Pigwackets useful than to send some of them to Annapolis Royal? Besides, had not Mascarene asked for "20 or 30 bold and warlike Indians . . . to keep in awe the Indians of this Peninsula who believe all the Indians come from New England are Mohawks of whom they stand in great fear?"[70] It is not surprising then that Shirley was certain that "Providence has, in so extraordinary a Way, cast them among us."[71] The remaining openings in the second incomplete company and in the third company were offered to the Pigwackets and eagerly accepted.

Believing that Mascarene was in no position to provision adequately the new Indian recruits, Shirley decided to have those who did not sail on July 31 remain in Massachusetts, supplied with food and other necessities by the government, until they were needed at Annapolis Royal. They were not sent to Mascarene until the latter part of September, and their arrival coincided with a major French-Indian siege of Annapolis Royal. Fifty Louisbourg regulars, together with 210 Micmacs and Malecites, had commenced the siege on September 8.[72] After the Pigwackets had landed, the French commanding officer in charge of the siege sadly noted in his journal: "The British yelled out many hurrahs. I had them carefully watched during the night. They were singing and enjoying themselves thoroughly; they probably spent the whole night drinking."[73] The arrival of the Pigwackets, however, was not responsible for the lifting of the siege during the first week of October. News that an expected French fleet was not coming to Annapolis Royal after all and instructions from Louisbourg's governor had brought the siege to an end. But as far as Shirley was concerned, his Massachusetts reinforcements had twice saved Nova Scotia.

Even the members of the Massachusetts House of Representatives were impressed with Shirley's uncanny sense of timing. They discovered in mid-October that his promise made on July 11 that the British government would reimburse Massachusetts for any money spent on the defence of Annapolis Royal was, in fact, considered binding by the Board of Trade.[74] This decision meant, of course, that a not inconsiderable sum of British money would be pumped into the sagging Massachusetts economy. The news from Annapolis Royal and from the Board of Trade added to Shirley's growing prestige and influence.

Within the entire context of the first few months of King George's War, Shirley's deep concern for Nova Scotia did not accurately reflect Massachusetts' attitudes. Few inhabitants seemed overly concerned with Mascarene's plight and only Shirley's persistent pressure finally squeezed a few reinforcements from the General Court. If it had not been for the Pigwackets, the entire recruiting campaign would have been a disaster. In the late summer and autumn of 1744, with the French privateers no longer considered a threat to the Massachusetts economy and with stability and peace on the frontiers, there was little popular enthusiasm for any major military commitment to be made for the protection of another colony. Opinions that had congealed during the first decade of the eighteenth century continued to influence Massachusetts' perception of its relationship with Nova Scotia.

9

William Shirley
and
Louisbourg,
1744-1745

Throughout the closing months of 1744, Governor William Shirley's concern persisted for what he called the "Preservation of his Majesty's Interest at Annapolis Royal."[1] He had come to realize that Nova Scotia's capital could not be kept out of French hands, in spite of the Massachusetts volunteers he had sent there, unless the surrounding seas were patrolled by ships of the Royal Navy. Such a British naval presence, he expected, would effectively counter any possible French decision to send a naval expedition from Louisbourg to capture the keystone of his northern military policy. Consequently, Shirley bombarded his patron Newcastle and the Lords of the Admiralty with requests for English warships to patrol the North Atlantic from Cape Sable to Boston. The Massachusetts governor wished to protect not only Annapolis but Massachusetts commerce from possible French naval encroachments.[2] On November 25, for example, Shirley wrote to the Lords of the Admiralty:

> By [Spring, 1745] . . . it is scarcely to be doubted but that the
> Enemy will send such a Naval force against it [Annapolis
> Royal] as will make 'em masters of it, if it is not protected
> against 'em by a Naval force from England. I need not
> observe to your Lordships how heavy the loss of the Garrison
> and Province of Nova Scotia would be on the one hand to

his Majesty's northern Colonies, and how much it would
affect the British Trade and Navigation to these parts.[3]

Shirley's persuasive persistence bore some fruit; early in the new year a formerly indifferent British government began to show some genuine concern about the defence of Nova Scotia. On January 14, 1745, the Duke of Newcastle wrote the following circular to the governors of the American colonies:

His Majesty having thought it necessary for the Security of the Collonys in North America, and particularly of the Province of Nova Scotia, (which has been already invaded by the French, & upon which there is great reason to apprehend that they will early in the Spring renew their attempts by the attack on Annapolis Royal) to employ such a strength of Ships of Warr in those Seas under the Command of Comodore Warren as may be sufficient to protect . . . the Trade and Fishery of His Majesty's Subjects in those parts and may also as Occasion shall offer, attack and distress the Enemy in their Settlements, and annoy their Fishery & Commerce.[4]

Expanding his strategic vision, Shirley soon began to consider seriously "the great consequences of the acquisition of Cape Breton."[5] He wished to see the French colony in British hands so that Annapolis Royal and Massachusetts would be safe from possible French attacks. Shirley's rather vague theorizing regarding the capture of Louisbourg was galvanized into definite expression by December 14, 1744. On that day he was reliably informed by recently released Massachusetts prisoners from Louisbourg that the French officer who had led the attacks on Canso and Annapolis Royal had sailed for France accompanied by three Louisbourg pilots intimately familiar with the coast of Nova Scotia and Massachusetts. They were expected to return in February of 1745 with "some Ships with Stores and Recruits for the Garrison at Cape Breton and also some Ships of Force to proceed to the coasts of Cape Breton, Nova Scotia . . . With a Design . . . To make a Descent on Annapolis Royal and to cruise on the Coasts of New England."[6] The aroused governor, now armed with evidence supporting his earlier predictions, immediately sent a letter to the Lords of the Admiralty in which he enunciated the broad outlines of his plan to drive the French from Cape Breton.

The plan was a simple one. Shirley merely wanted British warships to intercept the French fleet on its way to Nova Scotia, thereby dealing "a killing blow to the Enemy." Without reinforcements and supplies, he argued further, the "extremely ill mann'd" and "exceedingly discontented" Louisbourg garrison could be expected to surrender without any resistance to a blockading British naval force.[7]

Shirley's plan to capture Louisbourg had gradually evolved during the closing months of 1744; the plan may be regarded as the natural outgrowth of his Annapolis Royal policy. Four major factors seem to have influenced his thinking concerning Louisbourg: first, the difficulty he had experienced in Massachusetts in obtaining reinforcements and supplies for Annapolis Royal; second, the news about conditions in Louisbourg brought to him by returning prisoners of war; third, the views of Robert Auchmuty, judge of the Vice-Admiralty Court in Boston; and fourth, the policies advocated by Christopher Kilby, London agent of the Massachusetts government.

It is clear that most Massachusetts residents had shown little enthusiasm for Shirley's appeals for Annapolis Royal reinforcements. As a result, and also because of what had happened during the last war with France, the governor anticipated an even less enthusiastic response to the call for volunteers to attack the French fortress of Louisbourg. It seemed likely that the General Court, already faced with a sizeable debt and still not recovered from a serious economic recession, would oppose such a scheme if it involved the spending of any considerable sum of Massachusetts' money. Therefore Shirley was initially of the opinion that any expedition against Louisbourg would have to be carried out by a British fleet and by British regulars.

The second major factor was based on reports to Shirley from returning Massachusetts and Canso prisoners that Louisbourg was a ripe fruit ready to be plucked by an enterprising invading force. The walls of the fortress were in disrepair, and the troops, badly disciplined and inadequately supplied with arms, clothing, and foodstuffs, were on the verge of open revolt. Probably more than any other single factor, this information was responsible for Shirley's decision in December to press for a naval assault upon Louisbourg.[8]

Shirley's deliberations were also considerably influenced by the views of one of his close friends, Judge Auchmuty. In April, 1744, while acting as a special agent for the Massachusetts government in London, Auchmuty presented to the Board of Trade a memoir entitled

"The Importance of Cape-Breton to the British Nation." In all likelihood, Shirley was sent a copy of the memoir and studied its contents. Believing that his arguments regarding the economic potential of Cape Breton had proved that the "expense and danger in taking [Cape Breton] . . . will bear no proportion to the advantage and profits thereby resulting," Auchmuty concluded his memoir by describing in some detail his plan to capture Louisbourg. He proposed that by the beginning of April, 1745, a force of 3,000 men be raised in the colonies north of Virginia "under the specious pretence that [they] . . . are raised to defend the governments from invasion, or the surprise of an enemy." Not until the last possible moment were they to be told they were to attack "the Dunkirk of North America." Auchmuty further proposed:

> *A squadron of six sail of the line, with two thousand regular troops, and all things necessary for a formal siege, should take their departure from [Britain] the beginning of March next, so as to anchor in Gabaron [Gabarus] bay, within four miles of the rampart of Louisbourg, by the middle of April following; there to be joined by the American troops under convoy of the station ships. This may be executed without loss of men, no cannon commanding the entrance of this harbour, and where the navy of England may safely ride. It may be conceived advisable there to land the troops, and from thence to march and make regular approaches to the rampart. . . . It is judged by connoisseurs that the fire of their own cannon will shake down the works, and that they will not stand a battery.*[9]

What Joseph Dudley and Samuel Vetch had frequently advocated in the first decade of the eighteenth century with reference to a joint Anglo-American assault on French Nova Scotia, Auchmuty was now proposing concerning Cape Breton Island.

Three years earlier, Christopher Kilby had shown some interest in the capture of Louisbourg. In 1741 he had sent a "kinsman" to the French fortress to investigate its strength. The information Kilby received persuaded him that Louisbourg, because of inadequate "Fortifications and Garrison," was vulnerable to a combined land-sea assault.[10] On April 14, 1744, only a few days after Britain had declared war on France, Kilby submitted to the Board of Trade a detailed statement dealing with Louisbourg.[11] Kilby's document was remarkably similar in content to Auchmuty's memoir presented to the Board one week later. This similarity was no mere coincidence. The two men were close associates and both were interested not only in the general welfare of Massachusetts but also in their own ambitious commercial schemes. Might not the proposed expedition give them the opportunity to line their pockets from the profits resulting from their involvement in various supply contracts? In order to protect Nova Scotia and Massachusetts from French encroachments, Kilby urged that Louisbourg be attacked at once. When the British government refused to act immediately by sending a naval force to Cape Breton, Kilby proposed in October, 1744, that in the early part of 1745, "Six Ships of the line – three or four smaller ones, and a Bomb ship, with a compleat Regiment of Experienc'd Land forces, a proper Train of Artillery, and 4,000 Troops to be raised in America" should attack Louisbourg.[12] Kilby's October proposal was sent to the Duke of Newcastle and to Shirley. Kilby also informed Shirley that if a colonial force was raised, it would be "Effectually supported" by the British government.[13] In fact, however, Kilby had received no official assurance of any support whatsoever. But he knew that the odds were excellent that once Shirley began to recruit volunteers, the British government could be persuaded to provide financing for the expedition; it was a gamble certainly worth taking in his estimation.

Despite Auchmuty's and Kilby's emphasis upon a joint Anglo-American expedition, Shirley in early December stubbornly insisted that any assault should be the sole responsibility of the British government.[14] The governor had his sensitive political ear to the ground and heard no popular clamour for a massive Massachusetts initiative with respect to a Louisbourg attack. Only a small but vociferous minority led by Captain John Bradstreet, a returned Canso prisoner, and William Vaughan of Damariscotta in Maine pressed for a Massachusetts-led New England invasion of Cape Breton independent of any support from Great Britain.

Bradstreet was born at Annapolis Royal in 1714, the son of a British army officer, Lieutenant Edward Bradstreet, and Agathe de St. Etienne de La Tour, a granddaughter of the famous and controversial Charles de La Tour. In 1735 he had purchased an ensign's commission in Governor Philipps's Nova Scotia regiment and had been stationed at Canso. Here he became involved in numerous illicit commercial ventures with the French at Louisbourg. Captured at Canso in May, 1744, Bradstreet was imprisoned at Louisbourg until his release in October of the same year. While a prisoner at the French fortress, he had come to the conclusion that it could be easily captured by a small New England force.[15] The response to his daring proposal on the part of most Massachusetts inhabitants, however, was largely negative. Nonetheless, Bradstreet's plan did strike a responsive chord in one energetic man – William Vaughan.

A Harvard graduate and successful fishing and lumbering entrepreneur at Matinicus Island and Damariscotta in Maine, the forty-one-year-old Vaughan was somewhat dissatisfied with his lot in life in late 1744. Always a restless man, he was desperately looking for new worlds to conquer. Coveting fame and prestige, he felt that life in isolated Maine was providing him with neither. While visiting Boston, Vaughan talked to Bradstreet and saw in the Canso captain's proposal an extraordinary opportunity to achieve his own desired goals. If he could only organize and participate in such an expedition, there was always a chance that he could become a popular hero – another William Phips – and be rewarded perhaps with a colonial governorship. Had it not been said that his father had been appointed lieutenant-governor of New Hampshire in 1715 largely because he had participated in the Port Royal expedition of 1710?[16] If William Vaughan wished to achieve anything in his life, it was to follow in his father's footsteps.

Vaughan was gifted with boundless energy and with what has been described as a "daring, enterprising and tenacious mind."[17] Once decided upon a course of action, he stubbornly refused to permit any obstacle to prevent him from achieving his desired goals. In December, 1744, Vaughan began his propaganda offensive to persuade Massachusetts to capture Louisbourg. He travelled extensively throughout Maine, New Hampshire, and northern Massachusetts "Day and Night," enthusiastically advocating a "secret" New England expedition against the French fortress. Here was an itinerant preacher with a novel and exciting secular message to communicate. Vaughan sought to convince his sceptical audiences that Louisbourg could be captured by a "force consisting of 1500 raw militia, some scaling ladders, and few armed craft of New England." The scaling ladders would not be needed, Vaughan contended, if the expedition sailed immediately. For if a secret landing was made during the winter months, the invading force could easily enter the fortified town by scrambling up the snow that usually drifted, so it was said, up over the ramparts. As far as Vaughan was concerned, his proposed expedition could be readily transformed into an invigorating winter frolic. When he was not talking about his daring plan, Vaughan was patiently listening to observations made by men who had recently been in Louisbourg, and their reports strengthened his peculiar sense of mission.[18] Vaughan's enthusiasm, confidence, and persistence won him some converts, particularly in northeastern Massachusetts, including Maine where he was well known and where the fishing and lumbering interests had a lot to lose from Indian-French raids and from Louisbourg-based privateers.

Confident, perhaps a little too confident, of what he regarded as the considerable support which he had coaxed into existence in northeastern Massachusetts, Vaughan sometime in December approached Shirley with a "regular Scheme" to surprise and capture Louisbourg. Vaughan claimed sole authorship of the plan, as did John Bradstreet. In all likelihood, the plan placed in Shirley's hands by Vaughan was originally drafted by Bradstreet and then revised by Vaughan. Vaughan, of course, realized that his plan had little hope of success unless Shirley vigorously endorsed it. The governor was impressed, it was reported, with Vaughan's somewhat exaggerated account of "The General Spirit of the people in the eastern parts of the Province for [the] undertaking." He listened attentively to Vaughan's arguments as to why it was essential to organize the expedition immediately without waiting for assistance from Britain. To Vaughan and Bradstreet the immediate despatch of the expedition and the element of surprise were of far greater consequence for its success than was the eventual support of a large British fleet after a prolonged period of delay.[19] Besides, a successful Massachusetts expedition would mean laurels for American heads alone.

Shirley had firmly opposed the idea of any kind of independent New England expedition largely because he felt that such a plan lacked the support of an appreciable number of Massachusetts residents. On hearing Vaughan's description of the mood of the people in northeastern Massachusetts and after carefully weighing the political risks of supporting such an expedition, Shirley rather reluctantly decided to ask the General Court to finance and organize the effort. If it succeeded, and there was considerable evidence to suggest that it actually would, Shirley's position in Massachusetts and Westminster would be almost unassailable. If it failed, the governor could always argue that he had been pushed into accepting the Vaughan-Bradstreet proposal by an irresistible popular demand. Regardless of whether the expedition eventually failed or succeeded, Shirley would have a vast new reserve of patronage to dispense — patronage which could only strengthen and consolidate his political power and influence.

On January 20, 1745, at an unprecedented secret session of the General Court, Shirley stunned those present by strongly urging an immediate New England expedition against Louisbourg. The audacity of the governor's proposal lay in the recommendation, not that Louisbourg should be attacked, but that it should be attacked only by raw New England militia. After a brief, trenchant, introductory paragraph in which he commented on Louisbourg's "utmost annoyance" of Massachusetts' commerce, Shirley presented his plan:

> *From the best information that can be had of the circumstances of the Town and of the number of the soldiers and Militia within it, and of the situation of the Harbour, I have good reason to think that if Two Thousand men were landed upon the Island as soon as they may be conveniently got ready (which as I am credibly informed may be done in the proper part of the Island for that purpose with little or no risque) such a number of men would, with the blessing of Divine Providence upon their Enterprize, be masters of the field at all events, and not only possess themselves of their two most important batteries with ease, break upon their Out Settlements, destroy their Cable and Magazines, ruine their Fishery Works, and lay the town in ruines, but might make themselves masters of the Town and Harbour. . . . I would earnestly recommend it to you to make a suitable provision for the Expences of such an expedition, which, if it should succeed no further than with respect to laying open the enemies Harbour and destroying their Out Settlements and Works, must greatly overpay the expence of it, by its consequences to this Province, and if it should wholly succeed, it must bring an irreparable loss to the enemy, and an invaluable acquisition to this Country.*

Shirley did not want to discuss in "Detail . . . The manner of executing such an attempt."[20] He was primarily concerned with winning the support of the General Court for the idea of the expedition. Details regarding its actual implementation could be worked out later.

Most members, "struck with amazement at the proposal," were certain that the undertaking had "no rational prospect of success." In deference to Shirley's earnest plea, on the following day, January 21, a committee was appointed to consider the governor's proposal. For two days the committee members debated Shirley's recommendation. His supporters argued that unless the French fortress was captured, the Massachusetts cod fishery, as during previous wars with the French, would be dealt a serious blow by French privateers; Nova Scotia would be lost; and Louisbourg "would infallibly prove the Dunkirk of New-England." They predicted that the time was pro-pitious for a daring and imaginative assault. The French garrison was openly mutinous, provisions were scarce, and "the works mouldering and decayed, the governor an old man unskilled in the art of war." It was therefore considered necessary to launch an attack at once, since in "another year the place would be impregnable." A gamble had to be taken. If the expedition failed, the Massachusetts government would have "to grapple with the disappointment" of bearing the brunt of the entire cost of the episode. If it succeeded, however, "not only the coasts of New England would be free from molestation, but so glorious an acquisition would be of the greatest importance to Great-Britain and might give peace to Europe, and [the Massachusetts government] might depend upon a reimbursement of the whole charge."[21]

Those who opposed the scheme declared that some kind of arrangement could be made with the French whereby "both sides would be willing to leave the fishery unmolested." Moreover, they argued:

The accounts given of the works and the garrison at Louis-bourg could not be depended upon, and it was not credible that any part of the walls should be unguarded and exposed to surprise, that instances of disaffection rising to mutiny were rare and but few instances were to be met with in history where such expectation has not failed. The garrison at Louisbourg consisted of regular experienced troops, who, though unequal in number, would be more than a match in open field for all the raw unexperienced militia which could be sent from New-England ... that if only one 60 gun ship

should arrive from France, or the French islands, she would
be more than a match for all the armed vessels [New
England] could provide.

It was also pointed out that it was highly unlikely that a sufficient number of volunteers could be raised in Massachusetts, let alone supplied with arms, ammunition, and provisions and transported to Cape Breton all within a brief period of a few months. The Jeremiahs who attacked the scheme gloomily prophesied that if the expedition failed, and they knew it would, "such a shock would be given to the province that half a century would not recover us to our present state."[22] The men could not readily forget the embarrassing lessons learned from the previous two wars with France, and they drilled deep into this sensitive Massachusetts nerve.

The committee members were almost unanimously opposed to Shirley's scheme. On January 23 their report was quickly endorsed by the General Court and sent to the governor who was informed that the members were "fully convinced that all the Sea and Land Forces that can possibly be raised will be insufficient . . . in reducing the said French Settlement." It was further emphasized that it was solely the responsibility of the British government to organize and finance any Louisbourg assault. In the last sentence of its message to Shirley, almost as an afterthought, the General Court vaguely promised "as far as they are able, to exert themselves in conjunction with the other [colonial] Governments on such an occasion."[23] In its decision, the General Court was merely reaffirming the policy it had decided upon in the aftermath of the Port Royal fiasco of 1707.

Shirley accepted the Court's decision gracefully, and on January 26 he wrote to Newcastle in support of the General Court's request for British initiative in attempting "the Reduction of Cape Breton."[24] Shirley had quickly returned to his earlier position; he was now content, with the popular consensus behind him, to sit back and wait for the British government to make the next move. But William Vaughan had other ideas.

The irrepressible Vaughan, who regarded the Court's action as a personal affront, was determined singlehandedly to be responsible for reversing its decision. He swiftly executed a three-pronged campaign to achieve this end. First, he visited Essex County, the area that traditionally favoured a strong anti-French stance, where he was able to persuade over 100 leading fishermen to send a strongly worded petition to the General Court. In it these men, who felt their fishery threatened by Louisbourg-based privateers, promised "to furnish Vessels in 14 Days for 3,500 men" if Vaughan's plan for a surprise attack was accepted. Vaughan also urged "more than 200 principal Gentlemen in Boston" to petition the Court to accept his scheme. Most of these men were involved in commercial life and were concerned about the possible adverse effect of French privateering on their shipping. Second, Vaughan assiduously fanned the dying embers of Shirley's enthusiasm for the plan by inducing the somewhat reluctant governor to "make one push more at this time in the affair." Third, to strengthen Shirley's position in the renewed attempt to have the plan accepted by the Court, Vaughan urged that a detailed plan of the proposed expedition be presented to the members and defended in person by Bradstreet and a Captain Loring, who had returned in the preceding month from Cape Breton. Vaughan confidently expected that in such a confrontation those who opposed his scheme would be eventually won over to his side.[25]

The plan which was finally presented to the Court envisaged a surprise attack on Louisbourg early in the spring by a volunteer force of 3,000 New Englanders. These troops were to sail in fishing vessels to Canso, the "place of Rendezvous," and from there the fleet was to proceed to Gabarus Bay, a few miles southwest of Louisbourg, arriving there "by Dusk." Whaleboats, each equipped with two ladders, fifteen feet long, were to be used to land the troops under cover of darkness. Then various sections of the fortress were to be attacked simultaneously: "It will be Absolutely Necessary to appoint a time to strike the Blow all at Once which can be done by Agreeing upon a certain hour just before Day which is the Sleepiest time, and to the Commanding Officer of each Detachment to know the time, and when the time comes, by his Watch to begin without any further Ceremony. The Enemy finding themselves Attack'd at so many different places at Once probable that it will breed such Confusion among them that Our Men will have time to get in Unmolested." If for some unforeseen reason the original assault was repelled, the attacking force was to bombard the fortress with the "12 Nine Pounders and Two Small Mortars" in order "to make Breaches in their Walls and then to Storm them." If this bombardment failed to breach the walls, the besiegers were to be satisfied with awaiting "an attack by Sea from England."[26]

The petition of the Marblehead-area fishermen, which was sent to the General Court on January 30, was accompanied by a brief message from Shirley. The governor asserted that since it was abundantly clear that the fishing areas wanted the expedition, it was incumbent upon the General Court to reconsider its earlier decision. A committee of both houses was therefore appointed to take another look at the matter. Four days later, on February 3, along with a petition from "a great number of merchants, traders and other inhabitants of Boston . . . praying that an Expedition . . . may be undertaken," Shirley sent another message to the Court. In it he promised that the planned assault would be supported by the neighbouring colonies of New Hampshire, Connecticut, Rhode Island, and New York and that in all likelihood the British government would gladly reimburse Massachusetts for much of the expense involved in the expedition.[27]

After examining the proposed plan of action and questioning Bradstreet, Loring, and the other Massachusetts residents who had recently been at Louisbourg, the committee that had been formed on January 30 presented its eagerly awaited report on February 5. It was recommended

> that it is incumbent upon this Government to Embrace this favourable Opportunity to Attempt the reduction thereof; And they humbly propose that His Excellency the Captain General be desired to give forth his Proclamation to Encourage the Enlistment of Three Thousand voluntiers under such Officers as he shall appoint; That there be delivered to each man a blanket, that one month's pay be Advanc'd and that they be entitul'd to all the Plunder;
> That Provision be made for the furnishing of necessary Warlike Stores for the Expedition. . . . That a Committee be appointed to procure and fit Vessels to serve as Transports to be ready to depart by the beginning of March. . . . That Application be forthwith made to the Governments of New York, the Jerseys, Pennsylvania, New Hampshire, Connecticut and Rhode Island to furnish their respective Quotas of Men & Vessels to Accompany, or follow the force of this Province.[28]

The committee's controversial resolution was hotly debated in the House of Representatives until late in the evening of February 5. When the roll was finally taken, the resolution passed by the narrowest margin of one vote.[29] It was rumoured that the resolution passed only because "of the absence of several members who were known to be against it."[30]

Vaughan's so-called mad scheme had become Massachusetts' official policy. Supported by Shirley's shrewd political guidance and Vaughan's extraordinary tenacity, the coalition of the Essex County fishing interests, the Boston merchants, and some of the northeastern frontier spokesmen had succeeded in pressuring the House of Representatives to change drastically its earlier Louisbourg resolution, itself a continuation of a Nova Scotia policy adopted some forty years before. Without Vaughan's enthusiasm and persistence and the governor's active support, the plan clearly would never have been accepted in early February, 1745.

Specific preparations for the Louisbourg expedition began on February 5, 1745. After reluctantly agreeing to send the troops, the Massachusetts General Court outlined the broad framework of policy within which it expected Shirley would work. He was instructed to raise a force of 3,000 volunteers and to appoint all necessary officers. To facilitate recruiting, the governor was empowered to offer the volunteers one month's pay in advance, as well as to promise that they would be "entitul'd to all the Plunder."[31]

It must have been obvious to Shirley and to most members of the General Court that few men would volunteer unless an unusually popular commander-in-chief was appointed. One critical observer maintained that "Fidelity, resolution and popularity must supply the place of military talents. . . . It was necessary that the men should know and love their General, or they would not enlist under him."[32] Even though Shirley possessed the power to appoint such an officer independently, he preferred to consult the Court before making any final decision. He realized that if the General Court was to maintain its enthusiasm for the Louisbourg venture, its approval of his choice for commander-in-chief was absolutely essential.

Four men offered their services to Shirley — William Vaughan, Samuel Waldo, Lieutenant-Governor Benning Wentworth of New Hampshire, and John Bradstreet. Vaughan's offer was never taken seriously by Shirley, who like many members of the General Court, regarded Vaughan as a "whimsical wild projector" and an ambitious "outsider."[33] Waldo, on the other hand, was a leading member of the

General Court and one of Shirley's closest friends. A land speculator on a grand scale, Waldo had purchased in 1730 the old Temple-Nelson claim to Nova Scotia. In 1745, faced by serious financial difficulties, he saw in the Louisbourg project a heaven-sent opportunity for him to obtain large tracts of land in the western section of Nova Scotia from a grateful British government. Waldo, however, lacked the necessary popular appeal and his close association with Shirley was resented by some members of the General Court. As a result, he had to be satisfied with a brigadier-general's commission.[34] The gouty Wentworth's request to command the expedition was quickly rejected by Shirley who felt that such an appointment "would be attended with great risque, both with respect to our assembly and soldiers being intirely disgusted."[35] With respect to Bradstreet, Shirley was evidently tempted to select the confident Canso officer. But "finding it would be difficult to raise a Sufficient Number of Men Unless under the Command of one of their own Country Men," the governor resisted the temptation.[36] Bradstreet eventually joined the expedition as the commander-in-chief's special military adviser.

One man, William Pepperrell, a wealthy Piscataqua merchant and leading member of the General Court, seemed to tower above all other possible candidates, but he showed little enthusiasm at first to lead the expedition. Shirley soon came to realize that Pepperrell, who had been a member of the General Court since 1727 and who, in 1745, was president of the Council and colonel of the Maine militia, was the only man with the necessary qualifications to serve as commander-in-chief. Furthermore, he had played a key role in persuading the Court to reverse its Louisbourg policy; in order words, he was committed to the venture. Pepperrell's military experience may have been limited to the none-too-exacting inspection of frontier defences and to the general organization and training of the Maine militia,[37] but it was of greater importance that he was widely regarded as a gentleman "of unblemished reputation, of engaging manners, extensively known in Massachusetts and New Hampshire, and very popular."[38] Such a man, Shirley felt, would attract volunteers and help to transform the hitherto prevailing attitude of indifference towards a Massachusetts military commitment in the Nova Scotia–Cape Breton area into one of enthusiastic concern. Finally, Pepperrell's willingness to sacrifice his fortune and position for the greater good of his colony would be regarded as irrefutable proof that Louisbourg was, in fact, a sword of Damocles hanging over Massachusetts and threatening its very existence.

Almost immediately after the General Court had accepted the resolution of the special committee, meeting under the chairmanship of Pepperrell, to undertake the Louisbourg expedition, Pepperrell was approached by Shirley and leading members of the General Court "to head ye forces." Pepperrell politely yet firmly refused — "Mrs Pepperrell being in an ill state of health and my business unsettled." Pepperrell's initial rebuff spurred Shirley and the Court members into increasing their pressure upon the reluctant Piscataqua merchant. They bluntly argued that without him there would be no expedition and with no expedition the French from Louisbourg would soon invade "ye eastern part of New England, and Newfoundland would have stood but a poor chance, so that ye greatest part of ye codd fishery in a short time would have been in ye French hands, and great part of our trade to New England, Verginia, etc. intercept'd by ym." Pepperrell was made to feel that he alone would be responsible for the ensuing French devastation. He sincerely did not want "to undertake so dangerous and fatiguing an Enterprize," but he also did not wish to jeopardize the sending of the expedition.[39] Besides, Shirley's economic arguments must have struck hard at one of Pepperrell's vulnerable points — his considerable commercial empire. He was involved in the fishery, in lumbering, and in the North Atlantic carrying trade.

Thoroughly confused as to what he should do, Pepperrell sought the advice of a close friend, the English evangelist, the Reverend George Whitefield, who was then in Boston conducting "a hopeful Revival of Religion."[40] Whitefield assured Pepperrell that "if he did undertake it, he would beg the Lord God of armies to give him a single eye; that the means proposed to take Louisbourg, in the eye of human reason, were no more adequate to the end, than the sounding of rams' horns to blow down Jericho; but that, if Providence really called him, he would return more than conqueror."[41] After much prayer and after finally receiving the "free consent" of his wife, Pepperrell on February 11 accepted Shirley's offer and was commissioned lieutenant-general and commander-in-chief of all land and sea forces. Pepperrell obviously had a deep sense of responsibility towards his fellows in Massachusetts, and he was, as would be expected, concerned about protecting his investments and adding to his stature as a Massachusetts politician and leader. And as a pious Christian, believing that he was an instrument in the hands of the Almighty, Pepperrell, once decided on his course of action, could sanctify it by infusing it with the Holy Spirit's endorsement.

With Pepperrell's acceptance, the recruiting campaign began in earnest. The campaign was carefully planned by Shirley and his associates. A concerted propaganda barrage was intended to prepare the way for the recruiting officers. Across the length and breadth of Massachusetts, supporters of the expedition, led by the energetic Vaughan, proclaimed that the capture of Louisbourg was simply a matter of sailing there. The French fortress was "slenderly Fortified" and its garrison prepared to surrender to any invading force. It was also stressed that the Louisbourg merchants and officers possessed vast sums of money and other valuables, readily obtainable plunder that would doubtless make each volunteer a relatively rich man.[42] Some ministers of the Gospel, though not all, joined the propaganda chorus. By giving the expedition the motto *Nil desperandum Christo duce*, Whitefield tried to transform it into a Protestant crusade.[43] One poetic divine living in the afterglow of the Great Awakening, the religious revival which had swept New England in the late 1730s and early 1740s, declared:

> *For Zion's Sake hold not your Peace*
> *While She's in such Distress,*
> *Compressed by Vast Thousands of*
> *The Sons of Wickedness. . . .*
>
> *'Tis nothing less than Christ himself,*
> *These Anti-Christians fight,*
> *And if it were but in their Power*
> *They'd ruin his Kingdom quite. . . .*
>
> *Ev'n so, Lord Jesus, quickly come,*
> *In thine Almighty Power,*
> *Destroy proud Antichrist, O Lord,*
> *And quite consume the Whore.*[44]

Another pious worthy exclaimed:

> *And how sweet and pleasant will it be . . . to be the person*
> *under God that shall reduce and pull down that stronghold of*
> *Satan and sett up the kingdome of our exalded Saviour. O,*

*that I could be . . . in that single church [in Louisbourg] to
destroy ye images their sett up, and ye true Gospel of our
Lord and Saviour Jesus Christ their preached.*⁴⁵

To some ministers, the expedition was extremely important to test
whether in the post–Great Awakening period, the Almighty was
pleased with the spiritual state of Massachusetts. The capture of Louisbourg could be convincing proof, in their eyes at least, that their God
had remained their "great Preserver and Benefactor."⁴⁶ The selection
of the saintly Pepperrell was considered to be a step in the right
direction.

From the beginning of the campaign there was "a considerable
readiness in many to enlist," especially in northeastern Massachusetts
and Maine where Pepperrell and Vaughan both exerted considerable
influence.⁴⁷ Some wanted commissions because, as one citizen put it, of
"a hope, well or ill grounded, that if the place be taken they may have
their commissions confirmed at home, and so have either a full sterling
pay, if they are employed, and if they are dismissed at half-pay."⁴⁸
One frank father informed Pepperrell:

*The Prospect of Profit either by Wages or Plunder had no
Weight in ye Scale to induce my Son to engage in the
expedition . . . what he principally aimed at is a Capt's
Commission in the King's Pay. I have been told the Company
of Voluntiers who went to Annapolis last summer were (as
soon as advice of it got home) put in the British Pay and if
that be true, I suppose Cape Breton if it be reduced will be
garrisoned in part by New England Voluntiers upon the
Same Establishment and the Officers have commissions from
the Crown, as it should be so.*⁴⁹

For others the desire for plunder, as had been the case in earlier
Nova Scotian expeditions, was a major motivating factor. Only a few
years earlier, hundreds in Massachusetts had rushed to volunteer to
participate in the Cartagena expedition to the Caribbean. So many
volunteered in Massachusetts, in fact, that a large number had to be
turned away, thus precipitating an ugly crisis. These men were not
primarily interested in driving the Spanish from the West Indies;
rather, they wanted to fill their empty pockets with Spanish gold at a
time of economic recession when in some regions of the colony there

was a shortage of good inexpensive land for an expanding population. For many the Louisbourg expedition was regarded in a similar light, though some men were motivated by "The Expectation of Seeing Great things, etc.," and others were sure that if Louisbourg was not captured, the French fortress "was Like to prove Detremental if not Destroying to our Country." Some in enlisting showed their strong anti–Roman Catholic bias, and some blindly followed the example set by their friends or uncritically obeyed the command of a leading member of the community. There seemed to be a general excitement in the air and to refuse to participate in the expedition might be considered by some to be unpatriotic.[50]

After receiving their commissions from Shirley authorizing them "to beat . . . Drums" within a certain militia regiment "for the enlisting of Voluntiers," some officers went to great lengths to persuade men to enlist.[51] A Captain Sewell, for example, "called his men to his own house and generously entertained them all with a dinner and much encouraged them to engage in the present expedition, promising to as many . . . as would go that he wd give them out of his own pocket so much as with the Province pay they shd have 8 £ pr month. And if any of their familys were in want he would supply them so that they shd not suffer."[52] James Gibson, a Boston merchant and former officer in the Royal Regiment of Foot Guards in Barbados, raised "some hundreds" of volunteers at his own expense. Vaughan was so successful in recruiting men that the disconcerted Shirley eventually ordered him "to stop enlisting." A few audacious individuals recruited volunteers without first receiving commissions from Shirley. After they had collected together a company of men, they demanded commissions, a request which Shirley usually gladly met.[53]

In spite of these favourable factors, the recruiting campaign nevertheless met with some opposition in certain quarters, which was partly responsible for preventing the expedition from sailing on the intended date, March 12. There were evidently three main centres of opposition in Massachusetts. First, at least a few fishing entrepreneurs discouraged their workmen from volunteering in the hope that when the embargo on shipping was lifted after the fleet sailed, they would be able to fish off Cape Sable and elsewhere without any immediate fear of French attacks. Their fish would fetch high prices and their ships would be shielded from French privateers by the invading New England force. Second, a small number of clergymen vociferously argued that those who volunteered "would dye there [at Louisbourg] and be dammn'd to[o]." The souls of too many of the potential volunteers were still unregenerate and to enlist was to open the door to everlasting torment. Third, as had been the case in previous wars, frontier inhabitants, fearing possible Indian attacks, did all in their power "to keep the people at home." But the opposition could only delay, not halt, the recruiting program, and by April 4, some 3,000 Massachusetts residents had volunteered to serve in the land force and another 1,000 to man the expedition's ships.[54]

The unexpected postponement of the sailing of the expedition (the first Massachusetts contingent did not sail until April 4 and the second two days later) may also be traced to other factors. There was the unanticipated difficulty in obtaining supply and transport ships and sailors to man these vessels. There was, in addition, the belated and often negative response of the other colonial governments to Shirley's urgent appeal for aid. Finally, there was Shirley's decision to wait until the last possible moment to see whether British warships from the Caribbean might just possibly join the expedition.

In his negotiations with the General Court, Shirley had stressed that the neighbouring colonies would enthusiastically participate in the expedition. He was only partly right. When Pennsylvania and New Jersey were approached, they declined "to go and disturb those that neither meddle nor make with us; People with whom we have nothing to do."[55] New York was content to lend Massachusetts ten eighteen-pound cannon with their carriages and other siege equipment. Connecticut and New Hampshire each promised to raise 500 men, while Rhode Island offered an armed vessel. Including land and naval personnel in the expedition, Massachusetts contributed approximately 4,000 men, Connecticut over 600, New Hampshire 456, and Rhode Island 130. This army was, it should be stressed, the largest New England force recruited to fight a foreign war in the seventeenth and eighteenth centuries.

Since he had serious reservations regarding the emphasis placed upon the element of surprise in the plan to capture Louisbourg, Shirley on February 9 had written to Sir Chaloner Ogle, commander of the British squadron station at Jamaica, and to Commodore Peter Warren, commander of the Leeward Islands squadron, asking for naval assistance. Ogle's response was negative, but Warren's was not. In September, 1744, Warren, who had already developed a close commercial relationship with some Boston merchants, proposed to the Lords of the Admiralty that it was of vital importance for the British cause in North America to drive the French from Louisbourg. Warren had barely turned thirty when war had been declared. Having quickly moved up from the ranks, he had married into the New York élite and developed a huge appetite for financial profits and considerable military and political ambition. Warren was clearly a man looking for the main chance and a naval officer whose strategic thinking accurately reflected Shirley's. The Massachusetts governor's scheme had therefore struck an unusually responsive chord in the ambitious and North American — oriented Warren. On March 24 Warren boldly sailed from Antigua to Cape Breton with the *Superbe*, sixty guns, the *Launceston*, forty guns, and the *Mermaid*, forty guns. He also sent orders to the *Eltham* at Piscataqua and the *Bien Aimé*, a prize at Boston, to join him off Louisbourg. But Shirley knew nothing about Warren's departure until after the Massachusetts troops had left Boston for Canso.[56]

In organizing the expedition in a period of only two months, Shirley had performed a minor miracle. By using Vaughan's zeal and Pepperrell's popularity, he had been able to channel effectively the sudden outburst of enthusiasm for the Louisbourg venture into specific military proposals. At the outbreak of hostilities, Shirley had been determined to defend Annapolis Royal, which he considered to be Massachusetts' strategically located northeastern military outpost. He implemented his policy first by sending Massachusetts troops to the Nova Scotia capital and then by requesting the British authorities to send warships to cruise in Nova Scotia waters to prevent any possible French naval assault. He developed further this latter theme when he proposed late in 1744 that a British fleet should attack Louisbourg — the perceived source of most of Massachusetts' military problems. His growing obsession with the taking of Louisbourg made Shirley all the more receptive to Vaughan's enthusiastic arguments in favour of an independent New England expedition.

10

The Capture of Louisbourg and Aftermath, 1745-1748

By April 6, 1745, some 3,000 Massachusetts land troops had left Boston for Canso, the place of rendezvous, where Pepperrell was to make final plans for the taking of Louisbourg. While the commander-in-chief waited for the thick shore-ice to leave the Louisbourg waters, he ordered ashore his Massachusetts volunteers and those from New Hampshire, who had arrived earlier, to undergo some basic military training. On the inhospitable island of Canso, which one Massachusetts officer described as "the Strangest Country that I was ever in, in my life,"[1] the poorly organized training sessions took on a carefree carnival atmosphere. These chaotic sessions provided totally inadequate preparation for the projected landing and attack. Obviously, their aim was to keep the men busy during a longer than anticipated waiting period.

Pepperrell's troops, despite their inexperience and lack of training, naively expected the "Campaign will be very short . . . the place will surrender without any bloodshed."[2] Having recently thrown aside their fishing nets and their plows to volunteer to capture the "French Gibraltar of North America," these men soothed their underlying anxieties by constantly repeating the propaganda shibboleths they had come to regard as gospel truth. Their confidence, which at times blurred into a chauvinistic arrogance, was further strengthened on May 3 when Captain Durell's forty-gun *Eltham* arrived at Canso, to be followed the next day by Commodore Peter Warren with three additional British warships. Then on May 5 some 500 Connecticut volunteers finally landed on Canso. It was obvious to all that Shirley's promises were being honoured; indeed, the Almighty was carefully inserting the pieces of the puzzle which would eventually portray a glorious New England victory at Louisbourg.[3]

When it was discovered that Gabarus Bay, the planned landing area a few miles southwest of Louisbourg, was at last free of ice, the New England fleet set sail on May 10. Once in the bay, Pepperrell decided that since a surprise attack of the fort was definitely out of the question, a daring, amphibious daylight landing would have to be attempted just to build a beachhead on Cape Breton soil. Raw, untrained, and undisciplined New England militia were to carry out a manoeuvre that would have taxed the military ingenuity of the best-trained British regulars. Perhaps it was fortunate that New Englanders, ignorant of the accepted rules of war, adaptable and unorthodox in their approach to fighting, should have undertaken such a potentially difficult military assignment.

The actual landing took place on May 11. The shock troops were the Massachusetts Indians who had volunteered, men regarded as expendable cannon fodder, and they found it easy to make a landing. They were immediately followed by the less-adventurous Yankees, who quickly shouldered them to the periphery of the operation. It was an easy victory; no invader had been killed or seriously injured or captured. While some New Englanders madly pursued a few fleeing French "as dogs hunt foxes in ye woods," others began to look for plunder — a major reason why so many had volunteered. There was absolutely no discipline in the New England ranks. The volunteers were free to roam wherever they pleased, and roam they did. At this stage, Pepperrell was evidently content to have his men exhaust themselves by dashing off in all directions, for he refused to exert his authority on land, and instead, accompanied by most of his senior officers, he remained on board one of his transports in Gabarus Bay.[4]

By the evening of May 11, some 2,000 New Englanders were ashore within cannon shot of Louisbourg. While the French defenders were awaiting a daring New England thrust under cover of darkness, the more realistic Yankees were celebrating their great victory. As they roasted huge chunks of beef from the French cattle they had killed and washed their meat down with liquor, "There was Singing and

Great Rejoicing." Eventually the exhausted invaders went to sleep: "Wee Lay this Night in the open air — But wee Cut a few boughs to keep Us from the ground. Vastly the most Comfortable Nights Lodging This! Since I left Boston . . . wee should be Carefull to Rejoice in the Lord which has Done all for Us. it was a Very pleasent Evening it was the first time [we] heard any froggs Peep or Birds Sing for there was none at Canso."[5]

It was next planned to attack the Grand Battery, which commanded the mouth of Louisbourg harbour, a good distance from the fortress. John Bradstreet had been so confident the battery was indefensible from any large-scale attack that he had "a number of 42 pound Shott" cast in Boston to fit the forty-two pound French Grand Battery cannon. Even before a proper plan of attack had been drawn up, the indomitable William Vaughan and twelve men captured the formidable battery defended by twenty-eight forty-two-pounders and two eighteen-pounders.[6]

It is not surprising, after the unexpected easy capture of the Grand Battery, to find a New England volunteer rejoicing that "Providence seems to smile on us in every Shape."[7] There was no reasonable justification for such a precipitate abandonment of the Grand Battery by the French. Vaughan had found it gloriously empty. The battery could have been defended against the invaders — not indefinitely, of course, but at least for a respectable period of time. Furthermore, the valuable cannon should have at least been properly spiked. Even the inexperienced New Englanders had little difficulty in drilling them out and eventually using them to bombard Louisbourg.

For most of the New Englanders, the regular siege was the most disconcerting feature of the entire Louisbourg episode. Building siege batteries within shouting distance of the fortress was no easy job; manning these batteries was regarded as a fool's errand. Not only were the men subject to heavy French fire, but many were forced to use artillery for the first time. These amateur gunners all too often double charged their cannon in the hope that the shot would do twice as much damage. And so it often did, but to the wrong side. The bursting of various siege cannon resulted in a considerable number of New England casualties. One officer graphically described the sense of terror experienced by those who fought in the batteries:

We lay much Expos'd and ye french kept a firing small armes and great guns the greatest part of ye Day we had Kild and

wounded sundry men . . . it was such a day as new England
men never see that is very few of them. The bullets flew in
whole Showers as did bombs Cohorns and Cannon as well
from us as from our Enemies. May I have a proper sense of
gods covering me in that day Engagement when whole
showers of Death flew all around me and my company. . . .
The sky being darkened with Sulpher and Smoak.[8]

By May 21, in spite of their arduous siege activities, many of the invaders felt that little real progress had been made against Louisbourg. Morale had never been lower. There were two main reasons for the disillusionment that settled like a giant black cloud over the besieging Yankees late in May. News had reached Pepperrell's headquarters that about twenty volunteers had been "inhumanly butchered" by a scouting party of Micmacs and Frenchmen. Crazed by their hatred of Englishmen, the Micmacs "Scalped and Chopt and Stab'd and Prodigiously mangled" their enemy.[9] Later the same day, an attack against the Island Battery at the mouth of Louisbourg harbour had to be once again postponed. All sorts of vicious rumours began to be circulated, and Bradstreet was singled out for special abuse. It was said that Bradstreet — the man with La Tour blood — was a French spy and that he had ordered the cancellation of the attack on the Island Battery because he had not had time to warn the French defenders. Non – New Englanders were obviously not to be trusted. These rumours only added to the prevailing mood of gloom and disenchantment. A disgusted Commodore Peter Warren, hearing of the anti-Bradstreet gossip, urged Pepperrell: "For God's sake, Sir, put a stop to that disagreeable and ill-grounded suspicion that some unthinking people have pretended (for I can think it no other) to conceive of Collonel Broadstreet, it may otherwise be of fatal consequence to the expedition."[10] Captain George Curwen, one of Pepperrell's officers, glumly noted in a letter: "I must honestly tell you, yt if I was at home, I would not come again in this capacity, for we meet with a great deal of trouble."[11] Another New Englander observed to his father: "I am sorry to find our New England troops . . . Say that they want to go home, home is all ye Cry and if I was well at home, I'l ingage? They should never find me such a fool again this is the Language of those who are well Us'd as can be."[12]

In the following days morale continued on its downward trend. On

Sunday, May 23, some of the ministers who accompanied the expedition used the slaughter of the twenty New Englanders as the basis of their sermons. One preached from the text "for itt is a Pinted for Man once to Die," another from "thou are weigh'd in ye Ballances and found wanting."[13] The morbid sense of introspection emphasized by the ministers had only served to undermine morale even further. The troops began to be aware of the proximity of death as never before. Who would be the next man to be scalped by the Indians? When would a French cannon shot or an exploding New England cannon cut off another life? Some of the volunteers demanded to be returned home as "the smell of gun-Powder made them sick." Others were somewhat relieved when they discovered that they had dysentery and were therefore able to remain hospitalized in the camp. Others turned to rum in an attempt to flee from reality.[14] The fighting spirit of the invaders had been replaced by a feeling of defeat and war-weariness.

Only when the French warship, the sixty-four-gun *Vigilant*, was captured by Warren's blockading force on May 30 did morale significantly improve. The taking of the *Vigilant* was one of the turning points in the siege. If the vessel had been able to sail into Louisbourg, its men, guns, ammunition, and supplies would have dramatically upset the delicate balance of the siege.[15] The capture of the *Vigilant*, furthermore, strengthened Commodore Warren's position in his hard bargaining with his close friend Pepperrell. The men had known one another for almost a decade, but their friendship was strained during the siege. Warren, like Pepperrell, was looking for a colonial governorship and he, of course, wanted to be the man finally responsible for Louisbourg's capture. He understandably wanted the glory and fame and the ensuing rewards. But before Warren's fleet could sail into the harbour, the Island Battery would have to be dealt with, and he felt that the Yankees could at least do this for him.[16]

Late on Sunday, June 6, about 400 volunteers, most of whom came from Massachusetts, began to make final arrangements for the assault against the Island Battery. The flotilla of whaleboats pushed off from the beach near the Grand Battery just before midnight. The harbour was unusually calm and visibility was more than adequate. The projected landing place was the beach at the northwest corner of the island. As the leading boats ground to a stop on the narrow sandy beach, the volunteers, who had stubbornly selected their own officers, jumped into the water with their scaling ladders. A few who had consumed too much rum immediately bellowed out three hurrahs. The cheers aroused the French in the battery, but not before twelve ladders had been put up against the ten-foot-high walls. The Island Battery contained thirty or thirty-one twenty-eight-pounders, seven swivels, and two ten-inch brass mortars and was garrisoned by approximately 180 men. While the first attackers were landing, the French commanding officer was nervously pacing the platform of the battery. Until the wild hurrahs, he was apparently unaware of the assault, but because of the drunken yells, he had sufficient time to sound the alarm. Almost immediately "the battery was in a blaze from their cannon, swivells and small arms, their langrell cutting boats and men to pieces as they were landing."[17] A participant described the fierce battle in these words:

> *The Enemy played with Cannon upon the Boates which Distroyd Several Boates and Left the men floating on the water. Several Boates Landed their men But ye Enemy being Prepard Slew them at a Strange Rate Some of our Men after they fir'd all their Cartridges Retreated got into their Boates and made their Escape but Some were killd after they had got into yr. Boates. Some Boates Stove against ye Rocks. Some run a Drift. Some of our men fought manfully Till about Sunrise.*[18]

Sixty New Englanders were killed in the engagement and 116 taken prisoner. June 7 was a day of prolonged soul-searching for the invaders. Some of them, convinced that the Island Battery disaster was a clear indication that the Almighty was angry with them, called for a new spirit of repentance. Others, just as convinced that the defeat was meant to show that Louisbourg was, in fact, impregnable, wanted to sail home as quickly as possible. Morale was further undermined, and even Pepperrell was forced to admit, "Now things look'd something dark."[19]

During the first two weeks of June, the New Englanders continued with their siege but with little spirit. Most of the men were despondent, and the general atmosphere of hopelessness infuriated Warren who bitterly complained to Pepperrell, "For God's sake let us do something, and not waste our time in indolence."[20] After the Island Battery had been finally beaten into silence by New England cannon located on the side of the harbour immediately opposite Louisbourg, Pepperrell decided to do something about the indolence. He and Warren planned to lead a land-sea assault on the fortress on June 27. But, just before sunset on June 26, Du Chambon, Louisbourg's governor, decided to negotiate capitulation terms. With fewer than 600 regular troops at his disposal, and considering the widespread damage throughout the fort caused by over 6,000 New England cannonballs and shells, the governor felt that the siege had gone on long enough. Furthermore, he was under considerable pressure from the influential Louisbourg merchants to obtain immediately the best possible terms. These men had a lot to lose if Louisbourg was taken by storm and pillaged by the booty-coveting invaders.[21]

The terms finally agreed upon were extremely generous to the French merchant community, whose members were to be "treated with the utmost humanity, have their personal estate secured to them and have leave to transport themselves and said effects to any part of the French king's dominions in Europe." The French troops and the other residents also received sympathetic treatment. Warren and Pepperrell agreed, for example, that "if there are any persons in the town or garrison which you [Du Chambon] shall desire may not be seen by us, they shall be permitted to go off masked."[22]

Many of the New Englanders were bitter in their denunciation of the capitulation terms. There was "a great Noys and hubbub a mungst the Solders about the Plonder"; these men felt that they had been cheated out of what was rightfully theirs and what, furthermore, had been piously promised them.[23] One Massachusetts volunteer expressed in poetic form his disgust and that of most of his fellows:

Faire Well Cape:Britton
faire well all you fases
that Bread Such Dis:greases
against Solders that are True to their King
for I Boldely Do Say
If they once git a way
You Will Be hard Poot to it to Catch them agin.[24]

In the early afternoon of June 28, Warren's ships began to sail slowly into Louisbourg harbour. At four o'clock, before Warren's marines had landed, Pepperrell ordered his men to enter the fortress of Louisbourg: "The Colours were flying the Drums Beating Trumpets Sounding Flutes & Viols Playing Col Bradstreet att ye Head of the

Army The Genl. Lt. Genl. and Gentry in ye Rear."[25] With the landing of Warren's marines, bickering began in earnest between the New Englanders and the British regarding who was in fact responsible for the fall of Louisbourg.[26] The bickering had begun early in the siege when some British marines came ashore and denounced the Yankees for their military incompetence. This tactless and abrasive British sense of superiority infuriated the sensitive volunteers whose fathers had experienced the same British arrogance in 1707 during the unsuccessful Massachusetts attack on Port Royal. But both the British regulars and the Yankee volunteers should have realized that, as Thomas Hutchinson maintained, "neither would have succeeded alone," and that, as was remarked about another North American military episode, "there would appear in this celebrated campaign fully as much guid luck as guid guiding."[27]

It is noteworthy that the siege proper took so few lives. Only 53 French troops and 101 New Englanders were killed.[28] The capture of Louisbourg in 1745, which one Massachusetts resident declared "can scarce be parallel'd in History,"[29] showed what could be accomplished by a combined Anglo-American force and a combined sea and land force. But it also demonstrated that there was a widening chasm developing between Britain and the New England colonies, especially Massachusetts. The volunteers could not readily forget, nor would they permit their many friends at home to forget, the declaration of Captain Macdonald, commanding officer of the marines, that "the soldrs did not march as hansome as old regular troops, their toes were not turnd enough out, etc."[30] Nor would they soon stop complaining about what they conceived to be the callous disregard for their interests in the matter of booty.

The news of the capture of Louisbourg set off wild and unprecedented celebrations throughout New England. Never before had the inhabitants seen such brilliant displays of fireworks, such "universal and unaffected joy," such vast supplies "of good Liquor for all that would drink."[31] For some Massachusetts residents, the success against Louisbourg showed that "ye God of Heaven" was in fact "ye God of New England," since "the finger of God has been so conspicuous in every circumstance of this expedition."[32] The Reverend Charles Chauncy of Boston, in his "Thanksgiving Sermon for the Reduction of Cape Breton," declared: "I scarce know of a Conquest, since the days of Joshua and the Judges, wherin the Finger of God is more visible. . . .

The Lord hath *done great things* for us. The God of Jeshurun *hath rode upon the Heaven in our help, and in his Excellency on the Skie*. And this wonderful Appearance of God for us, should excite our Love, warm our Devotion, confirm our Faith and encourage our Hope."[33] For a brief moment Louisbourg brought together pro- and anti-Great Awakening factions, which had been previously at each other's throats. Because of their shared belief that the Almighty had reached down in June and given His people an extraordinary military victory, the two warring groups had at last found some common ground. For some of the Massachusetts New Lights, or Evangelicals, the stunning Louisbourg victory paradoxically triggered a growing interest in the West. They saw themselves compelled to spread their brand of the Gospel westward across the continent until their God "extends his empire from the *Eastern* to the *Western* Sea, and from the River of Canada to the Ends of *America*."[34]

The Louisbourg episode also strengthened a widespread view in Massachusetts that the colonial volunteer was a better soldier than the British regular. The Almighty may have been directly responsible for the capture of the French fortress, but it was contended that the "Supreme Contriver, Mover and Director" used the best instruments available – the New England volunteers – to achieve His goal.[35] The expedition must have strengthened in Massachusetts what Professor Daniel Boorstin has referred to as the "long-standing American myth of a constantly prepared citizenry."[36] Pragmatic Massachusetts volunteers brought up in the free and easy environment of colonial militia training had captured a fortress carefully designed by some of the faithful disciples of the famous French military engineer Vauban. Some of these volunteers were probably aware of the common saying in military circles in western Europe, "Ville assiégée par Vauban, ville prise; ville fortifiée par Vauban, Ville imprenable."[37] The New Englanders were proud as peacocks when they read the frequently reprinted paragraph from the British publication, *The Craftsman*: "But while I contemplate the virtues of the *New Englishmen*, I grieve and blush at the reproach of the *Old*, and I cannot conclude . . . without observing, that if a neglect of public *justice* prevails much longer in this land, we may possibly have reason to think this country no safe abode, and may find it necessary to seek a refuge in *New England*, where *justice* and *industry seem to have taken their residence*."[38] Nor could they forget the memorable pronouncement made by Morpain,

Louisbourg's port captain, "He tho[ught] the N. England men were cowards — but now he th[ought] that if they had a pick Ax and Spade — they would dig their way to Hell and storm it."[39]

In the Massachusetts response to the capture of Louisbourg, there was not only an articulate sense of Yankee moral superiority but also a clear manifestation of the conviction that New Englanders were, in fact, physically superior to European inhabitants. The Yankee volunteers were equal to "four times their number of regular troops"; they shot straighter, "picking off the enemy with their small arms from their walls in the city."[40] Unlike the British regulars, they were not given to "intemperances or universally debauched in their manners."[41] Instead, the New Englanders were "filled with more resolution" and were unequalled in their physical prowess.[42] One poetic correspondent to the *Boston Evening Post* felt moved to declare in July, 1745:

> *When Christian Lewis comes*
> *to hear what's done,*
> *With his strong fortress*
> *on the Isle Breton,*
> *He'll swear the valour*
> *of the British breed,*
> *In Western climes*
> *their grandsires far exceed.*[43]

This expression of New England moral and physical superiority seemed to flow directly and naturally into a new and dynamic feeling of Massachusetts community solidarity. All classes and groups, it was argued, had worked together to bring about the victory, and virtually everyone in Massachusetts joined together to celebrate the glorious joint endeavour. According to the *Boston Evening Post*, "The churl and niggard became generous and even the poor forgot their poverty," while the *Boston Gazette* observed, "The people of all ranks arose from their beds to joy and thanksgiving, and each one severally contributed their part . . . with a surprising decency and good order."[44] The Louisbourg episode was a decisive event in the historical development of Massachusetts, and in it there may be seen a cautious but nevertheless distinct secular provincial awareness. There was a new confidence in the air in Massachusetts — a new confidence in things American — as the colony moved away from its "theocratic" and recently turbulent past into the increasingly complex secular world of the 1750s.[45]

With the sense of Massachusetts superiority precipitated by Louisbourg and the new community solidarity and awareness, it is not surprising that many inhabitants violently objected to the attempt made by Warren "to take upon himself the chief command on Shoar" and to give the impression that his naval force had been entirely responsible for Louisbourg's surrender. As far as Shirley was concerned, and he was probably reflecting the point of view of most Massachusetts residents, Warren's policy was "an unwarrantable usurpation." Eventually Pepperrell, who was disturbed because of the powerful anti-Warren movement in Massachusetts, endeavoured to pour oil on the troubled waters by explaining that in spite of Warren's indiscretions, "These disputes are all over, as we both aim at ye good and security of this place."[46] Nevertheless, a large number of Yankees found it difficult to forgive Warren and his officers for their effrontery and seemingly brazen attempt to steal the spotlight from Pepperrell's volunteers.

When the British authorities heard about Louisbourg's fall, they did not hesitate to reward Warren, Pepperrell, and Shirley. Warren was promoted to the rank of rear-admiral and appointed Cape Breton's first English governor. Pepperrell was the first colonial to be granted a baronetcy, and he and Shirley also secured potentially profitable regimental commissions in the regular British army. Moreover, it was understood that in due course the British government would reimburse the various colonial governments for most of the expenses incurred in carrying out the Louisbourg expedition.

In July, August, and September, 1745, while many inhabitants in the thirteen colonies and Great Britain had been joyously celebrating Louisbourg's capture, the New England troops in Louisbourg were on the verge of mutiny. They continued to complain about not sharing as booty the considerable French private property they had originally been promised. Instead, they were humiliated by being "forst to Stand att there Dores to gard them."[47] These complaints were even more vociferous in August when Warren's ships had little difficulty in capturing three French vessels loaded with exotic goods and precious metals on their way home via Louisbourg from the East Indies. It was estimated that the total value of these ships was no less than £600,000 sterling.[48] The New Englanders received not one shilling of this prize money. They were understandably furious; one complained: " 'Tis Galling ... that the army should both fight for and afterwards Guard The City and yet they have none of the [Plunder] ... which Cost the Men of War nothing more than go and meet them which we could do was the City afloat."[49] What made the New Englanders even angrier was the fact that Warren's men, when on shore, strutted about and bragged about their prize money and good fortune. In contrast, "barefootd and their cloths tore almost in pieces," the Yankees had to be satisfied with their inadequate food rations and the hated boring garrison duty.[50] Most of the New Englanders by the early autumn of 1745 had had enough excitement and disappointment to last them a lifetime. They wanted to return home; their reaction to the Louisbourg episode was remarkably similar to the response of those Massachusetts residents who had been involved in the successful Port Royal expeditions of 1690 and 1710. It is noteworthy that in the various eighteenth-century joint expeditions against Nova Scotia – Cape Breton, there was considerable tension over the distribution of booty and the question of prolonged garrison duty. There was also thrust to the surface a recurring intense bitterness between the forces of Old and New England.

To deal with the explosive situation confronting him, Pepperrell urged Shirley to come to Louisbourg; he also wisely increased the rum ration to his troops. Pepperrell in addition permitted a surprisingly large number of his men to return to their homes in New England, hoping thus to get rid of the worst troublemakers. Consequently, by mid-September over 1,200 of the original Massachusetts and New Hampshire volunteers had returned home, leaving only about 2,000 to help defend the fortress. Later reinforcements, most of whom were likely conscripted, increased this number to 2,250 in November and 2,623 in December, 1745.[51]

Shirley, who arrived in Louisbourg harbour on August 27, did not return to Boston until December. His coming to Cape Breton indicated the seriousness of the morale problem facing Pepperrell. It showed too Shirley's extraordinary interest in the general region. No other Massachusetts governor, while in office, had ever visited Nova Scotia – Cape Breton. Shirley's obsession with the area and the emergency situation there impelled him to forget about the many dangers involved in making the trip. His sojourn there had a certain symbolic impor- tance: he wished to assert some Massachusetts control over the former

French territory and to neutralize some of Warren's growing influence. By increasing the monthly salaries of the Massachusetts troops and by promising all those who would winter in Louisbourg adequate clothing and food supplies as well as their discharges as soon as the British garrison arrived in 1746, Shirley, according to the official records of the Council of War, "quite appeased the late spirit of discontent." He also "put to . . . a stop . . . the Proceedings of the new Court of Vice Admiralty, and intended Sale of French Ships at Cansoe" and thereby helped to provide approximately £7 booty for each volunteer.[52]

It was a disastrous winter in Louisbourg for Pepperrell's Massachusetts troops. He wrote to Shirley on February 8, 1746: "From ye last of Nov. to this date we have buried 561 men, and have at this time 1100 sick. We flatter ourselves from ye burials of three or four days past not amountg to more than 3, 4, & 5, of a day, wn before were generally from 14 to 17, that the distemper abates." The epidemic, feeding upon the low resistance of the men brought about by excessive drinking and inadequate housing, did not, however, actually abate in February. Pepperrell had to admit in June, 1746, that "about 1200" troops had died. When the British regulars arrived in May, 1746, those Massachusetts citizens who had not enlisted in either Pepperrell's or Shirley's regiments sailed for home. They had had more than enough of the foggy, desolate deathtrap. In the future when they thought about Nova Scotia–Cape Breton, they remembered those seemingly endless gloomy epidemic days.[53] This experience, together with the negative aspects of the siege, significantly coloured the image of the region which they propagated on their return to New England. And this distorted image was superimposed upon an already unfavourable perception shared by many.

The Louisbourg expedition had driven the Massachusetts government to virtual bankruptcy. Because of inadequate accounts and because of a difference of opinion regarding the actual value in terms of sterling of the Massachusetts paper money used to pay for the expedition, it was not until 1748 that the British government decided on the actual sums to be reimbursed to the various New England colonies. In that year Massachusetts received £183,649.2.7, New Hampshire £16,355.13.4, Connecticut £28,863.19.1, and Rhode Island £16,322.12.10.[54]

The British authorities hoped that the massive injection of capital in 1749 would temper somewhat Massachusetts' disappointment at seeing Louisbourg returned to France, a stipulation of the Treaty of Aix-la-Chapelle of October, 1748. Massachusetts, on hearing of the official terms of the treaty early in 1749, was not taken entirely by surprise. Throughout 1748 the Boston newspapers had been preparing it for the shock.[55] A poem published in May, 1749, in the *Boston News-Letter* probably reflected the general Massachusetts response to the Treaty of Aix-la-Chapelle:

> *Vanquish'd by Peace, that Heros like withstood,*
> *Loud thund'ring Cannons, mix'd with Streams of Blood.*
> *The Gallics triumph — their Recess so short*
> *Joyful return, to that late conquer'd Fort,*
> *Where Monuments of English Arms will shew,*
> *When Time may serve, ye shall our Claims renew,*
> *New England's Fate insult! The Day is Yours,*
> *Constrain'd, we yield the Conquest that was ours.*[56]

Many Massachusetts residents must have felt betrayed and insulted on hearing of the return of Louisbourg. It was assumed that New Englanders would not respond as enthusiastically in another war against France. In such a war, Louisbourg, of course, would have to be recaptured, and as far as some Yankees were concerned, "The lobster backs could jolly well do the job themselves."[57] Besides, it seemed clear that more and more Massachusetts residents were turning their attention to the West — the "Rising American Empire." To these people, Nova Scotia was little more than an economic, political, and social backwater with a limited future and potential.

There were at least a few Massachusetts residents who viewed Cape Breton Island in French hands in quite a different kind of perspective than did the vast majority of colonists. Before the war, some of these merchants had carried on an extensive illicit trade with Louisbourg and were thus able, among other things, to penetrate the valuable French West Indies market. With Louisbourg once again under French control, such a trade could be and was resumed in earnest.[58] Such a readily available trade entrepôt provided the means to pierce cleanly through the tangle of English trade regulations.

The Louisbourg episode, including the return of the fortress to the French, and the anti-British bitterness engendered in Massachusetts in 1746 and 1747 because of the ruthless activities of the British navy's press gangs, had combined to produce a deep resentment in the colony against Great Britain.[59] While the chasm between Old and New England had evidently widened, there was also in Massachusetts a new sense of colonial moral and physical superiority and a dynamic awareness of community cohesiveness. Convinced that they were indeed the Almighty's special instruments for transforming the New World into a New Jerusalem, a growing number of influential residents became increasingly confident in what seemed to them to be their superior innate abilities and their superior way of life. The Louisbourg episode, which was far more than the military assault alone, should be viewed as a kind of catalyst producing a major change in the collective mood of Massachusetts.

The Louisbourg events did not make Governor Shirley forget about peninsular Nova Scotia. What had disturbed Shirley most about affairs there in the latter part of 1744 had been what he conceived to be the unforgivably traitorous behaviour of many of the Acadian inhabitants. Since he believed that they had supported with enthusiasm two attacks on Annapolis Royal late in October, 1744, he proposed to "take satisfaction of such of the French Inhabitants as have already revolted from their allegiance and join'd the French Enemy, by destroying and burning their Settlements and taking them prisoners, and to take hostages from among them, who have not yet revolted to be deliver'd to the Garrison as pledges for the fidelity of the Country."[60] What Shirley did not realize, or refused to realize, was that the vast majority of the approximately 10,000 Acadians inhabiting Nova Scotia had carefully walked the knife-edge of neutrality in 1744 and that only a handful had actually participated in the French-Indian attacks on Annapolis Royal. The Acadians may still have had some emotional ties with France at the outbreak of King George's War, but these ties were certainly of secondary importance when compared with the deep-grained Acadian pragmatic sense and their positive brand of neutrality. They had been ground between the millstones of contending imperial forces for so long, and they had no assurance that the French were capable of recapturing Nova Scotia. Consequently, most of them were content to live under what they referred to as the existing "mild and tranquil government" of the British at Annapolis Royal.[61]

Shirley's plan to teach the Acadians a lesson they could not readily forget was clearly an invasion of Paul Mascarene's sovereignty over

Nova Scotia. Obviously, Shirley felt that the sixty-year-old Mascarene's conciliatory policy towards the Acadians had failed and that much stronger measures were required. Shirley, in proclaiming his tough anti-Acadian policy, was not, in fact, responding to a fellow governor's urgent request for assistance. Rather, Shirley was blatantly seizing the strategic initiative in his friend's colony in an attempt to establish his and Massachusetts' suzerainty over Nova Scotia.

At the end of October, 1744, Shirley despatched a fleet of three small vessels to Annapolis Royal to carry out his tough Acadian policy. With the arrival of these ships, Mascarene was faced with an extremely thorny problem:

> [Shirley] felt that force alone would be sufficient to solve the annoying problem of the Acadians but Mascarene realized that such a method would only add to the difficulties as a punitive expedition against the Acadians would have served only to drive them to the French. This Mascarene was determined to prevent at all costs ... this ill-conceived plan would have wrecked in one day Mascarene's four years of patient conciliation. But how could Mascarene say no to Governor Shirley upon whom he depended to so great an extent? Mascarene was caught between his own beliefs and the forceful ideas of Shirley; he had to protect the Acadians but at the same time, he could not afford to alienate the Massachusetts governor.[62]

After discussing Shirley's proposal with the Annapolis Royal Council of War, Mascarene ordered the Massachusetts fleet to return to Boston. He observed to Captain Tyng, commander of the *Province Galley*: "It is very unlucky that the Season being so far advanc'd doth not allow you to go up the Bay. . . . I dare not urge it out of regard to yt Province of the Massachusetts as in case of any misfortune it might be thought the risk was out of proportion to the Service it perform'd."[63] Mid-November, of course, was not too late for an expedition against the Acadians to set out from Annapolis Royal. Mascarene, however, wished to give the impression that his decision was based upon a concern for the Massachusetts vessels. Shirley must have seen through Mascarene's flimsy excuse, but there was little the Massachusetts governor could do in late November to rectify the situation. He nevertheless tried to squeeze some face-saving political capital from the aborted assault attempt. In a letter to the Duke of Newcastle he contended that this fleet "must have struck such a terror into the french inhabitants of Nova Scotia as will discourage 'em from any thoughts of open Acts of Hostility for the present, and has already had the Effect to make 'em send Deputies to the Garrison, with Professions of their unshaken Allegiance & to open a free Communication between them and the Garrison for fresh Provisions & Material for finishing the Works of the Fort."[64] It was not Shirley's show of force which had been responsible for the return of some semblance of stability in the various Acadian communities. It was Mascarene's enlightened conciliatory policy and the sudden, disorganized retreat of the French invaders that had persuaded most of the Acadians that to abandon their carefully conceived policy of neutrality would be both stupid and disastrous.

The response of the Acadians to his show of force did not satisfy Shirley for long. In January, 1745, he exclaimed to the Duke of Newcastle that the Acadians "ought to be look'd upon (be their pretensions what they will) as ready in their Hearts to join with the Enemy, whenever a French force sufficient in their Imagination to subdue it shall appear in their Country."[65] Even while planning the Louisbourg expedition, Shirley had showed that he was determined to find a final drastic solution, if necessary, for the Acadian problem.

While the New Englanders were beginning to lay siege to Louisbourg in the middle of May, a combined French-Indian force numbering between 600 and 700 men was besieging Annapolis Royal. Like a bright flickering light attracting a moth, the Nova Scotia fort in 1744 and 1745 seemed to attract besieging French-Indian forces. The 1745 assault provided the most serious military threat to the fort during the war, but as was the case with the two earlier attacks, there seemed relatively little hope for a French victory as long as the invaders did not have any siege cannon.[66] On May 28 French hopes for success received an unexpected stimulus with the capture of two armed Massachusetts vessels, the *Montague* and the *Seaflower*, four miles below the fort. The *Montague* carried eight cannon and fourteen swivel guns, and for the first time the French could consider, at least, undertaking a formal siege. Realizing the seriousness of his situation, the distraught Mascarene could only send a whaleboat to Boston (he had no other ship to use) with letters to Shirley begging him for immediate assistance. John Henry Bastide, the fort's engineer, pleaded, "Pray hasten a man of War to us."[67]

What could Shirley do under the circumstances? Almost all of the available military resources of Massachusetts had already been channelled into the Louisbourg expedition. But Shirley did not want to see the French driven from Cape Breton at the same time the English were losing, as he later put it, "Annapolis Royal and the whole province of Nova Scotia to the French."[68] He therefore suggested to the commanding officer of the ex-Canso regulars, then stationed at Boston, that they break the terms under which they had been exchanged in order to ensure Annapolis Royal's "greater security and Defence against the Enemy." Shirley also sent a letter to Warren demanding that two ships be sent to Annapolis Royal "in order to deterr the inhabitants of Nova Scotia from revolting and joining with the enemy."[69]

Before the eighty or so ex-Canso regulars arrived at Annapolis Royal, the French had already lifted their siege. On June 3 a messenger from the governor of Louisbourg reached Annapolis with instructions to the commanding officer, Lieutenant Marin, urging him to come to Louisbourg "as quickly as possible . . . with the Canadien and Indian force that you command."[70] Marin's troops never reached the French fortress. When Louisbourg officially fell into Anglo-American hands on June 28, Marin's relieving force was encamped near Tatamagouche harbour on Northumberland Strait — at least a week's travelling distance from Louisbourg.

It was Shirley's Louisbourg policy, not his sending of the ex-Canso troops or his letter to Warren, that had been directly responsible for the lifting of the third French-Indian siege of Annapolis Royal. Shirley's long-term strategy had worked out superbly. By applying pressure at Louisbourg, he had relieved and protected the vulnerable Annapolis Royal. In the larger North American context, he was certain that his vigorous offensive policy had stopped the French from gaining control of "the whole Fishery and chief Navigation of those Seas" and "such a Footing upon the Northern Continent of America as might possibly in time make 'em think of disputing the Mastery of it with the Crown of Great Britain."[71]

With the capture of Louisbourg, the Acadians, the French officials in New France, and William Shirley and Peter Warren were all considering the implications of the expulsion of thousands of Nova

Scotia French inhabitants.[72] A growing number of Acadians and the New France officials feared that the support given to Marin by a tiny minority of the Acadians would encourage the English to adopt drastic retaliatory measures. Shirley and Warren were keen to remove any possible threat of a future French counteroffensive from the Nova Scotia–Cape Breton region. They felt that the French would be far less likely to attack Nova Scotia if they could not anticipate obtaining the overt support of thousands of French-speaking inhabitants. Besides, only if a large number of the Acadians were removed from their fertile farmlands could Shirley and Warren expect Anglo-American farmers to move in to "settle Nova Scotia upon a better foot for the future."[73] Only Mascarene seemed to favour a continuation of his conciliatory policy, the continuation of which amazed the governor and intendant of New France who reported to the minister of marine: "This policy appears to us extraordinary in the present conjuncture. We do not clearly perceive its motives, unless Mr. Mascarene calculates that mild measures will be more effectual than any other to detach the affections of the Acadians from France."[74]

By the late summer of 1745 Mascarene must have realized that it would be just a matter of weeks or months before Shirley would attempt to force his tough Acadian policy upon Nova Scotia. Events in 1745 had further strengthened Shirley's and Massachusetts' hold on the neighbouring colony. When the chips were down, Shirley and Massachusetts always delivered, and this growing dependence of Nova Scotia on Massachusetts would have to be paid for in one way or another. In November part of that payment had been decided upon — the expulsion of the Acadians.

On November 19, 1745, the Nova Scotia Council met at Annapolis Royal to consider the report of a committee appointed to investigate the general state of the colony. The committee members, some of whom were unquestionably influenced by Shirley, were extremely critical of the behaviour of the Acadian inhabitants during the three French-Indian invasions. Their arguments were precisely those Shirley had put forward earlier. The report concluded:

Upon consideration of the above Several Indisputable Facts, if they are not absolutely to be regarded as utter Enemies to His Majesty's Government they cannot be accounted less than unprofitable Inhabitants for their conditional Oath of

Allegiance will not entitle them to the Confidence and
Privileges of Natural British Subjects nor can it even be
expected in several generations especially whilst they have
French Priests among them. . . . Upon the whole it is most
humbly Submitted whether the said French Inhabitants may
not be transported out of the Province of Nova Scotia and
be replac'd by good Protestant Subjects.[75]

The debate over the merits of the report revealed a deep split
between Mascarene and the Council members, who were quite content
to accept Shirley's diagnosis and remedy. The phrasing of the report, in
fact, suggested that some of the Council members had carefully read
some of Shirley's correspondence regarding the Acadians. The
Council's unanimous decision to accept the committee's statement
further strengthened Shirley's hand and was a sharp repudiation of
Mascarene's conciliatory approach. What the Council members did on
November 19 was to declare publicly that with respect to the most
crucial problem facing their colony, they had no faith in their civil
and military commander. They had chosen to follow William Shirley
rather than Paul Mascarene. For them the political implications of
strategic and commercial realities could not be indefinitely evaded in
Nova Scotia, particularly at Annapolis Royal.

Mascarene waited for almost a month before he made Shirley
aware of his position concerning the Council proposal. In a carefully
conceived letter to the Massachusetts governor, Mascarene sought to
find some middle ground between his humane policy and the
anti-Acadian point of view in the Council report. He perceptively
observed that "it is less to be wonder'd att that the Enemy has so much
influence on this People lately as that he has not had much more."
For Mascarene, the Acadians were grasping at some form of identity
as they shifted about in a distressing kind of limbo between allegiance
to the king of France and the king of Great Britain. He looked at
them "as grafted in the Body of the British Nation as an unsound limb,
indeed, and therefore to be nurtured, and by time and good care to be
brought to answer the purposes expected from them; first to become
Subjects and after that good Subjects." The bilingual old Huguenot
realized that the process of making the French-speaking, Acadian
Roman Catholics into sound British subjects would be slow and
frustrating. But in his estimation it was certainly worth the effort. He

felt that there were excellent legal, strategic, and practical reasons why the expulsion should not take place, and he was hopeful that once Shirley considered these he would eventually abandon his plan. Yet if Shirley chose to disregard his advice, Mascarene was willing to accept "such a revolution . . . to be effected as most tending to the Publick Service." And as far as Mascarene was concerned, if Shirley finally decided to expel the Acadians, the Massachusetts governor was to do so without involving Nova Scotia in the nasty business. Mascarene had washed his hands of what he considered to be the inhumane aspects of Shirley's proposal.[76] In the process, he had surrendered to Shirley the ultimate right to govern in Nova Scotia.

In early 1746 Shirley's continued interest in Nova Scotia affairs, as expressed in his vigorous anti-Acadian policy, was an indication of the strategic importance he still placed on the region. This interest was also the means by which he could advance his own position in Nova Scotia at the expense of Mascarene and the absentee governor, Richard Philipps. Bluntly stated, Shirley wanted the governorship of Nova Scotia, and he was willing to use the Acadian issue to undermine Mascarene and Philipps. In a letter written to Newcastle in February, 1746, Shirley, as tactfully as possible, drove knives into the backs of these two men:

> Mr. Mascarene and his Council have not so good an harmony subsisting between them as could be wish'd, and that all the Officers have of late differ'd in Sentiments with him, particularly upon the Behaviour of the French inhabitants. . . . But I think there may be still danger of too much tenderness toward 'em on his part, and perhaps rigour on theirs in carrying any Orders of his Majesty's into Execution; So that by their Jarring, the Execution of the Orders may possibly be Obstructed, if they are left to themselves.

Only one man could introduce harmony at Annapolis Royal and only one man could effectively implement British imperial policy in Nova Scotia — and that man was the governor of Massachusetts. It was contended moreover that the rapidly deteriorating situation in Nova Scotia had been encouraged by "their Chief Governor's Age and health, and other Circumstances" and his not being "Upon the Spott."[77]

Shirley waited early in 1746 for the governorship to be offered to him by a grateful Newcastle. When it was not immediately forth-coming, the Massachusetts governor ordered his son, William, Jr., then in London, to petition for it. William, Jr., maintained that his father's "sole motive for applying for an appointment to the Govern-ment in present arrises from his Apprehensions that the preservation of that province [Nova Scotia] to his Majesty may depend upon a Speedy Settlement of it, a Service which Mr. Phillips on account of his great Age cannot be suppos'd capable of undertaking." Shirley's son then cut to the heart of his father's motives when he declared that since Shirley had "the Trouble of Settling" Nova Scotia's problems, "he hope[d] it will not be thought unreasonable that he should have the Benefits arising from it."[78] Newcastle rejected Shirley's request and urged him to wait patiently until Philipps died.

Newcastle's unexpected rebuff did not cause Shirley to lose interest in Nova Scotia. If anything, his concern intensified when he learned in the summer and autumn of 1746 that the French were planning a major counteroffensive to regain Louisbourg, to drive the English from Nova Scotia, and then to ravage the New England coast. This intelligence discouraged Shirley from pursuing his expulsion policy. In fact, by late August, the Massachusetts governor had already decided to accept Mascarene's conciliatory Acadian policy. Rather than expelling the French-speaking Roman Catholics, he decided that Anglicizing them would be a far wiser policy. By bringing in large numbers of English-speaking immigrants and by sending French-speaking Protestant teachers to the Acadian communities, Shirley hoped that "a sense of the true Protestant religion" would be cultivated together with a deep attachment to the British Crown.[79]

It was June 22, 1746, when the French expedition organized by the French minister of marine finally set sail for Nova Scotia. It consisted of ten ships of the line, three frigates, three bomb vessels, and approximately sixty transports carrying 3,500 regular troops. The fleet, under the command of the Duc d'Anville, sighted land on September 15, and a few days later most of d'Anville's ships lay anchored in the commodious Chebucto harbour at present-day Halifax. D'Anville was disheartened by his prospects. At least two of his frigates had been forced to return to France, and a terrible epidemic was sweeping the remaining ships, most of which had been badly battered by unusually severe North Atlantic storms. It has been estimated that by the end of September, no fewer than 2,300 French soldiers and sailors had died from scurvy and smallpox.[80]

On September 20 Shirley, who knew only of the arrival of "two large French ships" at Chebucto and of the landing of an undetermined number of French troops under the command of de Ramezay from Quebec at the northern extremity of the Chignecto Isthmus, asked the General Court to once again send reinforcements to Nova Scotia. He argued:

> *The danger which these motions of the enemy threaten us with will arise not from their present number, but our suffering 'em to continue in the province of Nova Scotia till they have gained over the French inhabitants (already ripe for a revolt) to join with 'em in attacking his Majesty's garrison, which may yet be prevented (as it has already most happily been twice before upon the appearance of succours from this government) by seasonably sending a sufficient strength of his Majesty's troops intended for the expedition against Canada to Annapolis Royal to drive the Canadeans ought of Nova Scotia, which seems not difficult to be done at present.*[81]

The General Court agreed to send reinforcements "provided there be fifteen hundred of said troops employed for the expedition to Crown Point, and your Excellency can give assurance that none shall be compelled nor allowed to remain in garrison at Nova Scotia or as a standing force for the protection thereof; and that no part of the pay, subsistence, nor charges of transporting them shall lay upon the Province." The members of the General Court were still unaware on September 20 and 21 of the size of the French fleet, and their response to Shirley showed that in spite of what the members admitted was "the exposed and hazardous condition of the province of Nova Scotia," they nevertheless regarded the planned offensive against Crown Point to the west to be of primary importance. Annapolis Royal was, in their estimation, of secondary concern to Massachusetts.[82]

It was probably only on the last day of September that Shirley received news about d'Anville's fleet. By this time Shirley had evidently despatched only 250 new troops to Annapolis Royal. The intelligence reports made Shirley forget about Nova Scotia for a moment and prepare instead for the defence of Massachusetts.[83] The inhabitants of the colony were terror stricken on hearing the news;

Thomas Hutchinson observed, "England was not more alarmed with the Spanish Armada in 1588 than Boston and the other North American seaports were with the arrival of this fleet in their neighbourhood."[84] Pious men dropped to their knees to petition the Almighty to destroy the French armada, while more practical men improved the coastal defences "so we may be ready to receive the enemy if they should come this Way."[85] An estimated 6,500 colonial troops from the interior were rushed to the coast to repel the anticipated assault.[86]

With Massachusetts actually threatened, nobody in the colony, including the governor, wanted to send Massachusetts soldiers to Annapolis Royal. Mascarene would have to make do with the small force at his disposal. Then on November 3 Shirley was informed that the French fleet was "in a very weak condition, and are gone (at least the bulk of them) to France or the West Indies."[87] The Massachusetts divines once again clearly "saw the immediate hand of divine providence in the protection, or rather rescue, of the British Colonies."[88] And Shirley viewed the French naval disaster and retreat as the signal for him to send another 700 men to Nova Scotia, supported by 200 from New Hampshire and 300 from Rhode Island, to "effectually drive the Canadians out of Nova Scotia, free it from the Danger, which may ensue by next Spring, from their Wintering there."[89] Shirley felt that his task was relatively easy, since the troops were already available, having been recruited for the postponed Crown Point expedition, and since they were also already being paid by the British government.

Before the new reinforcements could be sent, the de Ramezay force numbering only 300 Frenchmen from New France and a very small number of Indians attacked Annapolis Royal. The invaders provided no serious threat to the British fort and de Ramezay had no other choice but to wait for the expected French fleet to arrive. It, of course, never reached the Nova Scotia capital, and late on November 3 de Ramezay ordered his men to retreat to the safety of Minas, located at the head of the Bay of Fundy.[90] The overcautious Mascarene decided not to give chase even though it is probable that any concentrated British offensive would have driven the French from Nova Scotia. Shirley was furious when he discovered Mascarene's "indifferen[ce] about pursuing the advantageous Turn, which the Condition of his Majesty's Garrison & Government under his Command has taken, any further till next Spring."[91] The Massachusetts governor wanted an offensive organized immediately, and he proposed to force Mascarene to implement this policy. Shirley's determination was supported by those Massachusetts troops in Annapolis Royal and those in Boston, preparing to sail there, who did not look forward to a winter's confinement in the fort or on board the supply vessels in the basin. They wished to deal with the French threat as quickly as possible and return to their homes.[92]

Prodded by Shirley's sharp rebuke, Mascarene agreed to an early winter offensive and on December 16 ordered that 500 men, most of them from Massachusetts, set out for the Minas region. Under the command of Lieutenant-Colonel Arthur Noble, a Massachusetts veteran of the Louisbourg campaign, the men were to attack de Ramezay's force and then winter among the Acadians. On February 11, 1747, at about three o'clock in the morning in the midst of a blinding snowstorm, Noble's unsuspecting expedition was savagely ambushed near Minas by 240 French Canadians and about sixty Micmacs. Seventy New Englanders were killed, including Noble, and another forty-five were captured. The rest of Noble's men surrendered and marched back to Annapolis, having promised not to return to the Minas-Chignecto area for at least six months.[93]

The news of the "Massacre at Grand Pré," the first serious Massachusetts defeat suffered during the war, further strengthened the position of those men, especially in the General Court, who questioned Massachusetts' growing involvement in Nova Scotia affairs. For these men, Shirley's enthusiasm for the area had overreached reasonable limits. On the other hand, Shirley saw the massacre as convincing proof of Mascarene's total incompetence, a fact he did not hesitate to underline in his correspondence. Largely because of Shirley's intense lobbying, the Duke of Newcastle by the spring of 1747 had formally recognized the Massachusetts governor's "predominance in Nova Scotian affairs and all pretense of deference to Philipps and Mascarene was cast aside."[94] Newcastle consequently ordered Shirley and Charles Knowles, then governor of Cape Breton, to take upon themselves the responsibility for the defence of the Nova Scotia – Cape Breton area. Newcastle assumed that "Mascarene will, as he had already done, follow such orders as he shall receive . . . from Commodore Knowles and yourself [Shirley]."[95] The direction of all Nova Scotia affairs, not merely those dealing with military matters, was placed in the hands of these two men, and of the two, Shirley was clearly the dominant figure. There is almost no mention made of Mascarene in the official correspondence of this period; he was apparently satisfied with his role as Shirley's lackey and was content to permit others to find solutions for his colony's problems. For him as well as for Shirley and Newcastle, Nova Scotia had become a frontier county of Massachusetts.

Shirley's enthusiasm for Nova Scotia was clearly not shared by the members of the General Court, who in June, 1747, for example, demanded that all Massachusetts troops be withdrawn immediately from Nova Scotia.[96] The disconcerted governor reluctantly agreed to their demand. And when in the autumn Shirley asked the Massachusetts House of Representatives to send a vessel to help defend Annapolis Royal, the members showed little enthusiasm for the venture.[97] Shirley seemed oblivious in the summer and autumn of 1747 to the fact that ordinary Massachusetts inhabitants, as reflected in the decisions made by their representatives in the General Court, really were not interested in Nova Scotia and felt no real obligation to take upon themselves any special responsibility for its care. What Shirley did privately was his own business, but the General Court refused to endorse publicly the governor's obsessive enthusiasm about Nova Scotia. At the grassroots level in Massachusetts, the Louisbourg episode and the impressment riot in Boston, together with the Grand Pré massacre and a growing interest in the future of the West, had flowed together to counter effectively Shirley's northeastern imperialism. In December, 1747, Shirley felt compelled to inform Whitehall that his colony had lost interest in Nova Scotia, and he gloomily predicted that in the future "it will be difficult, if not impossible" to involve Massachusetts in the affairs of its neighbouring colony.[98]

The decision to fortify Halifax on Chebucto Bay to act, among other things, as a counterpoise to Louisbourg, and the appointment in 1749 of Edward Cornwallis as governor of Nova Scotia, were the final crowning blows to Shirley's Nova Scotia aspirations. The British were no longer satisfied in encouraging Nova Scotia's development as a colonial appendage of Massachusetts. In focusing so much attention on the strategic importance of Nova Scotia, Shirley had played a key role in bringing about a new British policy, which ironically destroyed whatever chance he might have had for the Nova Scotia governorship. Halifax and Cornwallis would not respond in the same way to Shirley's influence as Annapolis Royal and Mascarene had done. The construction of Halifax merely confirmed the already decreasing Massachusetts interest in the region. The Halifax British were now a significant buffer between the Louisbourg French and Massachusetts. In any moment of crisis British troops – and of greater importance British warships – would now be readily available to counter any French offensive threat. Massachusetts could, in 1749, feel safe in directing its interests elsewhere. William Shirley, however, still found it difficult to adjust to the new strategic and political realities.

11

William Shirley and Charles Lawrence, 1749-1756

For most New Englanders the Treaty of Aix-la-Chapelle was merely a temporary truce; they anticipated the outbreak of yet another major war that would probably determine, once and for all, which European nation would be supreme in North America. From 1749 to 1755, when hostilities broke out in North America, a year before the formal declaration of war in Europe, there was a growing concern in Massachusetts about the spectre of French encirclement. This widespread fear of what was called the "Encrouchments of our French Neighbours,"[1] and the "Grand Plan for Rendering the French Masters of all of North America,"[2] was concentrated and focused in Massachusetts upon the Gallic threat at Crown Point in the west and at the Chignecto Isthmus in the northeast.

By 1752 Crown Point, located at the southern extremity of Lake Champlain, had replaced Louisbourg in the eyes of some as "the Carthage of New England."[3] It was seen as the major military threat to the colony. Other Massachusetts residents were just as certain that the French troops located at the narrow neck of land joining peninsular Nova Scotia with the North American mainland were the real enemy to worry about, especially since they were in close contact with Louisbourg. These men contended that the French would quickly sweep into Nova Scotia from their Chignecto forts and eventually drive all the English out "of all their other Colonies in North America."[4] In presenting this simplistic argument, these Massachusetts Cassandras were articulating Shirley's strategic thinking that he had evolved during the early months of King George's War. In these two opposing conceptions of military realities was to be found the traditional Massachusetts interest in Nova Scotia in conflict with a new concern with the "Rising American Empire" of the West.

The Aix-la-Chapelle peace ushered in a period of violent political infighting in Massachusetts. Because of the virulent attacks of his enemies, who were determined to have him removed from the governorship, Shirley felt it necessary in September, 1749, to leave for London to defend himself in person. He skilfully countered the criticism directed against him and so impressed the Board of Trade officials that he was appointed to the commission established at Paris to decide upon the boundaries between the French and English in North America.[5] While at Paris, Shirley endeavoured at every opportunity to block any attempt on the part of the French to extend their boundaries in North America. He was particularly concerned with preventing the French from building fortifications in the disputed boundary area between present-day New Brunswick and Nova Scotia. Shirley feared that the French in this territory, once war broke out, would easily attract Indian support, capture Nova Scotia, and then threaten "the Security of New England."[6] But his uncompromising anti-French stance was an embarrassment to the English negotiators at Paris, and in March, 1752, Shirley was recalled to London; in August of the following year, he returned to Boston. Shirley's dismissal, as has been stressed by his most recent biographer, "implied a rebuke for a view of empire upon which he had set his heart as the only true course for Great Britain."[7] It is noteworthy that the rebuke did not shatter Shirley's "Imperial Vision"; rather, his conviction that France had to be driven from North America as soon as possible was substantially reinforced by his Paris experience, and so was his determination to do something about it.

While Shirley was negotiating in Paris, the Massachusetts merchants were re-establishing their commercial relations with Cape Breton and Nova Scotia. What is particularly striking is that New England trade with Louisbourg after the Treaty of Aix-la-Chapelle was much greater than it had been before 1744. In 1740, for example, it was estimated that the New Englanders imported from Louisbourg merchandise worth 70,678 *livres*. In 1752 they imported goods worth no less than

654,680 *livres*. Governor Edward Cornwallis of Nova Scotia estimated in November, 1751, that there had been no fewer than 150 New England vessels trading in Louisbourg during that year.[8] In 1754 Governor Charles Lawrence complained, "We sometimes see six or seven sloops in a day pass by this Harbour [Halifax] Loaded for that place; and we have certain intelligence of Thirty Vessels now in that Harbour who sail'd very lately from Boston loaded with Provisions."[9] By this time Louisbourg had grown dangerously dependent upon New England food supplies. Not only was there extensive New England commerce with the French of Cape Breton, but there was also probably much more trade than before the war with Nova Scotia. The thousands of troops and settlers in the Halifax region needed food and supplies, and in spite of the attractions of Louisbourg, many Acadians continued to trade with Massachusetts merchants. The existence of Halifax may have largely neutralized the political importance of Boston in Nova Scotia affairs, but much of the old economic dependency nevertheless remained.

At least twice while Shirley was in Europe, the governor of Nova Scotia requested Massachusetts' military assistance to facilitate the removal of the Indian-French threat from the Chignecto Isthmus region. This narrow neck of land is bordered on the northeast by Baie Verte, on the southwest by the Cumberland Basin, and on the northwest and southeast by the Sackville and Amherst ridges respectively. For the French the tiny Missiquash River running between the two ridges was the western boundary of Nova Scotia, and they were determined, by the building of Fort Beauséjour near the Cumberland Basin and the smaller Fort Gaspéreau on Baie Verte, to establish their claim to present-day New Brunswick and much of northern Maine.

In December, 1749, Governor Cornwallis proposed to Lieutenant-Governor Spencer Phips of Massachusetts that the General Court organize a "secret" assault on "the Savages" in the Chignecto region.[10] Sylvanus Cobb, a native of Plymouth and veteran of the Louisbourg campaign, was named by Cornwallis to lead the assault. Cornwallis however cancelled the attack because of what he regarded as Phips's unbelievable bungling. "By the first vessel from Boston," a disgusted Cornwallis informed the Duke of Bedford, "I heard that the Council had been assembled, Apthorp and Hancock [Boston merchants] called before them, and the whole affair known all over Boston." On seeing Phips's proclamation urging men to volunteer — "the most extraordinary advertisement ever published" — Cornwallis assumed that the intelligence "must, of course, reach both the French and Indians," and he therefore "judged it prudent to order Cobb not to proceed."[11] In advertising for volunteers, Phips was not committing the General Court to yet another Nova Scotia military adventure. Rather, he was assisting a neighbouring governor who wanted experienced Indian fighters and was willing to pay well for them.

In February, 1751, Cornwallis attempted once again to involve Massachusetts in the defence of his colony. He urged the General Court to join him in checking "the Designs of the French and Indians against Checanecto" in order to protect Massachusetts. Lieutenant-Governor Phips cogently summarized what he regarded as Cornwallis's "most convincing" argument concerning Massachusetts' need to preserve the safety of Nova Scotia, especially the Bay of Fundy area:

> *For if the French should make a strong Settlement on the South Coast in those Parts, and thereby gain a nearer Communication with the Indians on our Frontiers, and have the Opportunity of supplying them with Warlike Stores, and other things The Probability in that Case of the whole Province of Main as well as the Lands between that and the River of St. Croix, being soon swallow'd up by the French, is obvious to every Considerate Person.*[12]

A committee of six members of the General Court, including the hero of the Louisbourg episode, Sir William Pepperrell, met to consider the Cornwallis proposal. In all probability, Pepperrell played a key role in drafting the committee's surprising report. It was agreed that

> *considering the reduced state of this Province, both as to its Inhabitants and Money, by reason of their readiness in sending great numbers of their Men in the Expeditions against Cuba, Cape Breton, and to reinforce Anapolis in the last War, besides many more of its Inhabitants impressed on board His Majesties Ships of Warr and others employed on our large Frontiers for our immediate defence; And ye no small expense we were obliged to be at to defray ye Charge thereof and farther, considering, that it is highly probable this Government will be necessitated to furnish many more of their Men in a Short time for ye defence of its*

frontiers against ye Incursions of their Enemies as Governor
Cornwallis informs he is very apprehensive off, The Comtee
are humbly of Opinion that the Impoverished *state of this*
Province will not admitt that any of its Inhabitants be sent to
Nova Scotia at their own Charge. Nor will the safety of
this Province admitt it tho at the Charge of the Governmt
there which is Submitted.

After deleting the eight emphasized words and inserting a short
clarifying phrase, the General Court accepted the committee's recommendation.[13] What the Court was asserting in February, 1751, was its
independence of Halifax and its special brand of Massachusetts
isolationism. With their Kennebec River northeastern boundary secure,
the members of the General Court saw no good reason to adopt an
offensive policy that could benefit only Cornwallis. They had already
sacrificed enough in the Nova Scotia–Cape Breton area for an apathetic, if not hostile, mother country and, besides, Massachusetts had its
own major problems to solve. Without Shirley's consistent prodding,
the General Court had continued to disengage itself from the affairs
of what had once been known as "New England's Outpost."

When Shirley returned to Boston in August, 1753, he soon
discovered that most members of the General Court lacked his
enthusiasm for an aggressive British–North American imperialism.
Early in the winter session, at the urging of Shirley, the General Court
turned its attention to defence matters. As had happened in February,
1751, a special committee of the General Court under the chairmanship
of William Pepperrell met in early January, 1754, to discuss the
question of the French threat to Massachusetts. The committee members stressed that they were particularly concerned "by the late
Encroachments of the French, especially upon the St. John's River and
the West side of the Bay of Fundy . . . on the Isthmus of the Peninsular
near Bay-Verte" and "at Crown point." To provide "an effectual
Security against future Danger from any . . . Invasions of our French
Neighbours," the committee twice recommended that the British
government "be graciously pleas'd to cause them to be removed."
The "lobsterbacks," in other words, were to take the initiative in
protecting their North American colonies. The report solemnly
concluded: "Being thus expos'd on every side – having a large Frontier
to defend, the doing of which hitherto, has been a great Expence of

Blood and Treasure to us, we are very sensible of the Necessity of his Majestys Colonys affrding each other mutual Assistance, and we make no doubt but this Province will at all times with great Chearfulness, furnish their just and reasonable Quota toward it."[14] After the General Court accepted the Pepperrell committee report, it underlined its Massachusetts-first isolationism by withdrawing financial support for two western frontier forts located on New Hampshire territory.[15]

Shirley, who had suffered a stunning defeat, realized how politically vulnerable he had now become, and he felt it necessary to try to construct a new coalition to consolidate his position. What he needed was a vast new reservoir of patronage to tap. There seemed to be only one possible source, as his experience during King George's War had shown — military expeditions. His skilful distribution of military appointments and contracts had worked minor political miracles in 1744, 1745, and 1746. Could not the same miracle be performed in the same way once again? Shirley's opportunity came in March, 1754, two months before the May elections.

On March 28 Shirley announced to the General Court that he had received reliable intelligence concerning a large-scale French-Indian advance into the Kennebec region. Shirley gloomily predicted: "A Short Delay to dislodge them from their Incroachments near the River *Kennebeck* might give them an Opportunity of making themselves Masters of that River likewise, in the End; And in that Case we may Expect soon to see another Fort Built by them near the Mouth of it and the *French* in Possession of all the Sea Coast between that and the River St. John's."[16] Shirley's proposal for an expedition received enthusiastic support from leading Boston merchants like William Brattle, Thomas Hancock, Robert Temple, William Bowdoin, Charles Apthorp, and Samuel and Edward Gibbon. These influential Bostonians, the Kennebec Proprietors, owned large tracts of land on both sides of the Kennebec and did not want to see their potentially valuable land snatched away from them by anyone, especially the French. Moreover, Shirley's plan appealed to the Maine representatives who were becoming increasingly concerned about possible French-Indian frontier raids.[17] The General Court agreed on April 9 and 10 to "make Provision for the Pay and Subsistence of 500 Men," on condition that Shirley accompany the force. The General Court emphasized that it was not abandoning its isolationist policy but that it was merely "defending His Majesty's Territories against the Encroachments of the

French and the Ravages and Incursions of the Indians."[18]

The excitement generated by the news of the Kennebec expedition certainly assisted in the election of a larger number of Shirley supporters in May. On June 4 the new General Court voted that an additional 300 men be enlisted for the expedition.[19] John Winslow, a fifty-one-year-old native of Marshfield, Plymouth County, was selected by Shirley to command the troops. Winslow had been the captain of provincials in the ill-fated Cuba expedition of 1740 and had served as a regular officer in Governor Richard Philipps's Nova Scotia regiment. As far as the shrewd and calculating Shirley was concerned, Winslow was "extremely well qualify'd for the present Service. He hath the best reputation as a military man of any officer in this province and his character in every respect stands high with the Government and people and he is particularly well esteem'd and belov'd by the Soldiery."[20] He seemed even better qualified for his position than Pepperrell had been in 1745.

Even before the New Englanders sailed for Falmouth in late June, Shirley's "Grand Imperial Design" and his deep-rooted concern for Nova Scotia began to reassert themselves in his strategic thinking. The Kennebec expedition was seen as a giant step in the direction of the establishment of British control over all territory between the Missiquash and the Kennebec. As far as Shirley was concerned, he was simply reoccupying British territory; he was therefore not disobeying his instructions received in August, 1753, from the secretary of state: "But as it is His Majesty's determination not to be the aggressor, I have the King's commands, most strictly to enjoin you, not to make use of the armed force under your direction, excepting within the undoubted limits of his Majesty's dominion."[21] The Massachusetts governor had no doubts about these boundaries regarding Nova Scotia. Once stability was reintroduced in the valley of the Kennebec, according to Shirley, British troops from Halifax, "with the assistance of 1000 Men from New England," were to drive all remaining French troops from the Chignecto Isthmus and the St. John River region. Then "1000 Families . . . from New England . . . or from the North of Ireland" were to be settled at Chignecto, and British forts constructed at the mouths of the St. John and Penobscot rivers. The Acadians from the Chignecto area were to be moved to available land near Annapolis Royal, "where they might be properly look'd after." But they were not to be expelled from the colony. Shirley's policy, which owed much to Mascarene's influence, was intended to transform the Acadians into reliable British subjects:

> This propos'd Settlement in Chignecto, and Fort upon the Isthmus would likewise very much conduce towards reclaiming the Inhabitants of Minas and Annapolis River to a due sense of their Allegiance to his Majesty, and proper disposition towards his Government, by a constant inspection of their behaviour, promoting Traffik and all manner of Intercourse between them and the English, gradually introduce the English manners, customs, and language among them ... [this] might in a few generations make them good Subjects; which they would naturally incline to be, when they found the English would remain Masters of the Province and they could depend upon his Majesty's Government for protection both against the French and Indians.[22]

The June-July Kennebec campaign proved to be a pleasant diversion in an otherwise uneventful Massachusetts summer. Although Winslow's troops thoroughly scoured the Kennebec region, not one Frenchman was found, nor was there discovered any evidence of French military penetration. What Winslow had accomplished was to reassert Massachusetts' sovereignty over the disputed area and to overawe the Indian inhabitants. Shirley was happy to squeeze every ounce of political advantage out of the expedition. Few of the governor's efforts received so much popular acclaim. When he and Winslow returned to Boston early in September, "the vessels in the harbor, the wharves, streets, balconies and windows of the houses, by which his Excellency passed, were crowded with spectators; and there was the greatest concourse and acclamation of the people, that was ever known in Boston, upon this occasion."[23] The Kennebec Proprietors were ecstatic; the Boston merchants welcomed the opportunity to supply the troops; and the fishing and lumbering interests were delighted with the show of force that seemed to reduce a potentially dangerous threat to their investments and to their families.

It was not only the political ramifications of the expedition that were gratifying to Shirley. He observed that there was a sudden surge of interest among some Massachusetts residents concerning his continuing emphasis on Nova Scotia. For example, he heard the distinguished Massachusetts divine, the Reverend Jonathan Edwards, declare: "Tho peace is very desireable, upon just and honourable terms, yet we know very well that God's ancient people were not wont to be frightened out of their possessions. . . . I am sure there is not a true New-England-Man, whose heart is not already engaged in this contest . . . in a cause so just in the sight of God . . . a cause wherein our liberties, our lives, our bodies, our souls, are all so nearly concerned."[24] Shirley and all Massachusetts could read in the *Boston News-Letter* and the *Post-Boy* in early October that once war broke out, Nova Scotia "must unavoidably fall into their [French] Hands." "And if this should be the Case which it probably will very soon," a Halifax correspondent predicted, "you know better than I can tell you the fatal Consequences to all the rest of the British Colonies in North America." He argued that unless the French were removed from Chignecto and the St. John River region immediately, the residents of Massachusetts should "Tremble then not only for our [Nova Scotia] Fate, but your own likewise in its Turn."[25]

At this same time in 1754, one of Shirley's most enthusiastic supporters, a Dr. W. Clarke from Boston, was writing an influential propaganda pamphlet concentrated on Nova Scotia's special relationship with Massachusetts. He too maintained that once war was declared, the French would easily capture Nova Scotia and then strike at Massachusetts. The only way to save Massachusetts from devastating French-Indian raids was to drive out the unsuspecting French troops before any official declaration of war:

> One great and indeed main Security . . . against the fatal Effects of the French Encroachment, consists in this, that the French Settlements at present are not capable of subsisting a Body of Troops strong enough to over-run the English Settlements; but should the French make themselves Masters of Nova Scotia, which is a country fruitful of all kind of Grain and Provisions, they would be in a Condition to introduce and subsist a Body of Troops strong enough with the French Acadians, and inhabitants of Cape-Breton and Canada, together with the Indians, to reduce all the English Colonies.[26]

Another Boston propagandist appealed to New England pride and the long-standing suspicion and fear of the French and their Roman Catholicism. Part of the long title of the pamphlet summarized its basic thesis: *A Letter from Quebeck in Canada to M. L'Maine, a French Officer which contains a particular Account of the present Designs of the French upon the English in North America; What Force the French have collected, their several Divisions and the Place destin'd for each. Likewise an Account of the defenceless Condition of the English Provinces and Colonies*. . . . The author concluded his letter by putting these words into the mouth of a French official:

> *Those New-England Heretics . . . have a Tincture of Oliver Cromwell's Blood remaining. . . . For if they could take Cape-Breton (which we imagin'd to be impregnable) what can we suppose they could not effect, when their Indignation and Resentment provokes them to oppose our Encroachments on their territories? And they are sensible, that when once we become their Masters, Fire and Gibbet will be their Portion, if they do not fall down and worship the Images we shall set up.*[27]

The propaganda offensive and the rumours of war brought to Massachusetts by returning traders, together with Shirley's Kennebec success, had served to challenge by late 1754 the concept of Massachusetts isolationism. Furthermore, the secretary of state, Sir Thomas Robinson, appeared to add his considerable influence in support of Shirley's offensive stance. On hearing of the planned Kennebec expedition, Robinson ordered Shirley on July 5, 1754, to work closely with Governor Charles Lawrence of Nova Scotia so that Shirley would "have concerted the properest measure with him for taking all possible advantage in Nova Scotia itself . . . in case Mr. Lawrence shall have force enough to attack the Forts erected by the French . . . without exposing the English settlement."[28] Robinson informed Lawrence to consider the letter to Shirley "as an Instruction to yourself upon this important occasion." The Nova Scotia governor was further ordered to "take such effectual measures as will frustrate the designs of the French and will procure an essential Benefit to your own Government."[29] Even before receiving Robinson's instructions, Lawrence had proposed to the secretary of state that "a Body of Men in New-England, which joined to the few troops we could muster" be sent to demolish Fort Beauséjour, and "when that is done, the French Inhabitants on that side must either be removed to this, or driven totally away by Fire and Sword."[30] Quite independently of Shirley, Lawrence had come, at a critical time, to advocate precisely the same policy as that of the Massachusetts governor. By the closing months of 1754, Shirley, supported by a handful of propagandists, a neighbouring governor, and the British secretary of state, seemed to have a reasonable chance of dragging his somewhat reluctant colony once again into the affairs of Nova Scotia.

By the end of the first week of November, 1754, both Shirley and Lawrence had in their possession Robinson's instructions. Both men immediately wrote to one another but their letters crossed. Lawrence sent two of his officers, Lieutenant-Colonel Robert Monckton, commander of the garrison at Annapolis Royal, and Captain George Scott, to Boston with the letter and instructions to encourage the enlistment of 2,000 Massachusetts volunteers. In order to persuade the General Court to accept the proposal, Lawrence promised, "I do not propose to put your Excellency's Province to any expense upon this occasion but to defray all charges that may arise out of the money granted for this Colony concerning which I have already wrote to Ld. Halifax." Lawrence had, in fact, given Monckton "an unlimited credit upon Messrs. Apthorp and Hancock."[31] Shirley interpreted Robinson's rather vague instructions as permitting a joint Nova Scotia–Massachusetts expedition against Chignecto and the St. John River. He jubilantly informed Lawrence:

> *I construe the contents to be orders to us to act in Concert for taking* any *advantages to drive the French of Canada out of Nova Scotia when they may be done consistently with the safety of the English settlements there.*
>   *If that is your sense of them . . . I will endeavour to send you such assistance from this Province, as you shall want, in time, and shall readily Co-operate with you.*[32]

It is noteworthy that Shirley expected the initiative and leadership to come from Lawrence. Obviously, Lawrence was no Mascarene, and Halifax in 1754 was not Annapolis Royal in 1744. Two major difficulties, however, remained for Shirley. First, he had to gain the support of the General Court for the scheme and to ensure that a suitable number of volunteers could be recruited. Second, he wanted to be certain that he had interpreted Robinson's instructions correctly and that the secretary of state realized that the planned expedition was the Nova Scotia governor's special responsibility. Shirley therefore informed Robinson on November 11 that the military planning "is wholly with Colonel Lawrence to determine." He continued:

We shall be able to agree upon measures in a very few weeks for the reduction of the French Forts early in next year in case it should be his Majesty's pleasure to have that done.

These orders should arrive here by the latter end of March or first week in April to be in time for beginning the operations early in the year.[33]

Shirley certainly gave the impression that he did not expect the expedition to sail unless the British authorities gave their approval and provided suitable naval support.[34]

Monckton and Scott did not reach Boston until December 8. Two days later, before their instructions from Lawrence were fully digested by the delighted Shirley, the governor discovered that the scheme was in jeopardy. He received word from London that "his majy. had been pleased to order mine and Sir William Pepperrell's Regimts. to be forthwith reviv'd, and two Brish. Regimts. to imbark for Virginia upon an Expedition to be commanded by Major General Braddock."[35] Quite unexpectedly, the British had decided to push back the French threat on the Ohio River. Shirley was understandably worried that the recruiting for his and Pepperrell's regiments for the Ohio campaign would dry up the pool of available Massachusetts manpower and thus make recruiting virtually impossible for the Nova Scotia expedition. In an attempt to rescue his scheme from encroaching disaster, he despatched an urgent appeal to Robinson on December 14: "At this time particularly I am concerting Measures with Colonel Lawrence to drive the French out of Nova Scotia next Spring, in Obedience to his Majesty's Orders signify'd to me in your Letter, Sir, dated the 5th of July last, and propose that my Regimt should assist in the Service, unless I am forbid by different Orders."[36] Shirley had cleverly shifted the responsibility for the Nova Scotia expedition onto Robinson's shoulders and in the same sentence was daring enough to propose that a basic change in British North American strategy be undertaken. Shirley confided to Lawrence, in a letter also written on December 14, his reaction after reading the Robinson letter: "As the orders I received . . . seem'd at first sight to me to clash with the designed Expedition agt. the French in Nova Scotia this Spring, I was greatly embarrassed, but soon came to a determination to co-operate with you in the most vigorous manner."[37]

Shirley's "determination" was such that by January 6, 1755, he had decided to abandon his November 11 policy of first waiting to receive the permission of the British authorities before allowing the expedition to sail. He therefore informed Lawrence, "I shall not wait to hear further from England."[38] He was now certain, after carefully gauging the popular mood of his colony, as well as testing the strength of the new imperialism emanating from Westminster, that the proposed Nova Scotia expedition would receive sufficient support from the General Court and be enthusiastically endorsed by his British superiors. Shirley had little to lose in backing the expedition with vigour. Lawrence was willing to pay inflated Massachusetts prices for supplies and services, and Shirley could have his finger, if not his hand, in the deep patronage barrel being filled by a governor of another colony. If the expedition failed, Lawrence, not Shirley, would have to pay the political consequences. For Shirley the 1755 expedition was much less of a gamble than had been the Louisbourg assault of 1745, and the expected political and strategic dividends seemed to match those gained ten years earlier.

Having already ironed out the organizational and strategic difficulties with Monckton, whom Lawrence had appointed commander-in-chief of the expedition, Shirley called the General Court into emergency session on February 7, 1755. In a brilliantly argued address, Shirley explained why an expedition was essential and what Massachusetts' contribution should be. It was probably the governor's most effective speech to the Court. After discussing at considerable length his correspondence with Robinson and Lawrence and the fact that Nova Scotia was to pay for the proposed expedition, Shirley stressed the need for Massachusetts to participate. If the French troops were not driven from the Chignecto and St. John forts in what he regarded to be British territory, they would soon gain control of Nova Scotia, "which still remained the Northern Key of this Continent." The French would therefore be in a position to "pour in their Troops from France at Pleasure" and funnel them in a giant stream into Massachusetts. Eventually the Gallic invaders, supported by "Negro Slaves ... Roman Catholicks, Jacobites, and transported Convicts ... [and] Indians" would drive the English out of North America, "making

themselves Masters of this Continent." British North America, however, could still be saved. The proposed expedition promised salvation:

> *It is happy for us that we have now a fair Opportunity*
> *Offer'd of ridding the Province of its dangerous Neighbours,*
> *with all the Mischiefs that threaten'd it from their remaining*
> *so near: dislodging the French from their Forts upon the*
> *Isthmus and St. John's River, and driving them out of Nova*
> *Scotia would immediately cutt off their Communication*
> *between Louisbourg and Canada across the Peninsula and*
> *Bay of Funda, and break a principal link in the chain of*
> *Forts with which they have surrounded the English*
> *Colonies; it would be wounding the Serpent in the head,*
> *disconcerting their Scheme in its most essential part.*

To accomplish this end, Shirley asked that 2,000 volunteers be raised
in Massachusetts, and he announced that Monckton's second-in-
command would be the popular John Winslow. The troops were to
"receive the King's Bounty Money, pay, uniform, Cloathing (the most
proper that can be got here) and Arms, and have every thing provided
for them which is necessary for their comfortable Subsistence." The
enlistment period was to be for only twelve months.[39]

It is not known what the immediate response of the General Court
was to Shirley's long speech, since the deliberations were conducted in
secret. What is known is that six days later, Shirley again addressed
the Court and, on this occasion, made a significant addition to his
strategic argument. He now proposed that at the same time the
Anglo–New England force was capturing the French forts in the
disputed western frontier of Nova Scotia, Massachusetts would be
constructing "a Fort upon the rockey Eminence near Crown Point,
within the limits of his Majesty's Territories." Once war broke out,
Shirley declared that the Massachusetts troops would soon capture
Crown Point and "march . . . in a few days to the Gates of the City of
Montreal itself, and Pour our Troops into the heart of the Country."[40]
It is impossible to know for certain whether Shirley was serious about
building such a fort in the extreme west of Massachusetts. It is probable
that Shirley was being pressured by some of the western representatives
and by the isolationist diehards to introduce the Crown Point proposal
in exchange for their support for the Nova Scotia venture.[41] A
compromise had been worked out between the new forces involved in

"ye Rising American Empire" of the West and those Massachusetts inhabitants still tied to the traditional approach to "New England's Outpost."

On February 13, as an indication of the Court's support of the Nova Scotia venture, Winslow finally "Received Beating orders for that Purpose."[42] His recruiting skill was severely tested as he competed with other officers attempting to raise men for Pepperrell's and Shirley's regiments. Motivated by a deep desire to have his own regular regiment in the British army, Winslow was determined to impress the British authorities favourably and thus persuade them to reward him for his loyalty and service.[43] He was assisted in his recruiting by the high bounties offered and the reasonable monthly pay and other inducements,[44] and also by the shrill rhetoric of the anti-French and anti–Roman Catholic propagandists. The Reverend Isaac Morrill of Wilmington demanded that the men of his community put the Gallic interlopers "at the Muzzle of our Guns and at the Point of our Swords." All true New Englanders were expected to abandon their "Families and at present quiet Habitations" for the greater good of "the publick Service; the Service of your King, and the Defence of your Country." Morrill concluded his sermon by challenging his audience with a number of questions already answered, building to an emotional climax:

> And are we willing to give up our civil Rights and Privileges, and become subjected to Tyranny and arbitrary Government? Are we willing to give up our Religion, the Religion of Jesus, which we now enjoy in its Purity, and which should be more dear to us than our Lives? Are we willing to give up this for Ignorance, Error and Superstition? to resign our Bibles, and contentedly walk in the dark? . . . Can we calmly submit to give up this Land to usurping Powers, that our Forefathers purchased for us at the Price of their Blood? O! for God's sake, let us think of our Danger, and labour to prevent our Ruin. Let us determine to defend our Country though it be at the Price of our Blood. Let there not be an unwilling Mind, or a faint Heart in any son of New England. Let such as are willing, and may be called to go forth in the Defence of their Country, go out with Courage and Resolution.[45]

Massachusetts was battling, according to other ministers of the Gospel, against that "Mother of Harlots," "this Cockatrice Egg," "the Enemies of the Son of God . . . a Branch of the AntiChristian Romish Church."[46] Excessive anxiety and religious prejudice must have been responsible for the addition of at least a few men to Winslow's force. Unemployment, economic frustrations, and the desire for adventure must have motivated many others.[47]

By April 20 Winslow had recruited no fewer than 1,800 volunteers. By May 22, when the expedition finally sailed, there were almost 2,000 recruits. Originally Shirley and Monckton had planned to have the troops destined for Nova Scotia in Boston by March 25. Winslow had his men in the capital one month later, "waiting for the arrival of the 2000 stands of arms from England." The guns and ammunition, however, did not arrive until May 12, and on the following day Shirley returned from a meeting with General Braddock during which Braddock gave "his entire approbation of the measures . . . concerted for removing the French Incroachments in Nova Scotia." It seems that Monckton was reluctant to sail until Shirley returned with Braddock's approbation. In late April, as Shirley observed on May 31, there were already sufficient arms available in Massachusetts and Annapolis Royal for almost all the volunteers.[48] In addition, three twenty-gun frigates from Halifax, under the command of the Louisbourg veteran Captain John Rous, were anchored in Boston harbour ready to convey the thirty-three Massachusetts transport and supply vessels to Annapolis Royal and the Chignecto Isthmus.[49]

John Winslow kept a complete journal of the undertaking, partly for the edification of future Winslows and the British authorities, and also as an aid to Shirley and Lawrence in documenting the costs incurred. Of special interest is a list of all the volunteers, with their names, rank, age, birthplace, last residence, and occupation. Winslow's list provides by far the most complete population profile of any New England expedition to Nova Scotia. Of the 1,922 men referred to, 1,663 came from Massachusetts, 170 from Connecticut, 32 from New Hampshire, 27 from Rhode Island, and the others from Jamaica, New York, and other unidentified localities. It is not surprising that Massachusetts contributed 87 percent of the volunteers. It seems that Shirley's influence and Winslow's popularity were of limited importance in the neighbouring colonies. Furthermore, there was strong opposition to Winslow's recruiting forays in Connecticut and New

Hampshire because the governments of these colonies were not directly involved in the planning of the expedition and resented Shirley's interference in their internal affairs. Winslow discovered, for example, that in Connecticut his recruits were "for Frivolous Pretenses, arrested and imprisoned," while in New Hampshire, gouty Governor Wentworth "put a Stop to any enlistment."[50]

In Massachusetts, Barnstable County sent 23 men, Bristol 165, Essex 332, Hampshire 140, Middlesex 411, Plymouth 155, Suffolk 175, Worcester 218, and York only 44. When these numbers are compared with the approximate total male population over sixteen years of age in each of the counties, it is possible to make rough estimates of the percentage of men in each county involved in the expedition. In Barnstable it was .8 percent, Bristol 3.2 percent, Essex 3.6 percent, Hampshire 2.7 percent, Middlesex 1.2 percent, Plymouth 2.9 percent, Suffolk 2.2 percent, Worcester 2.8 percent, and York .8 percent. The regional response does not quickly fall into any discernible pattern. With its strong historical ties with Nova Scotia, and with its commerce and fishery threatened by French attacks, the reaction of Essex County is not surprising. What is noteworthy is the lack of response from York and Middlesex counties. York had sent hundreds of volunteers to Louisbourg; probably most of the available manpower in 1755 was being channelled into Pepperrell's regiment. It is difficult to speculate about Middlesex, but it may have been that Shirley's recruiters were hard at work there.

An age profile of the total expedition, as might be expected, reveals that 54 percent of the volunteers ranged in age from seventeen to twenty-two and 84 percent from seventeen to thirty. With respect to occupations, 840 were labourers, working for other people in towns or on farms, 406 were farmers, 176 were leather workers, 144 were involved in the building trades, 100 in smithing, 90 in the clothing industry, 84 were craftsmen, only 52 pursued maritime occupations, and the remaining 30 had miscellaneous occupations. It may be that the economic decline of the Boston region in the 1750s and the concomitant growth of unemployment among the young,[51] together with unthinking youthful enthusiasm, were key factors in the recruiting of volunteers. But the role of the propagandists should not be underestimated, nor should Winslow's attractive personality.

The Monckton-Winslow fleet reached Annapolis Royal on May 25 and May 26. At the former Nova Scotia capital it was joined by five supply vessels from Halifax, and on June 1 the expedition sailed for Fort Lawrence on the British side of the Missiquash River opposite Fort Beauséjour. Here the New Englanders landed on the following day and were "Joyned with 250 Regulars from Fort Lawrence and Fouer Fine Brass Field Peaces Six Pounder."[52] On June 12 the New Englanders began to build trenches and fascine batteries within mortar shot of the French fort. Beauséjour was defended by 160 French soldiers and by twenty-six cannon, most of which were six-, eight-, and twelve-pounders. The crumbling fortress also housed 220 Acadians.[53] It was merely a matter of time before the commanding officer de Vergor, the son of Governor Du Chambon of Louisbourg, who had surrendered to an Anglo-American force ten years earlier, would follow in his father's footsteps.

Taking advantage of their Louisbourg experience, the New Englanders dragged the four short brass field-guns into position. One volunteer described the siege warfare in the following manner:

> June 14: We Dugg Trenche all Night this Day we threw Bumbs all Day with Eight and Four Inch morter the Enemy threw from Thare Foart 150 Canon Shot and Four a Intch Bums. So that we Kept a warm Fire upon Each other all Day a Party of the Enemy Salley out on our Gards upon our Right wing I was ordered by Colonel Winslow to Detach 70 men from the Trenches and Go to the assistance of our Gards.[54]

Late on June 16 the French capitulated, and the invaders "Entered the Foart and Called it Foort Cumberland the Conditions of Agreement wore yt the Enemy Should Deliver up the Foort and King's Stores but Should be Transported to Lewisbuge with all thare Private Effects at the Expence of his majesty King George."[55] Two days later Monckton ordered Winslow to take 500 of his men and attack Fort Gaspéreau. After a fifteen-mile march, they easily captured the fort, which was "badly built and in Miserable order." Fewer than twenty invaders were killed during the siege. The rest of June and July was spent "in an Indolent Maner," and it did not take long for the frustrated New Englanders and the British regulars to begin to battle among themselves.[56]

Monckton, an arrogant and basically stupid man, treated the New Englanders with contempt and was irrational in his criticism of

Winslow whom he despised.[57] He cut off the supply of rum to
Winslow's regiment on July 5, precipitating a major crisis. Captain
Abijah Willard observed in his journal: "Weather fair but very Cold
for the Season att Evening Call Winslow Batallion the Souldiers beng
Lowed no Rum the Battallion was in an Uprore And Cried No Rum
till Late in Evening till the Souldirs Gott to such a Degree that the
officrs was obliged to go amongst the tents." A short time later,
Willard described "a grate uprore in the Camp Concerning the peese
for itt was thought that Coll Munckton had much Rather the Cattle
Should Eate the peess than the Souldirs that Come from New England."[58] With an abundance of supplies available to him, Monckton
had no good reason to treat the New Englanders with such callous
indifference. Probably only secret orders from Lawrence, arriving at
Fort Cumberland on August 6,[59] prevented further disturbances
"tending to muteny."[60]

Because of his fear of a possible French counteroffensive and
because the Acadians refused to take an unqualified oath of
allegiance, Lawrence and his Council in Halifax had unanimously
agreed on July 28 to deport all the Acadian inhabitants and "to
send them to be distributed amongst the several Colonies."[61] This
was a military decision made by an inflexible and insecure military
man. Shirley, who was then leading an expedition against Fort Niagara,
knew absolutely nothing about it and had for years opposed such a
policy. Nor was the Massachusetts General Court in any way involved
in influencing the decision made by Lawrence and the Nova Scotia
Council. By 1755 most Massachusetts leaders had learned to distinguish
between the aggressive agents of French imperialism and the pragmatic
Acadians.

On receiving his orders from Lawrence, Monckton commanded
the New England troops to begin the nasty business of burning the
Acadian settlements, slaughtering their livestock, and herding the
Acadians like cattle to various ports along the Bay of Fundy. Some of
the volunteers found the command "surprising" and "Very Disagreeable" to their "Natural make and Temper," but they nevertheless
obeyed.[62] It has been estimated that between 6,000 and 7,000 Acadian
men, women, and children, out of a total Acadian population on
peninsular Nova Scotia of no more than 9,000, were deported during
the last four months of 1755.[63] Over 1,000 Acadians were dumped
upon an unsuspecting Massachusetts. By August, 1763, the Acadians

"had drained the provincial treasury of nearly £ 10,000," since the British authorities refused to reimburse the General Court for considerable expenses involved in providing them with "food, shelter, clothing, employment and medical care."[64] Since 1630 Massachusetts had had considerable contact with the Acadians and had developed close economic ties with them. Massachusetts, on the whole, had viewed the Acadians – at a safe distance of course – with a reasonable degree of sympathy and understanding. The colony's humanitarian response to the plight of the Acadian exiles was perfectly consistent with Massachusetts' earlier Acadian policy. This charitable response was certainly no aberration;[65] it was the logical continuation of John Winthrop's Christian rule of charity.

Can Massachusetts be blamed for the expulsion of the Acadians? According to the classic and still widely accepted interpretation, all New England was, in fact, responsible. This explanation for *le grand dérangement* was put forward in 1927 by the distinguished and influential historian J. B. Brebner and has been almost universally accepted.[66] According to Brebner:

> If one is tempted to seek a single and therefore incomplete explanation of why the Acadians suffered as they did, it is far more likely to be found in the expanding energies of New England than in the character of Charles Lawrence, although the latter seems conclusively to have been the agent of the removal. . . . New England fisheries, commerce, and communications drew New England interest north and east. For a century and a half rivalry in empire, in religion, and in economic activity made New England regard Acadie or Nova Scotia as her section of the long Anglo-French frontier in North America.[67]

For Brebner, therefore, there was something of the inevitable in the expulsion of 1755. The activities of the New England fishermen and merchants and those of Sedgwick, Leverett, Phips, Church, March, Vetch, Shirley, Pepperrell, and Vaughan clearly pointed in this one direction. All events in pre-1755 Nova Scotia – New England relations obviously converged in the expulsion. Only when the French were finally forcibly removed from Nova Scotia could the "expanding energies of New England" be satisfied.

But on closer examination Brebner's analysis of the forces impinging on Nova Scotia in 1755 seems to break down. It is clear that the Winslow-Monckton expedition had little to do with the so-called expanding energies of Massachusetts, let alone New England. It was conceived by Lawrence and Shirley and financed from London via Halifax; all that Massachusetts provided were supplies and men – for a price, of course. Nobody in a position of political influence in the colony in 1755, including Shirley, had advocated the expulsion of the Acadians. There was no movement either at the governmental or popular level in Massachusetts in favour of a large-scale Massachusetts emigration to Nova Scotia. The absence of representative government in Halifax and the possibility of frequent French-Indian raids, in addition to the bad image of the colony, all discouraged Massachusetts settlement there. Furthermore, by using exactly the same episodes as does Brebner in New England–Nova Scotia relations during the 1630 to 1755 period, it may be argued that there was no causal link from decade to decade leading naturally to the expulsion. The nature of the relationship was obviously not this simple nor did it necessarily point solely in this direction. In fact, what is remarkable about the relation-ship is that in noneconomic matters, Massachusetts' expansion was virtually nonexistent except for a few outbursts of military expansion. These outbursts never developed into any kind of permanent imperial-istic thrust; they were largely defensive reflex actions and owed a great deal, not to popular demand, but to the political pressure of certain interest groups and the shrill rhetoric of various propagandists. If anything characterized Massachusetts' relationship with Nova Scotia in the pre-1755 period it was, first, a prevailing indifference and opposi-tion towards appropriating the neighbouring colony and, second, the widely held conviction that in spite of which European power was in actual possession of Nova Scotia, in times of peace or sometimes even in war, the New Englanders would still have an economic stranglehold on the region. If there was any expanding energy in Massachusetts in 1755, it was being pointed in a westerly direction.

During the closing months of 1755 it was not only the unanticipated arrival of the Acadian exiles that disturbed a growing number of Massachusetts inhabitants. The New Englanders discovered, soon after the capture of the French forts, that the fewer than 300 British regulars involved had shouldered the 2,000 New England volunteers aside and had taken upon themselves and upon Governor Lawrence the glory for the only successful British military achievement in North America in 1755. In his official report of the conduct of his troops, Monckton did not even mention Winslow's name.[68] The editor of the *Boston Gazette*, fully aware of the bitterness engendered ten years earlier by Warren's officers seeking to undermine the New England achievement at Louisbourg, led the counterattack. The Louisbourg scars were ripped open once again for all to see:

> Nova-Scotia *must have long since fallen intirely into the Hands of the* French, *had it not been once and again befriended and supported by the Province of the* Massachusetts Bay. *But it seems that they, who have been from Time to Time both imploring, and receiving Protection from us, now envy us the Honour of affording it to them, and strangely arrogate to themselves the Credit of whatever is generously done by others for their Defence and Security, as if it were both more blessed and more reputable* to receive than to give.[69]

Two other authors supported the *Gazette* point of view in a pamphlet entitled "An Account of the Present State of Nova Scotia." These men denounced Governor Lawrence's much-publicized letter to the secretary of state in which he declared that Monckton and his engineer, Captain Tonge, had been responsible for the capture of Beauséjour. Such a declaration, they contended, "was notoriously false, giving the merit of it to two poor creatures, who had not the least share in it, but who were glad to sit quietly and safely in their tents four miles off, and guarded by all the regular troops they had." The anonymous authors continued:

> The New England men . . . contrived everything did all the work and took the place, perhaps a little sooner than the Valiant C-1 in the tents expected; and for their forwardness he has borne them a grudge, and has done all that was in his power to starve them by cold and hunger ever since . . . yet it was thought better to give the praise of taking the place to these two contemptible animals, than to those who really deserv'd it because they were New England men and irregulars.[70]

What further exacerbated relations between Massachusetts on the one hand, and Monckton, Lawrence, and his Halifax cronies on the other, were Monckton's attempts to pressure the Massachusetts volunteers to enlist permanently in the British regiments then stationed in Nova Scotia. In early February, 1756, an angry General Court urged Shirley to ensure that all Massachusetts volunteers "may have Liberty, if they see Cause, at the Expiration of the Term of their Inlistment to return home." The members were disgusted with Monckton's arrogance and his questionable recruiting tactics. In reflecting the popular mood, the members of the General Court were determined to wash their hands of the unpleasant Nova Scotia business.[71] The anti-Monckton and anti-British army sentiment did not quickly disappear in New England. Benjamin Franklin perceptively observed in July, 1756, concerning the preparations for the Crown Point expedition:

> *The Provincials, it seems, apprehend, that Regulars join'd with them, would claim all the Honour of any Success, and charge them with the Blame of every Miscarriage. They say, that last year, at Nova Scotia, 2000 New England Men, and not more than 200 Regulars, were join'd in the Taking Beasejour; yet it could not be discovered by the Acct sent home by Govr. Lawrence, and publish'd in the London Gazette, that there was a single New England Man concern'd in the Affair.*[72]

By February, 1756, even William Shirley was losing interest in Nova Scotia. With the sudden death of General Braddock on the Monongahela River in July, 1755, Shirley had become commander-in-chief of all British forces in North America. Never had a commander-in-chief had such limited military experience. In his new position, Shirley viewed the French threat from a vantage point quite different from that at Boston. His shift of interest towards the West, towards the Ohio and the Great Lakes, shrewdly reflected British strategic thinking and the growing fascination with the area in the middle colonies. When he was removed from his military command and the governorship of Massachusetts in the summer of 1756, his colony had already turned its back on Nova Scotia. It may be argued that the Chignecto episode accelerated a movement already under way. It was an outstanding military victory, but it was also a source of bitterness and disillusionment in Massachusetts. It certainly did not further strengthen the ties between Massachusetts and Nova Scotia. Rather, in the eyes of a growing number of influential Massachusetts residents,

Nova Scotia could no longer be perceived as "New England's Outpost." Nova Scotia, as the *Boston Gazette* trumpeted in July, 1755, was only an "Asylum" for those Massachusetts settlers who lacked a proper "Regard to the *Credit* of their native Country."[73] Nova Scotia began to symbolize British arrogance and was now considered a suitable habitation for only the dregs of New England.

12

Massachusetts and Nova Scotia, 1757-1776

For some influential Massachusetts residents, Nova Scotia from 1757 to 1776 was considered to be a particularly corrupt and backward Anglophile colony incapable of political or ideological redemption.[1] It remained a kind of "Asylum" for those renegade New Englanders who had abandoned the pristine purity of "their native country" to settle in a colony ruled by an autocratic, military élite bent upon destroying hard-won colonial liberties.[2] But for some other Massachusetts inhabitants, especially in the 1760 to 1764 period, Nova Scotia was conceived as an "Asylum" from rapacious proprietors and from what seemed to be the increasingly grim realities of colonial life. For such people Nova Scotia was a virgin land with almost limitless economic and spiritual potential and promise. Thousands of New Englanders immigrated to Nova Scotia in the early 1760s and transformed it into what has been called a "New New England."[3]

The year 1758 witnessed three major developments in the Nova Scotia region which directly impinged upon Massachusetts affairs and which encouraged some residents, at least, to view the neighbouring colony in a rather more sympathetic light. First, on July 27, Louisbourg was captured by British regular troops. Massachusetts' contribution to the second siege of the French fortress was a few companies of Indian fighters and a contingent of carpenters, but the "lobsterbacks'" victory was nevertheless widely celebrated in Boston and other

Massachusetts towns. The *Boston Gazette* reported: "The Bells rang all Day; and in the Evening there was as beautiful and general an Illumination as perhaps has ever before been seen; and in every street there was a brilliant Appearance of Ladies and Gentlemen of Rank and Fortune."[4] The Massachusetts response to the news of the taking of Louisbourg was, as would be expected, not as enthusiastic as it had been in 1745. There were "Sentiments of Loyalty and Joy" and perhaps "A chearful Countenance appear'd in all Ranks of People,"[5] but there was little evidence of the frenzied jubilation that had exploded thirteen years earlier. The British victory in 1758 meant, nonetheless, that the French North Atlantic threat to New England had finally been destroyed, and the realization of this fact was a source of considerable relief to the Massachusetts population.

The second major occurrence in Nova Scotia affecting Massachusetts was the formal establishment of representative government with the first meeting of the colony's Assembly on October 2 at Halifax.[6] This development was considered by some a major victory for the relatively small New England element in the population, and it neutralized somewhat in Massachusetts the image of a Nova Scotia controlled by an Anglophile military-commercial élite.

The third Nova Scotia event sprung naturally from the former two. On October 12, 1758, Governor Charles Lawrence, who wished to see the vacant Acadian lands settled by loyal American subjects of the king, issued and propagated widely throughout New England a proclamation "declaring that I shall be ready to receive any Proposals that may be hereafter made to me, for effectually settling the said vacated or any other Lands within the Province aforesaid." In the proclamation he described the 200,000 acres of rich farmland newly available. There were "interval Plow-Lands, producing, Wheat, Rye, Barley, Oats, Hemp, Flax . . . cultivated for more than a Hundred Years past, and never fail of Crops, nor need manuring." There were also rich "Upland, clear'd and stock'd with English Grass, planted with Orchards, Gardens" and the "wild and unimproved Lands . . . well timber'd and wooded, with Beach, Black-birch, Ash, Oak, Pine, Fir."[7]

A surprising number of New Englanders greeted Lawrence's proclamation with a flurry of questions. They wished to know, among other things, "What terms of encouragement would be offered? How much land each person would get? What quit rent and taxes were to be exacted? What constitution of government prevailed? and what freedom in religion?"[8] Realizing that few settlers would even consider emigrating before these questions were adequately dealt with, Lawrence and his Council on January 11, 1759, issued a second proclamation — the so-called Charter of Nova Scotia. Lawrence emphasized in this new document that "the quantities of land granted will be in proportion to the abilities of the planter to settle, cultivate and enclose the same" and that quit rents would not be collected by the Crown until ten years after the issuing of the grant. After asserting that no "one person can possess more than one thousand acres by grant," the governor assured all potential immigrants that they would indeed feel at home in Nova Scotia. "The Government of Nova Scotia," both at the local township and provincial level, and the "Courts of Justice" were "constituted in like manner with those of Massachusetts, Connecticut and the other Northern Colonies." And as far as religious freedom was concerned, "full liberty of conscience . . . Papists excluded" was promised. It was also stressed that "Dissenters" were to be "excused from any rates or taxes . . . for the support of the Established Church of England." Finally, settlers were to receive protection from possible Indian raids from "his Majesty's troops" garrisoned in forts in close proximity to the lands to be granted.[9]

The generous terms offered by Lawrence were unquestionably far more attractive than those being circulated at the same time about New England holdings by many Yankee land speculators–proprietors. Unlike his competitors, Lawrence was promising to distribute the best available land in Nova Scotia, even that territory adjacent to the rivers and the Bay of Fundy, at no immediate cost to the immigrants, and he was willing also to provide them with military protection. Lawrence could not have selected a more propitious time to recruit settlers in eastern Connecticut, Rhode Island, and southeastern Massachusetts.[10] There were hundreds of farmers desperately looking for cheap yet rich land to cultivate, and there were hundreds of fishermen wanting to locate somewhere closer to the North Atlantic banks so that they could "Carry on the fishery to Greater Advantage."[11]

Eventually, the vast majority of settlers who finally came to Nova Scotia, whether farmers or fishermen, came from that relatively small corner of New England created when a line is drawn from New London, Connecticut, northward to Brookfield, Massachusetts, and then eastward to Plymouth. This area in 1759 and 1760 was under considerable tension and controversy between the proprietors, or landowners, and the noncommoners, or tenants, over the rights to common lands, as well as over the high prices charged by the owners for farming land.[12] It has been noted that the "Towns where the Proprietors guarded their rights most vigorously and where prolonged controversies show that the distinction between 'Proprietor' and 'Non-Commoner' was the most marked . . . were the towns from which most came to Nova Scotia."[13] Economic considerations may have motivated most settlers to emigrate, but there were some who, in retrospect at least, saw themselves as the special agents of the Almighty who "after previously Removeing our Enemies, planted us in this Infant Colony" in order to establish true Christianity.[14] A few others stressed the fact that the "principal Inducement [to emigrate] was the assurance of the Protection of the Government in all our civil and Religious Rights and Liberties as we enjoyed them in the Governments from which we came."[15] But despite Lawrence's attractive inducements and even the encouragement of New England's God, few would have settled in Nova Scotia if there had not been in certain areas of New England during the latter part of the Seven Years' War what has been called a "grass-roots revolt against privilege and a movement towards equality and freedom."[16] To leave the relative security of settled New England to become uprooted immigrants on the Nova Scotia frontier was not an easy decision to make, and the number of emigrants indicates something of the depth and extent of discontent with the economic and social status quo.

As would be expected of people who took the Old Testament seriously, some of those interested in Lawrence's offer sent five men in the spring of 1759 "to spy out the land of Canaan." When they visited the Minas Bay region in the middle of May, they saw the lush tidal plains and the heavily wooded uplands "showing unmistakeable signs of great fertility." When the five agents returned to New England, they did not bring back over their shoulders, as had the agents of Moses, a gigantic "single cluster of grapes." Instead they returned with information about a veritable Garden of Eden; Nova Scotia was, according to them, indeed a land flowing with milk and honey. They had seen it in the full splendour of a glorious May through their own disbelieving eyes.[17] Their glowing reports were swept across parts of New England, and only news about Indian depredations and the damage inflicted on the dyked lands by a violent hurricane prevented hundreds from emigrating in the late summer of 1759.[18]

The following year the great emigration began, and by the end of 1763, when the movement lost most of its original momentum, approximately 5,000 New Englanders had settled in Nova Scotia.[19] The Yankee farmers had pushed into the vacated Acadian lands on the south shore of the Minas Basin and around Cobequid Bay, in the Annapolis Royal area and the Isthmus of Chignecto. A few others had moved up the St. John River valley to Maugerville near present-day Fredericton. Probably less than half of these farmers, it should be emphasized, came from Massachusetts and even most of these came from regions contiguous to those sections of Connecticut and Rhode Island where the enthusiasm for emigration was probably greatest. This movement, therefore, was not basically a Massachusetts movement. Opposition to the emigration was particularly strong in Massachusetts, an opposition that owed a great deal to the existing traditional disenchantment with Nova Scotia, which had in fact intensified late in 1755 and in 1756 as a result of the impact of the Winslow-Monckton expedition.[20] But this anti–Nova Scotia feeling had not developed to the same extent in Connecticut and Rhode Island. Both of these colonies had never been as involved in Nova Scotia affairs and consequently had not experienced the same bitter reaction to the events of the 1740s and 1750s as had much of Massachusetts.

The fishermen and others who settled at Yarmouth, Barrington, Liverpool, and Chester were, on the other hand, almost to a man natives of Massachusetts. For decades these fishermen from southeastern Massachusetts and Essex County had regularly visited the hundreds of harbours on the southern shore of Nova Scotia. In the 1760s they were merely transforming what had been a kind of temporary residence into a somewhat more permanent one. It has been correctly noted:

The chief economic reason that led to the removal of this class was that the south shore of Nova Scotia lay four hundred miles nearer to the grand banks than the coast of Massachusetts. Losses suffered in the late war induced the establishment of new fishing stations. French privateers had captured many Nantucket and Cape Cod whalers and fishing schooners. Fishermen had been impressed into the naval service on board British ships of war. Recollection of these years of hardship made a change of scene desirable to some.[21]

What seemed to them to be the utter hopelessness of their position in Massachusetts had propelled them to move to a region which they knew well. Their own peculiar sense of disillusionment with Massachusetts had enabled them to close their ears to much of the propaganda then being directed at Nova Scotia.

By the middle of the 1760s, however, the influx of Yankee fishermen and farmers into Nova Scotia had virtually come to an end, and an outflow back to New England had begun. A serious economic recession in Nova Scotia, an intensifying dissatisfaction with the Halifax authorities, the availability of inexpensive, fertile land west of the Appalachian barrier, and the opening up of new areas in present-day Vermont and western New Hampshire had encouraged this development. Immigration to Nova Scotia from Great Britain, however, continued and even expanded. Some 2,000 Ulstermen, more than 750 Yorkshiremen, and some destitute Scottish Highlanders and Irish Roman Catholics entered the colony before the outbreak of the Revolution, strengthening considerably the non-Yankee element of the population.[22] By 1776, of an estimated total population of 17,000 to 20,000, approximately only one-half was of New England origin.[23] Nova Scotia in 1776, was, therefore, not a homogeneous New England colony; rather, it was little more than a political expression for a number of widely scattered and isolated communities. These stretched from Pictou on Northumberland Strait to Canso and to Halifax, from the colony's capital to Maugerville on the St. John River and to the tiny outpost of Passamaquoddy on the St. Croix. If there was a "New New England," it was only the coastal strip of peninsular Nova Scotia running from Liverpool to Yarmouth and along the south coast of the Bay of Fundy to present-day Truro, together with the relatively small St. John River settlement. There were then in the 1770s two Nova Scotias — the Yankee outsettlements and the rest.

In the social, religious, and economic sense, though not the political, the Yankee section of Nova Scotia retained very close ties with New England. Particularly strong emotional and family bonds existed, of course, between the two areas, and these ties produced a feeling of dependency that was especially strong in the area of religious practice and belief. Many of the Yankees were either Old Light or New Light Congregationalists, and their former church polity and theology were transplanted to Nova Scotia. Some of the Nova Scotia Yankees, especially those from an Old Light background, regarded their churches as frontier appendages of various Congregational associations in New England. When, for example, the church at Cornwallis was unable in 1769 to pay its minister, it requested immediate financial assistance from various Massachusetts churches:

> *And without Some Relief from Some other Quarter, Our*
> *Said Minister Cannot Continue much Longer with us which*
> *if after a Separation from the Society And Communion of*
> *our Christian friends in Newengland . . . Notwithstanding*
> *our many indeavours . . . We Say if After All this we Should*
> *be Left Destitute of Gosple Administrations by Neglecting*
> *to petition the Aid Of Such of our Christian Brethern As*
> *Are Able to Afford us Relief at So Critickle A Junctur as this,*
> *We Should be both wanting to Our Selves and posterity,*
> *And the Cause of Religeon among us, And be Reduced to A*
> *Worse Condition than At Our First Settleing. . . . It is*
> *Recommended that Any Donations for the Relief of our*
> *Revd Paster be paid into the hands of the Revd. Andrew*
> *Elliot of Boston.*[24]

In 1772 the colonial relationship of Nova Scotia Congregationalism to that of New England was graphically revealed in the ordination of Jonathan Scott of Yarmouth, Nova Scotia. On January 20, 1772, Scott was invited by the Chebogue church "to the work of the Ministry and Pastoral Office" on the condition that he be formally examined and ordained by "a Council of Ministers" from "the First Church in Middleborough [Plymouth County] and their associate Churches." On April 27 Scott noted in his journal: "Then in the evening the Council (13 in all) called for me and desired to see my Confession of Faith, which, where I had given it to them, was read before them, and they questioned me on the same as far as they saw fit. Then they inquired into my religious experience and dismissed me for the night." On the following day Scott was ordained, and "the ministers admitted me to their association as a member thereof."[25] Soon after his return to Yarmouth in May, "By the lifting up the Hand unanimously," the Chebogue church accepted Scott as its pastor.[26] He had to be properly ordained in New England, however, before he could serve the tiny Nova Scotia church. Scott's experience, as well as the appeal of the Cornwallis church, underlined the Nova Scotia Yankees' religious colonial relationship with their "mother country."

This religious relationship was carried on, from the Nova Scotia side, as if nothing had happened to the American world since 1763. The Nova Scotia Yankees were still viewing religious issues as they had done in New England in the 1750s. Their religious beliefs had not been transformed in the "intense political heat" of the 1760s into the new politico-religious ideology that had pressured traditional New England values into a justification for resisting a British "conspiracy" to destroy American liberties.[27] In a sense, therefore, the Nova Scotia Yankees were attached in the religious sphere to a New England which in the 1770s no longer really existed. They had missed a critical decade of American development, leaving New England before the Stamp Act crisis of 1765 and other issues had radically altered, among other things, the religious framework of society.

In the economic sense, the Nova Scotia Yankees were almost as integral a part of New England commercial life as they would have been if they had remained at home. The St. John River trade, as had been the case for decades, was funnelled through Boston. During the ten-year period preceding the outbreak of the American Revolution, the trading company at the mouth of the St. John controlled by William Hazen and James Simonds shipped to Massachusetts:

> *at least 40,000 beaver skins, 11,022 musquash, 6,050 marten, 870 otter, 258 fisher, 522 mink, 120 fox, 140 sable, 74 racoon, 67 loupcervier, 8 wolverene, five bear, two Nova Scotia wolf, 50 caribou, 85 deer, and 1,113 moose, besides 2,265 lbs of castor and 3,000 lbs of feathers, the value of which according to invoice was £11,295 or about $40,000. . . . In addition . . . large quantities of pollock, mackerel . . . codfish . . . gasperaux . . . limestone . . . [and] timber.* [28]

As far as the large agricultural settlements along the Bay of Fundy were concerned, a Halifax governmental official, Michael Franklin, accurately observed in September, 1766: "The produce of the fine fertile Marshes and other rich Lands in the Bay of Fundy, are now chiefly carried to Boston, as the Carriage by Water less Dangerous than coasting round to this and other Ports on the Sea Shore . . . we shall be a Province too much dependent on New England, and remain in a feeble, languid state."[29] This observation was just as valid for the colony during the next decade. Franklin could also have pointed out that Halifax, with a population of fewer than 3,000 inhabitants, could not compete effectively with the New England coastal cities, especially Boston. The commercial hinterland of Halifax was largely restricted to the Bedford Basin, while that of Boston stretched into the Bay of Fundy and around the south shore of Nova Scotia to Liverpool and beyond.

The south shore fishing and lumbering settlements of Yarmouth, Barrington, and Liverpool continued to be under the economic domination of New England, as the region had been since the middle of the seventeenth century. For over 100 years various Massachusetts fishing entrepreneurs had been able to control this region from a distance. In the 1760s and 1770s their agents and other New Englanders, by taking up permanent residence there, reaffirmed and strengthened this control. A random sampling of trade data from the valuable diary of Simeon Perkins, an influential Liverpool merchant, shows something of the extent of the commercial relationship:

Saturday, October 18th [1766] — Whittimore arrives in Mack's schr., 200 qtls. I settle with Capt. Annible for salt purchased last summer. Annible sails next day for Boston.
Monday, Oct. 20th — Capt. William Dean arrives in a schr. from Boston. . . .
Sunday, Nov. 9th — Sloop Liberty, and a schr. of Collins sail for Boston. . . .
Wednesday, July 29th [1767] A sloop from Cape Cod. . . .
Thursday, July 20th. . . . A schr. arrives from Nantucket. . . .
Monday, Aug. 3d — Ships 54 qtls. of fish in schr. Vigorous, for Boston. . . .
Sunday, Sept. 13th — Schr. Squirrell, Capt. Snow, sails for Boston. . . . A sloop from Connecticut puts in. . . .
Wednesday, April 22d [1772] Capt. William Dean arrives from Boston, wanting a cargo of oak boards. . . .
Sunday, April 26th — David Bears arrives in a small schr. from Boston, owned by Capt. Cobb & Co.
Saturday, May 30th — . . . Three Plymouth schrs. come in from the Banks. . . .
Saturday, July 2d [1774] . . . Seven vessels arrive from Plymouth. . . .
Sunday, July 10th — Captain Martin from Salem. . . .
Tuesday, July 12th — A sloop came from Boston last night. . . .
Monday, July 18th — Capt. William Davis, of Salem, arrived.[30]

It was only in the political sphere that the Nova Scotia Yankees discovered that the Halifax authorities were determined to break New England's control over the outsettlements. Halifax refused to give the settlers the same broad latitude in choosing local officials as they had enjoyed in New England. By the Act for the Choice of Town Officers and Regulating of Townships passed in 1765, the local Grand Jury was allowed to nominate two or more persons for each office. From these individuals, the Court of Quarter Sessions, carefully selected by the Halifax officials, was "to *choose* and *appoint*." As has been persuasively argued: "This Act was a complete repudiation of the New England form of Township government. . . . But it prevented the formation of some 20 little republics in Western Nova Scotia, and it enabled the central government both to establish communication with the Townships and to retain a check upon their activities."[31] Only at this one level did Halifax endeavour to neutralize what seemed to officials in the capital to be the disconcerting influence of New England. This governmental interference did not adversely affect those New England entrepreneurs involved in Nova Scotia's commercial life or those divines still interested in the colony. Nevertheless it must have been regarded by a growing number of Massachusetts critics of British imperial policy as yet another example of British tyranny.

It is worth repeating that in Massachusetts and elsewhere in New England during the late 1760s and early 1770s traditional colonial, political, legal, and religious values and attitudes were being transformed into a revolutionary ideology. During these years the "views men held towards the relationships that bound them to each other — the discipline and pattern of society" moved in a fundamentally different direction. In New England, but not in Yankee Nova Scotia, the "right, the need, the absolute obligation to disobey legally constituted authority" became what has been called the "Universal cry" of the patriots.[32] In Nova Scotia, on the other hand, the Yankees did not devote their political energy to insisting that their traditional rights and liberties could not be violated by the British government. Instead, they requested, hat in hand, that the British authorities "indulge" them with the "same Privileges" the New Englanders had possessed in the 1630s when they first settled in North America. In other words, while many in Massachusetts were vociferously protesting against the loss, real or imagined, of existing colonial liberties, the Nova Scotia Yankees were begging that they be given something that was obviously still missing in their new colony — any manifestation of the old New England "Rights and Privileges."[33]

This striking absence of what may be regarded as political development in Yankee Nova Scotia did not go completely unnoticed in some sectors of the Massachusetts population during the decade or so before the outbreak of the Revolution. For an articulate and influential minority led by the ardent patriots John Adams and James Otis, Nova Scotia possessed a despotic regime which had virtually nothing in common with the other New England colonies, in spite of the Yankee emigration. As far as this minority was concerned, the fundamental fault with the northern colony, one which became increasingly significant as tension with Britain mounted in the 1760s and early 1770s, was that the colony was clearly not a land of liberty. In the first place, and on this almost every observer of Nova Scotia affairs agreed, the colony had gotten off to a bad start. An "undigested synthetic System of civil and military Laws and Regulations" had profoundly affected representative institutions when they were finally introduced in 1758.[34] As a result, Nova Scotia possessed a corrupt and arbitrary government. In 1773 John Adams observed that when a governor was "entirely dependent on the Crown and the Council or in danger of becoming so," then "the Liberties of the Country would be totally lost, and everyman at the mercy of a few slaves of the governor."[35] According to the Adams analysis, Nova Scotia had been in such a state since the founding of Halifax in 1749. In such a hostile environment there was little hope and no future for the forces of liberty. As some early Yankee settlers in Nova Scotia had graphically expressed it, they had by emigrating merely been transformed into "the shameful and Contemptible By-Word of America; — The Slaves of Nova Scotia, the Creatures of Military Govrs; whose will, is our Law, and whose Person, is our God."[36] This negative self-image was superimposed on the existing extremely uncomplimentary Massachusetts stereotype of Nova Scotia.

Nova Scotia was obviously radically different from the New England colonies. What further emphasized this difference was the way the British authorities had built the new Nova Scotia. In their battle with the British authorities, some Massachusetts leaders felt it essential to stress that the New England colonies had not been founded by the English government. The argument usually followed a definite pattern. It was asserted, first, that the original settlements owed nothing

227

to the English government, and, second, that the settlements were not made in territory belonging either to the Crown or to the people of England. The point was, of course, that the colonists had only bound themselves indirectly to the English government by their voluntary consent to the various charters. They became, according to John Adams, "subject to the Crown upon certain Conditions which Contract, Subordination and Conditions were wrought into their Charters."[37] Nova Scotia did not fit into this pattern. The colonization of the colony since 1749 had been undertaken largely as a government project on territory belonging to the Crown of England. And the colonization, even the settling of many New Englanders, had been paid for by British taxpayers.

By the criteria of the New England critics, Nova Scotia in the 1760s and 1770s was one colony already enslaved by a despotic system. As early as 1759 Benjamin Franklin, a native of Massachusetts, had warned that Nova Scotia was the North American testing ground for the new colonial policies the British government eventually hoped to force upon the thirteen colonies. The British ministers, according to Franklin, thought that the North American colonies already had "too many and too great privileges." At the Board of Trade, the Earl of Halifax had led the way in his coddling of the military regime in Nova Scotia. "If his sentiment were no other way to be known," observed Franklin, "the fruitless Experiment he had try'd at the Nation's cost of a military Government for a Colony, sufficiently shows what he thinks would be best for us."[38] Franklin's assessment of the Nova Scotia situation was shared by others who denounced the "i–lg–l, high and a–b–y Measures" of the Nova Scotia government, which had compelled some disillusioned Yankees to take "their Flight, and return to a Land of Liberty."[39]

The contempt for Nova Scotia probably reached its peak in Massachusetts during the 1760s. It was felt that the British were actually using Halifax, and Halifax *was* Nova Scotia, as a base for operations against New England liberties. The tighter enforcement by the Vice-Admiralty Courts of the Navigation Acts significantly altered existing practices in the mainland colonies and meant that a vessel could be seized anywhere between Massachusetts and Georgia by customs officials, who then could "carry the trial to Halifax . . . and thither the owner must follow him to defend his property . . . among total strangers."[40] According to the British authorities, only the Court in Halifax could be trusted to treat the American offenders with any degree of impartiality.

During the Stamp Act crisis of 1764 and 1765 the publication of *A Letter from a Gentleman at Halifax* thrust to the surface in Massachusetts some of the existing bitter animosity concerning Nova Scotia.[41] In 1765 James Otis, while defending the colonies against the attacks of the Rhode Island author of the *Letter from a Gentleman at Halifax*, considered the most damaging epithet that he could use to attack personally the author was "Halifax." On several occasions Otis referred contemptuously to the "Halifax Tartar" or the "Halifax genius" or even simply to the "Halifaxian," a word which he and his readers must have regarded in itself as a term of abuse.[42] What also concerned Otis and other New England writers criticizing the Anglophile arrogance and anti–New England bias of the *Letter from a Gentleman at Halifax* was the emphasis placed in the pamphlet and its sequel on the crucial role played by Peter Warren and the British navy in the capture of Louisbourg in 1745.[43] The New England contribution had, apparently, been of little consequence. The debate served to turn at least some Massachusetts minds back to the bitter conflict that had raged in New England over the Louisbourg and Beauséjour episodes. There continued to be a deep pool of anti-British sentiment in Massachusetts which the successful propagandist could tap by evoking memories of 1745 and 1755. Moreover, Otis reminded his fellow Massachusetts inhabitants of the callous disregard of their interests in the midst of the Seven Years' War when, while they were "greatly alarmed and terrified at the rapid progress of the French . . . 10,000 of the best troops in the world were kept parading at Halifax and spent the summer in mock battles and sieges."[44]

In 1745 and 1755 the British had taken credit for what were, as far as Otis, Adams, and their supporters were concerned, major New England victories, and they had also made their own selfish use of the fruits of victory. Nova Scotia in the 1760s was, furthermore, the kind of colony the British authorities wanted Massachusetts eventually to become. The northern colony had had every ounce of freedom squeezed out of it by the arbitrary Halifax government. In early 1766, while noting, in the afterglow of the Stamp Act crisis, the "triumphant . . . Spirit of Liberty . . . everywhere" in America, John Adams could only "pity" his "unhappy fellow Subjects in Quebeck and Hallifax, for the great Misfortune that has befallen them." Adams could sympathize with the French and English in Quebec. They were "awed by an Army," but at least there seemed to be some signs of "Discontent" there. Halifax and Nova Scotia, on the other hand, as well as being "Kept in fear by a Fleet and an Army," showed no sign of "the Spirit of Liberty." The colony, declared Adams, "consists of a sett of Fugitives and Vagabonds."[45] Thus, one of the leading Massachusetts patriots in 1766 believed that there was a better chance for "the Spirit of Liberty" to spread among the Roman Catholic Papists of Quebec than among the Nova Scotia Yankees. Corrupt and despotic Nova Scotia, certainly not a "New New England," was both incapable and unworthy of ideological redemption. What it lacked, as one New Englander put it, was the essential *"Ecclaircisement"* which could telescope the transformation that had taken place in New England values between 1765 and 1775 into one great Nova Scotian act of understanding.[46]

Taking into account the negative image of the northern colony, one is hardly surprised that in the early years of the American Revolution, almost no one in Massachusetts was concerned about the liberation of Nova Scotia. The existing expansionist thrust was directed northwestward against Quebec. The only centre of organized activity against Nova Scotia during this period was the isolated tiny lumbering and fishing outpost of Machias, a few miles west of the St. Croix River. Many of the inhabitants of this settlement, led by the fiery Reverend James Lyon, formerly minister to a Presbyterian congregation at Onslow in Nova Scotia, wished to annex Nova Scotia and in the process plunder the settlements.[47]

In the summer of 1775 the Machias inhabitants informed General George Washington, commander-in-chief of the Continental Congress forces, that they would attack Nova Scotia if they were supported by a force of 1,000 men and four vessels.[48] Washington tactfully refused to agree to such a scheme, maintaining that all available men and supplies were needed for the proposed Quebec invasion. His arguments justifying his refusal help to explain why, in the strategic sense at least, Washington and also the Massachusetts authorities were unwilling to consider organizing any kind of offensive against Nova Scotia in 1775 and 1776:

I apprehend such an Enterprise inconsistent with the General Principal upon which the Colonies have proceeded. That

Province has not acceeded, it is true, to the Measures of
Congress; and therefore, they have been excluded from all
Commercial Intercourse with the other Colonies; But they
have not Commenced Hostilities against them, nor are any
to be apprehended. To attack them, therefore, is a Measure of
Conquest, rather than Defence, and may be attended with
very dangerous consequences. It might, perhaps, be easy,
with the forces proposed, to make an Incursion into the
Province and overawe those of the Inhabitants who are
Inimical to our cause; and for a short time prevent the
Supplying the Enemy with Provisions; but the same Force
must continue to produce any lasting Effects. As to the
furnishing Vessels of Force, you, Gentlemen, will anticipate
me, in pointing out our weakness and the Enemy's Strength
at Sea. There would be great Danger that, with the best
preparation we could make, they would fall an easy prey
either to the Men of War of that Station [Halifax] or some
who would be detach'd from Boston.[49]

Washington was undoubtedly accurate in his long-term strategic
analysis, but the inhabitants of Machias were certain in the summer of
1775 that much of Nova Scotia was vulnerable to a well-organized
American assault. Had not American economic pressure helped to
precipitate a serious recession in the colony? Had not Governor
Francis Legge of Nova Scotia alienated a large number of influential
inhabitants, and were not some Yankees, at least, sympathetic to the
revolutionary cause? In addition it was common knowledge that there
were only thirty-six British regulars guarding Halifax, and Legge, who
was certain "that many in this Town are disaffected," sadly observed
that "the fortifications [of Halifax] were in a dilapidated state, the
batteries . . . dismantled, the gun-carriages decayed, the guns on the
ground."[50]
   During the summer months of 1775, at the same time the citizens
of Machias were advocating a Nova Scotia expedition, an indigenous
revolutionary movement came into being in the Chignecto Isthmus
area of the colony. It was led by Jonathan Eddy and John Allan, both
of whom had represented Cumberland County in the Nova Scotia
Assembly. Eddy, a native of Norton, Massachusetts, had served under
Winslow in 1755 and had immigrated to the Chignecto region in 1763.[51]

Allan had come to Nova Scotia in 1749 at the age of three from Scotland, and after receiving his early education in Massachusetts, he had returned to the Chignecto region where he married into a Yankee family.⁵² Eddy, Allan, and their Yankee supporters had been greatly encouraged by the successful sacking in August of Fort Frederick, a small British military outpost at the mouth of the St. John River, by a small force of Machias freebooters. Towards the end of November, Eddy and Allan were given an excellent opportunity to precipitate a crisis that they hoped would eventually lead to armed insurrection in their colony.

The long-simmering discontent with the Halifax governmental authorities finally boiled over in the outlying areas of the colony in December when it was discovered that two unpopular acts had been passed by the Assembly which was controlled by the Halifax merchant clique. The first act stipulated that one-fifth of the militia was to be called out to defend the colony, and the second imposed a tax for the support of the militia. Almost immediately the two acts were denounced throughout the Yankee areas, but especially in the Chignecto region. Eddy and Allan, instead of immediately trying to channel the disenchantment into an armed uprising, decided instead to broaden first the popular basis of their support. To accomplish this, they sent a rather mildly worded remonstrance to Legge about the two new acts. In the protest, which was eventually signed by almost 250 inhabitants including some Yorkshiremen, the Chignecto settlers objected to the new tax and to the possibility of being forced to "march into different parts in arms against their friends and relations." Eddy and Allan had succeeded in winning a great deal of popular support for their assault upon the Halifax authorities, but almost at the moment when they attempted to use this support to emulate the example of the colonies in revolt, Legge suddenly pulled the rug from under their unsuspecting feet. Realizing the seriousness of the discontent as reflected in the Chignecto petition, the governor promptly suspended the two contentious acts and in this manner effectively neutralized much of whatever prorevolutionary feeling there was in the colony.⁵³

Failing to grasp the significance of Legge's clever manoeuvre, Eddy and Allan decided during January, 1776, that the time was propitious for fomenting a major insurrection. Nothing could have been further from the truth. When they sounded out their neighbours concerning their proposal, they were genuinely shocked to discover that the vast majority of Yankees, even though they would have welcomed an army of invasion, stubbornly refused to support the planned insurrection. Like many other Nova Scotia Yankees in early 1776, when most Chignecto inhabitants considered the meaning of the term revolution, it simply meant to them obtaining military assistance from New England. The American invaders would have to liberate the Nova Scotians and bring the Revolution to them. After their disconcerting sampling of Chignecto public opinion, Eddy and Allan, realizing that a Nova Scotia revolution was out of the question, were compelled to alter drastically their proposed policy.

In February, 1776, Jonathan Eddy set out from Chignecto with a band of fourteen men to persuade Washington and the Continental Congress to capture Nova Scotia. On March 27 Eddy met with the American general at Cambridge, Massachusetts. Washington carefully considered Eddy's often illogical arguments, but believing that the British forces that had abandoned Boston ten days earlier were then in Halifax, the general informed the ambassador from Chignecto that "in the present uncertain state of things . . . a much more considerable force [than that requested] would be of no avail." Washington reaffirmed the policy he had first enunciated in August of the preceding year when he had rejected the Machias plan. The disillusioned Eddy next went to the Continental Congress in Philadelphia, but as he expected, here too his urgent appeal fell on unresponsive ears. After his return to the isthmus in May, it was decided that, as a last resort, the revolutionary government of Massachusetts should be approached for military aid. The persistent Eddy immediately set sail for Boston, while Allan was left behind to prepare the way for the expected invaders.[54]

During the months of January and February, 1776, the Halifax authorities seemed to have been strangely indifferent to developments in the Chignecto Isthmus region. The loyalist leaders, the Yorkshireman Charles Dixon and the Anglican priest, the Reverend John Eagleson, had bombarded the governor and his Executive Council with frantic letters. A delegation had been sent, they reported, by the Yankees to General Washington; and on hearing a rumour that the American army had captured Bunker Hill, the supporters of Eddy and Allan had procured "a chaise and six horses, postillion and a flag of liberty, and drove about the isthmus, proclaiming the news and blessings of liberty." Dixon and Eagleson demanded immediate and vigorous government action. In March the Executive Council finally resolved to send the lieutenant-governor, Michael Franklin, "as soon as possible to [Chignecto] . . . and there make a strict inquiry into the behavior and conduct of the inhabitants and to make report thereof to the governor: also, that he will apprehend all persons, who, on due proof, shall be found guilty of any rebellious and treasonable transactions."[55] The pompous and arrogant Franklin was able to accomplish absolutely nothing.

It was not until June that the government exerted some semblance of authority on the troubled isthmus. This delay was at least partly the result of the recall of Legge in May and his replacement by Lieutenant-Colonel Arbuthnot. In June, 200 Royal Fencibles under the command of Lieutenant-Colonel Joseph Gorham, a native of Massachusetts, were sent to occupy Fort Cumberland, which had been abandoned by the British eight years earlier. Fort Cumberland, the reconstructed French Fort Beauséjour, was strategically located at the extreme southern tip of the Fort Cumberland Ridge which cuts through the Chignecto marshlands until it almost touches the waters of the Bay of Fundy. Gorham found the fort in a state of serious disrepair. He reported that "the face of the Bastions, Curtains etc., by being so long exposed to the heavy rains and frost were bent down to such a slope that one might with ease ascend any part of the fort." Gorham set about repairing the fort, and he went out of his way to overlook what he considered to be the harmless activities of the American sympathizers. He hoped that a simple show of strength would completely undermine the position held by the Eddy-Allan faction.[56]

It was not until July that the Halifax authorities, at last convinced of the seriousness of the revolutionary movement on the isthmus, considered it necessary to strike against the leaders of the "American Party." A proclamation was issued offering a reward of £200 for the capture of Eddy and £100 for Allan and two others. On hearing that he was a man with a price on his head, Allan decided to join his friends in Massachusetts and was content to leave behind a committee in charge of "the revolutionary interests."[57]

Eddy was unsuccessful in his attempt to persuade the Massachusetts authorities to send a military expedition, as it had frequently done in the past, "supplied with some necessaries, as provisions and ammunition . . . [to] destroy those [Nova Scotian] forts and relieve our brethren and friends."[58] Eddy had hoped that the prorevolutionary stance taken by some settlers in his community, as well as those at Maugerville up the St. John River and those at Passamaquoddy on the St. Croix, would finally force Massachusetts to defend the revolutionaries in western Nova Scotia by taking over the region. Had not the Maugerville inhabitants proudly resolved in May?

> *1stly . . . That we can see no shadow of Justice in that Extensive Claim of the British Parliament (viz.) the Right to Enacting Laws binding on the Colonies in all Cases whatsoever. This System if once Established (we Conceive) hath a Direct tendency to Sap the foundation, not only of Liberty that Dearest of names, but of property that best of subjects.*
>
> *2ndly . . . That as tyrany ought to be Resisted in its first appearance we are Convinced that the united Provinces are just in their proceeding in this Regard.*
>
> *3rdly . . . That it is our Minds and Desire to submit ourselves to the government of the Massachusetts Bay and that we are Ready with our Lives and fortunes to share with them the Event of the present Struggle for Liberty, however God in his Providence may order it.*[59]

All that Eddy was able to obtain from the Massachusetts authorities was a promise of "Two hundred pound weight of Gunpowder, five hundred weight of Musket Ball, three hundred Gun flints, and twenty barrels of Pork."[60] Massachusetts had no desire to expand into western Nova Scotia. Obsessed with its own defence problems and with providing men for Washington's army, Massachusetts had better things to do with its resources. Besides, if there were any lessons to be learned from her past relationship with Nova Scotia, it was for Massachusetts to keep clear of any entanglements whatsoever.

Eddy, in spite of the triple rebuff from Washington, the Continental Congress, and the Massachusetts General Court, refused to abandon his scheme. Instead he hurried off to Machias where he knew there were some men still vitally interested in attacking Nova Scotia. The Reverend Lyon was one man who sympathized with Eddy because of Eddy's treatment by the General Court. Lyon complained: "Some members of the Court consider the eastern country as a moth (costs more than it is worth and would be wise to let it suffer and sink). Should your honors believe the east to be a moth, dispose of it, and give us the right of dominion. We shall then become an independent state ourselves and we shall think of Nova Scotia as worth annexing to our dominion." He declared furthermore that he enthusiastically supported "the noble spirit and resolution of Captain Eddy and heartily wish[ed] him success and all the honour of reducing Nova Scotia."[61] But Lyon represented only a handful of Machias freebooters who were obviously out of touch with the Massachusetts consensus concerning Nova Scotia. Whatever enthusiasm there was for an invasion was restricted to the insignificant frontier backwater that was Machias.

Even with Lyon's endorsement, Eddy was able to recruit only twenty-eight men from Machias for the planned expedition against Nova Scotia. On August 11, just as the invading army was embarking, Allan arrived. Fully aware of the weakness of the so-called revolutionary movement on the isthmus and throughout Nova Scotia, Allan tried in vain to dissuade Eddy, the veteran of the Winslow-Monckton expedition, from carrying out what Allan was certain was now a rash and hopeless plan. Eddy refused to come to grips with the hard facts, and he regarded as inconsequential the movement of British troops into Fort Cumberland. Instead, Eddy naively hoped that his force would build up like a giant snowball at Passamaquoddy and Maugerville and that the Chignecto Yankees would eagerly rush to his revolutionary banner. He seemed to think that it would be only a matter of time before his liberating army, picking up hundreds of recruits as it rolled on to Halifax, would drive the British into the sea.[62]

At Passamaquoddy, a few miles northeast of Machias, Eddy added seven new recruits, and the invaders sailed in three whaleboats to Maugerville. The size of the flotilla was in sharp contrast to those of 1755, 1745, 1707, 1704, 1690, and even 1654, and it symbolized, in a sense, the dramatic decline of Massachusetts' interest in Nova Scotia. And without Eddy — the Nova Scotian — there would not have been even a Machias expedition. At Maugerville Eddy found the inhabitants "almost universally to be hearty in the cause," but he was nevertheless able to enlist only twenty-seven settlers and sixteen Indians. His liberating army, now numbering some eighty men, over half of whom were residents of Nova Scotia, returned to the mouth of the St. John River to await the arrival of some promised ammunition and supplies from Boston. Because of an unexpected prolonged delay, the force was unable to move eastward until the final week of October. On October 29 Eddy's men easily captured fourteen of Gorham's troops stationed at the military outpost of Shepody to the south of present-day Moncton. The invaders then swung sharply to the north and made their way up the Petitcodiac and Memramcook rivers to the Acadian settlement of Memramcook, where Eddy had little trouble in persuading a number of Acadians to support him. From Memramcook on November 5 Eddy and his men marched eastward towards their immediate objective — Fort Cumberland.

The supporters of Eddy and Allan on the isthmus loudly "expressed their Uneasiness at seeing so few [invaders] . . . and those unprovided with Artillery." They vehemently argued that taking everything into consideration, there was no possible chance of success. Even if Fort Cumberland was captured, and this was considered to be highly unlikely, British reinforcements would readily rout Eddy's motley collection of undisciplined freebooters, Indians, and Acadians. Eddy was forced to resort to outright intimidation and to false promises in order to win the unenthusiastic support of his friends. His arguments were objectively described by his associate Allan:

> *That they [Chignecto Yankees] had supply'd the Enemys of America which had much displeased the States. That the Congress doubted their integrity, that if they would not rouse themselves and oppose the British power in that province [Nova Scotia] they would be looked upon as enemys and should the country be reduced by the States they would be treated as conquered people and that if they did not Incline to do something he [Eddy] would return and report them to the States. But if they would now assert their rights publickly against the King's Govt., he was then Come to help them and in Fifteen days Expected a reinforcement of a large body of men.*[63]

These reinforcements, of course, existed only in Eddy's active imagination.

Apparently, only fifty Chignecto Yankees rallied to Eddy's banner, and they were joined a short time later by twenty-seven men from the Cobequid area. The invading army, now basically a Nova Scotian one, numbered roughly 180 men. Eddy deserves some credit for using his relatively small force to gain virtual control of the entire Chignecto

Isthmus, except of course, for Fort Cumberland. Most of the anti-American Yorkshiremen, fearing the destruction of their property if they supported Gorham, quickly surrendered their guns and ammunition to the invaders. It should be noted that well over half the Yankees supported neither Eddy nor Gorham but instead carefully balanced themselves between the two groups.

Eddy was neither a demagogue nor a megalomaniac. Rather, he was determined to transform revolutionary rhetoric into fundamental political change. He believed that all ties between Nova Scotia and Britain should be severed, and his almost fanatical enthusiasm for the revolutionary cause seriously dulled whatever sense of military strategy he might have possessed. In Massachusetts he would have probably been merely one of the thousands of rank-and-file revolutionaries, while in Nova Scotia he was the leader of the movement.

In spite of all sorts of fantastic rumours as to the size of Eddy's invading force, rumours which spread like wildfire across Nova Scotia during the months of October and November, the great majority of the Yankees could not be aroused from their profound sense of confusion and their acute case of collective disorientation. By missing the critical decade of ideological development in New England, the Yankees found themselves locked into the pre-1765 conceptual framework they had brought with them. Their world in 1775 and 1776 had suddenly assumed an unfamiliar shape; men with familiar names and from familiar places were using old words and phrases in a radically new and strange manner. Bitter civil strife, pitting New Englander against Briton, had engulfed their former homeland. American privateers and British press gangs were beginning to introduce further elements of instability into an already chaotic situation. The Eddy invasion provided no adequate answer to their frustrating dilemma; it merely added to the existing confusion.

As early as August, Gorham had heard of Eddy's strange invasion plans, but it was not until the beginning of November that he learned that Eddy was in the Chignecto area. With fewer than 200 troops at his command and believing that Eddy had at least 500 men, Gorham thought that it would be unwise to attack the invaders. Instead he waited in the fort for the siege to begin and for reinforcements from Windsor and Halifax to lift the siege.

During the early morning hours of November 7, Eddy's force experienced its only real victory during the Chignecto campaign.

Taking advantage of a thick fog that had settled over the coastal region, Zebulon Rowe, one of Eddy's lieutenants, set out with a handful of men thirsting for excitement and possible loot to capture a sloop filled with supplies for the Fort Cumberland troops. Because of the low tide, the sloop lay on the broad mud flats to the southwest of the fort. Eddy described the engagement:

> *After a Difficult March, they arrived opposite the Sloop; on board of which was a Guard of 1 Sergt and 12 men, who had fir'd at our People, must have alarmed the Garrison in such a Manner as to have brought them on their Backs. However, our men rushed Resolutely towards the sloop up to their Knees in Mud, which made such a Noise as to alarm the Centry, who hailed them and immediately called the Sergt of the Guard. The Sergt on coming up, Ordered his Men to fire, but was immediately told by Mr. Row[e] that if they fired one Gun, Every Man of Them should be put to death; which so frightened the poor Devils that they surrendered without firing a Shot, although our People Could not board her without the Assistance of the Conquered, who let down Ropes to our Men to get up by.*[64]

Only two attempts were made to capture Fort Cumberland, one on November 13 and the other nine days later. Both were fiascos and comic-opera episodes. Before Eddy could organize a third assault, British reinforcements arrived. On November 27 and 28 the British relieving force, consisting of two companies of marines and one company of Royal Highlanders, finally landed at Fort Cumberland. On the twenty-eighth, Gorham ordered Major Batt, an officer who had accompanied the reinforcements, to lead an attack on Eddy's camp one mile north of the fort. At five-thirty in the morning of the twenty-ninth, Batt marched out of Fort Cumberland with 170 troops, hoping to surprise the rebels. If it had not been for an alert young Negro drummer who furiously beat the alarm when he sighted the enemy, Eddy's men would have been slaughtered as they slept.[65] Wiping sleep from their eyes, Eddy's confused followers ran into the neighbouring woods in search of cover. In the skirmish that followed, only seven rebels and four British soldiers were killed. Seeing for the first time the utter hopelessness of the situation, Eddy ordered his men to retreat westward "to the St. John River . . . and there make a stand."

Batt refused to chase the enemy; instead he had his men put to the torch every home and barn belonging to the isthmus inhabitants who had openly supported Eddy. The billowing dark clouds of smoke, Eddy's legacy to Nova Scotia, could be seen by the defeated invaders as they fled in panic towards Memramcook.

Eddy's attempt to capture Fort Cumberland failed not only because he lacked siege weapons, but also because his inadequate force was poorly trained, undisciplined, and badly led. With British naval control of the North Atlantic firmly established, with the refusal of Washington and the Massachusetts leaders to mount a major offensive against Nova Scotia, and with the vast majority of Nova Scotians unwilling to support him, Eddy's task was from the very beginning a hopeless one. Even though the Eddy expedition was, by any strategic standards, quite insignificant in the larger revolutionary context, it nevertheless graphically demonstrates the weakness of the Massachusetts thrust into Nova Scotia during the critical months following the Declaration of Independence. It is difficult to imagine how Massachusetts could have cared less in 1776 about Nova Scotia. In a sense, its response was the logical culmination of events involving the two regions in the 1740s and 1750s.

13

Privateering and Revival: The Revolutionary Years, 1777-1784

Throughout the latter years of the revolutionary war, the Massachusetts General Court and most of the state's representatives in the Continental Congress remained coldly indifferent to peninsular Nova Scotia and the region's Yankee population. For the Massachusetts political leaders and for most of the inhabitants they represented, the settled area of Nova Scotia east of the Chignecto Isthmus was of little or no consequence in the larger revolutionary setting. The only Massachusetts residents, apart from the Machias settlers, who appeared interested in peninsular Nova Scotia were the Eddy-Allan refugees and the hundreds of privateersmen, especially those from Essex County, who played havoc with the colony's commerce and terrorized every coastal settlement, notably excepting Halifax. These privateersmen were attracted to the Nova Scotia coast not by any desire to propagate the revolutionary gospel or to push the territorial limits of Massachusetts significantly northeastward; rather, they were drawn by the expectation of seizing booty from British ships and from the Nova Scotia settlements.

Jonathan Eddy's only serious competitor in late 1776 and 1777 for the role of republican saviour of Nova Scotia was John Allan, his Chignecto neighbour. At the very moment, during the last week of November, 1776, when the quixotic Eddy was being chased by British troops away from Fort Cumberland into the wilds of western Nova Scotia, Allan was leaving Boston on horseback for Philadelphia and Baltimore to see George Washington and the members of the Continental Congress. Allan hoped to succeed where Eddy had failed and to persuade these seemingly uninterested men that it was vitally important to send immediately a large liberating army to Nova Scotia. Allan, using the argument that scores of propagandists had employed in Massachusetts since the time of Cotton Mather, maintained that unless this was done, the enemy would "influence the Indians more Westward to harass and disturb the eastern settlements of Massachusetts so as to annex those parts to that Colony [Nova Scotia]."[1]

Allan's concern for the liberation of his homeland reflected his ideological commitment to the revolutionary cause rather than any narrow economic motive. If he had been primarily concerned with retaining possession of his prosperous 348-acre farm — "one of the best in the two counties of Cumberland and Westmoreland" — and with continuing in his profitable Indian trade, he would not have publicly and enthusiastically espoused the revolutionary cause. Allan throughout the war was not afraid of sacrificing everything, including his own life, for his ideological principles. He had spent his impressionable boyhood years in Massachusetts during the turbulent 1760s and had been affected there by what he called the "Spirit . . . of Liberty."[2] When asked by some Indian friends in June, 1776, "How comes it that Old England & new Quarrel & come to blows?" Allan replied by giving what he described as "a short Historical Account of matters from the beginning of the settlement of America, the reasons of the first Emegrants leaving Europe; the different Charters of the Colonies, the unjust demand of Britain and breach of Faith – the usurp'd authority claimed by Britain, the different steps taken by the Americans for redress, and finally the design of Establishing Civil & religious Liberty."[3] Allan's political thinking, unlike most Nova Scotia Yankees', had been transformed in the late 1760s in Massachusetts, and the revolutionary rhetoric of 1774, 1775, and 1776 provided him with a perceptive and convincing analysis of Anglo-American relations.

After meeting with Washington on Sunday, December 22, 1776, Allan travelled to Baltimore where he discussed on January 4, 1777, with the members of the Continental Congress his plan to attack Nova Scotia. Moving the Congress from Philadelphia to Baltimore, further still from Massachusetts, had apparently made some of its members more receptive to arguments in favour of a Louisbourg-like expedition against Halifax and Fort Cumberland. What especially appealed to the Continental Congress was Allan's contention that 3,000 revolutionary troops would "destroy the immense Quantities of military Stores that are there deposited to be employed against us." John Hancock, one of Massachusetts' representatives and the president of the Congress, was fully convinced that "the Destruction of above Half a Million of Stores must be a severe Blow on the Enemy, and may possibly present a principal means of ridding our Country of those cruel Foes, who, with impious Hands have been spreading Pain and Desolation over it to the utmost of their Power."[4]

On January 8 the Continental Congress, in a significant shift in strategic policy, resolved that "a Body of Men not exceeding Three Thousand" be raised in Massachusetts for the projected "Expedition to Nova Scotia." The troops, who were to be paid by the Congress, were to be despatched "in the Course of the Winter, or early in Spring" only if the Massachusetts authorities decided "that an advantageous Attack" could be made. The Congress showed its concern for the Indians and the northeastern frontier by appointing Allan superintendent of the eastern Indians and a colonel in the Continental army.[5]

Before Allan's return to Boston on February 3, the Massachusetts Council had already discussed the resolution passed by Congress on January 8. By this time the news of Eddy's fiasco had reached Massachusetts, as had information about large numbers of British warships, "severel at Halifax and severel in the Bay of Fundy," and the recent arrival in Nova Scotia's capital of "eight or ten thousand Hessians." Confronted by these disconcerting pieces of evidence and the realization that troops, in all likelihood, could not be recruited, the Massachusetts Council on January 30 resolved that "it would be neither practicable nor calculated to advance the Interests of America to undertake the Expedition proposed at this time." This resolution reaffirmed the Legislature's earlier unwillingness to become militarily involved in Nova Scotia affairs. The Council, however, promised to "endeavour immediately to procure the best Intelligence with Regard to the force in that Province and, the practicability of such an Attempt and advise Congress thereof and in case they should, upon the Information we may obtain, think it expedient to prosecute such an Expedition we shall chearfully Comply with their desire and do all in our power to carry it into execution."[6] What the Massachusetts government was tactfully declaring on January 30 was that it would not at that point be pushed into Nova Scotia by the Continental Congress. The Bay state had far more important things to worry about.

The Massachusetts Council resolution and the Eddy disaster significantly altered Allan's military strategy regarding Nova Scotia. By February Allan realized that it was inconceivable that Massachusetts would agree to any large-scale land-sea assault on Halifax. He therefore proposed to the Massachusetts Council, instead, that an invading American force be sent to the St. John River, where two forts would be constructed to establish Yankee control over the general area. He contended that such a move would achieve important humanitarian ends as well as serve to protect the northeastern frontier of Massachusetts and perhaps even finally result in a major offensive thrust against Fort Cumberland. Preoccupied with the "Indigent Circumstances and Indispositions" of those Chignecto inhabitants who had supported Eddy, Allan maintained that a republican-controlled St. John River valley should be the "place of Retreat . . . for said Inhabitants with some aid and assistance to Enable them to Remove their Familys, as the Spring in all probability will produce a greater scene of distress." He argued further that the mouth of the St. John River was the base from which "a sufficient Force" could eventually "Expell those tyrants of the humane Race from the Country. . . . To Establish that system of Liberty which the U.S. are Contending for." If such an offensive thrust was impossible, at least the Massachusetts presence would win the wavering Indians to the republican side and "prevent the Britains from Annoying the Eastern Settlements and Opening a Communication into Canada."[7]

Allan's constant pressure finally forced the Massachusetts General Court in March, 1777, to consider seriously the plight of the Chignecto inhabitants and to re-examine its policy regarding the Indians on the northeastern frontier and in western Nova Scotia. In a remarkable reversal of policy, a committee of the two houses on March 25 enthusiastically endorsed Allan's proposal:

> That there be two fortresses erected on the River St. John in Nova Scotia . . . that a sufficient force be sent into Nova Scotia from this state, to Secure the Inhabitants in the possession of the remainder of their Estates, and to act as occasion may require . . . two Battalions raised in this State and one in the Province of Nova Scotia on the Continental Establishment for the term of one year, unless the service

*will admit of their being sooner discharged will be sufficient
to affect the business aforesaid.*[8]

In spite of the committee recommendation and some prodding
from the Continental Congress to "adopt and carry with Execution at
the Expence of the U.S." the planned expedition, nothing was done
about it in Massachusetts in March, April, or May. It was not until
the first week of June, almost ten weeks after the committee report,
that the Massachusetts Council was finally compelled by force of
circumstances to endeavour to transform strategic rhetoric into military reality. Allan reported that on May 26 a British armed sloop had
visited the St. John River area and that its crew had reported that the
British planned "to Return with all Expedition to Erect two Fortifications." Allan was certain, or so he reported to the Massachusetts
Council, that there was "intended . . . some secret Expedition near
your Honors plann'd by those Villians." Allan must have realized that
only such intelligence could possibly stir the obviously apathetic
Massachusetts authorities into actually doing something about their
March 25 resolution. He was right. On June 7, 1777, the Massachusetts
General Court agreed that "to preserve our Eastern Settlements and
to prevent a communication through said River [St. John] between
our Enemies in Nova Scotia with those in Canada . . . there be one
Regiment raised as soon as possible, in the Counties of Lincoln and
Cumberland Maine . . . to consist of 728 men." These men, after
leaving Machias "as soon as possible," were expected to protect
northern Massachusetts "against the depredations of the enemy to the
Independancy of the United States of America." They were to carry
with them "Six Field-Pieces, with two 12 pounders and two small
Mortars," and if a sufficient number of Nova Scotia Yankees volunteered to join them after their arrival at the St. John, it was anticipated
that the Maine troops would be dismissed and sent home.[9]

Possibly in an attempt to prime the flow of Massachusetts troops
to the St. John River valley as well as to establish a tiny Massachusetts
bridgehead there, Allan left Machias on May 30 with only forty men,
including Indians, in four boats and three birch canoes for western
Nova Scotia. A little more than a week later, before the actual news of
the Court's decision had arrived, "a Captain, a Lieutenant and forty
two men" set off "from Machias to the Assistance of John Allan." No
other troops left Massachusetts in 1777 for western Nova Scotia. In

late June a small flotilla of British warships arrived at the mouth of the St. John, and their presence and the troops they carried were responsible for driving Allan back to Machias in early August, after a difficult month of retreat.

Six days later the Massachusetts Council and House of Representatives agreed to abandon officially all future plans for a Nova Scotia expedition. Weeks earlier shrewd and sensitive Massachusetts observers must have predicted that such a decision would eventually have to be made, as it was common knowledge that few recruits could be found despite special bounties and other inducements. There was little enthusiasm in the venture outside of Machias even before it was reported that the British ships and troops had arrived in strength. The lack of effective military leadership for the expedition merely reflected this prevailing popular mood of indifference. The difficulty in recruiting, a general lack of interest, Allan's retreat, and news that Fort Ticonderoga had fallen to the British under Burgoyne on July 6, all help to explain why the August 8 decision was so quickly made. With Ticonderoga in British hands, it was argued, the way was clear for the enemy to rush into the "bowels of the state." Faced with this new emergency, Massachusetts found it relatively easy to abandon the Nova Scotia effort, which had been espoused with so little real enthusiasm in the first place.[10]

In a sense, Allan in 1777 had been far more successful than Eddy the previous year in involving Massachusetts militarily in Nova Scotia affairs. But in winning the grudging support of the Massachusetts General Court, Allan had not been taking advantage of a radical change in the opinions of the rank and file concerning the importance of Nova Scotia. For the vast majority of Massachusetts inhabitants, the British colony to the northeast must have remained of little interest and consequence.

Only in terms of privateering raids was there any significant Massachusetts involvement after 1777 in Nova Scotia affairs. Until July, 1782, the General Court had explicitly prohibited all privateers from operating above "the high water line." In other words, the freebooters were not permitted to plunder on Nova Scotia soil. The shrill complaints of some of the Nova Scotia Yankees and their friends and relatives in New England regarding the "continued outrageous and atrocious conduct" of the privateers on shore had persuaded the General Court to clarify its position in June, 1780. It agreed:

Whereas it appears to this Court that Several small privateers
have committed many Robberies above high water mark, on
the Inhabitants of Nova Scotia, — Therefore, —
Resolved, That this Court do highly disapprove the
Conduct of any persons belonging to, and Commissioned
from, this State, in the business of privateering who have
committed any such Robberies aforesaid. And also Resolved,
That when any Commissions shall be given out in future to
small armed Vessells, they give good & sufficient Bonds for
the purpose of preventing such evils again taking place.[11]

In passing the June resolution, the General Court was indicating
that it did not wish its privateers to encourage British retaliatory
raids on Massachusetts. Furthermore, there must have been at least
some consideration given to the advisability of keeping open the lines
of communication between southern Nova Scotia and Essex County,
the privateering centre. From the Yarmouth and Barrington region
of the British colony, especially during the early years of the war,
there was funnelled into Massachusetts, in Nova Scotia vessels, military
intelligence, fugitive or shipwrecked American privateersmen, and
badly needed dried cod, lumber and wood products, and salt.[12]

Two years later the General Court apparently disregarded its
previous humanitarian considerations with respect to privateering raids
on Nova Scotia soil when it specifically prohibited on shore only those
depredations "within the limits of the town of Yarmouth." After
August 1, 1782, "no commander of any armed vessel, or other person
belonging to this Commonwealth" was to "be permitted to go on
shore" there and "plunder any of the inhabitants thereof." It was
further stipulated that

[if] any . . . person shall notwithstanding this resolve,
presume to go on shore . . . and there take or seize any of
the articles hereinbefore enumerated, belonging to any of
the inhabitants thereof, such inhabitant or inhabitants, who
shall have any of the said articles thus taken, be and they
hereby are admitted, by themselves or their attorney, being
a leige subject of this Government, to appear within any
Courts of law within this Commonwealth, and there prosecute
the same to final judgment and execution, any law to the
contrary notwithstanding.[13]

Yarmouth was singled out for special favourable treatment because of its special relationship with Massachusetts in terms of commerce and the funnelling of prisoners back to New England. It was obvious, moreover, that Massachusetts was extending the limits of its legal system to include the southern extremity of the neighbouring British colony. There had been some seventeenth- and eighteenth-century precedents for what must have been regarded by many in Nova Scotia as a rather presumptuous undertaking on the part of the General Court. The new policy at least seemed to promise to introduce some limited order into an extraordinarily chaotic situation.

Few Massachusetts privateersmen had taken the 1780 resolve very seriously. Three months after its promulgation, for example, the town of Liverpool was attacked by two privateers, and in August of 1781, Annapolis Royal was plundered by the crews of two privateers, whose men even stole the shiny buckles from ladies' shoes. The following summer the foreign Protestants of Lunenburg were attacked by six privateers carrying almost 100 men. The town was systematically looted and goods worth an estimated £10,000 seized. A short time later the residents of Chester successfully turned back yet another projected assault. There then followed relative calm throughout virtually all coastal settlements of Nova Scotia. In spite of the implicit encouragement for privateering raids ashore in all areas outside of Yarmouth contained in the 1782 resolves, Massachusetts privateering raids on Nova Scotia territory had to all intents and purposes ended by 1782. There were at least two reasons for this development. First, a very effective counteroffensive against the Massachusetts privateers had been mounted by British warships, using Halifax as their base of operation, and also by a number of surprisingly effective Nova Scotia–based privateers. Second, many Massachusetts privateersmen had come to realize that most of the available booty in the outsettlements had already been appropriated. There is some evidence to suggest that the privateersmen, in 1781 and 1782, realizing that peace negotiations were drawing to some kind of final solution, had lost some of their earlier enthusiasm for daring military exploits, especially when the opposition was so much better organized and the rewards so inadequate.[14]

It would be too simplistic to conclude that the New England privateering raids drove the vast majority of wavering Nova Scotians into the welcoming arms of the mother country. Some Nova Scotia

Yankees certainly moved in this direction. The "horrid Crimes" committed by the "cruel . . . voracious" privateers resulted, according to John Allan, in the creation of "more Torys than 100 Such [Massachusetts] Expeditions Will make good."[15] But most of the Nova Scotia Yankees must have been able to distinguish clearly between the rapacious privateersmen and the people and government of Massachusetts. Moreover, the privateersmen usually preyed only upon the wealthy in the outsettlements and left the ordinary inhabitants undisturbed. Even after having lost a number of their ships to American privateers and after having suffered depredations ashore, the people of Liverpool, "much Discouraged," wanted to return to New England. They blamed their plight, not on the Americans, but on the indifference of the British authorities in Halifax, who seemed far more interested in impressing Nova Scotians than in defending them.[16] The New England privateering raids, together with the constant threat of British impressment, merely added to the confusion of the Nova Scotians, especially the Nova Scotia Yankees, during a period of acute disorientation.

It would be a mistake to emphasize in the Nova Scotia response to the Revolution what may appear to be the striking theme of the continuity of neutrality. According to this interpretation, the Yankees, despite their New England origins and ties, were forced into the same frustrating predicament as their immediate predecessors, "the neutral French-speaking Acadians." Far too much stress may be placed on the similar response of the Acadians in 1755 and the Yankees in 1776.[17] The Yankees were, without question, affected by many of the same strategic and geographical considerations that had impinged upon the Acadians two decades earlier. But Yankee society was grounded upon radically different beliefs and attitudes.

In 1775 and 1776, those Nova Scotians who had espoused the cause of the Revolution had asked to be liberated by American invaders. For these Nova Scotia Yankees, this American military thrust would result in the permanent subjection of the colony to the enlightened republican government of Massachusetts. In this manner the dream of William Shirley and other Massachusetts residents from an earlier age would have finally been realized. But instead of being absorbed by the new American imperialism, the Nova Scotia Yankees experienced during the Revolution an intense religious revival. This profoundly significant social movement helped to give the Yankees a new sense of identity in the midst of the extremely confused revolutionary situation. Henry Alline, the charismatic leader of the revival, was one Nova Scotian able to perceive a special purpose for his fellow Yankees during the Revolution. He was so convinced that, as he put it, he had an "omnicient eye" to read the "map of the Disordered world," that in the summer of 1783 he resolved to return to New England to "liberate" the new states for the Lord.[18]

Rather than being merely an explosion of religious emotionalism, the Great Awakening of Nova Scotia provided the means and the occasion for a basic reorientation in the value systems of many Yankees and other Nova Scotians. Alline, who had been born in Newport, Rhode Island, in 1748 and had immigrated with his parents to Nova Scotia in 1760, reflected this change in outlook in a dramatic fashion. In March, 1775, after experiencing his conversion, the young uneducated farmer naturally felt that he "must proceed to New England and endeavour . . . to get learning there." He unquestioningly regarded New England as the ultimate source of all that was of value in life. But eight years later, Alline's views had completely changed. The success of the revival he had helped coax into existence in Nova Scotia had convinced him that the northern colony was no longer inferior to New England. In August, 1783, although dying of tuberculosis, Alline was once again "determined to go to New England." This time he was not intending to go as a shy convert from the northern wilds. Instead, Alline was planning to proclaim "my Master's name" in corrupt Massachusetts, where the residents were now ensnarled by the agents of the Antichrist.[19] Alline felt called to redeem the American states. For Alline, the settlements of the Nova Scotia Yankees, and not New England, were "as CITIES ON HILLS."[20] By involving themselves in what Alline was convinced was a sinful war, the New Englanders had abandoned the mantle of Christian leadership in the world. At that moment of abandonment, "heaven's indulgent hand" had transformed the Nova Scotians into the "people highly favoured of God."[21]

It required considerable effort to believe that these isolated settlements, since 1763 a mere backwater even in terms of Massachusetts expansionism, had been selected by God for a special purpose. But Alline, striking deep into Puritan traditions concerning the virtues of self-abnegation and frugality and into a New England evangelical heritage that viewed too much education as a barrier to conversion, argued that the poverty and remoteness of the Nova Scotia Yankees had removed them from the corrupting influences of Britain and New England. Consequently, Nova Scotia was in an ideal position to lead the world back to God, for "wherever you find the Spirit of Christ altho' among the most poor and despised People on earth, believe there is more done in the Cause of Christ there, than in the greatest Corporation with the most Strictest Discipline of the highest orders of men."[22]

The amazing change in Alline's attitude towards Massachusetts and New England reveals the dramatic change that had taken place in the minds of many Nova Scotia Yankees during the revolutionary period. In 1775 and 1776 Nova Scotia was still regarded by revolutionary supporters and other Yankees as merely the northeastern frontier of Massachusetts. By 1783 Nova Scotia had become the vital centre of the Christian world. New England gone wrong had presented Nova Scotia with an opportunity to put things right. In 1783 it was Nova Scotia that was promising to lead Massachusetts and the rest of the world to the millennium. This was, indeed, an amazing twist to a relationship which had enmeshed the two regions for some 150 years.

Even after Alline died in New Hampshire early in February, 1784, many of his followers remained convinced that Nova Scotia was much purer than were any of the New England states.[23] As the Maugerville inhabitants declared in November, 1784, "God in his providence" had "smiled upon us" and had ensured that unlike the neighbouring United States, "vital piety" still continued to "flourish."[24] To the citizens of Massachusetts, of course, the view that Nova Scotia had taken over New England's mission to lead and to direct the forces of the Almighty was incomprehensible nonsense. For them, the British colony was still, as it had for so long been, that "detestable place."[25]

$\mathcal{Notes}$

PREFACE

1. A. H. Clark, *Acadia: The Geography of Early Nova Scotia to 1760* (Madison, Wis., 1968), pp. 99 – 100, 121 – 31, 201 – 12, 278, 345 – 51; J. B. Brebner, *New England's Outpost: Acadia before the Conquest of Canada* (New York, 1927), pp. 96, 165; *Historical Statistics of the United States, Colonial Times to 1957* (Washington, 1960), p. 756.
2. Brebner, *New England's Outpost*; idem, *The Neutral Yankees of Nova Scotia: A Marginal Colony during the Revolutionary Years* (New York, 1937).
3. Brebner, *The Neutral Yankees of Nova Scotia*, ed. W. S. MacNutt (Toronto, 1969), p. xix.
4. W. S. MacNutt, Introduction to *The Neutral Yankees of Nova Scotia*, p. xv.
5. This theme is developed in greater detail in G. Stewart and G. Rawlyk, *A People Highly Favoured of God* (Toronto, 1972), pp. 79 – 195.

CHAPTER I

1. J. K. Hosmer, ed., *Winthrop's Journal, A History of New England, 1630 – 49* (New York, 1908), I, 46; hereafter referred to as *Winthrop's Journal*. Old Style dates will be used in the text until the year 1744. Thereafter New Style dates will be used even though it was not until 1752 that the English adopted the Gregorian calendar. In the pre-1744 period, January 1 will be considered to be the beginning of the new year.
2. A. B. Forbes, ed., *Winthrop Papers* (Boston, 1929 – 47), II, 293 – 95; hereafter referred to as *Winthrop Papers*.
3. Ibid.
4. W. B. Weeden, *Economic and Social History of New England, 1620 – 1789* (Boston, 1890), II, 594 – 95.
5. *Winthrop's Journal*, I, 46.

6. Ibid., I, 97.
7. G. W. Brown, ed., *Dictionary of Canadian Biography (DCB)*, vol. I, *1000 – 1700* (Toronto, 1966), pp. 503 – 6, 567 – 69, 592 – 96; Gustave Lanctot, *A History of Canada* (Toronto, 1963), I, 144.
8. *Winthrop's Journal*, I, 97.
9. W. H. Whitmore and W. S. Appleton, eds., *Hutchinson Papers* (Albany, 1865), I, 29; hereafter referred to as *Hutchinson Papers*.
10. *Winthrop's Journal*, I, 97 – 98.
11. Ibid., I, 113.
12. Ibid., I, 146.
13. W. Bradford, *History of Plymouth Plantation* (New York, 1908), pp. 320 – 21; *Winthrop's Journal*, I, 59.
14. *Winthrop's Journal*, I, 201. For an excellent background to these developments, see B. Bailyn, *The New England Merchants in the Seventeenth Century* (New York, 1955).
15. E. S. Morgan, *The Puritan Dilemma: The Story of John Winthrop* (Boston, 1958), p. 177.
16. R. McFarland, *A History of New England Fisheries* (New York, 1911), p. 62.
17. *Winthrop's Journal*, II, 43.
18. Ibid., II, 85, 88.
19. Ibid., II, 105, 106 – 7.
20. A. H. Buffinton, "The Policy of the Northern Colonies towards the French to the Peace of Utrecht" (Ph.D. thesis, Harvard University, 1925), pp. 50 – 52. For a detailed treatment of Winthrop's Acadian policy in the 1640s, see R. E. Wall, Jr., *Massachusetts Bay: The Critical Decade, 1640 – 1650* (New Haven, 1972), pp. 65 – 74. Wall's book, unfortunately, was not available when this chapter was being written.
21. *Winthrop's Journal*, II, 107 – 9.
22. Buffinton, "Policy of the Northern Colonies," pp. 58 – 59.
23. G. L. Mosse, *The Holy Pretence: A Study in Christianity and Reason of State from William Perkins to John Winthrop* (Oxford, 1957), p. 98; *Winthrop Papers*, IV, 406.
24. Morgan, *Puritan Dilemma*, p. 182.
25. *Winthrop's Journal*, II, 104.
26. Buffinton, "Policy of the Northern Colonies," pp. 53 – 54, 62 – 63.
27. Lanctot, I, 286.
28. Buffinton, "Policy of the Northern Colonies," p. 61.
29. *Winthrop's Journal*, II, 136 – 37.
30. Ibid., II, 182.
31. Ibid., II, 203.
32. Ibid., II, 204.
33. Ibid., II, 197, 204, 206.
34. Ibid., II, 247.
35. Ibid., II, 275.
36. Ibid., II, 285.
37. Ibid., II, 356.
38. A somewhat different picture of New England – Nova Scotia relations is to be found in R. D. Cohen, "Colonial Leviathan: New England Foreign Affairs in the Seventeenth Century" (Ph.D. thesis, University of Minnesota, 1967), pp. 34 – 69.

CHAPTER 2

1. For a recent sympathetic account of d'Aulnay's Nova Scotia achievement, see Lanctot, *History of Canada*, I, 291 – 93. See also *DCB*, I, 505 – 6.
2. Massachusetts Historical Society (Mass. Hist. Soc.) *Collections*, 3d ser., VII, 114, Charnisay to Massachusetts General Court, March 2, 1651; *DCB*, I, 433.
3. Quoted in Lanctot, I, 296, from La Tour's patent, February 25, 1651. A partial translation of the patent is to be found in B. Murdoch, *A History of Nova-Scotia or Acadie* (Halifax, 1865), I, 119.
4. Excerpts from the La Fosse grant are quoted in Murdoch, I, 117.
5. Ibid., I, 119. The royal grant to Vendôme and Jeanne Motin, February 18, 1652. See also *DCB*, I, 514.
6. Mass. Hist. Soc. *Colls.*, 3d ser., VII, 114 – 15, Charnisay to the Massachusetts General Court, March 2, 1651. See also pp. 115 – 16, Jeanne Motin to the General Court, May 26, 1651, and Saint-Mas to General Court, May 29, 1651.
7. Ibid., VII, 117, Endecott to Madame d'Aulnay, July 12, 1651.
8. Lanctot, I, 296. See also Murdoch, I, 117.
9. The marriage contract, translated into English, is to be found in Murdoch, I, 120 – 23.
10. N. Denys, *The Description and Natural History of the Coasts of North America (Acadia)*, trans. W. F. Ganong, Champlain Society pub., II (Toronto, 1908), p. 99. See also *DCB*, I, 257, 434.
11. N. B. Shurtleff, ed., *Records of the Governor and Company of the Massachusetts Bay in New England* (Boston, 1854), IV, pt. I, 120 – 21; hereafter referred to as *Mass. Records*.
12. Ibid., p. 146.
13. Mass. Hist. Soc. *Colls.*, 3d ser., VII, 118, La Tour's debt to Gibbons, 1654.
14. *Mass. Records*, IV, pt. I, 157.
15. *DCB*, I, 434.
16. Denys, p. 100.
17. Public Archives of Canada (PAC), M.G. 18, F. 4, John Leverett Papers, Leverett to Cromwell, September 8, 1654.
18. For a brief biographical sketch of Sedgwick, see *DCB*, I, 604 – 5, and H. D. Sedgwick, "Robert Sedgwick," Colonial Society of Massachusetts (Col. Soc. Mass.) *Publications* (Boston, 1900), III, 156 – 73. For a recent study of the Sedgwick-Leverett expedition, see D. C. B. Doherty, "Oliver Cromwell, Robert Sedgwick, John Leverett and the Acadian Adventure of 1654" (M.A. thesis, Queen's University, 1969).
19. T. Birch, ed., *A Collection of the State Papers of John Thurloe* (London, 1742), II, 418 – 19, Sedgwick to Cromwell, July 1, 1654; hereafter referred to as *Thurloe Papers*.
20. Mass. Hist. Soc., Gay Transcripts, Robert Sedgwick Papers, Marke Harrison to Admiralty, July 1, 1654.
21. *Thurloe Papers*, II, 419, Sedgwick to Cromwell, July 1, 1654.
22. PAC, M.G. 18, F. 4, Leverett Papers, Leverett to Cromwell, July 1, 1654.
23. Ibid., Leverett to Cromwell, September 8, 1654.
24. See for example *Mass. Records*, III, 321.
25. *Thurloe Papers*, II, 419, Sedgwick to Cromwell, July 1, 1654.
26. See especially Buffinton, "Policy of the Northern Colonies," pp. 70 – 71.

27. Massachusetts Archives (Mass. A.), LXVII, 144, Massachusetts General Court to Sedgwick, 1654.

28. Mass. Hist. Soc., Gay Transcripts, Sedgwick Papers, Harrison to Admiralty, July 21, August 31, 1654.

29. *Collection de Manuscrits Relatifs à l'Histoire de la Nouvelle-France* (Quebec, 1883), I, 145 – 49, Capitulation of Port Royal.

30. Mass. Hist. Soc., Gay Transcripts, Sedgwick Papers, Harrison to Admiralty, August 30, 31, 1654.

31. Denys, p. 100.

32. *Calendar of State Papers, Colonial Series, America and West Indies, 1661 – 1668* (London, 1880), p. 39, Statement of the case of Thomas Temple and William Crowne, June 22, 1661; hereafter referred to as *Cal. S.P. Col.*

33. *Thurloe Papers*, II, 419, Sedgwick to Cromwell, July 1, 1654.

34. *Hutchinson Papers*, I, 286, Application of Sedgwick, Leverett, and others to the General Court, October 20, 1657.

35. *Mass. Records*, IV, pt. I, 251.

36. *Hutchinson Papers*, I, 306, Edward Rawson to Leverett, November 23, 1655.

37. *DCB*, I, 595.

38. A. H. Buffinton, "Sir Thomas Temple in Boston, a Case of Benevolent Assimilation," Col. Soc. Mass. *Transactions* (Boston, 1932), XXVII, 309 – 10.

39. *DCB*, I, 636.

40. Murdoch, I, 138, Patent of Oliver Cromwell to Latour, Temple, and Crowne, of Acadie, August 9, 1656.

41. Mass. Hist. Soc. *Colls.*, 3d ser., VII, 120, T. Lake to John Leverett, September 2, 1657.

42. Bailyn, *New England Merchants*, p. 110.

43. Buffinton, "Policy of the Northern Colonies," pp. 78 – 79.

44. *Cal. S.P. Col., 1669 – 1674*, p. 8, Temple to Sec. Lord Arlington, March 2, 1669.

45. Buffinton, "Policy of the Northern Colonies," p. 80.

46. Denys, pp. 101, 102.

47. *DCB*, I, 435 – 36.

48. See *Cal. S.P. Col., 1661 – 1668*, p. 628, Temple to Lords of Council, November 24, 1668; *1669 – 1674*, p. 8, Temple to Arlington, March 2, 1669.

49. Buffinton, "Sir Thomas Temple," p. 313.

50. *Cal. S.P. Col., 1669 – 1674*, p. 8, Temple to Arlington, March 2, 1669.

51. *Mass. Records*, IV, pt. I, 355 – 56.

52. Ibid., IV, pt. II, 74 – 75, 315.

53. Buffinton, "Sir Thomas Temple," pp. 314 – 15.

54. *Cal. S.P. Col., 1661 – 1668*, p. 417, John Winthrop to Arlington, October 25, 1666.

55. *Mass Records*, IV, pt. II, 316.

56. *DCB*, I, 435.

57. *Cal. S.P. Col., 1669 – 1674*, p. 25, Edward Rawson to Sec. Lord Arlington, May 20, 1669.

58. Quoted in Murdoch, I, 142.

59. *Cal. S.P. Col., 1669 – 1674*, pp. 153 – 54, Temple to the King, January 10, 1671.

CHAPTER 3

1. Public Archives of Nova Scotia (PANS), C.11.D., Microfilm Reel II, Memoire Acadie, 1686; Perrot Memoire, August 29, 1686.
2. Quoted in Buffinton, "Policy of the Northern Colonies," p. 119.
3. Bailyn, *New England Merchants*, pp. 134, 144.
4. Houghton Library, Harvard University, Nelson Papers, Nelson to the Duke of Shrewsbury, 1696.
5. J. C. Webster, *Acadia at the End of the Seventeenth Century* (Saint John, 1934), p. 193.
6. Murdoch, *History of Nova-Scotia*, I, 149.
7. *DCB*, I, 63.
8. *Collection de Manuscrits*, I, 207 – 8, Minister of Marine to Talon, February 11, 1671.
9. Ibid., I, 203, Talon's Memoire, November 10, 1670.
10. Ibid., I, 199, Treaty between Grandfontaine and Temple, July 17, 1670.
11. Buffinton, "Policy of the Northern Colonies," p. 99.
12. *Collection de Manuscrits*, I, 191, Instructions for Grandfontaine, March 5, 1670.
13. Buffinton, "Policy of the Northern Colonies," p. 99.
14. J. C. Webster, *Cornelis Steenwyck Dutch Governor of Acadie* (Shediac, N.B., 1929), p. 3.
15. *DCB*, I, 39 – 40, 573.
16. Ibid.
17. Webster, *Cornelis Steenwyck*, p. 3.
18. Mass. Hist. Soc. *Colls.*, 3d ser., I, 64, Frontenac to Leverett, May 25, 1675.
19. *Cal. S.P. Col.*, *1675 – 1676*, p. 469, Governor and Council of Massachusetts to Committee of Trade and Plantations, October 18, 1676.
20. Ibid.
21. Ibid.
22. Ibid., p. 470. See also ibid., *1677 – 1680*, p. 357, Van Bennington to the Lords of Trade and Plantations, May 11, 1679.
23. Webster, *Cornelis Steenwyck*, p. 3.
24. *DCB*, I, 573.
25. See Murdoch, I, 155.
26. *Hutchinson Papers*, II, 225.
27. The best study of King Philip's War is D. E. Leach, *Flintlock and Tomahawk: New England in King Philip's War* (New York, 1958).
28. *Hutchinson Papers*, I, 225.
29. Quoted in Buffinton, "Policy of the Northern Colonies," p. 101.
30. J. P. Baxter, ed., *Documentary History of the State of Maine* (Portland, 1900), VI, 96 – 97, Council Report, October 16, 1675; hereafter referred to as *Maine History*.
31. J. R. Brodhead, ed., *Documents Relative to the Colonial History of the State of New York* (Albany, 1853), III, 256, Andros to the Committee of Trade and Plantations, November, 1677.
32. Ibid.
33. *Mass. Records*, V, 169.
34. *Maine History*, VI, 96 – 97, Council Report, October 16, 1675.
35. Quoted from Samuel Gorton in Leach, 188.

36. *Collection de Manuscrits*, I, 238, Arrest of the Sovereign Council, October 31, 1678.
37. Murdoch, I, 155.
38. Increase Mather, *A Relation of the Troubles Which Have Hapned in New-England, by Reason of the Indians There* (Boston, 1677), p. 75.
39. Weeden, *Economic and Social History*, I, 263.
40. *Cal. S.P. Col., 1675 – 1676*, p. 409, Randolph to Secretary Coventry, June 16, 1676.
41. *Mass. Records*, V, 168.
42. B. T. McCully, "The New England – Acadia Fishery Dispute and the Nicholson Mission of August 1680," Essex Institute Historical *Collections*, XCVI (1966), 278.
43. *Collection de Manuscrits*, I, 286, Report of M. Duchesneau, November 13, 1681.
44. Ibid., I, 284.
45. R. S. Dunn, *Puritans and Yankees: The Winthrop Dynasty of New England, 1630 – 1717* (Princeton, 1965), p. 212.
46. Buffinton, "Policy of the Northern Colonies," p. 122.
47. *Mass. Records*, V, 373 – 74.
48. Buffinton, "Policy of the Northern Colonies," p. 123.
49. See *Winthrop's Journal*, II, 356.
50. *Cal. S.P. Col., 1677 – 1680*, p. 528, Bradstreet to Lords of Trade and Plantations, 1680.
51. Ibid., *1681 – 1685*, p. 689, Order of the Governor of Acadia, October 22, 1682.
52. Ibid., p. 688, ? to ?, September 15, 1684.
53. Ibid., p. 688, La Barre to La Vallière, October 4, 1683.
54. *DCB*, I, 89. See also Roger Comeau, "Pêche et Traite en Acadie Jusqu'en 1713" (Ph.D. thesis, University of Ottawa, 1949), pp. 48 – 59.
55. McCully, "New England – Acadia Fishery Dispute," p. 278.
56. *Collection de Manuscrits*, I, 292 – 93, Acadie Memoire, 1682.
57. Ibid., I, 293 – 96.
58. Ibid., I, 329, Acadie Memoire, November 6, 1684.
59. *DCB*, I, 90.
60. W. J. Eccles, *Canada under Louis XIV, 1663 – 1701* (Toronto, 1964), p. 129.
61. *Cal. S.P. Col., 1685 – 1688*, p. 142, Answer to the French concerning the fishing at Acadia, January 16, 1686.
62. Ibid.
63. Buffinton, "Policy of the Northern Colonies," p. 128.
64. W. I. Morse, ed., *Acadiensia Nova (1598 – 1779)* (London, 1935), I, 118, Voyage of Monsieur de Meulles to Acadie.
65. PANS, C.11.D., II, Perrot Memoire, August 29, 1686.
66. R. N. Toppan, ed., *Edward Randolph* (Boston, 1899), IV, 98, Randolph to Blathwayt, July 28, 1686; hereafter, together with volumes edited by A. T. C. Goodrick, referred to as *Edward Randolph*.
67. *Collection de Manuscrits*, I, 369, Dongan to Perrot, October 6, 1686.
68. Ibid., I, 403, Castin to Meneval, September 15, 1687; see also p. 388, Report to Denonville, November 10, 1686.
69. McCully, "New England – Acadia Fishery Dispute," p. 281.

CHAPTER 4

1. A detailed description of this policy is to be found in various letters in *Collection de Manuscrits*, I, 396 – 503; Webster, *Acadia*, pp. 22 – 24, Villebon's Account, 1690; Morse, *Acadiensia Nova*, I, 165 – 72, Sojourn of Gorgas in Acadie, 1687 – 1688, and Letter of Vincent de Saccardy relating to Acadie ... 12th January 1690.

2. Morse, I, 176 – 77, 198.

3. *Collection de Manuscrits*, I, 403, Castin to Meneval, September 15, 1682.

4. Ibid., I, 435, Meneval to the Minister of Marine, September 10, 1688; see also p. 437, Memoire of the Compagnie de l'Acadie, 1688.

5. Ibid., I, 415, Minister to the Compagnie de l'Acadie, February 21, 1688.

6. Morse, I, 166, 216 – 17.

7. McCully, "New England – Acadia Fishery Dispute," p. 289. Nicholson to Blathwayt, September 5, 1687.

8. *Edward Randolph*, VI, 216, Randolph to Blathwayt, March 14, 1687.

9. *Cal. S.P. Col., 1685 – 1688*, p. 352, Andros to the Earl of Sutherland, March 30, 1687.

10. Mass. Hist. Soc. *Colls.*, 5th ser., V, 185, *Diary of Samuel Sewall*; hereafter referred to as *Sewall Diary*.

11. McCully, "New England – Acadia Fishery Dispute," pp. 288 – 89, Nicholson to Blathwayt, September 5, 1687.

12. Ibid., pp. 289, 285, 290, Nicholson to Blathwayt, September 5 and September 1, 1687.

13. *Collection de Manuscrits*, I, 399, Castin to Denonville, July 2, 1687.

14. *Edward Randolph*, IV, 224 – 25, Randolph to Povey, June 2, 1688.

15. Ibid., IV, 225.

16. For a good description of this raid, see Webster, *Acadia*, p. 207, and *Collection de Manuscrits*, I, 469 – 70.

17. *Cal. S.P. Col., 1689 – 1692*, p. 164, ? to Board of Trade, October 24, 1689.

18. Cotton Mather, *Magnalia Christi Americana* (London, 1702), p. 61; see also J. Belknap, *The History of New Hampshire* (Philadelphia, 1812), I, 196.

19. C. Mather, *Decennium Luctuosum* (Boston, 1690), in J. F. Jameson, ed., *Original Narratives of Early American History Series* (New York, 1913), p. 190.

20. Buffinton, "Policy of the Northern Colonies," pp. 200 – 205.

21. *Cal. S.P. Col., 1689 – 1692*, p. 46, Randolph to the Lords of Trade and Plantations, May 29, 1689.

22. R. E. Moody, "The Maine Frontier, 1607 to 1763" (Ph.D. thesis, Yale University, 1933), p. 233.

23. *Cal. S.P. Col., 1689 – 1692*, p. 46, Randolph to the Lords of Trade and Plantations, May 29, 1689.

24. Moody, "Maine Frontier," p. 234.

25. *Maine History*, VI, 471, Edward Tyng to Massachusetts Council, 1689.

26. *Collection de Manuscrits*, I, 481, Monsieur Thury Relation, 1689.

27. *Cal. S.P. Col., 1689 – 1692*, p. 167, Bradstreet to Lords of Trade, October 26, 1689, and ? to Lords of Trade, October 24, 1689.

28. *Maine History*, VI, 485.

29. Buffinton, "Policy of the Northern Colonies," p. 235.

30. PANS, C.11.D., II, Meneval to the Minister of Marine, September 7, 1689. See also *Edward Randolph*, VII, 340, Randolph to Blathwayt, March 27, 1690.

31. J. D. Phillips, *Salem in the Eighteenth Century* (Boston, 1937), p. 24.
32. Mass. A., XXXV, Salem Petition, 1689.
33. Buffinton, "Policy of the Northern Colonies," p. 236.
34. PAC, M.G. 6, III, Meneval to the Minister of Marine, September 7, 1689.
35. *Maine History*, V, 16, Thos. Danforth, Elisha Cooke, Thos. Hinckley, John Walley, and Wm. Vaughan to the Massachusetts General Court, December 6, 1689.
36. *Edward Randolph*, VI, 318 – 19, Randolph to Blathwayt, December 16, 1688.
37. *Maine History*, V, 19, E. Prout Statement, December 16, 1689.
38. This thesis is developed in considerable detail in P. Miller, *The New England Mind from Colony to Province* (Boston, 1966), pp. 149 – 72.
39. Ibid., p. 164.
40. *Maine History*, V, 26 – 27, Proposals of John Nelson, January 4, 1690.
41. Ibid., V, 25.
42. Ibid., V, 30 – 31, Gedney, Browne, Redford, Nelson, Oliver, Foster, and Alden to the Council, January 16, 1690.
43. Mass. A., VI, Encouragement to such as undertake an Expedition against Port Royal, February 6, 1689/90.
44. *Cal. S.P. Col.*, *1689 – 1692*, p. 264, Journal of Benjamin Bullivant, May 19, 1690.
45. *Sewall Diary*, V, 310 – 11.
46. *Maine History*, V, 57, W. Vaughan and R. Martyn to N.H. Council, 1690.
47. Murdoch, *History of Nova-Scotia*, I, 193, M. de Lagny to ?, February 21, 1690. See also *Collection de Manuscrits*, I, 432, Observations on the State of Affairs in Canada, November 18, 1689.
48. *Maine History*, V, 52.
49. *Sewall Diary*, V, 316.
50. *Cal. S.P. Col.*, *1689 – 1692*, p. 264, Journal of Benjamin Bullivant, May 19, 1690.
51. *DCB*, I, 544.
52. *Sewall Diary*, V, 219.
53. *Cal. S.P. Col.*, *1689 – 1692*, p. 264, Journal of Benjamin Bullivant, May 19, 1690.
54. *Maine History*, V, 60 – 61, Payment of Soldiers ... March 20, 1690.
55. Cotton Mather, *The Present State of New England* (Boston, 1690), pp. 32 – 33, 35 – 36, 38, 45. For a brilliant analysis of Mather's career, see R. Middlekauff, *The Mathers: Three Generations of Puritan Intellectuals, 1596 – 1728* (New York, 1971), pp. 191 – 367.
56. W. Phips, *A Journal of the Proceedings in the late Expedition to Port Royal* (Boston, 1690), pp. 15 – 16.
57. Brebner, *New England's Outpost*, p. 50.
58. The following narrative is based almost entirely on Phips's *Journal* and owes a great deal as well to D. Chard, "Pagans, Privateers and Propagandists: New England – Acadia Relations, 1690 – 1710" (M.A. thesis, Dalhousie University, 1967), pp. 22 – 25.
59. *Maine History*, V, 128 – 29, Southack to his parents, June 18, 1690.
60. Mass. Hist. Soc. *Colls.*, 3d ser., I, 114 – 17. Meneval to the Governor of Boston and the Council, December 4, 1690.
61. *Cal. S.P. Col.*, *1689 – 1692*, p. 376, James Lloyd to the Board of Trade, January 8, 1691.
62. Phips, *Journal*, pp. 13 – 15.

CHAPTER 5

1. *Maine History*, V, 167 – 68, Bradstreet to the Massachusetts Agents, November 29, 1690.
2. Webster, *Acadia*, pp. 22 – 25, Villebon to the Marquis de Chevry, 1690.
3. Eccles, *Canada under Louis XIV*, p. 194.
4. *Collection de Manuscrits*, II, 206, State of the Indian Presents, March 3, 1696.
5. Webster, *Acadia*, pp. 45, 41, Villebon's Memoir.
6. Ibid., p. 42.
7. A detailed description of the controversy is to be found in F. Parkman, *Count Frontenac and New France under Louis XIV* (Boston, 1899), pp. 250 – 52.
8. Quoted in Murdoch, *History of Nova-Scotia*, I, 197.
9. *Maine History*, V, 159, The Court to Alden, November 6, 1690.
10. *Cal. S.P. Col., 1689 – 1692*, p. 564, Information of Marke Harrison, 1691.
11. Buffinton, "Policy of the Northern Colonies," p. 303; see also Webster, *Acadia*, p. 50, Villebon's Memoir, 1693.
12. Mass. A., XXXVII, Faneuil to Boudrot, April 22, 1691.
13. Ibid., XXXVI, Council Minutes, June 4, 1691.
14. *Cal. S.P. Col., 1689 – 1692*, pp. 560, 561, Foxcroft to Nicholson, October 21, 1691; Jeffreys to Usher, November 19, 1691.
15. Webster, *Acadia*, p. 200.
16. Buffinton, "Policy of the Northern Colonies," p. 304.
17. Webster, *Acadia*, p. 31, Villebon's Memoir.
18. For good, brief, biographical sketches of Nelson, see Webster, *Acadia*, pp. 184 – 86, and *DCB*, II, 493 – 94.
19. Webster, *Acadia*, p. 33.
20. Moody, "Maine Frontier," p. 255.
21. *Maine History*, V, 316, George Burroughs and others to Mass. Governor and Council, January 27, 1692.
22. Webster, *Acadia*, p. 36.
23. S. G. Drake, ed., *The History of Philip's War ... by Thomas Church* (Boston, 1827), p. 213.
24. Moody, "Maine Frontier," p. 299.
25. Webster, *Acadia*, pp. 40 – 41.
26. *Maine History*, V, 379, Southack's Instructions, March 31, 1693.
27. Webster, *Acadia*, p. 39.
28. Ibid., pp. 55, 57.
29. Belknap, *New Hampshire*, I, 217.
30. Webster, *Acadia*, p. 56.
31. T. Hutchinson, *The History of the Colony and Province of Massachusetts Bay*, ed. L. S. Mayo (Cambridge, 1936), II, 65; hereafter referred to as Mayo, *Hutchinson's History*.
32. Webster, *Acadia*, pp. 77, 81.
33. Ibid., p. 140.
34. *Mass. Acts and Resolves* (Boston, 1892), VII, 132, Vote and Order For Suspending the Clause in the Act of August 17, 1695.
35. Webster, *Acadia*, p. 82.
36. Mass. A., II, 408, Stoughton to the Governor of New York, November 11, 1695.
37. Drake, p. 215.

38. Mass. A., VI, General Order, June 16, 1696.
39. Drake, pp. 215 – 16.
40. For a graphic description of the short siege, see *Cal. S.P. Col., 1696 – 1697*, pp. 142 – 45, Stoughton to the Lords of Trade, September 24, 1696.
41. Mather, *Magnalia Christi Americana*, p. 48.
42. See Church's instructions, Drake, pp. 216 – 17.
43. Ibid., pp. 228, 232.
44. Ibid., pp. 232 – 33.
45. Ibid., pp. 233 – 34.
46. Ibid., pp. 220 – 39.
47. Mayo, *Hutchinson's History*, II, 74.
48. See ibid., and Webster, *Acadia*, pp. 89 – 94.
49. *Mass. Acts and Resolves*, VII, 123, Mass. General Court to the King, September 24, 1696.
50. Mass. A., II, Vote of the House, December 18, 1696.
51. *Sewall Diary*, V, 465.

CHAPTER 6

1. *Cal. S.P. Col., 1697 – 1698*, pp. 501 – 3, Villebon to Stoughton, September 5, 1698.
2. PANS, C.11.D., III, 182 – 86, Villebon to the Minister of Marine, June 27, 1699.
3. *Cal. S.P. Col., 1697 – 1698*, p. 500, Stoughton to the Council of Trade and Plantations, October 24, 1698.
4. *Mass. Acts and Resolves*, VIII, 194 – 95, Mass. General Court to King William, November 19, 1698.
5. Ibid., VIII, 195.
6. *Cal. S.P. Col., 1697 – 1698*, p. 502, Nelson to Council of Trade and Plantations, January 26, 1698.
7. Webster, *Acadia*, p. 117, Villebon's Memoir.
8. *Collection de Manuscrits*, II, 307, Complaints against Villebon, 1698; see also Webster, *Acadia*, p. 121, Villebon's Last Journal.
9. Webster, *Acadia*, pp. 138 – 39, Villebon's Last Journal.
10. Murdoch, *History of Nova-Scotia*, I, 247.
11. *Collection de Manuscrits*, II, 333, King to Brouillan, March 23, 1700.
12. Mayo, *Hutchinson's History*, II, 84.
13. *Cal. S.P. Col., 1700*, p. 65, Bellomont to ?, November 29, 1699; p. 90, Bellomont to Council of Trade and Plantations, February 28, 1700; p. 180, Bellomont to Council of Trade and Plantations, April 20, 1700.
14. Ibid., pp. 414 – 15, Bellomont to Council of Trade and Plantations, July 15, 1700; p. 399, Minutes of Massachusetts Council, July 9, 1700.
15. E. Kimball, *The Public Life of Joseph Dudley* (New York, 1911), p. 75.
16. *Cal. S.P. Col., 1701*, p. 155, Stoughton to Council of Trade and Plantations, April 10, 1701.
17. Ibid., p. 390, Minutes of Council, August 5, 1701.
18. Ibid., p. 469, Addington to Mr. Popple, August 25, 1701; p. 390, Minutes of the Council, August 5, 1701.
19. Murdoch, I, 273.

20. See PANS, C.11.D., IV, 4, Brouillan to Minister of Marine, October 6, 1701; see also *Collection de Manuscrits*, II, 1701, Brouillan to Minister of Marine, October 30, 1701.
21. *Cal. S.P. Col.*, *1701*, p. 470, Brouillan to Government of Massachusetts Bay, August 8, 1701.
22. Ibid., pp. 470 – 71, Massachusetts Council to Brouillan, August 22, 1701.
23. Ibid., *1702*, p. 355, Minutes of Massachusetts Council, May 29, 1702; p. 372, Minutes of Massachusetts Council, June 2, 1702.
24. Buffinton, "Policy of the Northern Colonies," p. 362.
25. See Kimball, *Dudley*, pp. 1 – 75.
26. Mayo, *Hutchinson's History*, II, 160.
27. Ibid., II, 105.
28. *Cal. S.P. Col.*, *1702*, p. 434, Minutes of Massachusetts Council, June 30, 1702.
29. Ibid., p. 483, Dudley to the Council of Trade and Plantations, July 23, 1702.
30. Ibid., pp. 592 – 95, Dudley to the Council of Trade and Plantations, September 17 – 19, 1702.
31. *Collection de Manuscrits*, II, 1702, Brouillan to the Minister of Marine, October 30, 1702.
32. *Cal. S.P. Col.*, *1702 – 1703*, p. 34, Dudley to the Earl of Nottingham, December 10, 1702.
33. Ibid., p. 597, Minutes of Massachusetts Council, September 17, 1702.
34. Ibid., p. 483, Dudley to Council of Trade and Plantations, July 23, 1702.
35. Ibid., p. 594, Dudley to Council of Trade and Plantations, September 17, 1702.
36. Ibid., p. 709, Dudley to Council of Trade and Plantations, November 10, 1702.
37. Quoted in ibid., p. 598, Minutes of Massachusetts Council, September 17, 1702. See also Mass. A., II, 604, Brouillan to Dudley, August 29, 1702.
38. *Cal. S.P. Col.*, *1701*, p. 471, Massachusetts Council to Brouillan, August 22, 1701.
39. PANS, C.11.D., IV, 211, Brouillan to the Minister of Marine, December 30, 1702.
40. Murdoch, II, 269, Brouillan to ?, October 4, 1705.
41. Mass. A., VII, Massachusetts Council Minutes, March 25 – 27, 1703.
42. Murdoch, II, 275, Bonaventure to Minister of Marine, November 5, 1705.
43. Ibid., II, 269, quoted from an unidentified letter written by Brouillan.
44. Belknap, *New Hampshire*, I, 264.
45. For a graphic description of the raids, see Samuel Penhallow, *The History of the Wars of New England With the Eastern Indians* (Boston, 1726), pp. 4 – 7.
46. Belknap, *New Hampshire*, I, 265.
47. Mayo, *Hutchinson's History*, II, 106.
48. *Cal. S.P. Col.*, *1702 – 1703*, p. 665, Massachusetts Council Minutes, September 3, 1703.
49. *Sewall Diary*, VI, 96.
50. *Cal. S.P. Col.*, *1704 – 1705*, pp. 213 – 14, Dudley to Council of Trade and Plantations, July 13, 1704.
51. Mass. A., VIII, Massachusetts Council Minutes, March 20, 1704.
52. B. Church, *The History of the Eastern Expeditions of 1689, 1692, 1696, and 1704*, ed. H. M. Dexter (Boston, 1867), p. 251; hereafter referred to as Church, *Expeditions*.
53. Ibid., p. 253.

54. See *A Memorial of the Present Deplorable State of New England* (Boston, 1707).
55. Mayo, *Hutchinson's History*, II, 109, Mather to Dudley, January 20, 1707.
56. Church, *Expeditions*, p. 255, Dudley to Church, May 4, 1704.
57. Penhallow, p. 18; see also Church, *Expeditions*, pp. 257 – 80.
58. Penhallow, p. 18.
59. Church, *Expeditions*, p. 270.
60. *Collection de Manuscrits*, II, 419 – 20, Smith, Southack, Rogers to Brouillan, June 24, 1704.
61. Church, *Expeditions*, pp. 280 – 81, 256.
62. Ibid., pp. 284 – 85.
63. Penhallow, p. 18.
64. *Cal. S.P. Col.*, *1706 – 1708*, pp. 30 – 31, Dudley to Council of Trade and Plantations, February 1, 1706; see also p. 265, Lt.-Governor Usher to Council of Trade and Plantations, October 13, 1706.
65. *The Deplorable State of New England* (London, 1708), p. 126.
66. Church, *Expeditions*, p. 286.
67. For a detailed description of these negotiations, see A. H. Buffinton, "Governor Dudley and the Proposed Treaty of Neutrality, 1705," Col. Soc. Mass. *Pubs.*, XXVI (1924 – 26), 221 – 29; see also *Collection de Manuscrits*, II, 449 – 56, for various letters from the French point of view.
68. For details concerning the episode, see *Memorial of the Present Deplorable State of New England*, pp. 1 – 41; *A Modest Enquiry* (London, 1707), pp. 1 – 30; *Deplorable State of New England*, pp. 1 – 39.
69. *Deplorable State of New England*, p. 19.
70. *Cal. S.P. Col.*, *1704 – 1705*, p. 482, Council of Trade and Plantations to Dudley, April 12, 1705.
71. Quoted in G. M. Waller, *Samuel Vetch: Colonial Enterpriser* (Chapel Hill, N.C., 1960), p. 83.
72. *Cal. S.P. Col.*, *1706 – 1708*, p. 278, Minutes of General Assembly, August 7, 1706.
73. Mass. Hist. Soc. *Colls.*, 6th ser., III, 367, Dudley to Winthrop, February 10, 1707.
74. *Mass. Acts and Resolves*, VIII, 674 – 83; see also Mass. A., LXXI, 282 – 90.
75. *Mass. Acts and Resolves*, VIII, 683.
76. Mass. Hist. Soc. *Colls.*, 6th ser., III, 371, Winthrop to Dudley, February 25, 1707.
77. Mass. Hist. Soc. *Proceedings*, *1884 – 88*, 2d ser., I, 159, John Marshall's Diary.
78. *Sewall Diary*, VI, 184.
79. See Mass. Hist. Soc. *Colls.*, 3d ser., V, 189 – 90, Autobiography of Rev. John Barnard. See also *Mass. Acts and Resolves*, VIII, 690 – 91, Roster of the Expedition.
80. See especially, Mass. Hist. Soc. *Proc.*, *1884 – 88*, 2d ser., I, 159, Marshall's Diary.
81. F. Parkman, *A Half-Century of Conflict* (Boston, 1899), I, 98.
82. Mass. Hist. Soc. *Colls.*, 3d ser., V, 190 – 91, Barnard Autobiography. For biographical data about six Harvard graduates involved in the expedition, see C. K. Shipton, *Biographical Sketches of Those who Attended Harvard College, 1701 – 1712* (Boston, 1937), V, 22 – 23, 181, 240, 246, 258, 315; hereafter referred to as *Sibley's Harvard Graduates*.
83. *Mass. Acts and Resolves*, VIII, 686 – 87.

84. Mass. Hist. Soc. *Colls.*, 6th ser., III, 376, Winthrop to Dudley, April 4, 1707.
85. The description of the expedition is based upon *Mass. Acts and Resolves,* VIII, 699–729; Mass. Hist. Soc. *Colls.*, 3d ser., V, 189–96, Barnard Autobiography; and J. C. Webster, ed., *Dièreville: Port Royal* (Toronto, 1933), pp. 210–15.
86. PANS, C.11.D., VI, Bonaventure to Minister of Marine, July 5, 1707.
87. Mass. Hist. Soc. *Colls.*, 3d ser., V, 193, Barnard Autobiography.
88. *Mass. Acts and Resolves,* VIII, 725.
89. Mass. Hist. Soc. *Colls.*, 6th ser., III, 388, Fitz-John Winthrop to Dudley, August 14, 1707.
90. Ibid., III, 388–89, John Winthrop to Fitz-John Winthrop, July, 1707.
91. Ibid., III, 389.
92. Ibid., 3d ser., V, 194, Barnard Autobiography.
93. Ibid., and 6th ser., III, 392, 394–95, Dudley to Winthrop, July 14, August 4, 1707, and Fitz-John Winthrop to Dudley, August 14, 1707.
94. Ibid., 3d ser., V, 195, Barnard Autobiography.
95. Ibid., V, 196.
96. Mass. Hist. Soc. *Proc., 1884–88,* 2d ser., I, 159, Marshall's Diary.
97. *Mass. Acts and Resolves,* VIII, 747–48.
98. *Cal. S.P. Col., 1706–1708,* pp. 590–92, Dudley to the Board of Trade, 1707.

CHAPTER 7

1. For an excellent biographical study of Vetch, see Waller, *Samuel Vetch.*
2. Quoted in ibid., p. 102.
3. *Cal. S.P. Col., 1708–1709,* pp. 41–51, Vetch to the Board of Trade, July 27, 1708.
4. Ibid., *1706–1708,* pp. 590–92, Dudley to Council of Trade and Plantations, November, 1707.
5. Ibid., *1708–1709,* p. 22, Vaughan to Council of Trade and Plantations, July 6, 1708.
6. Ibid., pp. 41–51, Vetch to the Board of Trade, July 27, 1708.
7. Ibid., p. 232, H.M. Instructions to Vetch, March 1, 1709.
8. Ibid., pp. 147–50, Vetch to the Board of Trade, November 17, 1708.
9. Ibid., pp. 314–16, Massachusetts General Court to the Queen, October 20, 1708.
10. Waller, *Samuel Vetch,* p. 119.
11. *Cal. S.P. Col., 1708–1709,* p. 285, Lord Sunderland to Dudley, 1709.
12. Mass. A., LXXI, 71, Nicholson, Vetch, Dudley Proclamation, May 9, 1709.
13. Mass. Hist. Soc. *Proc., 1884–88,* 2d ser., I, 160, Marshall's Diary.
14. Belknap, *New Hampshire,* I, 278.
15. *Cal. S.P. Col., 1708–1709,* p. 446, Dudley to Popple, August 16, 1709.
16. Mass. A., LXXI, House of Representatives Declaration, May 30, 1709, and June 2, 1709.
17. *Cal. S.P. Col., 1708–1709,* p. 437, Vetch to Sunderland, August 2 and 12, 1709.
18. *New England Historical and Genealogical Register (New Eng. Hist. and Geneal. Register)* (Boston, 1870), XXXIV, 110–11.
19. Mayo, *Hutchinson's History,* II, 135.
20. J. B. Brebner, "Paul Mascarene of Annapolis Royal," in G. A. Rawlyk, ed., *Historical Essays on the Atlantic Provinces* (Toronto, 1967), p. 19.

21. *Cal. S.P. Col.*, *1708 – 1709*, pp. 438 – 39, Vetch to Sunderland, August 2 and 12, 1709.
22. Mass. A., LXXI, House of Representatives to Dudley, May 27, 1709.
23. Ibid., Report of Committee, July 15, 1709; Petition to General Court, September 9, 1709; Petition of some Boston inhabitants, 1709.
24. *Cal. S.P. Col.*, *1708 – 1709*, p. 488, Dudley, Nicholson, Vetch, and Moody to Sunderland, October 24, 1709.
25. See Waller, *Samuel Vetch*, pp. 154 – 55.
26. Mass. Hist. Soc. *Colls.*, 6th ser., I, 385, Sewall to Ashhurst, October 27, 1709.
27. *Cal. S.P. Col.*, *1708 – 1709*, pp. 490 – 92, Congress of the Governors, October 14, 1709.
28. See the relevant correspondence in ibid., pp. 443 – 46.
29. Ibid., *1710 – 1711*, pp. 29 – 30, Account of Charges, October 12, 1709.
30. PANS, C.11.D., VII, Subercase to Minister of Marine, January 3, 1710; see also *Cal. S.P. Col.*, *1708 – 1709*, p. 438, Vetch to Sunderland, August 2 and 12, 1709.
31. PANS, C.11.D., VII, Subercase to Minister of Marine, January 3, 1710.
32. *Cal. S.P. Col.*, *1708 – 1709*, p. 497, Dudley, Vetch, Moody to Sunderland, October 25, 1709.
33. Ibid.
34. Ibid., pp. 492 – 93, Address of the principal inhabitants and merchants at Boston, October, 1709.
35. Ibid., pp. 407 – 8, Memorial of Col. John Higginson, 1709.
36. See Chard, "Pagans, Privateers and Propagandists," p. 131.
37. Nova Scotia Historical Society (N.S. Hist. Soc.) *Collections* (Halifax, 1879), I, 60 – 62, Nicholson's Instructions, March 18, 1710.
38. Waller, *Samuel Vetch*, p. 175.
39. *Cal. S.P. Col.*, *1710 – 1711*, pp. 103 – 4, Nicholson to ———, May 16, 1710; p. 215, Nicholson and Vetch to Lord Dartmouth, September 16, 1710.
40. Mass. A., LXXI, House of Representatives Order, July 21, 1710.
41. *Cal. S.P. Col.*, *1710 – 1711*, p. 174, Massachusetts General Court to the Queen, August 22, 1710.
42. Ibid., p. 215.
43. Mass. A., LXXI, Encouragement of Volunteers, July 27, 1710.
44. See ibid., Dudley to Suffolk County Sheriff, August 19, 1710, and Gedney to Dudley, September 4, 1710.
45. Mass. Hist. Soc. *Proc.*, *1884 – 88*, 2d ser., I, 161, Marshall's Diary.
46. Mayo, *Hutchinson's History*, II, 135.
47. N.S. Hist. Soc. *Colls.*, I, 65, Nicholson's Journal.
48. Penhallow, *Wars of New England*, p. 52.
49. N.S. Hist. Soc. *Colls.*, I, 65 – 66, Nicholson's Journal; *Sibley's Harvard Graduates*, IV, 199 – 200.
50. Murdoch, *History of Nova-Scotia*, I, 313.
51. N.S. Hist. Soc. *Colls.*, I, 67 – 85, Nicholson's Journal.
52. Penhallow, p. 55.
53. N.S. Hist. Soc. *Colls.*, I, 86, Nicholson's Journal.
54. T. Hesketh, *Divine Providence Asserted and Some Objectives Answered a Sermon Preach'd October the 10th 1710 (at Annapolis-Royall in America)* (Boston, 1710).
55. See *Cal. S.P. Col.*, *1710 – 1711*, pp. 225 – 27, Proclamations of General Nicholson and the rest of the Council of War, October 12, 1710.

56. N.S. Hist. Soc. *Colls.*, I, 102, Dudley's Proclamation, October 8, 1710.
57. *Sewall Diary*, VI, 298.
58. For the extent of this trade, consult the various letters written by Annapolis Royal officers in A. M. MacMechan, ed., *Nova Scotia Archives* (Halifax, 1900), II, 1 – 54.
59. Waller, *Samuel Vetch*, pp. 235 – 77.
60. Brebner, *New England's Outpost*, p. 70.

CHAPTER 8

1. D. E. Leach, *The Northern Colonial Frontier, 1607 – 1763* (New York, 1966), pp. 135 – 36.
2. MacMechan, *Nova Scotia Archives*, II, 22, Caulfield to Costabille, August 16, 1715.
3. Quoted in J. S. McLennan, *Louisbourg from its Foundation to its Fall, 1713 – 1758* (Toronto, 1918), p. 62.
4. *Cal. S.P. Col.*, *1719 – 1720*, pp. 103 – 4, Memorial of James Pitts, Oliver Noyes, John Marshall, Nathl. Cunningham, and Benjamin Alford, June 9, 1718.
5. For a more detailed examination of the Massachusetts fishery at Canso, see Clark, *Acadia*, pp. 227 – 29.
6. *Cal. S.P. Col.*, *1719 – 1720*, pp. 104 – 5, Shute to Smart, 1718.
7. Ibid.
8. Ibid., p. 69, Southack's Journal.
9. Ibid., p. 99.
10. See McLennan, *Louisbourg*, p. 63.
11. *Cal. S.P. Col.*, *1719 – 1720*, p. 115, Council of Trade and Plantations to Lords Justices, June 5, 1719.
12. Ibid., p. 32, Young to the Council of Trade and Plantations, October 21, 1720.
13. McLennan, *Louisbourg*, p. 67.
14. Ibid., p. 68, Armstrong's Journal, 1722.
15. *Cal. S.P. Col.*, *1722 – 1723*, p. 3, Armstrong to Council of Trade and Plantations, February 22, 1722.
16. McLennan, *Louisbourg*, pp. 69 – 70.
17. *Cal. S.P. Col.*, *1722 – 1723*, p. 142, Philipps to Council of Trade and Plantations, September 19, 1722.
18. *Massachusetts House Journals, 1721 – 1722* (Boston, 1922), p. 82.
19. *Cal. S.P. Col.*, *1722 – 1723*, p. 142, Philipps to Council of Trade and Plantations, September 19, 1722.
20. Ibid.
21. MacMechan, *Nova Scotia Archives*, III, 110, 164, Minutes of H.M. Council.
22. Quoted in Murdoch, *History of Nova-Scotia*, I, 428, Articles of Submission.
23. H. A. Innis, ed., *Select Documents in Canadian Economic History, 1497 – 1783* (Toronto, 1929), pp. 158 – 59, Extent of the Canso Fishery. *Cal. S.P. Col.*, *1735 – 1736*, pp. 109 – 10, State of codd fishery, 1735; p. 324, State of codd Fishery . . . Whale Fishery, 1736; *1737 – 1738*, p. 270, Account of fish made at Canso . . . Whale fishery, 1737.
24. Clark, *Acadia*, p. 227.
25. W. Douglass, *A Summary, Historical and Political, of the First Planting, Progressive Improvements, and Present State of the British Settlements in North America* (London, 1760), I, 302.

26. Innis, *Select Documents*, p. 162, Decline of Canso Fishery, P. Warren, July 9, 1739.
27. See J. G. Lydon, "North Shore Trade in the Early Eighteenth Century," *American Neptune*, XXVIII, no. 4 (October, 1968), 261 – 74; see also W. S. MacNutt, *The Atlantic Provinces: The Emergence of Colonial Society, 1712 – 1857* (Toronto, 1965), p. 23.
28. PAC, Admiralty Papers, II, 483, T. Corbett (Sec. to the Admiralty) to John Scrope, May 31, 1744.
29. *Mass. House Journals, 1724 – 1726*, p. 88.
30. *Cal. S.P. Col., 1720 – 1721*, p. 80, Philipps to Council of Trade and Plantations, August 6, 1720.
31. Innis, *Select Documents*, p. 222, Report of a Committee of His Majesty's Council for the Province of Nova Scotia, May 29, 1732.
32. MacMechan, *Nova Scotia Archives*, III, 227, Petition of Henry Cope, June 19, 1732.
33. Ibid., II, 191, Instructions to Mascarene, September 10, 1732.
34. Ibid., II, 120, Council to Philipps, June 10, 1738; Mass. Hist. Soc. *Colls.*, 6th ser., VI, 329, J. Belcher to J. L. Gyse, October 6, 1735.
35. MacMechan, *Nova Scotia Archives*, III, 227 – 32, Minutes of H.M. Council, June 19, June 21, 1732.
36. "Journal of a Voyage to Nova Scotia Made in 1731 by Robert Hale of Beverly," Essex Institute Historical *Collections*, XLII, no. 3 (July, 1906), 230.
37. C. B. Fergusson, ed., *Minutes of His Majesty's Council at Annapolis Royal, 1736 – 1749* (Halifax, 1967), p. 14.
38. Clark, *Acadia*, pp. 257 – 59, 315 – 29.
39. *Mass. House Journals, 1718 – 1720*, pp. 329 – 30.
40. Ibid., pp. 359, 369, 379.
41. *Cal. S.P. Col., 1726 – 1727*, p. 38, Bradstreet to Council of Trade and Plantations, March, 1726.
42. Innis, *Select Documents*, p. 132, Hibbert Newton's Report, September 1, 1743.
43. See the superb chart in McLennan, *Louisbourg*, p. 382.
44. New Style dates will be used from this point on in this and in succeeding chapters, even though it was not until 1752 that the British adopted the Gregorian reform of the calendar. G. S. Kimball, ed., *The Correspondence of the Colonial Governors of Rhode Island, 1723 – 1775* (Boston, 1902), I, 258 – 60, Governor Clinton to Governor Greene, May 28, 1744.
45. See the excellent biography, J. A. Schutz, *William Shirley: King's Governor of Massachusetts* (Chapel Hill, N.C., 1961).
46. V. Parsons, *The Life of Sir William Pepperrell, Bart.* (Boston, 1856), pp. 41 – 42, Shirley to Pepperrell, October 10, 1743.
47. G. A. Wood, *William Shirley: Governor of Massachusetts, 1741 – 1756* (New York, 1920), pp. 114 – 31.
48. For a good account of Shirley's successful drive for the control of patronage, see Schutz, *William Shirley*, pp. 80 – 85.
49. *Mass. House Journals, 1744 – 1745*, pp. 8 – 11.
50. Ibid., pp. 15 – 16, 31.
51. Ibid., pp. 28, 36.
52. PAC, Archives des Colonies (AC), C11B, XXVI, Du Quesnel and Bigot to Maurepas, May 9, 1744.

53. Ibid., Archives Nationales (AN), G.5, CCLIII, Carton 258, Amirauté et Conseil des Prises; *Pennsylvania Journal*, June 28 to August 2, 1744, and also *Boston News-Letter* for the same period.
54. *Pennsylvania Journal*, July 4, 1744, and PAC, AN, G.5, CCLIII, Carton 258, Amirauté et Conseil des Prises.
55. H. M. Chapin, *Rhode Island Privateers in King George's War, 1739 – 1748* (Providence, 1926), p. 11; *Pennsylvania Journal*, November 1, 1744.
56. *Pennsylvania Journal*, November 1, 1744.
57. PAC, AC, C11A, LXXXIX, Hocquart to Maurepas, October 9, 1744.
58. Ibid., AN, G.5, CCLIII, Carton 258, Amirauté et Conseil des Prises.
59. See G. A. Rawlyk, *Yankees at Louisbourg* (Orono, Maine, 1967), pp. 4 – 5.
60. C. H. Lincoln, ed., *The Correspondence of William Shirley* (New York, 1912), I, 137, Shirley to the Lords of Trade, July 25, 1744; hereafter referred to as *Shirley Correspondence*.
61. *Mass. House Journals, 1744 – 1745*, p. 29.
62. PAC, A 26, Mascarene to Shirley, June 8, 1744.
63. *Mass. House Journals, 1744 – 1745*, pp. 39 – 40, 42.
64. Ibid., pp. 49, 58.
65. Brebner, *New England's Outpost*, p. 104.
66. Rawlyk, *Yankees at Louisbourg*, pp. 9 – 10.
67. PAC, A 26, Mascarene to Shirley, July 7, 1744.
68. *Shirley Correspondence*, I, 135, Shirley to the Lords of Trade, July 25, 1744.
69. *Mass. House Journals, 1744 – 1745*, p. 57.
70. PAC, A 26, Mascarene to Shirley, June 9, 1744.
71. *Mass. House Journals, 1744 – 1745*, p. 57.
72. T. B. Akins, ed., *Selections from the Public Documents of the Province of Nova Scotia* (Halifax, 1889), p. 146, Mascarene to Shirley, December, 1744; hereafter referred to as Akins, *N.S. Documents*.
73. PAC, A.C.E. 169, Du Vivier's Journal.
74. *Mass. House Journals, 1744 – 1745*, p. 85.

CHAPTER 9

1. *Shirley Correspondence*, I, 153, Shirley to Jonathan Law, November 19, 1744.
2. Ibid., I, 159, Shirley to the Duke of Newcastle, January 5, 1745.
3. PAC, Admiralty Papers, I, 3817, Shirley to the Lords of the Admiralty, November 14, 1744.
4. Clements Library (Cl. Lib), University of Michigan, George Clinton Papers, Newcastle to Clinton, January 3, 1745. See also *Shirley Correspondence*, I, 155 – 56, Newcastle to Shirley, January 3, 1745.
5. Ibid., I, 152, Shirley to Benning Wentworth, November 10, 1744.
6. PAC, Admiralty Papers, I, 3817, Shirley to the Lords of the Admiralty, December 7, 1744.
7. Ibid.
8. Ibid., Shirley to the Lords of the Admiralty, December 4, 1744.
9. *Mass. Hist. Soc. Colls.*, 1st ser., V (1798), 202 – 5, The Importance of Cape-Breton to the Nation, April 9, 1744.
10. PAC, A 26, Kilby to Newcastle, October 8, 1744.
11. Quoted in Wood, *William Shirley*, p. 227, Kilby to the Board of Trade, April 3, 1744.
12. PAC, A 26, Kilby to Newcastle, October 8, 1744.

13. Ibid., C.O., 5900, Kilby to the Earl of Harrington, April 22, 1745.
14. Ibid., Admiralty Papers, I, 3817, Shirley to the Lords of the Admiralty, December 7, 1744.
15. *Dictionary of American Biography* (New York, 1929), II, 578; Murdoch, *History of Nova-Scotia*, I, 263; L. E. DeForest, *Louisbourg Journals, 1745* (New York, 1932), p. 171, Colonel John Bradstreet's Journal.
16. W. Goold, "Col. William Vaughan of Matinicus and Damariscotta," Maine Historical Society *Proceedings* (Portland, 1881), VIII, 293 – 313; New Hampshire Historical Society (N.H. Hist. Soc.), Vaughan Papers, The Memorial of William Vaughan sent to the King, 1745. See also McLennan, *Louisbourg*, pp. 361 – 65.
17. Belknap, *New Hampshire*, II, 154.
18. McLennan, *Louisbourg*, p. 366, J. T. Mason to Newcastle, October 25, 1745; see also Douglass, *A Summary, Historical and Political*, I, 348; Belknap, *New Hampshire*, I, 155.
19. McLennan, *Louisbourg*, pp. 361 – 62, Memorial of William Vaughan; see also DeForest, *Louisbourg Journals*, p. 171, Bradstreet's Journal; McLennan, *Louisbourg*, p. 365, Shirley to Newcastle, March 23, 1745.
20. *Shirley Correspondence*, I, 159 – 60, Shirley to the General Court, January 9, 1745.
21. Mayo, *Hutchinson's History*, II, 309 – 12.
22. Ibid., II, 312.
23. Mass. A., Court Records for Massachusetts, January 12, 1744/45.
24. *Shirley Correspondence*, I, 163, Shirley to Newcastle, January 15, 1745.
25. McLennan, *Louisbourg*, p. 360, Vaughan to Shirley, January 14, 1745.
26. Rhode Island Archives, Memorandum for an Attack upon Louisbourg, enclosed in Shirley's letter to Governor Greene, January 29, 1745; N.H. Hist. Soc., Cape Breton Expedition — Plan of Operations, February 1, 1745. It is interesting to note that Shirley had serious reservations regarding certain features of the plan. He referred to it as "a rough, inaccurate and imperfect scheme." See Wood, *William Shirley*, p. 246.
27. Mass. A., Court Records, January 19, January 23, 1744/45.
28. Ibid., January 25, 1744/45.
29. Mayo, *Hutchinson's History*, II, 411; Douglass, *A Summary, Historical and Political*, I, 349; Kimball, *Correspondence of the Colonial Governors of R.I.*, I, 364, Governor Wanton to Richard Partridge, July 26, 1745. For a discussion of this vote, see Rawlyk, *Yankees at Louisbourg*, p. 172.
30. Belknap, *New Hampshire*, II, 155.
31. *Shirley Correspondence*, I, 169 – 70, Massachusetts General Court Action on the Cape Breton Expedition.
32. Belknap, *New Hampshire*, II, 155.
33. McLennan, *Louisbourg*, p. 360, Vaughan to Shirley, January 14, 1745; Douglass, *A Summary, Historical and Political*, I, 348.
34. Schutz, *William Shirley*, pp. 31, 33, 92; J. Williamson, "Brigadier General Samuel Waldo, 1696 – 1759," Maine Historical Society *Collections* (Portland, 1887), IX, 75 – 93; PAC, C.O. 5, 753, The humble Petition of Wyndham Beawes of London and Samuel Waldo of Boston (n.d.), and The Case of Samuel Waldo of Boston (n.d.).
35. N. Bouton, ed., *Documents and Records Relating to the Province of New Hampshire from 1738 to 1749* (Nashua, N.H., 1871), V, 936, Shirley to Wentworth, February 16, 1745.

36. DeForest, *Louisbourg Journals*, pp. 171 – 72, Bradstreet's Journal.
37. See B. Fairchild, *Messrs. William Pepperrell: Merchants at Piscataqua* (Ithaca, N.Y., 1954), pp. 174 – 75.
38. Belknap, *New Hampshire*, II, 158.
39. Mass. Hist. Soc. *Colls.*, 6th ser., X (1899), 392, Pepperrell to Silas Hooper, November 9, 1745. See also, W. Pepperrell, *An Accurate Journal and Account* (London, 1746), p. 3, Pepperrell to Henry Stafford, November 4, 1745.
40. *Boston Gazette*, January 22, 1745.
41. L. Tyerman, *The Life of the Reverend George Whitefield* (New York, 1877), II, 150, Whitefield to ?, July 29, 1745.
42. McLennan, *Louisbourg*, pp. 365 – 67, Shirley to Newcastle, March 23, 1745, Mason to Newcastle, October 25, 1745; J. Eliot, *God's Marvellous Kindness* (New London, 1745), p. 19. Consider as well H. M. Burrage, *Maine at Louisbourg in 1745* (Augusta, Maine, 1910), pp. 14 – 15, Jonathan Edwards to a friend in Scotland, (n.d.): "The state of the place [Louisbourg] was strangely concealed from us, which if it had been known, would have effectually prevented the design. . . . It was unaccountable that so many, that had been conversant there, should be kept in such ignorance. If one-half of the strength of the place had been known, the expedition had never been thought of."
43. Tyerman, *George Whitefield*, II, 151, Whitefield to ?, July 29, 1745.
44. John Carter Brown Library, Brown University, Providence, R.I., *Moses Pleading with God for Israel . . . With a Word to our Brethren gone and going out on the present Expedition against Cape-Breton, 1745.*
45. Mass. Hist. Soc. *Colls.*, 6th ser., X, 106, John Gray to Pepperrell, February 22, 1745.
46. See especially W. McClenachan, *The Christian Warriour* (Boston, 1745), and T. Prince, *Extraordinary Events* (Boston, 1745).
47. Mass. Hist. Soc. *Colls.*, 6th ser., X, 99, Alexander Bulman to Pepperrell, February 4, 1745. See also C. E. Clark, *The Eastern Frontier: The Settlement of Northern New England, 1610 – 1763* (New York, 1970), pp. 280 – 92.
48. Ibid., p. 102, A. Le Mercier to Pepperrell, February 8, 1745.
49. N.H. Hist. Soc., Waldron Papers, R. Waldron to Pepperrell, March 19, 1745.
50. H. L. Osgood, *The American Colonies in the Eighteenth Century* (New York, 1924), III, 498 – 99. Examine, for example, the various journals in DeForest, *Louisbourg Journals*.
51. Mass. Hist. Soc., Belknap Papers, Shirley's Beating Orders, February 5, 1745.
52. Mass. Hist. Soc. *Colls.*, 6th ser., X, 99 – 100, Bulman to Pepperrell, February 4, 1745.
53. J. Gibson, *A Journal of the Late Siege by the Troops from North America Against the French at Cape Breton* (London, 1747), p. v; Bouton, *Documents Relating to N.H.*, V, 937, Shirley to Wentworth, March 1, 1745; Mass. Hist. Soc. *Colls.*, 6th ser., X, 104, Ammi Cutter to Pepperrell, February 20, 1745.
54. Mass. Hist. Soc., Belknap Papers, Waldo to Pepperrell, February 19, 1745; Mass. Hist. Soc. *Colls.*, 6th ser., X, 109, Jothan Odiorne, Jr., to Pepperrell, February 27, 1745. See also *Shirley Correspondence*, I, 196, Shirley to Newcastle, March 27, 1745; H. M. Chapin, *New England Vessels in the Expedition against Louisbourg, 1745* (Boston, 1923), pp. 3 – 8.

55. L. W. Larabee, ed., *The Papers of Benjamin Franklin* (New Haven, Conn., 1961), III, 15, Notes on Assembly Debates. For a detailed treatment of the response of the various colonies to the Massachusetts initiative, see Rawlyk, *Yankees at Louisbourg*, pp. 49–54.

56. Rawlyk, *Yankees at Louisbourg*, pp. 54–56. A great deal of useful information about specific New Englanders involved in the expedition is to be found in *Sibley's Harvard Graduates*, IV, 356–64; V, 165, 594, 612; VI, 9, 29, 110, 241, 264, 277, 431, 486; VII, 58, 132–36, 195, 507; VIII, 16, 24, 459, 631–32, 641, 772; IX, 62, 274–75, 301, 437, 509, 513, 584; X, 32, 275, 289–90, 338, 411, 497–98, 506, 509, 528–29.

CHAPTER 10

1. Essex Institute Historical *Collections*, III (1861), 187, George Curwen to Mrs. Curwen, April 22, 1745.

2. Ibid.

3. C. H. Lincoln, ed., *The Journals of Sir William Pepperrell Kept during the Expedition against Louisbourg, March 24–August 22, 1745* (Worcester, Mass., 1910), pp. 14–15; Essex Institute Historical *Collections*, XLVIII (1912), 298, Journal Kept by Lieut. Daniel Giddings of Ipswich During the Expedition Against Cape Breton in 1744–5.

4. E. M. Bidwell, ed., "Journal of the Rev. Adonijah Bidwell," *New Eng. Hist. and Geneal. Register* (Boston, 1873), XXVII, 154; Mass. Hist. Soc., David Papers, ? to ?, n.d. See also *New Eng. Hist. and Geneal. Register* (Boston, 1912), LXVI, 117, Benjamin Cleaves's Journal.

5. DeForest, *Louisbourg Journals*, p. 10, First Journal, Anonymous. See also *New Eng. Hist. and Geneal. Register*, LXVI, 117, Benjamin Cleaves's Journal; S. A. Green, *Three Military Diaries* (Groton, Conn., 1910), p. 13, Dudley Bradstreet's Diary.

6. DeForest, *Louisbourg Journals*, p. 174, John Bradstreet's Journal. For a detailed description of the taking of the Grand Battery, see Rawlyk, *Yankees at Louisbourg*, pp. 89–97.

7. *Boston Evening Post*, May 20, 1745, ? to ?, May 4, 1745.

8. N.H. Hist. Soc., Waldron Papers, T. Waldron to R. Waldron, May 20, 1745.

9. DeForest, *Louisbourg Journals*, p. 76, Fifth Journal, Anonymous; Green, *Three Military Diaries*, p. 17, Dudley Bradstreet's Diary.

10. Mass. Hist. Soc. *Colls.*, 6th ser., X, 162, Warren to Pepperrell, May 11, 1745.

11. Essex Institute Historical *Collections*, III, 187, George Curwen to Mrs. Curwen, April 22, 1745.

12. Cl. Lib., Louisbourg Papers, T. W. Waldron to R. Waldron, June 6, 1745.

13. DeForest, *Louisbourg Journals*, p. 86, Sixth Journal, Anonymous; Green, *Three Military Diaries*, p. 20, Dudley Bradstreet's Diary.

14. Cl. Lib., Louisbourg Papers, R. Waldron to T. W. Waldron, June 21, 1745; DeForest, *Louisbourg Journals*, p. 76, Fifth Journal, Anonymous; Green, *Three Military Diaries*, pp. 15, 19, Dudley Bradstreet's Diary; Mass. Hist. Soc. *Colls.*, 6th ser., X, 1–7, Waldo to Pepperrell, May 13, 1745.

15. McLennan, *Louisbourg*, pp. 156–57.

16. DeForest, *Louisbourg Journals*, p. 197, Warren to Pepperrell, May 23, 1745.

17. Connecticut Historical Society *Collections*, I (1860), 152, Journal of Roger Wolcott.

18. Green, *Three Military Diaries*, p. 20, Dudley Bradstreet's Diary.

19. Pepperrell, *An Accurate Journal*, p. 21; W. P. Upham, ed., "Craft's Journal of the Siege of Louisbourg," Essex Institute Historical *Collections*, VI (1864), 186; Lincoln, *Pepperrell Journal*, p. 27.
20. Mass. Hist. Soc. *Colls.*, 1st ser., I, 34, Warren to Pepperrell, May 26, 1745.
21. Parkman, *Half-Century of Conflict*, II, 305 – 7, Du Chambon to Maurepas, September 2, 1745. PAC, AN, F. 3, L, pt. I, Inhabitants of Louisbourg to Du Chambon, 1745.
22. Connecticut Historical Society *Collections*, I, 144 – 45, Pepperrell and Warren to Du Chambon, June 16, 1745.
23. DeForest, *Louisbourg Journals*, p. 92, Sixth Journal, Anonymous.
24. Ibid.
25. Green, *Three Military Diaries*, p. 26, Dudley Bradstreet's Diary.
26. Mass. Hist. Soc., Louisbourg Papers, ? to ?, n.d.; Davis Papers, W. Clarke's Account of the Louisbourg Siege, December 13, 1745.
27. Mayo, *Hutchinson's History*, II, 421; C. P. Stacey, *Quebec, 1759: The Siege and the Battle* (Toronto, 1959), p. iii, Lord Selkirk's Diary, 1804.
28. Prince, *Extraordinary Events*, p. 31.
29. *Boston Evening Post*, July 15, 1745.
30. Mass. Hist. Soc. *Colls.*, 6th ser., X, 330, Pepperrell to Shirley, July 4, 1745.
31. See for example ibid., X, 308 – 9, T. Hubbard to Pepperrell, July 4, 1745.
32. Ibid., X, 307, Benjamin Colman to Pepperrell, July 3, 1745; p. 308, Hubbard to Pepperrell, July 4, 1745.
33. C. Chauncy, *Marvellous Things, done by the right Hand and holy Arm of God in getting him the Victory* (Boston, 1745), pp. 12, 21.
34. Prince, *Extraordinary Events*, p. 35. See also A. Heimert, *Religion and the American Mind: From the Great Awakening to the Revolution* (Cambridge, Mass., 1966), pp. 82 – 84.
35. Prince, *Extraordinary Events*, p. 33.
36. D. J. Boorstin, *The Americans: The Colonial Experience* (New York, 1964), p. 356.
37. E. Eis, *The Forts of Folly* (London, 1959), p. 221.
38. Dalhousie University Library, J. G. Bourinot Transcripts, p. 73, The Virtue of the New England People, from *The Craftsman*, August 3, 1745.
39. DeForest, *Louisbourg Journals*, p. 130, Ninth Journal, Chaplain Stephen Williams.
40. *Boston News-Letter*, July 25, 1745; *Boston Gazette*, July 16, 1745.
41. Chauncy, *Marvellous Things*, p. 14.
42. *Boston Evening Post*, July 15, 1745.
43. Ibid., July 29, 1745.
44. Ibid., July 8, 1745; *Boston Gazette*, July 9, 1745.
45. This thesis is developed at greater length in S. Shortt, "Symbolic Louisbourg: The Secularization of the City on a Hill" (Unpublished paper presented at Queen's University, March 17, 1970).
46. Mass. Hist. Soc. *Colls.*, 6th ser., X, 322 – 33, Shirley to Pepperrell, July 7, 1745; p. 330, Pepperrell to Shirley, July 17, 1745.
47. DeForest, *Louisbourg Journals*, p. 92, Sixth Journal, Anonymous.
48. Cl. Lib., Papers of Sir James Douglas, Journall Kept on Board His Maj. Ship 'Vigilant' Commencing May the 23, 1745; and DeForest, *Louisbourg Journals*, pp. 35 – 36, First Journal, Anonymous.
49. Cl. Lib., Louisbourg Papers, T. W. Waldron to R. Waldron, July 26, 1745.
50. Mass. Hist. Soc. *Colls.*, 6th ser., X, 329, Pepperrell to Shirley, July 17, 1745.

51. Ibid., X, 30 – 31, Records of the Council of War; *Shirley Correspondence*, I, 264, 293, Shirley to Benning Wentworth, September 2, 1745, Shirley to Newcastle, December 14, 1745.

52. Mass. Hist. Soc. *Colls.*, 6th ser., X, 47, Records of the Council of War; Maine Historical Society, Falmouth Papers, I, Plunder Accounts, 1745.

53. Mass. Hist. Soc. *Colls.*, 6th ser., X, 442, Pepperrell to Shirley, January 28, 1746; PANS, XIX, Pepperrell to Newcastle, May 21, 1746.

54. McLennan, *Louisbourg*, p. 167.

55. *Boston News-Letter* and the *Independent Advertiser* carried reports from the peace negotiations.

56. *Boston News-Letter*, May 11, 1749.

57. H. H. Peckham, *The Colonial Wars, 1689 – 1762* (Chicago, 1964), p. 119; see also R. W. Van Alstyne, *The Rising American Empire* (London, 1960), pp. 16 – 21.

58. Rawlyk, *Yankees at Louisbourg*, p. 159.

59. J. Lemisch, "Jack Tar in the Streets: Merchant Seamen in the Politics of Revolutionary America," *The William and Mary Quarterly*, XXV, no. 3 (July, 1968), 387.

60. PAC, C.O. 217, A 26, Shirley to the Lords of Trade, October 16, 1744. For Shirley's involvement in Nova Scotia affairs for the 1744 – 48 period, see B. Moody, "Paul Mascarene, William Shirley and the Defence of Nova Scotia, 1744 – 1748" (M.A. thesis, Queen's University, 1969).

61. Akins, *N.S. Documents*, p. 135, The inhabitants of Mines to DeGanne, October 10, 1744; Rawlyk, *Yankees at Louisbourg*, pp. 11 – 15.

62. Moody, "Paul Mascarene, William Shirley and the Defence of Nova Scotia," p. 133.

63. PANS, XXI, Mascarene to Tyng, November 3, 1744.

64. Ibid., XXI, Shirley to Newcastle, December 8, 1744.

65. *Shirley Correspondence*, I, 164, Shirley to Newcastle, January 14, 1745.

66. See Moody, "Paul Mascarene, William Shirley and the Defence of Nova Scotia," pp. 150 – 56.

67. Mass. Hist. Soc., Belknap Papers, Bastide to Shirley, May 19, 1745, and Mascarene to Shirley, May 19, 1745.

68. *Shirley Correspondence*, I, 163 – 64, Shirley to Newcastle, January 14, 1745.

69. PANS, XIII, Shirley to Major Aldredge, May 26, 1745; Mass. Hist. Soc. *Colls.*, 6th ser., X, 206, Shirley to Pepperrell, May 22, 1745.

70. Mass. Hist. Soc., Parkman Transcripts, Du Chambon to Morin, May 16, 1745; V. H. Paltsits, ed., *The Journal of Captain William Pote* (New York, 1896), pp. 16 – 17.

71. *Shirley Correspondence*, I, 164, Shirley to Newcastle, January 14, 1745.

72. Canadian Archives *Report, 1905*, II, Appendix C, p. 39, Warren to Newcastle, October 3, 1745; *Shirley Correspondence*, I, 219 – 20, Shirley to Pepperrell, May 25, 1745; E. B. O'Callaghan, ed., *Documents Relating to the Colonial History of the State of New York* (Albany, 1858), X, 4 – 5, Beauharnois and Hocquart to Maurepas, September 12, 1745.

73. *Shirley Correspondence*, I, 220, Shirley to Pepperrell, May 25, 1745.

74. O'Callaghan, *Documents Relating to N.Y.*, X, 17, Beauharnois and Hocquart to Maurepas, September 12, 1745.

75. PAC, A 27, Representation of the State of His Majesty's Province of Nova Scotia, November 8, 1745.

76. Ibid., Mascarene to Shirley, December 7, 1745.

77. Moody, "Paul Mascarene, William Shirley and the Defence of Nova Scotia," p. 179; PANS, XIII½, Shirley to Newcastle, February 11, 1746.
78. PAC, C.O. 5, 900, William Shirley, Jr., to Andrew Stone, March 9, 1746.
79. *Shirley Correspondence*, I, 337, Shirley to Newcastle, August 15, 1746.
80. G. Lacour-Gayet, *La Marine-Militaire de la France Sous Le Règne de Louis XV* (Paris, 1902), pp. 181 – 84.
81. *Shirley Correspondence*, I, 346 – 49, Shirley to the General Court, September 9, 1746.
82. Ibid., I, 350, General Court to Shirley, September 10, 1746.
83. Ibid., I, 355, Shirley to Benning Wentworth, September 10, 1746.
84. Mayo, *Hutchinson's History*, II, 328.
85. *Shirley Correspondence*, I, 355, Shirley to Wentworth, September 20, 1746.
86. Douglass, *A Summary, Historical and Political*, I, 323.
87. *Shirley Correspondence*, I, 360, Shirley and Warren to William Greene, October 23, 1746.
88. Mayo, *Hutchinson's History*, II, 328.
89. *Shirley Correspondence*, I, 364, Shirley to Greene, October 27, 1746.
90. PAC, AC, C11A, LXXXVII, pt. 3, Journal of the Acadia campaign.
91. Ibid., C.O. 5, 901, Shirley to Newcastle, November 1, 1746.
92. PANS, XIII, John Gorham to Shirley, November 15, 1746.
93. Ibid., Mascarene to Newcastle, January 23, 1747; PAC, M.G. 18, Charles Morris, A Brief Survey of Nova Scotia; ibid., AC, C11A, LXXXVII, pt. 3, Journal of the Acadia campaign.
94. Moody, "Paul Mascarene, William Shirley and the Defence of Nova Scotia," p. 228.
95. PANS, XIII½, Newcastle to Shirley, May 30, 1747.
96. Parkman, *Half-Century of Conflict*, II, 351, Shirley to Newcastle, June 25, 1747.
97. *Massachusetts House Journals, 1747 – 1748*, p. 181.
98. PAC, Admiralty Papers, I, 3818, Knowles and Shirley to Thomas Corbett, November 28, 1747.

CHAPTER 11

1. I. Morrill, *The Soldier exhorted to Courage in the Service of his King and Country, from a Sense of God and Religion In a Sermon Preach'd At Wilmingston, April 3, 1755, To Capt. Phinehas Osgood and His Company of Soldiers* (Boston, 1755), p. 13.
2. T. C., *A Scheme to Drive the French Out of All the Continent of America* (Boston, 1755), p. 7.
3. New York Public Library, Massachusetts Papers, J. Willard to W. Shirley, December 28, 1752.
4. W. Clarke, *Observations On the Late and Present Conduct of the French, With Regard to their Encroachments Upon the British Colonies in North America* (Boston, 1755), p. 26.
5. Schutz, *William Shirley*, pp. 145 – 65.
6. Mass. A., V, 348 – 60, Shirley's Some Points Stated concerning the Importance of Nova Scotia, with Observations upon 'em, 1749.
7. Schutz, *William Shirley*, p. 165.
8. Clark, *Acadia*, p. 324.
9. Quoted in ibid., p. 323.

10. Mass. A., V, Cornwallis to Phips, December 18, 1749.

11. Akins, *N.S. Documents*, p. 182, Cornwallis to the Duke of Bedford, March 19, 1750.

12. *Mass. House Journals, 1750 – 1751*, p. 164.

13. *Maine History*, XII, 125 – 26, Pepperrell Report, February 15, 16, 1750.

14. Ibid., XII, 236 – 41, Pepperrell to Shirley, January 4, 1754.

15. Ibid., XII, 241 – 42, Shirley to Phinehas Stevens, March 4, 1754.

16. *Mass. House Journals, 1754*, pp. 263 – 66, Shirley to the General Court, March 28, 1754.

17. *Maine History*, XII, 210 – 11, Kennebec Proprietors to Phips, May 30, 1753.

18. *Shirley Correspondence*, II, 47 – 51, General Court to Shirley, April 9, 1754.

19. *Maine History*, XII, 280, General Court Vote, June 4, 5, 1754.

20. Akins, *N.S. Documents*, pp. 271, 396, Shirley to Lawrence, January 6, 1755.

21. *Shirley Correspondence*, II, 13, Earl of Holderness to Shirley, August 28, 1753.

22. Ibid., II, 62 – 64, Shirley to Sir Thomas Robinson, May 8, 1754.

23. *Boston Gazette*, September 8, 1754.

24. J. Edwards, *A Sermon Preach'd in the Audience of His Excellency William Shirley* (Boston, 1754), pp. 35 – 36.

25. *Boston News-Letter*, October 10, 1754, ? to ?, September 29, 1754; *Boston Post-Boy*, October 14, 1754, ? to ?, September 29, 1754.

26. W. Clarke, *Observations on the Late and Present Conduct of the French*, pp. 27 – 28.

27. *A Letter from Quebeck*... (Boston, 1754), p. 6.

28. Akins, *N.S. Documents*, p. 383, Robinson to Shirley, July 5, 1754.

29. Ibid., pp. 383 – 84, Robinson to Lawrence, July 5, 1754.

30. S. M. Pargellis, ed., *Military Affairs in North America, 1748 – 65* (New York, 1936), p. 29, Lawrence to Lord Halifax, August 23, 1754.

31. Akins, *N.S. Documents*, pp. 377 – 79, Lawrence to Shirley, November 5, 1754.

32. Ibid., p. 380, Shirley to Lawrence, November 7, 1754.

33. Ibid., p. 388, Shirley to Robinson, November 11, 1754.

34. Ibid., pp. 388 – 89.

35. Ibid., p. 389, Shirley to Lawrence, December 14, 1754.

36. *Shirley Correspondence*, II, 109, Shirley to Robinson, December 14, 1754.

37. Akins, *N.S. Documents*, p. 389, Shirley to Lawrence, December 14, 1754.

38. Ibid., p. 393, Shirley to Lawrence, January 6, 1755.

39. *Maine History*, XII, 350 – 62, Governor Shirley's speech, February 7, 1755.

40. *Shirley Correspondence*, II, 127 – 30, Shirley to the General Court, February 13, 1755.

41. Ibid., II, 121 – 22, Israel Williams to Shirley, February 1, 1755.

42. N.S. Hist. Soc. *Colls.*, *1884*, IV (1885), 179, Winslow to Halifax, June 27, 1755.

43. *Shirley Correspondence*, II, 134 – 36, Shirley to James Delancey, February 24, 1755; N.S. Hist. Soc. *Colls.*, IV, 177 – 82, Winslow to King Gould, June 16, 1755, Winslow to Thomas Lane, June 26, 1755, Winslow to Halifax, June 27, 1755, Winslow to Charles Gould, June 27, 1755.

44. Ibid., IV, 116 – 17, Shirley to Winslow, February 12, 1755.

45. Morrill, *The Soldier exhorted to Courage*, pp. 15 – 16, 20.

46. J. Ballantine, *The Importance of God's Presence with an Army, going against the Enemy* (Boston, 1756), p. 19; S. Checkley, *The Duty of God's People when engag'd in War* (Boston, 1755), p. 28.

47. See, for example, J. A. Henretta, "Economic Development and Social Structure in Colonial Boston," *The William and Mary Quarterly*, 3d ser., XXII, no. 1 (January, 1965), 75–92, and K. A. Lockridge, *A New England Town: The First Hundred Years* (New York, 1970), pp. 139–59.

48. Akins, *N.S. Documents*, pp. 406–7, Shirley to Lawrence, May 31, 1755.

49. N.S. Hist. Soc. *Colls.*, IV, 129–33, Winslow's Journal; *New Eng. Hist. and Geneal. Register* (October, 1879), XXXIII, 385, Diary of John Thomas.

50. See Mass. A., Winslow's Journal, pp. 20–64.

51. Henretta, "Economic Development," pp. 75–92.

52. *New Eng. Hist. and Geneal. Register*, XXXIII, 386, Thomas Diary.

53. J. C. Webster, *The Forts of Chignecto* (Shediac, N.B., 1930), p. 42.

54. *New Eng. Hist. and Geneal. Register*, XXXIII, 388, Thomas Diary.

55. Ibid.

56. N.S. Hist. Soc. *Colls.*, IV, 176, 215, Winslow's Journal.

57. D. S. Graham, "The Making of a Colonial Governor: Charles Lawrence in Nova Scotia, 1749–1760" (M.A. thesis, University of New Brunswick, 1962), pp. 70–72.

58. J. C. Webster, "Journal of Abijah Willard, 1755," New Brunswick Historical Society *Collections*, no. 13 (1930), pp. 28, 45.

59. N.S. Hist. Soc. *Colls.*, IV, 221–22, Monckton to Winslow, August 6, 1755.

60. *New Eng. Hist. and Geneal. Register*, XXXIII, 389, Thomas Diary.

61. Akins, *N.S. Documents*, p. 267, N.S. Council Minutes, July 28, 1755; pp. 267–69, Lawrence to Monckton, July 31, 1755.

62. Webster, "Journal of Abijah Willard," p. 37; and C. B. Fergusson, Introduction to *Evangeline: A Souvenir of the Evangeline Country* (Winnipeg, 1971), p. 35.

63. G. F. G. Stanley, *New France, The Last Phase, 1744–1760* (Toronto, 1968), p. 122.

64. R. G. Lowe, "Massachusetts and the Acadians," *The William and Mary Quarterly*, 3d ser., XXV, no. 2 (April, 1968), 221.

65. For a perceptive study of this problem in the 1755–63 period, see Lowe, "Massachusetts and the Acadians," pp. 212–29.

66. See, for example, MacNutt, *The Atlantic Provinces*, pp. 1–51.

67. Brebner, *New England's Outpost*, p. 233.

68. Webster, *Forts of Chignecto*, p. 116, Monckton's Journal.

69. *Boston Gazette*, July 14, 1755.

70. J. B. and W. M., *An Account of the Present State of Nova Scotia* (London, 1756), pp. 1–12.

71. For an excellent statement of the General Court's reaction to the Chignecto affair, see *Mass. House Journals, 1756*, pt. II, pp. 315–16, General Court to Shirley, February 7, 1756.

72. Pargellis, *Military Affairs*, p. 185, Franklin to Sir Everard Fawkener, July 27, 1756.

73. *Boston Gazette*, July 14, 1755.

CHAPTER 12

1. L. H. Butterfield, ed., *Diary and Autobiography of John Adams* (Cambridge, Mass., 1961), I, 285.

2. See, for example, James Otis, *Brief Remarks on the Defence of the Halifax Libel on the British-American Colonies* (Boston, 1765), pp. 3–15; and by an unknown author, *An Essay on the Present State of the Province of Nova Scotia* (Halifax, 1773), p. 5.

3. Brebner, *Neutral Yankees*, pp. 172–206.

4. *Boston Gazette*, August 21, 1758.

5. *Boston News-Letter*, August 24, 1758.

6. Brebner, *New England's Outpost*, p. 261.

7. *Boston News-Letter*, November 2, 1758.

8. Murdoch, *History of Nova-Scotia*, II, 359.

9. See T. C. Haliburton, *An Historical and Statistical Account of Nova Scotia* (Halifax, 1829), I, 220–23.

10. A. W. H. Eaton, *The History of Kings County, Nova Scotia: Heart of the Acadian Land* (Salem, Mass., 1910), pp. 65–72.

11. E. D. Poole, *Annals of Yarmouth and Barrington in the Revolutionary War* (Yarmouth, N.S., 1899), p. 51, Simon Burns to Massachusetts Council of State, November 17, 1778.

12. I. F. MacKinnon, *Settlements and Churches in Nova Scotia, 1749–1776* (Montreal, 1930), pp. 40–42; R. H. Akagi, *The Town Proprietors of the New England Colonies* (Philadelphia, 1924), pp. 115–229.

13. MacKinnon, *Settlements and Churches*, p. 42.

14. *Mass. Hist. Soc. Proc.*, *1887–89*, 2d ser., IV, 67, Samuel Beckwith, Caleb Huntington … Elkanah Morton, Junr, to Rev. Andrew Elliot, November 8, 1769.

15. PANS, 284, Memorial of the People of the Townships of Horton, Cornwallis, Falmouth, and Newport to the Board of Trade (1762).

16. MacKinnon, *Settlements and Churches*, p. 42.

17. A. W. H. Eaton, "Rhode Island Settlers on the French Lands in Nova Scotia in 1760 and 1761," *Americana* (January, 1915), p. 15.

18. Ibid., pp. 10–12; Murdoch, II, 364–65.

19. PANS *Report, 1933* (Halifax, 1934), pp. 21–27, State and Condition of the Province of Nova Scotia together with some observations, etc., 29th October, 1763; MacKinnon, *Settlements and Churches*, pp. 24–26; J. S. Martell, "Pre-Loyalist Settlements around Minas Basin" (M.A. thesis, Dalhousie University, 1933), pp. 62–180; Eaton, "Rhode Island Settlers," pp. 1–43; A. W. H. Eaton, "The Settling of Colchester County, Nova Scotia, by New England Puritans and Ulster Scotsmen," Royal Society of Canada *Transactions*, VI (1912), sec. II, 221–65.

20. See Lieutenant-Governor Belcher's letter to the Board of Trade, December 12, 1760, quoted in Eaton, "Rhode Island Settlers," p. 14.

21. MacKinnon, *Settlements and Churches*, p. 22.

22. M. Armstrong, *The Great Awakening in Nova Scotia* (Hartford, Conn., 1948), pp. 21–22; Brebner, *Neutral Yankees*, p. 95.

23. See the article by C. B. Fergusson, "Pre-Loyalist Settlements in Nova Scotia," *N.S. Hist. Soc. Colls.*, XXXVII (1970), 5–22.

24. Mass. Hist. Soc. *Proc., 1887–89*, IV, 68–69, Samuel Beckwith, Caleb Huntington . . . Elkanah Morton, Junr, to Rev. Andrew Elliot, November 8, 1769.
25. C. B. Fergusson, ed., *The Life of Jonathan Scott* (Halifax, 1960), pp. 28–29.
26. PANS, Records of Church of Chebugue.
27. See B. Bailyn, *The Ideological Origins of the American Revolution* (Cambridge, Mass., 1967), and Heimert, *Religion and the American Mind*.
28. W. O. Raymond, *The River St. John* (Saint John, 1910), pp. 309–23.
29. PANS, LXXVIII, Franklin to Board of Trade, September 30, 1766.
30. H. A. Innis, ed., *The Diary of Simeon Perkins, 1766–1780* (Toronto, 1948), pp. 13, 27–30, 44, 76–77.
31. D. C. Harvey, "The Struggle for the New England Form of Township Government in Nova Scotia," Canadian Historical Association *Report* (1933), p. 22.
32. This thesis is superbly developed in Bailyn, *Ideological Origins of the American Revolution.*
33. PANS, 211, 250, Liverpool Memorial, July 24, 1762; ibid., 284, no. 10, Horton, Cornwallis, Falmouth, and Newport Memorial, n.d.; PAC, M. G. 9, B-9, Nova Scotia Local Records, 4, Cornwallis Town Meeting, April 14, 1771.
34. *Essay on the Present State of the Province of Nova Scotia*, p. 6.
35. Butterfield, *Diary and Autobiography of John Adams*, I, 298.
36. PAC, N.S.A. LXII, 2–5, Petition of John Parison, January 27, 1758.
37. Butterfield, *Diary and Autobiography of John Adams*, I, 283.
38. Larabee, *Papers of Benjamin Franklin*, VIII (1959), 293–94, Franklin to Isaac Norris, March, 1759.
39. *A Letter from a Merchant in Halifax to a Merchant in Boston Trading in Halifax* (Boston, 1757), pp. 2–3.
40. (Stephen Hopkins), *The Rights of the Colonies Examined* (Providence, 1765), p. 15.
41. Martin Howard, Jr., *A Letter from a Gentleman at Halifax to his Friend in Rhode-Island* (Newport, R.I., 1765).
42. Otis, *Defence of the Halifax Libel on the British-American Colonies*, and James Otis, *A Vindication of the British Colonies* (Boston, 1765).
43. Martin Howard, Jr., *A Defence of the Letter from a Gentleman at Halifax* (Providence, 1765).
44. Otis, *A Vindication*, p. 4.
45. Butterfield, *Diary and Autobiography of John Adams*, I, 285.
46. E. C. Burnett, ed., *Letters of the Members of the Continental Congress* (Washington, 1928), IV, 246, James Lovell to Horatio Gates, June 3, 1779.
47. D. C. Harvey, "Machias and the Invasion of Nova Scotia," Canadian Historical Association *Report* (1932), p. 17; J. H. Ahlin, *Maine Rubicon: Downeast Settlers during the American Revolution* (Calais, 1966), pp. 11–43.
48. J. C. Fitzpatrick, ed., *The Writings of George Washington* (Washington, 1931), III, 415.
49. Ibid., III, 415–16.
50. Canadian Archives *Report* (1893), pp. 334–35, Legge to Lord Dartmouth, July 31, 1775; see also W. B. Kerr, "Nova Scotia in the Critical Years," *Dalhousie Review*, XII (1932), 97.
51. J. W. Porter, *Memoir of Col. Jonathan Eddy of Eddington, Me.* (Augusta, Maine, 1877), pp. 3–9.
52. Brebner, *Neutral Yankees*, pp. 317–18.

53. See G. A. Rawlyk, "The American Revolution and Nova Scotia Reconsidered," *Dalhousie Review*, XLIII (1963), 383 – 84.
54. Fitzpatrick, *Writings of George Washington*, III, 437 – 38; see also W. B. Kerr, *The Maritime Provinces of British North America and the American Revolution* (Sackville, N.B., n.d.), p. 73.
55. Canadian Archives *Report* (1894), p. 345, Dixon to Butler, January 14, 1776, Eagleson to Butler, January 27, 1776; Murdoch, II, 568.
56. Canadian Archives *Report* (1894), p. 360, Gorham Journal.
57. F. Kidder, *Military Operations in Eastern Maine and Nova Scotia During the Revolution* (Albany, N.Y., 1867), p. 12.
58. P. Force, ed., *American Archives, Fifth Series* (Washington, 1851), II, 734, Petition of Jonathan Eddy, August 28, 1776.
59. Mass. A., CXLIV, Maugerville Committee of Safety to the Massachusetts General Court, May 21, 1776.
60. Ibid., XXXV, Resolution of the Council, August 31, 1776.
61. Ibid., CXCV, Lyon to the Massachusetts General Court (Sept.) 1776.
62. The description of the expedition is based upon the relevant Allan papers found in Kidder, *Military Operations*; Eddy's journal reproduced in Harvey, "Machias and the Invasion of Nova Scotia," pp. 22 – 24; and Gorham's journal in Canadian Archives *Report* (1894), pp. 359 – 66.
63. Mass. A., CXLIV, Allan Petition, February 19, 1777.
64. Harvey, "Machias and the Invasion of Nova Scotia," p. 22.
65. Rawlyk, "The American Revolution and Nova Scotia Reconsidered," p. 389.

CHAPTER 13

1. Kidder, *Military Operations*, p. 13 and p. 310, Allan's Report on the Indian Tribes.
2. Ibid., pp. 11, 188, Allan's Official Report from Aukpake, June 18, 1777.
3. Ibid., pp. 170, 173, Allan to Massachusetts Council, November 21, 1776.
4. Mass. A., CXCVI, Hancock to Massachusetts Council, January 10, 1777.
5. Ibid., CCXII, Resolve of Congress, January 8, 1777.
6. Ibid., CXCVI, Massachusetts Council to Hancock, January 30, 1777.
7. Ibid., CXLIV, Allan to Massachusetts Council, February 19, 1777, and February 25, 1777.
8. Ibid., CXLIV, Allan to Massachusetts Council and House of Representatives, March 7, 1777; Allan to Massachusetts Council, March 18, 1777; Committee Report, March 25, 1777.
9. Ibid., CXCVII, Hancock to Massachusetts Council, May 13, 1777; Allan to Massachusetts Council, May 30, 1777; Resolve for raising a Reg for relief of . . . Nova Scotia, June 7, 1777.
10. Ibid., CXCVII, George Stillman to Massachusetts Council, June 18, 1777. See also Ahlin, *Maine Rubicon*, p. 84; Kidder, *Military Operations*, pp. 91 – 124, Allan's Journal, 1777; Mass. A., CXCIX, F. Shaw to Massachusetts Council and House of Representatives, June 6, 1777; CCXV, Resolve of General Court, July 1, 1777; CCXIV, Report, June 18, 1777.
11. Poole, *Annals of Yarmouth*, p. 86, Resolve of General Court, June 22, 1780. For a recent and exhaustive study of the impact of American privateering in Nova Scotia during the revolutionary period, see J. D. Faibisy, "Privateering and Piracy: The Effects of New England Raiding upon Nova Scotia during the American Revolution" (Ph.D. thesis, University of Massachusetts, 1972).

12. O. T. Brown, "Beverly Privateers in the American Revolution," Col. Soc. Mass. *Transactions, 1920 – 22* (Boston, 1923), XXIV, 394 – 99.
13. Poole, *Annals of Yarmouth,* p. 126, Resolve ... July 5, 1782.
14. D. C. Harvey and C. B. Fergusson, eds., *The Diary of Simeon Perkins, 1780 – 1789* (Toronto, 1958), pp. 41 – 42; *Nova Scotia Gazette,* September 4, 1781, July 9, 1782; M. B. Des Brisay, *History of the County of Lunenburg* (Toronto, 1895), pp. 65, 270, 271; Brebner, *Neutral Yankees,* pp. 294 – 95.
15. Kidder, *Military Operations,* pp. 255 – 56, Allan to General Court, August 17, 1778.
16. Innis, *Diary of Simeon Perkins,* p. 203.
17. See Brebner, *Neutral Yankees,* pp. 255 – 310.
18. H. Alline, *A Sermon on a Day of Thanksgiving ... 21st November, 1782* (Halifax, n.d.), p. 23. See also J. M. Bumsted, *Henry Alline* (Toronto, 1971).
19. H. Alline, *Life and Journal* (Boston, 1806), pp. 42, 171.
20. H. Alline, *A Gospel Call to Sinners* (Newburyport, Mass., 1795), pp. 30 – 31.
21. H. Alline, *A Sermon on a Day of Thanksgiving,* pp. 9, 23.
22. H. Alline, *Two Mites on Some of the Most Important and Much Disputed Points of Divinity* (Halifax, 1781), p. 234.
23. G. E. Levy, "Diary of the Rev. Joseph Dimock," N.S. Hist. Soc. *Colls.,* XXVIII (1949), 62 – 67.
24. J. Hannay, "The Maugerville Settlement," New Brunswick Historical Society *Collections,* I, no. 1 (1894), 84 – 86.
25. Levy, "Diary of the Rev. Joseph Dimock," pp. 62 – 63.

Bibliographical Note

Because of the number and the detail of the notes to be found in this book, I have decided not to repeat in a long essay or even a long list the titles of all the various sources used. I have been greatly dependent upon a large number of manuscript collections in various New England and Canadian archives, as well as upon hundreds of volumes of printed collections of documents. The manuscript and printed primary sources from the Massachusetts Archives and the Massachusetts Historical Society, as would be expected, proved to be of particular importance.

What the notes do not show, however, are the many newspapers, pamphlets, and sermons produced in pre-1784 Massachusetts which were examined and which provided so little relevant material. Contemporary newspapers, the *Boston News-Letter*, 1707–1776, the *Boston Gazette*, 1719–1783, the *New England Courant*, 1721–1727, the *Boston Post-Boy*, 1734–1769, and the *Boston Evening Post*, 1735–1775, apart from a few brief outbursts of interest, contained virtually no mention of Nova Scotia–Acadia. Seemingly relevant pamphlets and sermons cited in Evans's *American Bibliography* as well provided relatively little information about Massachusetts perceptions of Nova Scotia. A great deal of my research, therefore, much to my dismay, produced negative results. And this fact, more than anything else, strengthened my conviction that especially in the eighteenth century, apathy, indifference, and ignorance characterized Massachusetts' response to Nova Scotia.

For my treatment of the pre-1717 period, I am especially indebted to the pioneering work of A. H. Buffinton, "The Policy of the Northern Colonies towards the French to the Peace of Utrecht" (Ph.D. thesis, Harvard University, 1925) and also to G. M. Waller, *Samuel Vetch: Colonial Enterpriser* (Chapel Hill, N.C., 1960), D. Chard, "Pagans, Privateers and Propagandists: New England – Acadia Relations, 1690 – 1710" (M.A. thesis, Dalhousie University, 1967), and D. C. B. Doherty, "Oliver Cromwell, Robert Sedgwick, John Leverett and the Acadian Adventure of 1654" (M.A. thesis, Queen's University, 1969). For the post-1717 period, I owe a great deal to J. A. Schutz, *William Shirley: King's Governor of Massachusetts* (Chapel Hill, N.C., 1961), B. Moody, "Paul Mascarene, William Shirley and the Defence of Nova Scotia, 1744 – 1748" (M.A. thesis, Queen's University, 1969), and to my close friend Professor Gordon Stewart of Michigan State University, some of whose penetrating insights concerning Massachusetts – Nova Scotia relations, 1763 – 1784, are to be found in *A People Highly Favoured of God* (Toronto, 1972).

Index

Cape Sable: and Alexander, 2; and
Andros, 53, 54; and Bergier, 47;
and Cromwell, 27; and d'Aulnay,
14; and fisheries, 18, 43, 59, 63;
and Indian raids, 129; and
Ipswich fishermen, 10; and
King George's War, 138, 145;
and La Tour, 4, 13; and Louis-
bourg expedition of *1745*, 162;
Massachusetts economic control
of, 34; and privateers, 80, 85, 92
Cape Sable Indians, 130
Carignan-Salières regiment, 36
Cartagena expedition, 161
Carter, William, 46
Casco Bay, 58, 95, 98, 104
Castin. *See* Saint-Castin, Jean-
Vincent d'Abbadie de
Catholic missionaries. *See*
Missionaries, Jesuit
Chamberlayne, John, 109
Chambly, Jacques de, 37, 38
Charles II, 29, 30, 32, 33, 37, 44, 49
Charter of Nova Scotia, 219
Chauncy, Reverend Charles,
172 – 73
Chebogue church, 223
Chebucto Bay, 186, 190
Chedabucto, 46; French fort at,
53; and Phips expedition, 68
Chester, 221, 248
Chignecto Isthmus, 82; and Church,
97; and Eddy-Allan insurgents,
231 – 34, 236 – 39; expedition of
1755, 203, 206, 208, 215; French
threat at, 193, 195, 201, 205;
immigration to, 221; and
Kennebec expedition, 199; and
King George's War, 187, 189;
and La Vallière, 44; proposed
fort on, 200; and Revolution, 241.
See also Minas Basin
Church, Benjamin, 76, 81 – 83; and
Acadian expulsion, 212; and
Dudley, 96 – 98, 102
Church of England, 121, 219
Clarendon, Lord Chancellor, 29
Clark, Thomas, 37
Clarke, W., 201
Cobb, Sylvanus, 195, 196
Cobequid Bay, 221, 237

Cod fisheries. *See* Fisheries
Coffin, Ebenezer, 100
Collective mentality: colonial
mentality, 83 – 84, 112, 123; and
Louisbourg expedition of *1745*,
173 – 75, 179. *See also* British –
New England friction;
Massachusetts, and interest in
the West
Compagnie des Pêches sédentaires
de l'Acadie, 46, 47
Congregationalists, 101, 222 – 23
Connecticut, 32; and Chignecto
expedition of *1755*, 208, 209; and
Church expedition, 81; and
Dudley, 101, 102; emigration
from, to Nova Scotia, 219, 221;
and Louisbourg expedition of
1745, 156, 163, 177; trade with
Liverpool, 225; and Vetch, 111,
114, 115, 119
Connecticut River, 95
Connecticut Valley, 125
Continental Congress: and Allan's
proposed expedition, 241 – 42,
243, 245; and Eddy-Allan
insurgents, 233, 235, 237; and
Machias freebooters, 230 – 31;
Revolution and Nova Scotia, 241
Cope and Company, Major Henry,
133
Cornwall County, 37
Cornwallis, Edward, 191, 195 – 97,
223
Council of War, 177
Court of Quarter Sessions in Nova
Scotia, 226
Cromwell, Oliver, 21 – 27, 29
Crowne, William, 26 – 27, 28
Crown Point, 193, 197, 206;
expedition, 187, 188, 215
Cuba, 196, 199
Cumberland, Fort, 210 – 11; and
Allan's proposed expedition,
242, 244; and Eddy-Allan
insurgents, 234, 236, 237, 238,
239 – 40, 241
Cumberland Basin, 195
Cumberland County, 231, 242
Curwen, George, 168

Virginia, 111, 148, 159; and
Massachusetts trade, 6

Wainwright, Francis, 106
Waldo, Samuel, 157 – 58
Waldron, William, 38
Walker expedition, 122
Warren, Peter: and Annapolis
Royal, 182 – 83; and British –
New England friction, 229; and
Canso fishery, 130 – 31; and
Louisbourg expedition of *1745*,
163 – 64, 166, 168 – 72, 175 – 77,
214
Washington, George: and Allan's
proposed expedition, 241, 242;
and Eddy-Allan insurgents, 233,
234, 235, 240; and Machias
freebooters, 230 – 31
Wells, 59
Wentworth, 157 – 58, 209
West Indies, 6, 37
Westminster, Treaty of, 38
Westmoreland County, 242
Weymouth, 119
Whitefield, Reverend George, 159,
160
Willard, Abijah, 211
William, King, 83, 84, 86
William and Mary, 68
William of Orange, 38, 58, 61

Wilmington, 207
Winslow, John: and Chignecto
expedition of *1755*, 206 – 9, 211,
213 – 14; and Eddy, 231; and
Kennebec expedition, 199 – 200
Winslow-Monckton expedition,
213, 221, 236. *See also* Chignecto
Isthmus, expedition of *1755*
Winthrop, Fitz-John, 100 – 101
Winthrop, John: Christian rule of
charity of, 212; and defence, 3;
and La Tour, 4 – 5, 7 – 14; and
Nova Scotia, 1 – 2, 15, 45
Winthrop, John (grandson of
John Winthrop, Jr.), 105
Winthrop, John, Jr.: governor of
Connecticut, 32; and Indian
trade, 100; and John Winthrop,
105; and La Tour, 9, 11
Worcester County, 209

Yarmouth, 221 – 23; privateers
during the Revolution, 247, 248;
trade with New England, 225
York, 59; massacre at, 76
York, Duke of, 37, 39, 41
York County, 209
Yorkshiremen, 222; and Eddy-
Allan insurgents, 232, 233, 238
Young, Benjamin, 127